LEARNING WAR

Studies in Naval History and Sea Power

Christopher M. Bell and James C. Bradford, editors

Studies in Naval History and Sea Power advances our understanding of sea power and its role in global security by publishing significant new scholarship on navies and naval affairs. The series presents specialists in naval history, as well as students of sea power, with works that cover the role of the world's naval powers, from the ancient world to the navies and coast guards of today. The works in Studies in Naval History and Sea Power examine all aspects of navies and conflict at sea, including naval operations, strategy, and tactics, as well as the intersections of sea power and diplomacy, navies and technology, sea services and civilian societies, and the financing and administration of seagoing military forces.

LEARNING WAR

THE EVOLUTION OF FIGHTING DOCTRINE IN THE U.S. NAVY, 1898–1945

TRENT HONE

NAVAL INSTITUTE PRESS
Annapolis, Maryland

This book has been brought to publication with the generous assistance of Edward S. and Joyce I. Miller.

Naval Institute Press
291 Wood Road
Annapolis, MD 21402

Library of Congress Cataloging-in-Publication Data
Names: Hone, Trent, author.
Title: Learning war : the evolution of fighting doctrine in the U.S. Navy, 1898–1945 / Trent Hone.
Description: Annapolis, Maryland : Naval Institute Press, [2018] | Series: Studies in naval history and sea power | Includes bibliographical references and index.
Identifiers: LCCN 2018005736 (print) | LCCN 2018016010 (ebook) | ISBN 9781682472941 (ePDF) | ISBN 9781682472941 (ePub) | ISBN 9781682472934 (hardcover : alk. paper) | ISBN 9781682472941 (ebook)
Subjects: LCSH: Naval tactics—Study and teaching—United States. | Military doctrine—United States—History—20th century. | United States. Navy—History—20th century. | United States. Navy—Officers—Training of. | Naval strategy—History—20th century. | Naval tactics—History—20th century.
Classification: LCC V169 (ebook) | LCC V169 .H66 2018 (print) | DDC 359.4/20973—dc23
LC record available at https://lccn.loc.gov/2018005736

Maps created by Lauren S. Hillman.

For Eleanor Zelliot
who taught me that history never ends

CONTENTS

ILLUSTRATIONS

PREFACE
HOW DID THE NAVY TRANSFORM?

War is the acme endeavor of man.

—Bradley A. Fiske, 1916

On the evening of 7 December 1941, the core of the U.S. Navy's Pacific Fleet—its battle line—was sitting in the mud at the bottom of Pearl Harbor. Prewar plans were shattered. For seven months, the Japanese held the initiative in the Pacific, seizing positions from the Aleutians to Singapore and creating a strong defensive perimeter. Yet by the following December—just a year later—Adm. Chester W. Nimitz, the Pacific Fleet's new commander, had wrested the initiative from the Japanese in the Guadalcanal campaign and begun advancing in the South Pacific. A year after that, in November 1943, the Central Pacific offensive began in the Gilbert Islands. It would destroy the remnants of the Imperial Japanese Navy (IJN) and take the Pacific Fleet to Japan's shores.

The Pacific Fleet's success raises a series of questions:

- How did it recover so quickly from the Pearl Harbor attack?
- How did it seize the initiative from the Japanese without its battle line?

- How did it transform from a centralized battle fleet to a collection of carrier task groups?
- How did these task groups break through Japanese-held island groups, defeat the IJN, and win the war in the Pacific?

The traditional answer to these questions is that the shock of Pearl Harbor forced the Navy out of its stodgy conservatism. The devastating strike of Japanese carrier airpower not only sank the battle fleet but forced the Navy to leave behind the "gun club" philosophy that had dominated its tactical thought in the interwar period (1919–39). "Battleship admirals" had failed to appreciate the nature of the technological changes taking place around them, had restricted experimentation, and had inhibited the development of modern approaches; the raid on Pearl Harbor freed the Navy of its shackles. It is a compelling narrative that has appeared in popular histories, authoritative analyses, and rigorously researched articles.[1] It is also incorrect.

The true story of how the Navy rapidly transformed is a remarkable one of innovative change in the face of dynamic technologies, budgetary constraints, and wartime stress. In the early years of the twentieth century, the Navy transitioned from a traditional institution to a modern, professional organization. This change was triggered by a new concept of American naval power and a revised view of the role of a modern naval officer. New approaches to officer education and new organizational structures followed, along with processes for experimenting with new ideas, gathering feedback from the experience, and continually improving. These processes were core aspects of the Navy; as officers worked to understand how best to coordinate a modern fleet in combat, they collaboratively refined their tactics and kept their minds open to the possibility of new approaches, triggering a series of innovations.

Throughout this process, the Navy of the early twentieth century demonstrated an ability to learn, innovate, and evolve that places it at the forefront of modern ideas regarding management, organizational structure, and innovation. Numerous theories have been advanced about how best to foster sustained organizational learning. Over a century ago, the Navy introduced a successful approach to harnessing new technologies advantageously in an extremely dynamic environment. It conducted regular experiments, engaged in cycles of learning, and continuously improved. During World War II, the pace of these cycles accelerated, and the Navy rapidly transformed. Victory in the Pacific was a result of the Navy's ability to foster evolutionary changes in its doctrine, an ability that had been developed and refined over prior decades.

This book describes the development of that ability. It charts the evolution of the Navy's surface-warfare doctrine during the first half of the twentieth century. Chapters 1 through 4 discuss the development of that doctrine from the end of the Spanish-American War through the beginning of World War II; they describe the Navy's transformation from a traditional organization to a modern one and the emergence within it of a learning system. In these years, the Navy developed its first coherent tactical doctrine, introduced processes to refine it, and institutionalized learning approaches. Then, during the interwar period, the Navy exploited them.

By the time war came in 1941, a sophisticated doctrine was in place. It stressed flexibility and eschewed the dogmatism later attributed to "battleship admirals." Because the Navy's doctrine had emerged from, and was now refined by, regular cycles of learning, it was capable of rapid evolution. The last three chapters describe that evolution during World War II and explain the shift from a centralized battle fleet to a distributed collection of mutually supporting carrier task forces.

The best vehicle for assessing the Navy's innovative approach is the history of its surface-warfare doctrine. Surface ships were a core element of the Navy throughout this period; to follow the evolution of the Navy's approach to coordinating them in combat provides the most coherent view of how the Navy sustained innovation. Regardless of the dominant technologies or ship types, the key to success in naval war remained the coordinated action of a modern fleet. As the Navy's officers developed more sophisticated approaches to coordinating such a fleet in battle, a new approach to doctrinal development emerged. This book describes that process and its implications.

The dynamics involved have relevance to a broad audience, including military historians, students of organizational learning, and managers interested in fostering innovation in their organizations. The history of the Navy's surface warfare doctrine is a story of innovation: the following chapters explore how to foster it, how to develop it, and how to exploit it. They leverage a central assumption: that the evolution of the Navy's surface-warfare doctrine is best understood by viewing the Navy as a "complex adaptive system" (CAS)—a lens that clarifies the dynamic nature of the mechanisms that foster and sustain innovation. These mechanisms allowed the Navy to explore new technologies rapidly and exploit wartime opportunities quickly. The following chapters describe the development of those mechanisms and how they helped win World War II in the Pacific.

ACKNOWLEDGMENTS

Like all works of complexity, this volume is the product of multiple interactions. I am indebted to many others for its final form. Alicia Juarrero and Robert Artigiani encouraged my study of complexity and helped me apply it to the U.S. Navy. I would not have been introduced to them without the encouragement of Tonianne DeMaria Barry and Jim Benson, who expanded my view of management and knowledge of organizational concepts. Roger Jackson's patient guidance when I was an undergraduate set me on a path that led me to explore the interdependent nature of our world.

Evelyn Cherpak of the Naval War College Archives and Barry Zerby, Rick Peuser, Mark Mollan, and Charles W. Johnson of the National Archives provided invaluable assistance locating archival records. Capt. Wayne P. Hughes Jr., Vince O'Hara, Jon Parshall, and Craig C. Felker gave feedback on early drafts. David Dickson, Keith Allen, and David Rosenberg provided important primary sources. Pelham Boyer used his editing talent to correct errors and suggest valuable improvements. Camille Coy helped with revisions, and Lauren Hillman, my wife and best friend, produced the maps and diagrams. All their collective efforts have found their way into this work, but all mistakes remain my own.

ABBREVIATIONS

BatDiv	battleship division
BuOrd	Bureau of Ordnance
CAS	complex adaptive system
CIC	Combat Information Center
CINC	commander in chief
CNO	Chief of Naval Operations
COMINCH	Commander in Chief, U.S. Fleet
IFF	identification, friend or foe
IJN	Imperial Japanese Navy
JCS	Joint Chiefs of Staff
MPI	mean point of impact
NA	National Archives
NHC	Naval Historical Center
NHHC	Naval History and Heritage Command
ONI	Office of Naval Intelligence
OODA	observe, orient, decide, act
OPNAV	Office of the Chief of Naval Operations
OTC	officer in tactical command
PPI	plan position indicator
RAN	Royal Australian Navy
RG	Record Group

RN	Royal Navy
TF	Task Force
TG	Task Group
USN	U.S. Navy
VHF	very high frequency

PROLOGUE
COMPLEX ADAPTIVE SYSTEMS
AND MILITARY DOCTRINE

You cannot cause innovation, but you can catalyze
conditions to enable innovation to emerge.
—Alicia Juarrero, 2015

To understand the Navy's innovative approach fully, we must take a long view across several decades. Most histories of innovation in the Navy during the early twentieth century have focused on the interwar period. This is logical. Aircraft, along with the specialized ships that carried them, emerged as a decisive weapon of war during those years. This, combined with the established narrative surrounding the "gun club," has led many historians to focus on how the Navy successfully adopted airpower and employed it in World War II, distorting our view of the historical record.[1]

The Navy of the early twentieth century employed a combined-arms approach—it did not favor one specific type of ship or weapon—and innovated in all aspects of naval warfare. The focus on aviation has obscured the integrated nature of the Navy's combat doctrine; innovative approaches to surface warfare have largely been ignored by historians and analysts. When these approaches have been described, they have been presented as outdated and backward-looking. The result is an incomplete and biased perspective, akin to Walter Licht's observations regarding industrialization in the United States:

> The creation of a new political economic order occurred slowly, in fits and starts, and over a good fifty-year period. Historians have tended to foreshorten this story, seeing America critically reconstructed during the so-called Progressive Era of the first decades of the twentieth century or during the New Deal period of the 1930s and 1940s. In fact, the process began in the last decades of the nineteenth century and continued through the Second World War.[2]

The history of the Navy has been similarly foreshortened. To get a clear picture of the Navy's approach to innovation, it is necessary to start in the late nineteenth century. Viewing the Navy as a CAS increases the depth of our understanding, overcomes the limitations of traditional interpretations, and allows an accurate assessment over the entire period.

COMPLEX ADAPTIVE SYSTEMS AND EVOLUTIONARY CHANGE

Our modern view of the world is based on the concept of linear causality. We believe we can separate specific causes from their effects and trace the relationship between them. If it rains, it is because of the condensation of water vapor in the sky. If we succeed in business, it is because we have made the right choices. We believe we can explain the world if we can break it into components and understand the causal chain, from *A,* to *B,* to *C.* This assumption is deeply embedded in classical mechanistic science and in how we view the events of our everyday lives. It is also the lens through which we traditionally approach history and describe the process of military innovation.[3]

Historians examine the past in an effort to explain it. If they cannot derive causal links through deductive reasoning, they use inductive approaches based on probabilities. They sift through documentary evidence to ascertain the "how" and "why" of past events and assume a linear causal chain. This allows them to construct a coherent narrative so that history "makes sense."[4] However, by imposing the assumption of linear causality, we often establish unjustified linkages between causes and effects. We develop narratives that reflect the known outcomes and ignore what might have been; this is called "retrospective coherence." When we do this, we focus on history that makes sense rather than making sense of history.[5]

This work attempts to avoid those difficulties by assuming that the U.S. Navy of the twentieth century can best be described as a complex adaptive system. CAS approaches have increased our understanding in numerous fields, including biology, economics, and artificial intelligence. They offer explanations that more traditional approaches cannot. Treating the Navy as a CAS will permit new avenues of investigation into how organizations innovate, adapt, and evolve over time. It will provide a deeper understanding of the mechanisms involved in organizational learning, with important ramifications for students of modern organizations. A CAS approach also embraces the inherent diversity of human systems, making it ideal for understanding the varied ways the Navy transformed into an innovative learning organization in the early years of the twentieth century. As Jean G. Boulton, Peter M. Allen, and Cliff Bowman have described, "Systems thinking deals with stable patterns and history deals with the particularity of events, conditions, and individuals—but complexity thinking marries the two and provides us with a sophisticated and unique theory of change. . . . It is detail and variation coupled with interconnection that provide the fuel for innovation, evolution, change, and learning."[6]

A CAS evolves and changes over time through the interaction of its components with each other and with the external environment. These components include the individuals within the system, the constraints that channel their behavior, and the world that surrounds them. The basic concepts were described well by the French biologist François Jacob:

Complex objects, whether living or not, are produced by evolutionary processes in which two kinds of factors are involved: the constraints that, at every level, specify the rules of the game and define what is possible with those systems; and the historical circumstances that determine the actual course of events and control the actual interactions between the systems. The combination of constraints and history exists at every level, although in different proportions. Simpler objects are more dependent on constraints than on history. As complexity increases, history plays a greater part.[7]

In the Navy, both factors—historical circumstances and constraints—were very important. They created the dynamics that led to dramatic, innovative changes in the Navy's approach to doctrinal development and surface combat. Before examining them in detail to illustrate how the Navy evolved from a traditional institution to a modern, learning organization, it is important to describe how complex systems evolve and change.[8]

Constraints are essential to CAS; they govern the dynamic processes that lead to increasingly sophisticated organization and specialization. Constraints channel the behavior of individuals in the system and focus their efforts. This activity can often foster the development of new approaches. In the strictest sense, Jacob's "historical circumstances" constitute a special type of constraint. They are the initial conditions that define the starting point of the system and limit its potential future. Therefore, constraints—both the historical initial conditions and the current "rules of the game"—are the key to understanding the evolutionary behavior of complex systems.

French physicist Léon Foucault demonstrated a sophisticated, but relatively simple, complex system in 1851, when he hung a large pendulum from the dome of the Panthéon in Paris. The motion of the weight at the end of the pendulum was constrained by a long wire; it swung back and forth. But it did more than that. The motion of the pendulum was also influenced by the rotation of the Earth. To an observer on the floor of the Panthéon the plane of the pendulum's swing rotated, and it did so at a predictable rate.

The simple constraint of the wire interacting with the rotation of the Earth created a timing device. This was a new, *emergent* property of the system, a higher level of complexity enabled by the interaction of all the components. The constraint allowed that increased level of sophistication to appear; in complex systems, constraints become "relational properties that parts [of the system] acquire in virtue of being unified—not just aggregated—into a systematic whole."[9] In other words, constraints become integral parts of systems.

These same mechanisms are at work in human systems. Language helps us organize and communicate our thoughts by imposing a structure on writing and speech. Language constrains us to a limited number of syllables and specific ways of tying those syllables together. Contextual arrangement of syllables into words and sentences permits the communication of extremely sophisticated ideas with relatively little effort. As Alicia Juarrero has explained, "Language's increased capacity to express ideas rests not on newly invented grunts and shouts but on relationships and interconnections established by making interdependent the sounds in a sequence of grunts or shouts."[10] This is the fundamental nature of constraints; they create specific categories—like syllables—that allow greater differentiation and specialization. In language, syllables come together to make words and increase the "signal-to-noise" ratio. From these specializations, higher levels of order and complexity emerge.

It is useful to categorize constraints into two basic types. *Enabling constraints* create a coherent relationship between previously independent components and, by so doing, produce a newly emergent property or behavior. In some cases, the constraint and the behavior then begin to modify each other through feedback cycles. *Top-down constraints* arise at the systemic level and exert their influence on the lower component levels of that system. They have less contextual sensitivity and less potential for fostering the emergence of new, complex approaches. The difference is subtle but important; enabling constraints produce innovation.

We see this at work today in the concise language of texting with emojis. Each symbol has individual meaning, but the overall message of a text is conveyed by their contextual arrangement. Clever individuals are pushing the boundaries of convention and creating a new language, with new patterns and norms. Letter writing, in contrast, remains much more formalized. It is governed by a series of top-down constraints that create specific expectations in terms of formatting, layout, and spelling. Emails reside in between.

The mechanisms we use to control traffic flow at intersections provide another useful example.[11] Two of the most common methods are stoplights and traffic circles. While both are top-down constraints—imposed from above by the designers of the traffic network—they foster very different behavior. Traffic circles are contextually sensitive; they allow the flow of traffic to respond dynamically to the current situation by forcing drivers to self-organize. Traffic lights impose rigid control without knowledge of context. When the light is red, all traffic in that direction stops and waits, regardless of the flow of traffic in the other direction. Drivers at a traffic light are unable to collaborate; they conform to the light's signals and are reduced to automatons. Because traffic circles leverage the skill and knowledge of drivers, they are much more resilient. Traffic lights sacrifice resiliency to increase stability and predictability but can fail in unanticipated circumstances.

When the power to the light goes out, drivers approaching an intersection self-organize and generally treat it as a four-way stop. Recognizing the need for some degree of order, they introduce an enabling constraint into the system. They wait their turn and proceed when appropriate. The intersection functions effectively despite the loss of power. This process illustrates how enabling constraints can emerge dynamically through the behavior of individuals in a system. It also demonstrates how enabling constraints—a self-organized four-way stop at an unmarked intersection—can become a top-down constraint—the traffic light—when a specific mechanism becomes codified.

When a set of interlocking constraints triggers a higher level of self-organized complexity, the transition is called a *symmetry break*. The symmetry of the system has been "broken" because a higher degree of specialization has emerged. Individuals, processes, or constraints that previously performed identical roles have changed and are now performing different ones; they have lost their "symmetry." New capabilities are created by the increased specialization.[12] Embryonic development is an excellent example. In its earliest stages, all the cells within an embryo are identical. As the embryo develops, those fundamental cells lose their symmetry. Some become muscle tissue; some become bones; and others develop into organs. They form more sophisticated and specialized networks, like the nervous system and digestive tract. Embryos go through a series of symmetry breaks as cells become increasingly specialized, each break enabling a new level of complexity.

When a symmetry break occurs, the characteristics of the new system—the constraints governing it, the individuals within it, and the interaction of all the various components—will reflect the conditions that were in place immediately before the symmetry break occurred. In an embryo, the arrangement of cells reflects a specific set of initial conditions: the location where the sperm entered the egg. That positioning determines the alignment of the embryo's body plan.[13]

Human organizations exhibit similar mechanisms. Greater complexity emerges through the creation of increased levels of specialization that contextually embed the organization's history. Hierarchies are a clear example. They constrain the behavior of members of the organization, granting specific authority to some and not others, while allowing the organization to achieve "economies of scale" and accomplish challenging endeavors that less well-organized collections of people would find impossible. The hierarchy contains specializations—a broken symmetry—that reflect the organization's past accomplishments and future objectives.

When a symmetry break occurs and a CAS achieves an increased level of self-organized complexity, the event is called *emergence*. The use of "emergence" is important; it reflects the fact that the increased level of complexity originates from within the system itself and not through external factors. The most famous example is the Bénard cell. A Bénard cell is a macroscopic structure that spontaneously appears in a liquid when it is heated from below. Before the heat is applied, there is no significant difference in the overall temperature of the liquid. As the heat increases, the lower levels of the liquid heat up; once they reach a certain threshold, the dynamics of the fluid change. The random movements of the molecules become ordered; they create convection cells. In each of these cells, billions of molecules "rotate in a coherent manner along a hexagonal path, either clockwise or anti-clockwise, and always in the opposite direction from that of its immediate neighbors."[14] The Bénard cell is an *emergent property* of the fluid and its environment. The cell exhibits properties that were not present and not possible in the molecules that created it. The rotation of the Bénard cell becomes a contextual, top-down constraint that limits the movement of the molecules and makes them conform to a pattern; symmetry breaks as they become more organized and more constrained. This dynamic interaction illustrates how the concepts of constraints, emergence, and symmetry breaks are linked.

In biology, Jacob described innovation through constraints as "tinkering" (or *bricolage,* in his native French). He claimed that "evolution does not produce innovation from scratch. It works on what already exists, either transforming a system to give it a new function or combining several systems to produce a more complex one." The analogy is useful; from this perspective, innovation stems from a series of contingent events, each building on the last, rather than a grand design.[15]

The capability of a system to introduce increased levels of complexity is described by two very similar terms, *emergent potential* and *evolvability.*[16] A system with greater emergent potential is more likely to support the introduction of self-organized complexity. Evolvability is the capability of an organization, organism, or other system to evolve and modify its behavior. Both are related to the level of freedom that exists within the lower levels of the system. Daniel R. Brooks and E. O. Wiley have described the relationship this way: "So long as there remains an element of probabilistic indeterminism ('randomness') at the lowest level of hierarchical systems, there does not seem to be any limit on the degree of complexity that may evolve."[17] In the example above, a traffic circle has greater emergent potential than a traffic light. Both mechanisms constrain traffic flow, but the circle supports more variability and fosters more self-organization.

If the individuals in an organization have sufficient freedom to self-organize and develop new ways of interacting, they have the potential to introduce a constraint that will trigger the emergence of increased complexity. If this freedom does not exist, or if it is more limited—through, for example, the imposition of inflexible, top-down constraints—the evolvability of the system is reduced, and it becomes more difficult to foster new approaches. But a balance is required. Too much variability and too little constraint prevent effective ideas from being channeled and focused; they can arise and quickly disappear. Emergence and evolutionary change are maximized in the space between these two extremes, where constraints lend focus without inhibiting experimentation. This space has often been described as "the edge of chaos."[18]

To retain the capacity for evolvability, a system must develop mechanisms to support *safe-to-fail* experimentation.[19] This runs counter to our traditional view of safety and robustness, which emphasizes fail-safe mechanisms. Fail-safe approaches assume that the future is predictable; they anticipate failure modes and design them out. The "dead man's switch" that turns a machine off when there's no hand on the handle is a common fail-safe mechanism; we put them on hedge trimmers, lawn mowers, and airport baggage carts. Fail-safe approaches work under anticipated circumstances but are vulnerable to variability, the "black swan" events made famous by Nassim Nicholas Taleb. The levees around New Orleans, for example, were designed to withstand a standard hurricane; Katrina, when it struck in August 2005, was anything but standard, and the levees failed catastrophically. Safe-to-fail mechanisms, in contrast, do not rely on assumptions about the future. Instead, they leverage redundancy, flexibility, and dynamic responses. Like a raft moving through rapids in a river—the rubber hull bending as it flows around the rocks—safe-to-fail systems absorb failure, continue functioning, and even thrive.[20] They are far more effective at responding to stress in unpredictable environments.

The concepts of evolvability, emergent potential, and safe-to-fail are tied together by variability. Evolvable, safe-to-fail systems leverage variability to explore the potential of unforeseen and unexploited opportunities; they do this under the influence of constraints that enable self-organization and trigger the emergence of new, more sophisticated approaches. These systems refrain from becoming overly standardized and maintain "clouds" of possible options. While this may initially appear redundant and inefficient, it enables the system to survive, or even thrive, in the face of major shocks and disruptions. This is extremely valuable for a military organization, which is regularly subjected to stressors in wartime, and it is arguably the most important criterion for assessing the effectiveness of military doctrine.

The Navy in the first half of the twentieth century behaved as a CAS. Increasingly sophisticated tactics and doctrine for surface action emerged from the development and application of enabling constraints. The Navy's approach to doctrinal evolution was resilient and demonstrated high levels of evolvability. It leveraged safe-to-fail approaches and parallel experimentation to explore new possibilities and exploit variability. This allowed the Navy to sustain a period of successful innovation and transformation over several decades.

Transformation—a symmetry break, in the language of CAS—requires the development of radically new potential through the application of advanced technologies and procedures. Modern organizations, especially military ones, aspire to leverage transformation. Clear examples illustrate its potential: the German army's blitzkrieg, the decisive use of carrier airpower in World War II, and the introduction of nuclear weapons. Transformation is a force multiplier, one that will deliver victory if properly harnessed. For business organizations, transformation is a path to commercial success. Organizations that innovate and transform the lives of their customers will flourish; those that do not will perish. The growth of literature on this topic has led to a wealth of theories about how to create, sustain, and drive innovation. This work builds upon and adds to this body of literature, with a specific focus on the concept of evolvability. The approach is designed to allow students of innovation to draw potential lessons from the Navy's experience, regardless of their area of specialty.

COMPLEXITY AND MILITARY DOCTRINE

The best vehicle for understanding the Navy's approach to innovation in the early twentieth century is the development of its surface-warfare doctrine; before getting into the details of that evolution, it is important to define "doctrine." The following section addresses three important questions: What is doctrine? Why is it important? And how can viewing the Navy as a CAS help understand doctrine and its evolution more fully?

Doctrine is the set of implicit and explicit assumptions that govern the behavior of a military force. It is what officers and sailors fall back on to guide their decisions when precise instructions are not available. It has a parallel to "culture" or "ethos" but greater specificity than either one. From the perspective of CAS, doctrine is the set of constraints that influence decision making in combat.[21]

Clues to an organization's doctrine are found in manuals and other published materials, but these are only part of the picture. An officer brings a specific mind-set to these manuals, and that contextual understanding is far more important than the printed text. The full meaning and influence of published materials cannot be understood without re-creating the contexts in which they were used. This makes it difficult to assess doctrine effectively.

A sports team offers a useful analogy. The Pittsburgh Steelers are an American football team; they have a detailed playbook that documents their plays and formations. However, none of us would become familiar with their offensive and defensive schemes by merely reading the playbook. The "magic" is in the way the players and coaches interpret its contents and collectively adjust to circumstances during the game. These two elements—the published material and the contextual interpretation—come together to form doctrine.

Effective doctrines enhance resiliency by increasing the ability of ships and crews to coordinate their actions in the absence of direct communication. In battle, this necessitates some level of decentralization. Command authority must be delegated to account for loss of communications and the "friction" that develops in encounters with the enemy. Decentralization is made easier when commanders and their subordinates share common sets of assumptions and predilections. The Navy's 1938 manual *Tentative War Instructions and Battle Doctrine, Light Cruisers* explained the concept well: "The purpose of a written battle doctrine is to promote effective coordinated action in battle through mutual understanding. In the absence of instructions, the doctrine should serve as a guide to sound decisions and appropriate actions."[22]

The importance of doctrinal resiliency should not be overestimated. Military officers recognize this, but the predominant image within the civilian world is that military organizations promote a "command and control" mind-set, where independent action and thought are stifled by rigid orders.[23] This view is mistaken. Successful military forces invest in developing the flexibility required by their primary mission: victory in war. Doctrine is the most effective mechanism for achieving that end. A doctrine's constraints allow the various elements of a force to overcome unanticipated circumstances by using a common set of assumptions. Doctrine becomes a shared mind-set—a shared context for action—that allows coordinated operations without real-time communication. This is exactly what Vice Adm. Horatio Nelson cultivated within his fleet before the battle of Trafalgar in October 1805, and what the Prussian army created among its commanders before the Franco-Prussian War of 1870.

It is valuable to view the shared decision-making framework that doctrine creates as a set of heuristics. Heuristics are guides that inform decision making; they are not rules that give definitive answers but frames that help make sense of different types of problems. The Nobel laureate Daniel Kahneman, who explored the use of heuristics in his work on behavioral economics, defined them as "a simple procedure that helps find adequate, though often imperfect, answers to difficult questions."[24] Kahneman and his colleague Amos Tversky discovered that people tend to employ decision rules rather than thinking through difficult problems, particularly if the full scope of the problem is not immediately apparent. Instead of thoroughly analyzing possible outcomes, our tendency is to select an applicable heuristic and quickly solve the problem.

In many cases, heuristics serve us well. When problem-solving, we tend to use a "similarity heuristic," by which we quickly gravitate toward approaches that were used to solve similar problems in the past. This permits a rapid decision but at a cost. A heuristic embeds certain assumptions, and when we use a similarity heuristic, we assume that the current problem is the same as others in our experience. If that is not the case, we risk wasting time and effort. Maj. Blair S. Williams has noted this flaw: "In the course of intuitive decision making, we use mental heuristics to quickly reduce complexity. The use of these heuristics exposes us to cognitive biases."[25] The specific impact of these biases will vary. Sometimes it is minimal; at other times, it might lead to a catastrophic mistake. The difference will depend on how well the assumptions embedded within in the heuristic reflect the current problem.

Repetition and experience develop the mental patterns that create heuristics; once they are ingrained, we apply them subconsciously. This is why military forces place such emphasis on practice, drill, and routine. Once embedded, the heuristics become constraints that enable faster decisions. At the same time, they limit the number of possible options and introduce potential biases. Ultimately, this process permits a higher level of sophistication to emerge, through the cooperative action of many individuals. Doctrine, activated through heuristics, is a set of enabling constraints that allows resiliency and sophisticated responses to unanticipated circumstances. The interwar Navy leveraged this process.

Understanding the Navy's doctrine is made more difficult because the Navy used the term "doctrine" in two very different ways during the first half of the twentieth century. The uses were similar but varied depending on the situation. In some contexts, "doctrine" referred to instructions issued to a specific task force; in others, it referred to guidance applicable to the entire Navy. These differences make it easy to misinterpret the Navy's doctrine and its development.

Doctrine was most commonly used to refer to low-level guidance issued by task force commanders. This included the communication protocols, plans, and approaches developed for a specific collection of ships and subordinates. Task-force doctrines like these were generally relatively sparse collections of instructions that assumed a rich shared context. They were flexible, adaptive, and often very brief. These doctrines changed frequently, according to the ships in the task force and their capabilities.

The Navy also used "doctrine" to refer to a set of implicit and explicit assumptions that governed the behavior of the fleet in combat. This "Navy doctrine" addressed how the Navy approached combat, educated its officers, and developed plans for battle. It was, most succinctly, how the Navy fought and how it learned to fight. Although a few historical documents described doctrine this way, most viewed it as a lower-level, task-force concept.

This book will investigate both levels. Its central thesis is that the evolution of the Navy's surface-warfare doctrine in the first half of the twentieth century was an example of sustained and repeated innovation. These innovations occurred through a series of transformations, or—in the language of complexity—symmetry breaks. Examining this evolution—how doctrine changed, when it changed, and who facilitated it—will provide a window into broader lessons about the processes that drive innovation. Navy surface-warfare doctrine becomes a vehicle for understanding organizational development through the lens of complexity. The chapters of this book examine different evolutionary threads, each of which had a significant impact on the outcome of World War II in the Pacific.

The focus on Navy doctrine makes this a work of military history. The leaders who shaped the Navy's organization, doctrine, and strategy knew that their business was war. However, the lessons of the Navy's experience are broadly applicable. The Navy faced challenges common to most organizations: limited budgets, rapidly advancing technology, and constant pressure to keep ahead of—or at least even with—determined competitors. The Navy proved particularly adept at leveraging new technologies to enhance its fighting power. The following chapters explain why. They illustrate that the ways organizations approach and integrate new technologies are generally more important than the technologies themselves. The case of the Navy in the first half of the twentieth century is therefore particularly relevant, not only for students of military history but also for those interested in organizational learning, innovation, and transformation in times of rapid technological change.

A secondary thesis of this work is that the most critical attribute of military doctrine is its ability to change and reconfigure with unanticipated circumstances. The link between effective doctrine and success in battle is relatively clear; effective doctrine allows decentralized decision making and permits the members of a military force to act cohesively in the unpredictable conditions of combat. What is less clear is the importance of maintaining a doctrine's emergent potential. Most doctrinal analysis rests on an unchallenged assumption that the key attribute of doctrine is the guidance it contains and the actions it triggers in battle. This view considers war a struggle between forces with relatively static methods; the side with the "best" theory will win. This incorrect belief is predicated on the artificiality that the dynamic nature of combat is limited to the battlefield and not a common element of all human endeavor.[26]

War, like any human activity, is a constantly adaptive discipline. New challenges constantly emerge, as opponents seek to adapt, change, and continually alter their approaches to achieving superior levels of "fitness" for current circumstances. The key to victory rests not upon developing the theory of combat that is the "best" but on creating an environment—a framework—that allows for the rapid identification and exploitation of new concepts and opportunities, so that doctrinal "fitness" is continually improving. In this model, the war-winning doctrine is not the "best" doctrine but the one that is most effective at adapting, evolving, and innovating. A doctrine's ability to do so requires an effective balance between the *exploration* of new ideas and *exploitation* of successful ones.

Cultivating the emergent potential of military doctrine is therefore an essential activity, both in peace and war, so that new concepts and lessons can be discovered and then leveraged effectively. The Navy accomplished this with its surface-warfare doctrine in the years before World War II. Sufficient emergent potential was retained to allow the rapid absorption of wartime lessons and the evolution of emergent, more sophisticated approaches. The perspective of CAS is essential to understanding this success. Victory in the Pacific came through repeated practice at adapting and innovating. The following chapters describe how this process emerged in the U.S. Navy.

1

A PROFESSIONAL
OFFICER CORPS

All organizations are composed of human beings. . . .
[T]he iron and brass, and steam, and coal employed are
merely inert matter[;] . . . the work of organizations
must be done by human beings.

—Bradley A. Fiske, 1907

Our story begins with an insurgency, a struggle to change well-established approaches, to improve them in light of modern technologies, and to bring them into line with contemporary ideas. The struggle was over fundamental definitions: *What did it mean to be a naval officer? How could the Navy best promote and develop the skills of its leaders? What should be the relationship between military and civilian authority in the American republic?* Ultimately, the process of answering these questions transformed the Navy into a modern, professional institution.

In the mid-nineteenth century, the Navy was a traditional organization. It relied on apprenticeship and hands-on experience to grow the skills of its men and develop its leaders. Officer promotion was based exclusively on seniority; if a man lived long enough, he would advance in the ranks. Officer education stressed the core principles of seamanship: sailing across the oceans, navigating by the sun and stars, and fearlessly bringing a ship into battle. These principles imbued the Navy and were reflected in popular culture. Famous phrases—Adm. David G. Farragut's "Damn the torpedoes, full speed ahead"; Capt. James Lawrence's "Don't give up the ship"; and Capt. John Paul Jones' "I have not yet begun to fight!"—exemplified the traditional view of a naval officer.

By the late nineteenth century, this traditional view was becoming inadequate. Technology was changing rapidly; steam, electricity, and steel were revolutionizing human endeavor. Navies, with their great capital investments in large vessels of war, were more vulnerable to rapid technological change. The Navy's leaders—both military and civilian—recognized that they had to come to grips with these technologies; they had to understand how to leverage them to design modern ships and command them in battle.

To do that, they had to overcome a multifaceted problem. They had to learn how to discover, acquire, and leverage the most effective modern technologies for naval warfare. They had to develop a skilled officer corps conversant with the details of those technologies. In the late nineteenth century, the Navy could do neither of these things effectively, and many men, within both the Navy and its civilian leadership, failed to recognize the complex nature of the challenge. This created a climate ripe for an insurgency. The insurgency's leaders recognized that the dominant paradigms and the structures based on them—the Navy's systems of organization, education, and promotion—no longer reflected the operational environment. The established norms were based on a small force, composed mainly of wooden sailing vessels, that focused on coastal defense and did the bulk of its work by hand. By the 1880s, these conditions were being invalidated. The new ships were steel, powered by steam, and used machinery for their operations. The insurgents began to suggest that these ships could become an oceangoing fleet that could project power over the seas, helping to increase the influence of the United States across the world.

AN INSURGENCY BEGINS

One of the initial leaders of the insurgency was Rear Adm. Stephen B. Luce. He argued persuasively for a series of changes, including the introduction of a naval general staff built upon the Prussian model and a new conception of the naval profession based on the art of naval strategy, an elusive concept that did not yet formally exist. He impressed upon his fellow officers the need to recognize that war was the essence of their profession: "The conduct of war, under any conditions, calls for the very highest proficiency as a strategist and as a politician, using that much abused term in its broadest sense. The chief of that office [the Navy commander in chief] must be conversant with the basic principles of military science. He must be familiar with the laws of war, and of our international relations. He must be . . . an officer of the highest professional attainments. To cover this broad field of knowledge requires years of study and reflection."[1]

Luce's most lasting impact was in the founding of an institution where naval officers could investigate that emerging field of knowledge. He worked with Senator Nelson Aldrich (R-R.I.) and Representatives Henry Cabot Lodge (R-Mass.), Washington C. Whitthorne (D-Tenn.), and Charles A. Boutelle (R-Mass.) to introduce a new school dedicated to the professional education of naval officers, the Naval War College, established at Newport, Rhode Island, in 1884. Luce became its first president and set the institution on an important path. Small classes of attendees wrestled with the challenges of naval command and refined the Navy's approach to officer education. The college became a laboratory ashore that explored key questions of tactics, doctrine, and war planning. It would become extremely influential in the early years of the twentieth century as its faculty and students defined the American art of naval strategy.

In his time at the Naval War College and in the fleet, Luce influenced a cadre of like-minded reformers who carried on his work and pushed for further improvements. They included Alfred Thayer Mahan, Henry C. Taylor, and Bradley A. Fiske. These officers were the first wave of insurgents; their arguments for reform often appeared in the U.S. Naval Institute *Proceedings,* a professional journal introduced in 1873. A young member of the New York State Assembly, Theodore Roosevelt, was also impressed by Luce's arguments and became an important ally.

Other American professions were also beginning to embrace formal education, formal licensing boards, and formal studies of how to apply their skills in complex organizations like the industrial enterprise. The American Medical Association, for example, was founded in 1847 and incorporated in 1897. The American Dental Association was founded in 1859. Increasing specialization was not restricted to medicine; the American Society of Civil Engineering was founded in 1852 and the American Bar Association in 1878. Management science followed. In 1881, Frederick W. Taylor introduced his time-motion studies to understand factory work better and to try to make it more efficient. His efforts ultimately led to the theory of "scientific management," which exerted a significant influence on American industry in the early years of the twentieth century. Taylor claimed that "the best management is a true science, resting upon clearly defined laws, rules, and principles." He argued that "whenever these principles are correctly applied, results must follow which are truly astonishing."[2]

The similarity to Luce's thinking is clear. Unsurprisingly, Taylor's "scientific" approach influenced the Navy. His methods were introduced into the Navy yards, bastions of traditional practices. Younger, college-educated naval constructors felt Taylor's approach would improve the efficiency of both public and private building yards. They would wage a campaign to impose scientific management methods on shipyards, a campaign that would last until World War II.

Taylor's concepts turned out, however, to be a poor fit for officer education. With its emphasis on formulaic calculation and repeatability, Taylor's method was ineffective for military planning and combat. Luce's vision for the Naval War College was therefore subtly altered by its second president, Capt. Alfred Thayer Mahan. Mahan grasped "the importance of judgment in war [and] offset a tendency towards the mechanical application of principles" that was apparent in much contemporary "scientific" thinking.[3]

Mahan emphasized a collaborative approach whereby officers developed contextual solutions to problems using their collective knowledge and experience; after Mahan, the college taught war as an art, not a science. The distinction he and his contemporaries made between the two was best expressed by Bradley A. Fiske: "In any human art and science—say medicine, music, or navigation—it is the art and not the science by which one gets results[;] . . . the science is merely the foundation on which the art reposes, and . . . it is by the practice of the art and not the knowledge of the science that skill is gained."[4] Although some officers found common ground between these ideas and Taylor's "scientific management," the core of the Navy's approach remained more flexible and more collaborative.

Through this emphasis on contextual knowledge, skill, and practical learning, Mahan and his fellow insurgents tempered the increasing emphasis on science as the basis for American professionalism. Nonetheless, that backdrop acted as an important constraint on their behavior. They followed prevailing models for defining a modern profession, borrowed from scientific concepts, and sought to develop specialized knowledge. However, in the last decades of the nineteenth century, that specialized body of knowledge did not exist. It would emerge gradually, through the interaction of the Naval War College and the fleet, a process described in more detail in the following two chapters.

The frontier was an additional constraint on naval officers, influencing their outlooks and attitudes. Frederick Jackson Turner explained the frontier's unique impact on the North American character: "The frontier is productive of individualism. . . . It produces antipathy to control, and particularly to any direct control. . . . Frontier individualism has from the beginning promoted democracy."[5] Turner did not mean the romanticized image the term "frontier" calls to mind today; Turner's frontier was the interface between established society and the wilderness, a zone where small communities of hardy families worked collaboratively to harness their livelihoods from the natural world: "To the frontier the American intellect owes its striking characteristics. That coarseness and strength combined with acuteness and inquisitiveness; that practical, inventive turn of mind, quick to find expedients; that masterful grasp of material things, lacking in the artistic but powerful to effect great ends; that restless, nervous energy; that dominant individualism, working for good and for evil, and withal that buoyancy and exuberance which comes with freedom—these are traits of the frontier, or traits called out elsewhere because of the existence of the frontier."[6]

Service in the Navy enhanced many of these elements. Because ships could be alone at sea for months, officers and men became accustomed to an ambitious self-reliance, honed by a distinctive American practicality that Turner described as an "inventive turn of mind" and "masterful grasp of material things." Mahan's collaborative approach exploited these attributes by bringing officers together to share their perspectives and learn from each other. Practicality informed their preparation for war and influenced their efforts to transform the Navy into a modern professional institution. It also illuminated the obstacles standing in their way.

OBSTACLES TO IMPROVEMENT

Despite the emergence of new technologies in the nineteenth century, the Navy refused to change its approach to officer education. Instead, it incorporated specialized knowledge through the introduction of staff roles, which were separate and distinct from the corps of line officers (that is, in the British phrase, "seaman officers"). "By 1842, staff officers included surgeons, chaplains, naval constructors, pursers, professors of mathematics, and engineers."[7] These officers became experts in their fields and used their knowledge to augment the Navy's capabilities. However, their responsibilities, promotion mechanisms, and educational systems remained separate. Line officers enjoyed a privileged status and reserved sole responsibility for commanding ships and men in battle.

The growing importance of machinery in the late nineteenth century began to expose the weaknesses in this approach. Engineering officers were essential to shipboard operations, but they remained outside the established hierarchy of command. Ships were organized as if engineers were useful augmentations, not integral parts of shipboard operations. This made little sense for modern ships, which relied heavily on machinery. The engineer in chief, Rear Adm. George W. Melville, summarized the problem:

> The Engineers . . . were a vital part of the military organization, exercising military command over a large and increasing body

of men, and yet classified as civilians. . . . Furthermore, on board ship, when there was any possibility of doing so, the engineers were invariably humiliated, and reminded on all occasions that they were not as good as line officers. This naturally resulted in the bright men of the [Engineering] Corps seeking civilian employment, and those who found it necessary to remain, from a financial standpoint, became disgruntled, disgusted, and always discontented.[8]

The separation of the engineers began to harm efficiency and threatened to undermine command authority. The root cause went beyond command relationships; the new ships were sophisticated, complex machines and required specialized knowledge to command them. As Donald Chisholm has pointed out, the challenge presented by the increasing assertiveness of the engineers went directly to the core of what it meant to be a naval officer: "Line-staff conflicts were manifested in practical issues of rank, pay, and privilege, but were really battles over how professional 'naval officer' would be defined."[9]

An added source of friction was the Navy's promotion system. In the late nineteenth century, promotion was based on seniority. This caused two problems. First, there was no incentive to demonstrate exceptional talent. Promotions would come in seniority order, regardless of merit. The second problem was that the process was glacially slow. The Navy had grown significantly during the Civil War and added many young officers to the rolls. When the conflict ended, the Navy shrank back to a peacetime size. The officers remaining in the service formed a "bubble" that slowly moved through the ranks, holding the officers behind them back. Officers who did reach the highest grades did so at such advanced age that they reached mandatory retirement before they could develop the necessary skills for high command.

As the Navy grew in the late nineteenth century, the flaws in this system became more apparent. Commanding larger formations of ships requires its own level of skill and expertise, one that can only be developed through practical experience. The current system made it nearly impossible to acquire that experience. The insurgents chafed at this inefficiency. It not only inhibited the development of a modern Navy but prevented their own professional growth. Many of them were young, ambitious, and talented; they would directly benefit from an improved system that placed skill and initiative over time in service. But the pursuit of improved *efficiency* by the reform-minded Navy officers and civilian secretaries had to be tempered by the desire of members of Congress to preserve *equity*—fairness to the existing officers—and *economy.*[10]

Another difficulty was the assumption of civilian authority that was embedded in the Navy's command structure. The president was commander in chief. He appointed a civilian Secretary of the Navy, who was responsible for the administration of the Navy Department and possessed command authority in wartime. Underneath the secretary there were five major squadrons at sea—the North Atlantic, Pacific, Asiatic, European, and South Atlantic—and eight bureaus ashore. The Navy's bureaus were semiautonomous administrative organizations; they had their own budgets and were led by rear admirals or officers of equivalent standing. The bureaus specialized in various technical matters and procured material that fell under their respective spheres of responsibility. The Bureau of Ordnance (BuOrd), for example, was responsible for guns, gun mounts, and the sights used to aim them; the other bureaus performed similar duties in their specializations. In 1898, the bureaus were Yards and Docks, Equipment and Recruiting, Navigation, Ordnance, Construction and Repair, Steam Engineering, Provisions and Clothing, and Medicine and Surgery. The Bureau of Navigation, whatever its name might suggest, was responsible for personnel assignments; its chief had significant influence on officer appointments.

With this organization, there was no effective mechanism for planning or coordinating operations during war. "Because the bureau chiefs were immersed in those areas over which they had cognizance, the bureau system was ill suited to provide professional direction to plan and control naval operations."[11] Planning fell to the secretary, but he often lacked the professional knowledge and experience to perform this role effectively. There was no established staff structure to assist him, inform his decision making, or plan for future contingencies.

Many naval officers could see these deficiencies clearly. The insurgents, such as Luce and Taylor, used them to support arguments in favor of a naval general staff. Capt. A. P. Cooke, writing in 1886, supported their case:

> Its importance cannot be overestimated, and its services should be utilized to the fullest extent. Its chief labors would be directed to one important end—the preparation for war—so that when the time arrived there might not be a moment's delay. In war the General Staff would be the mainstay and reliance of the department and of the admirals afloat. . . . Previous knowledge and preparation are so essential to success in war, that without a perfected and thoroughly worked-out system of this nature the best ships and equipment will be unavailing.[12]

A recent example underpinned these arguments. The Prussian General Staff had successfully planned and executed the victory over France in 1870 and in doing so had caught the attention of the world. The Prussian system held that "war was a distinct body of knowledge that could be taught in school." This aligned well with Luce's beliefs and reinforced the arguments he had used in support of the Naval War College.[13] The civilian Navy secretaries and their allies in Congress viewed the idea of increased military authority with great suspicion. They feared naval officers would create an alternative command structure that would undermine the security of the republic and promote imperialism. Organizational improvements had to balance these concerns with the insurgents' desire for an enhanced ability to plan and prepare for war.

In today's terms, the Navy of the late 1890s had become ripe for disruption. It was not long in coming. On the morning of 25 January 1898, the battleship *Maine* arrived in Havana Harbor. Cuba was embroiled in a rebellion against Spanish colonial rule, and *Maine* had been sent to protect American interests. Three weeks later, on the evening of 15 February, she exploded, triggering the Spanish-American War. That conflict was the shock that would push the Navy out of a traditional organizational model into a modern, professional one.

Naval power was a critical component of the American victory over Spain. Off Cuba, Rear Adm. William T. Sampson's North Atlantic Squadron and Commo. Winfield Scott Schley's Flying Squadron blockaded Adm. Pascual Cervera y Topete's fleet in the harbor at Santiago. They destroyed Cervera's fleet when it attempted to break out the morning of 3 July 1898. Two months earlier, the Asiatic Squadron under Commo. George Dewey had sailed aggressively into Manila Bay. Dewey's victory over Adm. Patricio Montojo's flotilla the morning of 1 May ended Spanish rule in the Philippines.

For the United States, the Spanish-American War was primarily a naval war; victory established the United States as a global power. New territorial obligations extended the sphere of American influence and created new roles for the Navy. The Philippines, Puerto Rico, and Guam were acquired from Spain; Hawaii was annexed in 1898; Tutuila (American Samoa) was occupied in 1900; and in 1903 a base was officially established at Guantanamo Bay in Cuba. Power projection—the ability to sail vast distances and successfully fight a naval battle—became a core aspect of the Navy's professional thinking.

The defeats of the Spanish at Santiago and Manila Bay demonstrated that the ships of the new steel navy could successfully project power, at least on a modest scale. The ships had come together from a variety of dispersed stations to fight and win. However, they had not fought cohesively; victory had resulted as much from Spanish errors and inefficiency as American skill. Officers were accustomed to showing the flag on distant stations, not operating in fleets. The war made these limitations clear and motivated the insurgents to turn their practical eye toward improvements.

THE GENERAL BOARD

One of the most critical problems exposed by the Spanish-American War was the Navy's inadequate capacity to plan and wage war. Because of the emphasis on civilian control, responsibility for planning rested with the Secretary of the Navy. To aid him in this work, there was an assistant secretary. When the war came, these posts were held by John Davis Long and Theodore Roosevelt, respectively.

TABLE 1. Timeline

Year	Month	President	Secretary of the Navy	Event
1897	March	William McKinley	John D. Long	
1898	April–August			Spanish-American War
1899	March			Naval Personnel Act • Integrates engineers and the line • Introduces plucking boards
	September			Open Door Policy announced
1900	March			General Board established
1901	September	Theodore Roosevelt		
	November			Hay-Pauncefote Treaty
1902	May		William H. Moody	
1904	July		Paul Morton	
	December			Roosevelt Corollary to Monroe Doctrine announced
1905	July		Charles J. Bonaparte	
1906	December		Victor H. Metcalf	
1908	January			"The Needs of Our Navy" published
	February–March			Senate Naval Committee hearings
	July–August			Newport Conference
	December		Truman H. Newberry	
1909	March	William Howard Taft	George von L. Meyer	
	December			Naval Aides introduced
1913	March	Woodrow Wilson	Josephus Daniels	
1915	May			William S. Benson appointed CNO
1916	August			Line Personnel Act signed, introducing promotion by merit for officers
1917	April			Congress declares war on Germany

Long, a former governor of Massachusetts and member of Congress, admitted that he had "no special aptitude for the Navy Department."[14] He firmly believed in the primacy of civilian control and resisted calls for a general staff, arguing that the existing structure was more "efficient" because there was no way a naval officer could dispute his own authority as secretary or undermine his decisions. In peacetime, Long effectively managed the operations of the department, using his authority to resolve disputes between the bureau chiefs. During the war, Long controlled the major movements of ships and squadrons; it was he who deliberately sent Dewey to the Philippines to operate against the Spanish fleet.[15]

However, difficulties in coordinating naval operations during the war revealed the limitations of the current organization. Part of the problem had been apparent before the war even started. When Long entered office in 1897, he was presented with three alternative plans for a war with Spain. One had been created by Lt. William Kimball, of the Office of Naval Intelligence (ONI). The Naval War College had a plan written by Capt. Henry C. Taylor, then its president. A third plan had been developed by a special planning board headed by Rear Adm. Francis M. Ramsay, chief of the Bureau of Navigation. Although the plans had similarities, there were distinct differences. Kimball and Ramsay called for operations off the coast of Spain; Taylor advocated isolating Cuba.

This planning process reflected institutional friction within the Navy Department. The three plans were not just alternative approaches to war; they represented different opinions about where responsibility for planning should reside. Both ONI and the Naval War College had the capability to develop plans; the college had more sophisticated mechanisms, but not all officers supported it. Rear Admiral Ramsay actively opposed the college. He had convinced Long's predecessor, Secretary Hilary A. Herbert, to create the special planning board specifically to counter Taylor's plan and reduce the influence of the college. The lack of an official approach led to confusion, wasted effort, and internecine struggle.[16]

To try to make sense of his alternatives, Long convened his own board in June 1897. Headed by Rear Adm. Montgomery Sicard, commander in chief (CINC) of the North Atlantic Squadron, the board recommended a course that struck a balance between the competing approaches. The Navy had been fortunate to emerge from this convoluted process with plans that were feasible despite the absence of a defined planning apparatus. Long astutely recognized this. To avoid similar problems during the war, he appointed a Naval War Board— more commonly known as the "strategy board"—to advise him and President William McKinley on the conduct of naval operations. The board was staffed with senior officers and chaired by Rear Admiral Sicard. Long retained command authority, using the board's knowledge and insights to help him make effective decisions. Although a far cry from a general staff, the Naval War Board was a significant step toward a more centralized, efficient authority for planning a war and operating naval forces; it proved its value during the conflict.

After the war, however, the insurgents and other like-minded individuals renewed their arguments for a general staff. Captain Taylor drew a parallel between the concept of a general staff and modern approaches to management: "The need for a General Staff in our Navy is not unnatural: All military organizations, afloat and ashore, experience the same necessity, as do all large business enterprises in civil life, though under other names than that of General Staff."[17]

Secretary Long began to see value in these arguments. At his request, Capt. Asa Walker drafted a memorandum that expanded on the parallels between a naval general staff and management structures used in the business world, such as boards of directors. Walker argued that these bodies were necessary to "think" and "watch the future" so that the organization could anticipate new developments and make the most of them when they occurred.[18]

> The American Navy has for some years felt that this [a general staff] . . . was needed for future efficiency. Evidence of this is apparent in the creation many years ago, of a War College at Newport and an Office of Naval Intelligence in the Navy Department. In

those two institutions are to be found many of the elements of a General Staff, requiring only a slight drawing together by a common head—such as the Assistant Secretary or the Chief [of the Bureau] of Navigation—to create a nucleus of effort around which would form a body of great usefulness. . . . It would grow of itself, needing but one care and precaution on the part of the Navy[:] . . . that of selecting always for that duty officers best known for their practical success in the handling of ships and command of men, and forbidding any continuous staff duty, in order that frequent tours of active service afloat, alternating with the General Staff work ashore, may prevent that over-theorizing in which exists always the initial germ of decay for any practical calling, and especially for the profession of arms.[19]

Captain Walker proposed as an initial step the creation of a board of officers to meet regularly and consider future plans. This suggested a potential compromise; Long could employ the approach he used with the Naval War Board and create an advisory board. This body could "watch the future," address many of the shortcomings of the current organization, and move the Navy closer to a general staff without compromising the supremacy of civilian authority. The secretary would remain in control, supported by a skilled group of experienced officers.

Long embraced this idea and issued General Order 544 in March 1900; the order created an advisory entity called the General Board. To help explain the reasoning behind the decision, Taylor published Walker's memorandum as an article in the U.S. Naval Institute *Proceedings* in the fall of 1900.[20] Adm. George Dewey, the victor of the battle of Manila Bay, was appointed the General Board's first chairman. Captain Taylor, who had long argued for a general staff, was named one of the inaugural members. Additional members included the president of the Naval War College, the Navy's senior intelligence officer, the chief of the Bureau of Navigation, and a handful of other senior officers. It was one of the most significant and influential changes ever in the Navy's organization.

The introduction of the General Board was a uniquely American solution, marrying the increasingly sophisticated professional knowledge of military officers with the need to retain civilian authority over military plans and operations. The board allowed the Navy to bring an increased focus to war planning and preparation and exerted a positive influence on ship designs, tactics, and war plans. It developed a long-term vision for the size and composition of the fleet that informed congressional appropriations and the Navy's building programs. It became an effective mechanism for reflecting upon current experience and learning from it. The board was an extremely important development in the increasing professionalism of the Navy.

ENGINEERING OFFICERS

The Spanish-American War also marked the start of a transition toward a more professional system of officer education and promotion. The existing emphasis on seniority began to be replaced by a focus on merit, ability, and professional skill. These changes helped motivate officers to embrace learning and knowledge as essential aspects of the American naval profession. The first and most significant change was the merging of the line and the Engineering Corps. The division between them—between the technical specialists and the ship handlers—had been a source of tension, as has been seen, throughout the latter part of the nineteenth century. By the first year of Secretary Long's tenure, the friction had become acute, as Charles Paullin described:

> By 1897 the differences between the line officers and the engineers engaged the attention of the [Navy] department even more than the evils of infrequent promotions. . . . [T]he development of steam power, machinery and engineering on board naval ships had . . . gradually and continually enhanced the importance of the engineer corps, which had correspondingly increased in importance, risen in rank and in the education of its officers, and grown in dignity and consideration. . . . In 1897 the chief controversy between them and the line related to their demand for certain

rights and privileges which were enjoyed by the line and which the line was unwilling to share with them.[21]

Secretary Long knew he had to improve the situation. He convened a panel to investigate the issue and provide recommendations: on 4 November 1897, the Naval Personnel Board was formed to "consider the matter of a reorganization of the personnel of the navy." To prevent either the line officers or engineers from biasing its work, Long appointed Assistant Secretary Roosevelt the board's president, assuming he would act as a moderator. The officers of the board represented a mix of disciplines, balanced between engineers and line officers.[22]

Before the first meeting, Roosevelt formulated a proposal for the board's consideration. He was interested in an amalgamated officer corps, one that combined the engineers and line officers into a single professional organization. The Engineering Corps would be abolished, and engineering would become a core part of officer education. The approach—"amalgamation"—had been originally proposed by Ira N. Hollis, a Harvard University professor who had once served as a naval engineer. The merits of Hollis' arguments convinced the board; the members favored amalgamation by a vote of nine to one. The board presented the recommendations to Secretary Long on 9 December in a report written by Roosevelt; he hoped to encourage adoption by characterizing the change as natural:

> Every officer on a modern war vessel in reality has to be an engineer whether he wants to or not. Everything on such a vessel goes by machinery, and every officer, whether dealing with the turrets or the engine room, had to do with engineers' work. There is no longer any reason for having a separate body of engineers responsible for only a part of the machinery. What is needed is one homogeneous body, all of whose members are trained for the efficient performance of the duties of the modern line officer. The midshipmen will be grounded in all these duties at Annapolis. . . . We are not making a revolution; we are merely recognizing and giving shape to an evolution.[23]

Roosevelt was correct that amalgamation was a natural consequence of changes that had already occurred. However, he was misrep-
resenting the nature of the change. Redefining what it meant to be an
American naval officer was not an evolutionary change; it was a revolutionary one, and it would have extremely important consequences,
particularly for the Navy's approach to technology. If every officer was
expected to be an engineer, the emphasis of education would naturally
shift from traditional methods to modern, professional techniques.

In addition to this dramatic shift, the board also recommended
improvements to the promotion system. To accelerate the movement
of officers through the grades and prevent younger, talented officers
from staying too long in the lowest ranks, it called for the creation of a
new board that would periodically review the officers in lower grades
and select the least effective ones for early retirement. Removing the
least competent officers would allow the best—as well as the average—
to continue to be promoted by seniority. It was a compromise; the new
mechanism would not promote the best, as demonstrated by skill and
ability, but only remove the worst.

Roosevelt prepared a draft bill summarizing the board's recommendations, and Long passed it to Congress. Senator Eugene Hale,
chairman of the Senate Committee on Naval Affairs and a Republican
from Maine, introduced it in January 1898. His fellow senators agreed
with the proposals. Debate in the House began that spring. After sum-
moning Roosevelt and prominent officers for hearings, the House Naval
Affairs Committee issued its report in May. The Spanish-American
War prevented further progress that year, but Congress took the legislation up again in January 1899, and on 3 March it was signed into
law by President McKinley.[24]

The resulting Naval Personnel Act was "the most important legislation concerning the officers of the Navy that had passed since the
Civil War."[25] It created a new, modern definition of the naval profession. The traditional concepts of seamanship, navigation, and bravery
were integrated with modern ideas of engineering and scientific investigation. The act accelerated officer promotions by forcing some early
retirements. The secretary was authorized to maintain a list of "applicants for voluntary retirement" and select officers of a given grade

from this list if the number of available openings in the next higher grade was not large enough. If there were still insufficient openings, the secretary was permitted to convene a "plucking board" to select officers for retirement.

The Naval Personnel Act was structured to provide for a smooth amalgamation of engineers and line officers. Engineering officers above the rank of commander moved to shore duty. Older officers below this rank were given a choice; they could remain engineering specialists and move ashore or assume line-officer duties. The youngest engineers were expected to become line officers. All engineers wishing to become line officers were required to pass a special examination to prove their competence. If they failed, they would be restricted to engineering duties and not allowed to join the line. However, the merging of the line and engineering officers did not initially proceed as planned. Line officers tended to avoid engineering duty and failed to gain the necessary experience in it. By 1905, a reversal was being considered, but the Navy secretary at the time, Charles Bonaparte, disagreed. He favored a "thoroughgoing and persevering enforcement" of the established law. This course was ultimately successful, and by 1910, the new system was working as intended.[26]

From that point on, all Navy officers were expected to be competent engineers as well as (potentially) ship commanders. The distinction between the different types of officers began to blur. All quickly recognized that "almost every act of the line officer aboard ship has to do with machinery and with engineering."[27] The broader scope of knowledge among the officer corps had distinct benefits for efficiency and maintenance. By 1911, the annual cost of repairs was only 2 percent of the Navy's overall expense on machinery maintenance; in the merchant marine, it consumed 9 percent.[28] This was particularly important for a service that expected to sail thousands of miles to defend the country's strategic interests.

By redefining what it meant to be an officer, the Navy began to create new possibilities. A parallel had taken place in England in the eighteenth century, when the roles of master and commander—the ship handler and the warrior—had merged to form a new naval profession.

This was a vital step for Britain's dominion of the seas; Norbert Elias has pointed out that it was possible thanks largely to the looser social constraints that existed in Britain at that time.[29] The U.S. Navy's environment at the dawn of the twentieth century—influenced as the service was by the independence, self-reliance, and practicality of the frontier—was similar, and it enabled the redefinition of the naval profession. As the lines between engineers and line officers blurred, innovative approaches emerged as more officers began to apply their technical knowledge to the problems of ship handling and war fighting. That would become extremely important in the coming decades as new technologies—fire-control computers, oil fuel, airplanes, superheated steam machinery, radar, and many others—made their way into the fleet. With engineering a core part of officer education, the Navy was particularly well positioned to exploit these new technologies.

THE INSURGENCY PROGRESSES

Theodore Roosevelt became president of the United States in September 1901, after the assassination of William McKinley. In his continued pursuit of a more effective naval organization, Roosevelt was joined by a younger wave of insurgent officers who tried to introduce increasingly professional approaches. Among them were William S. Sims, Albert L. Key, Reginald R. Belknap, George B. Bradshaw, Richard D. White, and C. R. Plunkett. These officers pursued three specific improvements: a more effective ship-design process that recognized the needs of the fleet; the introduction of a naval general staff; and promotion of officers by selection rather than seniority.

Powerful congressmen opposed their efforts to reform the Navy Department. Among them was Senator Hale. Although Hale had helped to pass the Naval Personnel Act, he was dubious about Roosevelt's aggressive foreign policy and used his position as chairman of the Senate Naval Affairs Committee to stifle reform and prevent the Navy from becoming, as he feared, a tool of imperialism.

The potential for reform during Roosevelt's tenure was further limited by frequent turnover at the position of Navy secretary; six separate individuals held the post under Roosevelt. Of the six, only one saw merit in a general staff; none of the others pursued the idea.

The lack of support for organizational reform at the secretariat level was partially balanced during the first Roosevelt term by Henry C. Taylor, now a rear admiral. Taylor had been president of the Naval War College, served on the General Board, and commanded the battleship *Indiana* at the battle of Santiago. He was "regarded as one of the most gifted men of his generation."[30] Roosevelt appointed Taylor to be chief of the Bureau of Navigation on 29 April 1902, promoting him ahead of many others. He would hold the post until his untimely death in July 1904.

As chief of the Bureau of Navigation, Taylor proposed a transformation of the current General Board into "a board of seven members, consisting of the Admiral of the Navy, the Chief of the Bureau of Navigation, the President of the Naval War College, the Chief Intelligence Officer, and three officers of the line that would devise measures for the effective preparation and maintenance of the fleet for war."[31] Secretary William H. Moody agreed. He prepared legislation along these lines that would have created a legitimate general staff. However, the bill was crippled in Congress. Hale and his allies saw that it went nowhere. The insurgents, frustrated by the lack of progress and the difficulty of pursuing reforms under a "revolving door" of Navy secretaries, looked for alternative mechanisms.

They began to lobby legislators directly, hoping to gain allies for their agenda, of which one of the most important elements was ship design. The fleet's new battleships were some of the largest and most complicated machines in the world, but they did not incorporate lessons from operational experience. This had become particularly apparent during the voyage of the Great White Fleet, which exposed the Navy's new battleships to real operating conditions. A new approach was needed, and the insurgents would let the world know.

In late July 1899, then-Secretary Long had placed primary responsibility for ship design with the Bureau of Construction and Repair. Construction and Repair coordinated with the Bureau of Steam Engineering, which had responsibility for propulsion systems, and BuOrd, which provided guns and armor. Together, the three bureaus collaboratively developed new designs. To help coordinate their work, a Board on Construction was established, composed primarily of the chiefs of the relevant bureaus, which defined the characteristics of new ships.[32]

However, the Board on Construction was unable to coordinate the bureaus effectively, and its members did a poor job of incorporating feedback from the fleet. The design of the battleships of the *Virginia* class, authorized by Congress in March 1899, exemplified the issues. As part of the first shipbuilding appropriation after the Spanish-American War, the designs incorporated lessons from the fighting. *Virginia* and her sisters would be larger and more powerful than any previous American battleships. Substantial time was spent agreeing on their required speed and exact displacement. Their armament—and the choice of whether to employ superimposed turrets—led to more controversy. It took three different boards to arrive at a final agreement on the requirements, and the official design was not approved until February 1901, almost two years after authorization. This delay caught the attention of congressional leaders. Concerned, the congressmen injected themselves into the process, asking Secretary Long to supply them in the future the rationales behind designs.

The debacle with the *Virginia* class gave valuable ammunition to the insurgents. Many officers were starting to conclude that the Board on Construction was overly conservative and unable to keep pace with the rapid changes taking place in warship design. It was an unfortunate time to have a cumbersome and controversial process: in February 1906, Great Britain launched a battleship of unprecedented size and power. HMS *Dreadnought* displaced more than 18,000 tons, had ten 12-inch guns, could reach twenty-one knots—the speed of an armored cruiser—with her steam turbines, and was twice as powerful as any other battleship afloat. All other capital ships in the world were rendered obsolete overnight. The U.S. Navy's future battleships would have to match or exceed this new standard.

Congress now became more receptive to the arguments of the insurgents and their lobbying. Senator Hale, however, was opposed. Cdr. William S. Sims, then inspector of target practice, was frustrated with the resulting lack of congressional action and contributed to an article by Henry Reuterdahl that appeared in *McClure's Magazine* in January

1908. "The Needs of Our Navy" was one of several contemporary muckraking pieces criticizing the Navy and supporting the cause of the insurgents. Through Reuterdahl, Sims pointed out flaws in battleship designs, the problems with the existing promotion system, and inefficiencies resulting from the lack of a general staff.[33]

Senator Hale was incensed. He used a series of Senate hearings convened to investigate the charges in Reuterdahl's article to stifle reform. Much of the testimony focused on the design of battleships, particularly the Navy's latest, *North Dakota*. Hale and his Naval Affairs Committee, unsympathetic to Sims and the reformers, made it impossible for them to present their arguments effectively. Having failed to achieve their ends in Congress, Sims and the others appealed directly to President Roosevelt.

The appeal to Roosevelt led to the 1908 Newport Conference. Ostensibly an investigation of the design of battleship *North Dakota,* the conference was "actually an inquiry into the general problem of battleship design and the *process* of battleship design."[34] Roosevelt believed it was essential that the senior officers of the Board on Construction incorporate feedback from fleet officers. He invited several younger officers—ship captains, executive officers (seconds in command), and department heads—to share their views.[35] Roosevelt was frustrated by the immediate results; he was unable to change the ship-design process, and the characteristics of the next two battleships—*Florida* and *Utah*—would be fundamentally the same as those of *North Dakota*. However, when William Howard Taft became president in March 1909, his new Secretary of the Navy, George von Lengerke Meyer, dissolved the Board on Construction and passed responsibility for new ship designs to the General Board.

This shift had far-reaching ramifications. The General Board lacked the authority of a true general staff, but it had proved its ability to take a long-term view and advise the secretary effectively on complex naval subjects. Since its establishment, it had provided detailed recommendations on the size and composition of the Navy. The board coupled this perspective and its skill at effectively soliciting opinions from across the Navy's organizational structure to address the deficiencies identified in Reuterdahl's article and by the Newport Conference. The result was a much closer alignment between the design of new ships and the roles they were expected to fulfill in wartime.

The General Board's approach allowed the Navy to harness a diverse set of perspectives—strategic, tactical, and technical—and integrate them into the designs of new ships. Diversity was ensured by the board's use of confidential hearings, which allowed naval officers to testify privately, without fear of reprisal. A preliminary design section was established within the Bureau of Construction and Repair; it worked closely with the board to prototype new ideas rapidly and provide quick feedback on what was feasible with respect to the limitations of current technology. Inputs from these various sources fed into internal deliberations, where the board reviewed available information and refined its recommendations.[36]

The first battleship design that went through this process clearly demonstrated its advantages. The *Nevada* class, authorized in 1911, represented a radically new, forward-looking approach. Anticipating the increasing battle ranges that would result from improving gunnery techniques, *Nevada* and her sister *Oklahoma* were the first battleships in the world explicitly designed to fight at ranges over ten thousand yards. They marked a milestone in the Navy's design process and introduced a new "standard" type that would dominate the Navy's battleship designs until after World War I. It was the first of many innovations that emerged from the process of ship design used and refined by the General Board.

THE CHIEF OF NAVAL OPERATIONS

The new approach to ship design did not satisfy the insurgents. Sims, Fiske, Key, and Belknap had all pushed for the creation of a naval general staff in the lead-up to the Newport Conference of 1908. Many of the civilian secretaries, along with members of Congress like Senator Hale, had consistently opposed the idea. They feared that even if the introduction of a naval general staff improved the Navy's ability to plan and prepare for war, the constitutional cost would be too great. Too much power would be in the hands of the naval officers and too little in those of their civilian masters, threatening the future of the republic.

President Roosevelt disagreed. In his annual message in December 1908, he argued for a naval general staff: "There is literally no excuse whatever for continuing the present organization of the Navy."[37] In mid-January 1909, the president hosted a large commission composed of retired Navy secretaries and current and retired officers to investigate the problem of naval administration; as in 1908, he was disappointed with the results. On 27 January, he created a new commission of just eight men and asked it to pursue the question further; this was the Moody Board, comprising two former secretaries of the Navy, a former member of the House Naval Affairs Committee, and Admirals Mahan, Luce, William M. Folger, William S. Cowles, and Robley D. Evans. They recommended that the Navy Department be organized into five divisions, one of them dedicated to developing war plans and policy. Unfortunately, Roosevelt lacked the political influence needed to turn the board's recommendations into legislation, and they died in committee during the waning hours of his administration.[38]

However, Roosevelt had developed an effective relationship with George Meyer, President Taft's Navy secretary. Meyer kept alive the issue of how best to organize the Navy Department, convening several boards to investigate relevant questions. In his first annual report, Meyer characterized the problems he observed with the current organization: "As the business of the department has grown beyond the personal coordinating power of the Secretary, it is necessary that he have assistants in the different logical divisions of duties, who will present matters of business for his verbal decisions or for his signature. He will thus act as does the president of a railroad or other large business establishment, and be able to decide matters quickly, while being kept thoroughly informed as to the business of the department."[39]

Meyer envisioned four logical divisions: Operations (i.e., of the fleet), Personnel, Material, and Inspections. Of these, he felt the greatest need was Operations: "The most serious defects in the existing organization are the lack of a branch dealing directly with the military use of the fleet and the lack of responsible expert advisors to aid the Secretary in reaching conclusions in case of disagreement between the coordinate branches of the department."[40]

To address these problems, Meyer built on the approach advocated by the Moody Board. Meyer divided the Navy Department into his four divisions and assigned an officer with the title of "Aid" (hereafter "aide") to each of them. Aides were senior officers who could provide the secretary direct advice and coordinate activities within their spheres of responsibility. Meyer stressed that the naval aides, like the General Board, were purely advisory and lacked executive power and authority. They had to coordinate their efforts and work through the secretary; the Aide for Operations, for example, would "advise the Secretary as to strategic and tactical matters in conjunction with the General Board, and also advise regarding the movements and dispositions of naval vessels."[41]

It was within Meyer's authority to introduce this reorganization without congressional approval, and he did so in December 1909, while Congress was in recess. This avoided a fight for legislative approval, but it meant that the aide system was without legal foundation. Meyer hoped that once the positive effects of the new organization were seen, the aides could be given legal recognition and four-year terms, a need he repeatedly emphasized in his annual reports. However, legal recognition was not forthcoming. Although the aides improved the workings of the department, their existence remained tenuous.

When President Woodrow Wilson took office in March 1913, he appointed Josephus Daniels as his Navy secretary. Daniels, like many secretaries before him, firmly believed in the preeminence of civilian authority. He opposed the creation of a naval general staff, fearing it would undermine that authority. When Rear Adm. Bradley A. Fiske, the Aide for Operations, approached Daniels to argue that the aides should receive legislative sanction, Daniels responded, "Absolute control of the Navy by a military head or by a general staff composed solely of naval officers is contrary to the spirit of our institutions."[42]

Undeterred, Fiske continued to argue strongly for a general staff organization. He lobbied Congressman Richmond P. Hobson of Alabama, a Democratic member of the House Naval Affairs Committee. Hobson was a former naval officer who had served in the Spanish-American War. He was supportive of reorganization and arranged to have Fiske testify before the committee in the deliberations on the 1915 Naval Appropriations Bill. Afterward, Fiske, Hobson, and six other officers met and prepared legislation introducing a Chief of Naval Operations (CNO); Hobson inserted their language into the bill. It called for "a Chief of Naval Operations . . . responsible for the readiness of the Navy for war and . . . charged with its general direction."[43] Fiske logically expected to hold the new post as a natural evolution of his current position.

Fearing that Hobson's provision would unacceptably compromise civilian control, Daniels leveraged the extremely cordial and harmonious relationships he had developed with congressmen and senators to revise the language. He could not stop the creation of the CNO position, but he did ensure that authority remained with the secretary. The final appropriation bill read: "There shall be a Chief of Naval Operations, who shall be an officer on the active list of the Navy appointed by the president, by and with the advice and consent of the Senate, from the officers of the line of the Navy not below the grade of Captain for a period of four years, who shall, under the direction of the Secretary, be charged with the operations of the fleet, and with the preparation and readiness of plans for its use in war."[44]

Daniels reinforced his authority over the new office by choosing Capt. William S. Benson as the first CNO. In doing so, Daniels passed over several well-qualified more senior officers, including Fiske, whose tenure as Aide for Operations ended with Benson's appointment. Daniels had hoped to select a talented individual who would respect civilian authority. He chose wisely: Benson was diplomatically skilled and got along well with Daniels. Despite the limited scope of the office, in fact, Benson performed impressively.

Greater authority for the CNO came sooner than expected. By the middle of 1916, it had become apparent that the United States might be drawn into World War I or face a hostile coalition after its end. This spurred an increase in military preparedness, despite the country's neutral stance. The resulting 1916 Naval Appropriations Bill dramatically increased the size of the Navy and called for construction that would make it the largest in the world; it also provided several organizational improvements, including additional power for the office of the

CNO. Daniels welcomed these changes. In the intervening year, he had become an enthusiastic supporter of the office and now recognized the need to give it more weight. At the end of 1916 Daniels claimed that the Navy possessed "the best naval organization that human wisdom has devised." During World War I, Daniels allowed Benson to operate effectively in his new role, proving the value of the office and the soundness of the concepts underpinning it.

The introduction of the office of the CNO was the closest the Navy would come to a naval general staff. It was a compromise solution and, like the General Board, distinctly American. The CNO was responsible for planning and preparation but lacked command authority. That remained with the secretary and the fleet commanders afloat. The structure necessitated conversation and compromise.

A SYSTEM OF PROFESSIONALS

The Naval Personnel Act of 1899 was a remarkable piece of legislation and an important milestone. However, it failed to address the problems inherent in the existing officer promotion system. The "plucking boards" allowed more rapid movement through the ranks but did not advance the most deserving officers. The assumption of equity—equal treatment for each officer—remained the basis for the promotion system. This had a mixed impact on morale; officers knew they could advance through the ranks but that advancement was out of their control. If they lived long enough and remained competent, they would become admirals. This explains the title of Donald Chisholm's comprehensive study of the Navy's officer personnel system; they were all but literally *Waiting for Dead Men's Shoes*.

The insurgents, with the tacit approval of President Roosevelt, argued for promotion based on merit. The most talented and skilled officers would be selected for higher rank; that would promote "efficiency." Lieutenant Commander Sims had efficiency in mind when he introduced a new system of target practice in 1902. It ranked ships by the accuracy of their fire, so that the entire fleet knew who had performed best and who was the worst. The consequences of this system are described in more detail in the next chapter, but it is important to note that it helped trigger interest in a system that promoted officers on the basis of competence rather than seniority.

In January 1905, the General Board issued a report on the personnel problem. The report represented a year's effort and broke the problem into several components. The most serious was the age of senior officers. The board argued that "unless more vacancies are produced in the rear admiral's, captain's, and commander's lists, officers will attain those grades too old." It called for mandatory retirement ages for various grades. This would help ensure that officers entering the higher ranks would be young enough to serve effectively. It was a significant change, one that threatened the current assumption of equity, but it addressed one aspect of the problem with the promotion process—the reliance on seniority. The Secretary of the Navy, now Paul Morton, submitted draft legislation to Congress based on the General Board's recommendation, but nothing came of it.

In November, the General Board revisited the question, prompted by a memorandum by Cdr. S. A. Staunton, currently at the Naval War College. Staunton argued against mandatory retirement ages, contending that "age does not impair great qualities, [and] ill health frequently fails to blunt them."[45] He believed a better approach would be to select the best officers for promotion to the highest ranks and remove those who had been passed over once they reached a certain age. The General Board agreed and sent the new Navy secretary (Morton having resigned in June), Charles Bonaparte, a draft bill. Bonaparte, less familiar with the nature of the challenges, had his own ideas and modified the proposal to Congress; the legislation again went nowhere. However, the proposal had touched on the other major aspect the promotion process—rewarding those most talented.

In August 1906, Secretary Bonaparte appointed a board to consider the personnel problem. His assistant secretary, Truman Newberry, served as the board's president. Newberry solicited opinions from a variety of officers before the board convened. Two of the most detailed were provided by Sims and Key. Sims argued that promotions should be based on merit. He proposed, to defeat bias, a complex system that relied on gathering the opinions of many officers. He felt that if the pool was large enough, the potential for favoritism would drop and the best officers would rise to the top. Key's detailed proposal was one that he had previously published in *Proceedings*. Rather than urging the promotion of the best-qualified officers, Key argued for extending the plucking boards. He would have them remove officers who did not meet the qualifications for promotion to the next higher grade. This would improve the flow through the ranks by removing the worst. Newberry's board thought Key's plan was the better fit and developed a set of recommendations based on it.[46]

Bonaparte adjusted these recommendations slightly for his annual report in December. President Roosevelt followed with recommendations of his own, declaring that there was an "urgent need for the establishment of a principle of selection which will eliminate men after a certain age if they cannot be promoted from the subordinate ranks."[47] Congress was not moved; Senator Hale opposed the measure, and no legislation was forthcoming. It was soon thereafter that Sims and his fellow insurgents shared their frustrations in Reuterdahl's article.

One final effort at reform was made during President Roosevelt's tenure. Cdr. Roy C. Smith, at the Naval War College, wrote a paper on the personnel problem and sent it to the General Board in December 1908. It discussed the relative merits of two approaches. One selected the most talented for promotion; the other involuntarily retired the least capable. Like Key, Smith concluded the latter would be the best fit for the needs of the service. The recommendation found its way to Congressman Hobson, who introduced a bill based on it. The chairman of the House Naval Affairs Committee forwarded the bill to the Navy secretary, now Truman Newberry, on 10 December. Newberry queried his department and responded to the committee with an extremely detailed report on 12 January 1909. The report did not recommend approval, but the rapidity of the response, its detail, and the variety of organizations providing input illustrates "how well developed . . . [the Navy's] institutional capacity for problem-solving had become."[48] The professionalism of the department was increasing, even if the problem of promotion remained unsolved.

George von Lengerke Meyer brought an emphasis on operational efficiency to his work. Conscious of the limits of his knowledge, Meyer relied on officers for advice. The aide system was a visible example of this; less visible was Meyer's willingness to consult with Sims and the other insurgents. In 1909, in his first annual report, Meyer pointed out the flaws he observed in the promotion system:

> It is necessary to invite your attention to the urgent need for legislation to improve the conditions which have existed for some years, and still exist, in the higher grades in the line of the navy. The senior officers of our navy are old for the responsibilities and arduous duty required in the modern battle ship. They are much older than similar officers in the other principal navies of the world. . . . [F]lag officers arrive at the grade of rear admiral so late that even those of longest possible service do not get adequate training as subordinate flag officers before assuming the chief command.[49]

At the time Meyer wrote his report, the average age of the Navy's rear admirals was sixty. Captains averaged fifty-six years old. They were about a decade older, on average, than their counterparts around the world.[50]

However, even though he could recognize the problem, clearly frame it, and provide recommendations for improvement, Meyer was unable to spur congressional action. Meyer's efforts failed because he and his officers were unable to convince Congress that the existing system was seriously flawed, in spite of the fact that it failed to allow officers to reach the highest ranks while they were still youthful enough to be effective. The General Board had helped promote understanding of the problem and was improving the Navy's ability to describe the complex, interrelated factors. However, the arguments offered were insufficient to change the law. "Until the Navy, which now recognized this fundamental component of the personnel problem, found a way to educate Congress, no personnel bills were very likely to pass."[51]

In the meantime, the majority opinion in the service was turning against the existing system. Promotion by seniority, augmented occasionally by the plucking boards, assumed that the characteristics of a good naval officer remained constant as an individual moved through the grades. As the insurgents gained experience themselves at higher levels of command, they realized this was not the case. Fiske devoted considerable attention to this topic in a June 1907 article in *Proceedings*, "The Naval Profession." Fiske described three separate skill sets required for effective leadership in a modern organization—"driving," "managing," and "directing"—and noted that different levels of command required distinct approaches with different mixes of these skills.[52] Other officers were becoming more convinced of the merits of promotion based on skill.

Under President Wilson, Josephus Daniels capitalized on these changes of opinion within the service to introduce a modern system of officer promotion. He had already instituted a shipboard education system, created postgraduate programs, and made attendance at the Naval War College a requirement for promotion to high command. Daniels looked favorably on the idea of promotion by selection because it would ensure talented officers were placed in the most important positions. He considered efficiency more important than equity.

Daniels quickly familiarized himself with the core problems of the existing promotion system. The best officers were not being promoted, and the current laws prevented the officer corps from growing as the Navy increased in size. To investigate the problem and propose solutions (yet again), Daniels appointed a personnel board in July 1914. The board was headed by the assistant secretary, Franklin D. Roosevelt; other members were Rear Adm. Victor Blue and Chief Constructor David W. Taylor. Daniels gave the board specific instructions: he wanted it to propose a system "causing a healthy flow of promotions through the various grades, enabling the most capable and efficient officers to reach the higher grades at an age when they are capable of rendering the most efficient service."[53]

The board conducted a thorough investigation; it interviewed a variety of officers and examined previous congressional testimony. It issued in January 1915 a report recommending a system that selected the best and most talented officers for promotion. Daniels drafted legislation on the basis of this recommendation and sent it to the House

Naval Affairs Committee, along with the board's report. The draft bill would abolish the plucking boards and replace them with a system of competitive selection.[54]

The chair of the House Naval Affairs Committee was Lemuel P. Padgett, a Democratic representative from Tennessee and a Daniels ally. Padgett favored the bill and worked to educate other congressmen about its importance. In the Senate, Virginia Democrat Claude Swanson worked to similar ends. Senator Benjamin R. Tillman of South Carolina, another Democratic ally of Daniels, chaired the Senate Naval Affairs Committee. They were unable to secure passage of the bill, but a few changes did appear in the final 1915 legislation. The plucking boards were abolished, and the ranks of admiral and vice admiral were established as permanent grades, something Navy secretaries had been pushing for since the early 1890s.[55]

Daniels was determined to try again. He told the personnel board to make further recommendations. With his annual report for 1915, Daniels addressed the problem directly. In a section entitled "Officers Should Be Promoted for Merit and Not by Seniority," he stated: "It [promotion by seniority] is a deterrent to efficiency, gives no incentive toward excellence, and is contrary to every rule guaranteeing that merit shall win its just reward, the only proper American system. There is no industrial or commercial business . . . which promotes equally men of average ability and men of proven excellence."[56]

Victor Blue augmented these arguments with a plea for congressional action:

An abnormal condition exists in the line of the Navy . . . which will adversely affect efficiency by causing stagnation in promotion. The longer remedial legislation is delayed the greater will be the cost and the more drastic the action, to say nothing of the consequent loss of efficiency. The most serious situation which confronts the personnel of the Navy today is the advanced ages at which captains are being promoted to the rank of rear admiral, as well as the large number of junior lieutenants and ensigns compared with the number of officers in grades senior to them. Until

Congress enacts remedial legislation the ages of captains when promoted to rear admiral will continue to increase and there will be little in prospect for junior officers.[57]

Blue and his colleagues forwarded another draft law to the congressional committees in March 1916. Through the late spring and early summer, with the war in Europe raging, the bill was vigorously debated in Congress. Attention was fixed on the need for a large and powerful Navy to protect the nation's interests; President Wilson went on a speaking tour, calling for "the greatest Navy in the world" and proposing the largest building program the world had ever seen. Talented officers would be needed to command these ships.

By early August, the details of an agreement had been roughed out. All promotions to command grade—the rank of commander and above—would be by selection; selections would be made by a board of rear admirals. Starting in 1920, mandatory retirement ages would be introduced, to ensure that there would be openings for younger and .more talented officers. Officers would need two years of sea service in their current grades to be eligible for promotion, a provision emphasizing the value of commanding ships and formations at sea. On 29 August 1916, President Wilson signed the Line Personnel Act into law, ushering in a new officer promotion system. The massive 1916 naval building program was more conspicuous, but this act was more important. The Navy finally had a modern system for its officer corps, with promotion predicated on demonstrated performance at sea. Victor Blue called it, with justification, his "proudest achievement."[58] It perfectly complemented the General Board and Office of the Chief of Naval Operations (OPNAV).

PROFESSIONAL ENLISTED MEN

The Navy's shift to an increasingly professional organization affected enlisted men as well as officers. The dynamics of the change were different for the enlisted, but many of the drivers were the same. The rapid growth of the fleet required the Navy to bring in many more recruits. These recruits had to be trained to operate the machinery of the Navy's increasingly modern warships. The result was an increasingly effective educational system that developed the skills of sailors, increased their professional knowledge, and helped the Navy retain them.

In the late nineteenth century, the Navy relied almost exclusively on enlisted men who came to the service already in possession of nautical skills. Sailors, in the traditional interpretation of the word, formed the core of the Navy's enlisted force. There was a significant reliance on foreign nationals and seamen from the eastern seaboard. "Landsmen"—as those without nautical skills were known—were not recruited. All this allowed the Navy to leverage a traditional apprenticeship model for education and devote little attention to the professional development of enlisted men.

The situation changed after the Spanish-American War. The increasing size of the Navy necessitated recruiting landsmen, many of whom came from the Midwest. Unlike sailors, landsmen required training before they could serve effectively on board ship. The Navy introduced a series of training stations to educate the new recruits and familiarize them with their responsibilities, at Newport, Rhode Island; Norfolk, Virginia; San Francisco, California; and Lake Bluff, north of Chicago, Illinois. These stations provided generalized education for new recruits, but the increasing complexity of shipboard duties necessitated more specialized knowledge as well. For seamen-gunners, a class was created at the Naval Gun Factory (within the Washington Navy Yard) in Washington, D.C. A similar course on torpedoes and mines was introduced at the Naval Torpedo Station in Newport. To help promote the accuracy of the fleet's gunnery, small-arms target ranges were established at various stations; these familiarized officers and men with the basics of ballistics.

In 1898, a school for the fundamentals of electricity was established at the Boston Navy Yard. A year later, similar schools were established in the yards at New York and Mare Island, California. Additional specialty schools followed. Newport and Mare Island gained schools for yeomen and musicians; an artificers' school for carpenters, blacksmiths, plumbers, and other trades was added at the Norfolk Navy Yard in 1902; and a machinists' school was introduced at Charleston,

South Carolina. There were schools for firemen, who tended the ships' boilers, cooks, and bakers. Charles Oscar Paullin noted in 1914 the impact of these schools:

> These various schools and means of instruction have greatly enhanced the efficiency of the sailorman. They have specialized his training to meet new naval needs, and have enabled him to use and understand the complicated machinery with which ships are now fitted. He is coming to know less and less about sails, and more and more about machines. . . . The bluff, jolly, illiterate, profane and picturesque man-of-war's men of the old school is disappearing. The newcomers are men of better morals, more booklearning, and more specialized skill, though less indigenous to the sea and more likely to abandon a seafaring life.[59]

The composition of the Navy's enlisted force was changing as it grew. It was becoming better trained and more skilled, and its reliance on foreigners was decreasing. These changes were taking place while the force dramatically increased in size. In 1898, the authorized strength of the enlisted force was 13,750. By 1902, it had doubled to 28,000, and by 1913 it had nearly doubled again, to 51,500. Most of the new recruits were landsmen from the interior of the country; in 1901, such men accounted for 4,198 of the new enlistments.[60] Soon, the publicity generated by the cruise of the Great White Fleet would draw even more of them to the service.

Secretary Daniels, who believed in the power of education, encouraged enlistment. He was convinced that the Navy had great value as an educational institution, one that could better the lives of sailors. In his first annual report, he emphasized this point:

> It is my ambition to make the Navy a great university, with college extensions afloat and ashore. Every ship should be a school, and every enlisted man, and petty and warrant officer should be given the opportunity to improve his mind, better his position and fit himself for promotion. . . . Training produces skill, and skill not only produces efficiency but enhances self-respect. It is admitted

by naval officers that . . . seamen and even petty officers have too little accurate knowledge. . . . They know a thing is habitually done but not always why it is done. This will be corrected.[61]

Daniels established an academic department on every ship and at every naval station. Starting in 1914, academic and practical instruction was mandatory for every enlisted sailor for the first two years of his enlistment. It became optional thereafter, but many continued to participate; in 1915, 60 percent of the Navy's enlisted men were involved in educational activities in their spare time. Daniels expected the emphasis on education to have a positive impact on retention and lead to an increasing rate of reenlistment.[62]

He was correct. Service in the Navy soon became so attractive that by May 1914 a waiting list was established for new recruits. There were more applicants than there were spots to fill, and the service became more selective. By 1915, only about one-sixth of those applying for service in the Navy were accepted; the rest did not meet the new standards. The number of reenlistments also increased. Daniels highlighted in 1915 the fact that 85 percent of those eligible reenlisted, a significant increase over the 54 percent that had reenlisted in 1912 and part of a growing trend over his tenure to that point.[63]

Daniels' efforts to promote the education of enlisted men were paralleled by his emphasis on professional education for officers. He hired the first civilian head of the English Department at the Naval Academy to give midshipmen more familiarity with the liberal arts and humanities and to help them learn to write clear, concise orders. Daniels so increased the class sizes at the Naval War College that by the end of 1914, seventy officers were attending class at Newport and over four hundred were participating in a correspondence course.[64]

The improving educational system for officers and enlisted men was a new, enabling organizational constraint, one triggered by specific requirements. The Navy needed additional recruits to man the larger and more powerful ships that were joining the fleet. The increasing sophistication of the equipment on those ships required new and more specialized knowledge. An educational system satisfied both needs, by giving enlisted men the knowledge they needed to do their jobs effectively while simultaneously providing them with an incentive to stay in service.

The constraint had an additional, unanticipated result. It contributed to a culture that emphasized learning and knowledge. The educational system began to integrate with the processes inherited from the nineteenth century—which focused on seniority and apprenticeship—and augmented them by increasing the importance of gaining skill and ability through study. The "skilled seamanship of the disciplined sailor" remained "an art developed through trial and error," but the first trials became more successful and the initial errors less significant.[65] The Navy began to become a learning institution.

CONCLUSION

On 2 April 1917, President Wilson asked a joint session of Congress to declare war on the German empire and enter the world war. The Navy that would fight Germany was radically different from the one that had triumphed over Spain. In the intervening eighteen years, the organizational structure of the Navy had been transformed by the efforts of the insurgents and their supporters. It had changed from a traditional organization to a modern, professional one, with a series of new organizational constraints in place that would influence its work over the next several decades.

Two of those constraints were visible in the Navy's organizational structure. The General Board had become the Navy's senior advisory council. It worked closely with the Naval War College to develop plans and force structures, providing the secretary with effective advice and allowing the department to develop a long-term view. The CNO was now responsible for planning and preparing the fleet for war. Between these two organizations, the Navy finally possessed an effective apparatus to act as, in effect, a naval general staff. It fell short of what the insurgents wanted, but it met their goals admirably while preserving the preeminence of civilian authority.

A third constraint was less visible, but no less important. The Navy had taken steps to become a learning institution; it had begun to stress the importance of knowledge and professional development. The establishment of the Naval War College was the initial step in a broad transition that culminated in the introduction of the merit-based promotion system. The educational systems introduced for enlisted men supported and reinforced this trend. In the fleet, merit-based scoring systems for gunnery and engineering performance built on this foundation, encouraging officers and enlisted men to apply their best knowledge and skill to the challenges of steaming and fighting their ships.

The transition to a merit-based promotion system further redefined the role of a naval officer, building on the changes introduced by the integration of the line officers and the engineers. The need to acquire a diverse collection of specialized knowledge—in tactics, strategy, machinery, electricity, and gunnery—helped expand the perspectives of the officers entering the service in the early years of the twentieth century and fostered new, innovative approaches. These new constraints interacted with the relatively small size of the Navy's officer corps to shape its leadership. Throughout this period, the Navy had relatively few officers. Even with the increases during the preceding years, there were just over two thousand line officers in service by July 1915.[66] The small numbers allowed each officer to become familiar with his peers, subordinates, and superiors.

Personal relationships and connections, in fact, dominated their work. More senior officers requested that proven and familiar individuals be transferred with them to new commands. The career of William V. Pratt is an excellent example. Pratt graduated from the Naval Academy in 1889 and came to the attention of Cdr. M. R. S. MacKenzie while serving on *Chicago* and on *Petrel* soon thereafter. When MacKenzie was fitting out the converted yacht *Mayflower* for service during the Spanish-American War, he specifically requested that Pratt join him.[67] Pratt was handpicked again in 1913, when Sims asked him to join the Atlantic Fleet's Torpedo Flotilla as his chief of staff. His close relationship with Sims served him well when Rear Admiral Benson asked Pratt to serve as Assistant Chief of Naval Operations in 1917.

Ernest J. King was one of a new breed of younger officers who benefitted from the organizational constraints introduced in this period. The emphasis on learning, the new system of officer promotion, and the amalgamation of the Engineering Corps and the line created new opportunities for talented, ambitious men like King who had graduated from the Naval Academy in the early years of the twentieth century. His contemporaries were the leaders who were, again like him, to see the Navy through World War II. Harold R. Stark, a future CNO, graduated in 1903; William F. Halsey graduated a year later; Chester W. Nimitz was a graduate of the class of 1905; and Frank J. Fletcher and Raymond A. Spruance followed in 1906.

King graduated in 1901. Forty years later, with the battleships of the Pacific Fleet sunk in Pearl Harbor, President Roosevelt made King the Navy's commander in chief. To prevent the confusion in command both had observed in 1917, Roosevelt took the unprecedented step of also making King CNO, in March 1942. This move ensured unity of command and direction during World War II. With King as both CNO and commander in chief, the Navy obeyed a single authority. Working successfully with his peers, he became the architect of the defeat of Japan in the Pacific and the projection of American power across the Atlantic.

The work of the insurgents was an important foundation of that later victory. Ultimately, they were successful in their efforts, and the changes they triggered transformed the Navy into a modern institution. Elting E. Morison praised their perseverance when he dedicated his biography of William S. Sims to "the insurgent spirit and to those officers who have maintained it within the United States Navy in time of peace."[68] Published soon after the American entry into World War II, Morison's note foreshadowed how important that spirit would be in the Pacific.

2
THE GUNNERY SYSTEM

Hit hard, hit fast, hit often.
—William F. Halsey, 1942

At the dawn of the twentieth century, the predominant weapon of naval warfare was the gun. Torpedoes and mines had roles, but gunfire decided major naval battles. American victories in the Spanish-American War and the Japanese triumph at Tsushima during the Russo-Japanese War were won with naval artillery. However, hitting one moving ship from another was difficult. Analyses of the battles of Santiago and Manila Bay revealed a surprising level of inaccuracy. Only 2.5 percent of shells hit the target at Manila Bay; at Santiago, just 1.3 percent found their mark.[1] The Navy needed to improve. Efforts to increase accuracy of gunfire led to increasingly sophisticated approaches and ultimately to the Navy's first shipboard information-management system, a merging of skilled men and sophisticated machines that modeled the movements of the firing ship and the target. This information-management system was called "fire control"—it controlled the fire of the ship's guns. It was the Navy's first major innovation of the twentieth century.

The fire-control system had several unique characteristics that made it particularly effective. Its components were loosely coupled together in what today we would call an "open architecture," one that allowed it to leverage and integrate new technologies as rapidly as they became available. The system contained multiple feedback loops, allowing accurate assessments of system performance and permitting output to be continually refined. Automation was incrementally applied to the parts of the system most susceptible to human error, increasing accuracy and freeing operators to concentrate on more complex challenges requiring human judgment. Redundant and flexible connections made the system resilient, "safe to fail," and highly tolerant of damage from enemy fire. All these features combined to make the Navy's fire-control system the most effective of its kind during the battleship era.[2]

As the Navy's fire-control system was refined and improved, it began to exert a strong influence. It became an enabling constraint for battle tactics—permitting accurate fire at longer ranges and during more complicated maneuvers—and enhanced the capabilities of the battle fleet. As the Navy's first true system of distributed cognition, it influenced later developments, like the radar plot and the Combat Information Center (CIC). Because of its impact on tactics, doctrine, and the Navy's approach to shipboard organization, the fire-control system was arguably the most important technological development in the evolution of the Navy's surface-warfare doctrine.

A SYSTEM FOR IMPROVEMENT

Adm. William S. Sims exerted a powerful influence on the development of the Navy's fire-control system. As described in the previous chapter, Sims was an insurgent, an officer who repeatedly challenged existing approaches and consistently pushed for more systematic methods. He has been described as the "father" of the Navy's fire-control system—working as an individual champion, struggling alone against institutionalized resistance. Reality was more complex. Sims had sponsors and supporters, and he began his work at a time when there was a willingness to adopt new methods. His efforts are best understood against the backdrop of substantial change taking place in the Navy Department in the early twentieth century. Enlightened officers and men saw Sims' techniques as a way to grow their own careers, triggering a revolution that ultimately led to a new system of fire control.

The first step was the introduction of a "feedback loop" that assessed current performance; that system of feedback was Sims' greatest contribution.

His efforts began before the Spanish-American War. In January 1898, Sims was serving as the naval attaché in Paris. There he wrote reports about the superiority of European methods of gunnery training. These caught the attention of Theodore Roosevelt, then the Assistant Secretary of the Navy. The war intervened before the pair could promote any changes, but an important precedent had been set. In 1900, as a lieutenant in the Asiatic Squadron, Sims met Capt. (later admiral) Sir Percy Scott of Great Britain's Royal Navy (RN). Scott had developed a new method for controlling gunfire and was employing it on cruiser HMS *Terrible*. Scott's method, "continuous aim," dramatically increased the accuracy and effectiveness of shipboard gunfire.

Hitting one moving ship from another is a complex problem. Moving targets must be "led," so that shells are aimed not at where the target is but at where it will be when they arrive. When the firing platform is also moving—not only along its course but rolling and pitching in the waves—the challenge increases dramatically. The difficulties become more pronounced as the range increases. Minor errors in aiming, either in direction ("line") or distance (range) are magnified as the distance to the target increases. These difficulties explain why, although potential battle ranges increased with improvements in the technology of naval artillery during the late nineteenth century, effective combat range was limited by how well the guns could be aimed and controlled by individual gunners.

Continuous aim addressed this problem by improving the control of individual guns. Before continuous aim, the gun "pointer" had to pick a specific point in the ship's roll to fire. There were two possible choices. Firing at either end of the roll would work well in that the ship would be momentarily stationary, but the plane of the deck, to which the gun was attached, would be at an angle. The sights of the gun would need to be "offset" to compensate for this, and there was no guarantee that the angle would be the same every time. The other alternative was to fire in the middle of the roll, at the moment when the ship's deck was horizontal. The sights would not need to be offset, but the pointer's timing had to be perfect. With continuous aim, pointers elevated and depressed their guns in harmony with the ship's roll, always at the correct elevation with respect to the horizon. Scott made this dramatic change possible by modifying the gearing for gun elevation, allowing the gun pointers to keep their sights on target while the ship was rolling. Accuracy increased. The rate of fire also increased, because the gun could be fired whenever it was ready, rather than having to wait for the proper moment in the ship's roll. In timed practices, ships employing continuous aim hit six times more often.[3]

Sims detailed the effectiveness of the new approach in a series of reports to the Navy Department. He argued that it should be adopted throughout the Navy without delay. Although Adm. George C. Remey, the commander of the Asiatic Squadron, endorsed the reports, no action was taken. When Theodore Roosevelt became president in September 1901, Sims saw an opening. In a dramatic breach of protocol, he wrote to the new president directly. Roosevelt responded warmly and ordered that Sims' reports be printed and distributed.[4] In Roosevelt, Sims had a powerful champion for change.

Sims may not have recognized it, but he had another important ally as well. The chief of the Bureau of Navigation was Rear Adm. Henry C. Taylor, an "enlightened" insurgent who worked to modernize the Navy's culture and institutions. Taylor was now responsible for personnel matters. In October 1902, despite resistance from other officers, Taylor appointed Sims to the post of Inspector of Target Practice and gave him the opportunity to experiment with continuous aim and introduce it to the fleet. Taylor's choice of Sims was crucial for the development of the Navy's fire-control system.

Improvements came quickly. In the 1903 gunnery practice, the battleship *Alabama* gave an unprecedented shooting performance, with 60 percent hits. Other ships demonstrated similar levels of increased proficiency. But the exercise had not been especially challenging: ranges had been less than two thousand yards and the target stationary. However, these results were sufficient for Sims to declare the experiment with continuous aim successful.

Continuous aim improved accuracy, but the more important result was increasing standardization of procedures for aiming and firing. Before the introduction of continuous aim, gunners had developed their own techniques, based on their own experience or that of the most seasoned individuals in their ships. The approach was unsystematic and relied heavily on master-apprentice relationships, making it difficult to generate broad improvements. With continuous aim, the Navy had standard procedures for the first time. Sims codified them in a new drill book, *Instructions Governing the Training and the Target Practice Required for the Development of Expert Gun Pointers and Gun Crews*. Standard procedures were a constraint that helped enable the emergence of new approaches.

Under Sims' influence, practices became more systematic, more rigorous, and more competitive. Standardized procedures enabled the creation of a culture of continuous improvement as gunners and ships strove to improve their scores. Cdr. Mark C. Bristol described some of the ramifications in a 1906 lecture at the Naval War College:

> The new system of training of gun pointers and gun crews was established beyond question by the results of these target practices. This system is based, (1) upon fair competitive target practice, (2) enlistment of the personnel [*sic*] initiative of all officers, and, (3) the dissemination of information gained at each target practice and other sources, amongst all officers concerned. A direct effect of this is to keep all defects in ordnance material under the criticism of hundreds of competent officers, who are directly interested in getting the best results and winning distinction. Consequently, there has been a rapid improvement in all ordnance material.[5]

The material did need improving. Along with other problems, the practices demonstrated that the Navy's "gun sights were mechanically defective and optically inefficient." Rear Adm. Newton E. Mason, chief of BuOrd, gathered lessons and helped to drive improvements. At Sims' urging and under pressure from Roosevelt, Mason installed new sights. These more than doubled the average number of hits. In addition to the new sights, Mason procured range finders, computing devices, and other equipment essential to improving fire control.[6]

The Secretary of the Navy, Victor H. Metcalf, described the influence of the recent gunnery practices in his annual report of 1908:

> The present system of competitive target practice between individual guns and ships has enlisted to such an extent the enthusiastic interest of officers and men that not only has the practice of each year . . . shown a marked increase in rapidity of hitting over those of previous years, but the advance in skill and knowledge of scientific gunnery methods and requirements resulting from this competition has stimulated a similar and no less important improvements [sic] in all ordnance material. The increase in skill has brought about a demand for more efficient appliances, which, in turn, have permitted greater refinements of skill, a process of development which there is every reason to believe will be continued.[7]

The feedback loop Metcalf describes is a clear example of increasing complexity through the introduction of an enabling constraint. The competitive practices drove the gunners to improve, and better techniques and new material resulted. These in turn increased the challenge of the competitive exercises and drove further interest in improvement.[8]

The changes triggered by continuous aim and the new system of practice were crucial. However, the new way of aiming and firing was only an incremental improvement. Shipboard communication mechanisms had not changed. Gunners still aimed and fired their weapons individually. Additionally, accuracy remained limited at longer ranges, and the large main batteries of battleships could not benefit from continuous aim because their elevation machinery was too slow. As potential fighting ranges increased, these limitations became more important.

Potential ranges were increasing because the size and power of battleships were growing. The battleship *Indiana* was commissioned in 1895 and fought at Santiago; she displaced just over ten thousand tons and was armed with short 13-inch guns. *Connecticut*, authorized in 1902, displaced 16,000 tons and was armed with modern 12-inch guns. Although *Connecticut*'s guns were smaller than *Indiana*'s, they were far more powerful because they used more modern powder. Slower burn rates allowed *Connecticut*'s guns to impart 40 percent more energy to their shells. Maximum range and accuracy increased accordingly.

Sims recognized the need for a more centralized approach. At longer ranges, individual gunners would not be able to see their targets or the "fall of shot" well enough to correct their fire. He proposed what amounted to a symmetry break. The guns would be coordinated from a central point, high in the ship; from there an officer would observe the flight of the shells and, given their points of impact relative to the target, order changes to the range settings for all guns at once. Individual gunners would no longer correct their own misses; instead, they would focus on doing their best to fire at the ordered time and at the ordered range. This was rudimentary "fire control," and in 1904 Sims, building on the work done with continuous aim, began experimenting with it.

> The officer in the tops—called a spotter and located in a fire control station—estimated the range at which the battery would open—that is, with the aid of a range-finder he estimated how far away the target was. This range he communicated to all sight-setters, who set their sights accordingly. When this had been done, a "ranging salvo" was fired. If it fell short of the target, the spotter estimated how far short, and communicated with the sight-setters below, telling them to advance their range—let us say fifty yards—calling out, "Up fifty."[9]

The battleship *Alabama* performed the initial experimental exercise. The changes led to greater accuracy and earlier hits after fire was opened. Sims and his colleagues became convinced that fire control was not only possible but essential. At six thousand yards—the expected battle range at the time—a spotter in the masts could observe the splashes and determine when changes needed to be made to the estimated range. Sims had found a solution that permitted centralized control of the guns and incorporated feedback. It became the foundation of the Navy's fire-control system.

Lieutenant Commander Bristol described the importance of spotting and its value as a feedback loop in his 1906 lecture: "It was evident, as soon as the subject was carefully considered, that there were variable errors of gun fire, and . . . [that] the sight bar range necessary to hit a target or ship must always be different from the actual distance measured; therefore, it was necessary to note the fall of the shot and make the necessary correction in the sight bar to bring the shots on the target. This has been termed 'spotting.'"[10]

The results of the initial experiments with fire control led to the convening of a special board by the Secretary of the Navy in 1905. The board's recommendations led to the adoption of such "fire control" as the Navy's standard approach. At BuOrd, Admiral Mason remarked on the impact in his annual report of 1907: "The most striking feature . . . during the last few years has been the progress in gunnery. Results of single-gun shooting have been such as were thought impossible a few years ago, and in the target practices that have been conducted in accordance with the new rules it has been made apparent that team work by the whole battery is not only possible, but that by such team work the effective fighting power of ships can be immensely increased."[11] Ranges also increased. By 1910, battleships were firing in target practices at over nine thousand yards. In the autumn of 1911, *Delaware* conducted an experimental practice at 16,000 yards; she hit a small target 3 percent of the time. In 1912, *Utah* scored 21 percent hits at over 11,000 yards.[12]

The system of fire control was Sims' greatest legacy as inspector of target practice, but it must be understood as part of a broader system of improvement. Continuous aim led to standardized approaches. These allowed the introduction of competitive gunnery practices, a self-organizing constraint that fostered new and more complex methods. Fire control was the first and most significant step along this path—a symmetry break that opened the door to a significantly greater potential—but it was not the last. Sims and Mason developed a system that encouraged experimentation and improvement using consistent regulations and competitive trials. Embedded within it was the assumption that no single technique was the end goal, that continuous refinement was desired. The fire-control system was the visible result of this work; less visible was the cultural change it triggered. The fire-control system, once developed, would be continually refined and improved.

In 1916, Secretary Daniels illustrated the ongoing improvements in his annual report:

> Exceptional records were being made in the fall practice of 1914 ... [by] the *North Dakota* under command of Capt. C. P. Plunkett ... with old guns of inferior caliber. The latter's report attributed the splendid record which his ship made ... to a system for locating errors, and ... to a plan for determining with reasonable certainty the causes of practically all misses. The system was then put into effect by Admiral [Henry T.] Mayo in the first division of the Atlantic Fleet, and an improvement followed similar to that which was noted on the *North Dakota*.[13]

Daniels went on to note that periodic analysis of approaches to fire control were eliminating poor methods, increasing the standardization of effective ones, and generally building knowledge of the underlying principles required for effective gunfire. Officers were layering their new knowledge upon the initial improvements triggered by Sims and Mason, spurred on by the system of gunnery exercises—the enabling constraint—established over a decade before. One of the reasons why they were seeking to eliminate faulty methods and improve standardization was that the approach to fire control, much like the Navy's gunnery before the introduction of continuous aim, had yet to be standardized.

FRAGMENTED SOLUTIONS

In the immediate aftermath of the decision to move to a centralized fire-control system, several fragmented approaches emerged. Different ships employed different tools in a variety of configurations, each attempting to develop a system that would allow accurate fire and high practice scores. Their approaches relied heavily on the skill and experience of individuals and did not immediately lend themselves to standardization. However, the period of experimentation was valuable because it allowed the Navy to gain experience with different techniques and prevented premature convergence on a suboptimal solution.

The most difficult problem confronting these early fire-control systems was determining the initial range to the target and then predicting how the range would change as the firing ship and target moved. A report on the target practice of 1905 noted, "In order to keep the . . . range . . . , it is necessary frequently to change the [range] setting by exactly the right amount[;] . . . it is necessary to establish the rate of change of range."[14] This rate of change in range was called the "range rate." Determining it was more complicated than might appear.

The situation of two ships approaching each other on parallel but opposite courses best illustrates the problem. When the two ships are distant from each other, the range rate is nearly constant and equals the combined speed of the two ships. However, as the ships get closer, the range rate slows down; when they are opposite each other, the range is constant and the range rate is zero. Thereafter, the range increases again, and the range rate accelerates, approaching once again the combined speed of the two ships. The geometries involved are not complicated, but accurately modeling them requires that range, courses, and speeds all be known. Early approaches to fire control involved measuring one or more of these factors.

Range finders were one of the most important tools. A range finder provided initial estimates of range to the target and, once a model of the target's movement had been developed, a check on the model's accuracy. At first, range finders were mounted in the tops of masts, but this limited their size and therefore accuracy, because accuracy was primarily determined by the base length of the range finder. Starting with the battleships *New York* and *Texas,* authorized in 1910, range finders were placed in turrets, permitting them to be large, accurate, and protected behind armor. In 1908, the crew of the battleship *Vermont* employed another method of finding the range—a "down ladder."

Three guns from the 7-inch secondary battery were fired in quick succession, the first three hundred yards beyond the range indicated by the range finder, the second at the range-finder range, and the last three hundred yards short. These three shells "bracketed" the target, allowing a quick and accurate determination of the actual range.[15]

Range finders and ranging salvoes could determine the current target range, but a proper solution to the problem required not only the range but an estimation of how it would change over time. To address this, the Navy introduced two new devices, the "range projector" and the "range clock." The "Change of Range Projector" had been invented by Lt. Cdr. Joseph M. Reeves and Lt. R. D. White in 1907. It supplied a rough physical model of the movements of the firing ship and the target, one that allowed a quick determination of the range rate. The range projector took in the range to the target, the target course, and the target speed. Using mechanical linkages, it solved the associated trigonometric functions and calculated the range rate. Previously, these calculations had been done manually.[16]

Initial experimentation with the range projector took place on board the battleship *Virginia*. The report of the ship's ordnance officer was very positive: "Used with the range clock there is but little more difficulty in keeping on the target than when the ship is at anchor."[17] A 1908 article in *Proceedings* was similarly positive, and Admiral Mason moved quickly to produce and install the new tool. Navy yards on the East Coast—at Washington, D.C., New York, and Philadelphia—manufactured them and shipped them to the West Coast to be installed in the ships of the Great White Fleet before their voyage across the Pacific. By mid-1909, the change-of-range projector had been provided to every battleship, cruiser, and gunboat in the fleet.[18]

The design of the range projector was clever. It visually represented the orientation of the firing ship and the target, using slotted disks. The one representing the target was turned to align with the target's relative course, and a pin within the slot was moved to represent the target's speed. The firing ship's disk was similar. This approach made it easy to assess the configuration of the device very quickly; the basic layout would be used by future devices.[19]

The range projector rapidly calculated the range rate, but if the guns were to shoot accurately, they had to be set to fire at a future range. To find that, the current range, range rate, and time required to aim and fire had to be factored together. These calculations could be performed manually, but that was time-consuming and error-prone. When the Navy discovered that the British firm Vickers had developed a device for the purpose called a "range clock," one was acquired for evaluation. The range clock, which looked much as the name suggests, incremented the range up or down according to an initial setting of the range and the range rate. If the range rate did not change and had been set correctly, the "hands" of the clock would always indicate the correct range.

Those conditions did not always hold true, but the range clock was a significant improvement over manual processes. Initial trials were very positive: "[It] automatically allows for the change of range, thus permitting the fire-control officer to devote his attention to obtaining the correct . . . range by spotting, in almost the same manner as if the ship were at anchor. Of course, when the spotter's observations, or those made by the range finder or range projector, show the rate of approach has changed, the rate of the instrument must be changed."[20] Spurred on by Sims, the Navy procured range clocks as standard equipment, manufactured under license by an American company, Sloan & Chase.

Once the future range to the target was determined, it had to be communicated to the guns. When individual gunners aimed and fired their own weapons, that communication was done only once, before firing began. The fire-control system, in contrast, required a network of communications; it had to allow the ship's captain to designate a target, spotters to provide their observations, range-finder operators to communicate the range, and fire-control officers to transmit orders to the guns. All this required a system of telephones, backed up by voice tubes. To support the increasingly complex nature of the connections and allow rapid reconfigurations, the telephone system was routed through a central control station (known as "central") containing a large switchboard. It connected all the various stations but did not guarantee the smooth and error-free transmission of information. Protocols had to be established to communicate the relevant information precisely and bring the guns on target quickly. The wiring was the easy part. Different ships, spurred on by the regular exercises, began to experiment with new fire-control vocabulary.

One of the most important components of the fire-control system was "spotting," performed by specially trained personnel high in the masts. Spotting provided the feedback that determined if the predictions of the fire-control system were accurate and, if not, how they should be modified. This was a fundamental change; before spotting, as we have seen, individual gunners corrected their own aim. With the introduction of fire control, the Navy created a closed-loop system. Observations of the target established the range, course, and speed and estimated the range rate. These were used to create a model of the target's movements, the guns were fired, and the spotter provided corrections. Corrections refined the model and brought the guns on target.

The importance of spotting was reflected in many ways. The 1905 board proposed new masts made of a redundant lattice framework to resist shellfire; these became the "cage" masts—metal structures resembling birdcages—that became standard on the Navy's battleships until the 1930s. They gave spotters a lofty and durable vantage point. The unusual masts were designed to be safe to fail—that is, to survive multiple direct hits from heavy-caliber shells. To make the task of spotting easier and more precise, the Navy emphasized "full" salvos, in which all the ship's main guns fired simultaneously. The large number of splashes made it easier to discount random errors and determine the location of the mean point of impact (MPI).

As spotting was refined and improved, it developed into a precise art. Extensive training familiarized officers with the science and probability of achieving hits on moving targets with naval guns. The associated textbooks are replete with example calculations and challenging problems designed to familiarize students with the many variables involved and how to account for them. Spotters had to be highly skilled to quickly determine the corrections necessary to bring the guns onto the target. Rigorous training provided a solid background in theory so that individual spotters could tailor their own practices to their specific situations. Deep knowledge of the ballistics involved was helpful; it was not unusual for talented spotters to be excellent marksmen as well.

The Navy's textbook on exterior ballistics included detailed discussions on spotting and the probabilities of hitting:

> Experienced spotters generally adhere to the rule that after the hitting range has . . . been established, a correction for a subsequent error of the MPI should not be applied unless the error occurs at least twice in the same direction. . . . This rule is . . . well founded in the laws of probability. We know that the spotter must not attempt to apply corrections for the accidental errors of gunfire, which manifest . . . not only in the dispersion of the shots of a salvo but also in the dispersion of the MPIs of successive salvos. We also know that it is a characteristic of accidental errors that they are as likely to occur in one direction as in the opposite direction and that most likely they will alternate in direction.[21]

These "accidental errors" were common. Even if estimates of enemy course, speed, and range were perfect, the values had to be transmitted to the guns correctly. Transmissions could be late or wrongly applied; guns could fire at the wrong moment. These errors were considered "accidental," to distinguish them from flaws in the model of the target ship's motion: "It must be borne in mind that the spotter is not justified in applying corrections for control errors of the accidental type, any more than he is justified in applying corrections for the accidental errors of the gun."[22] It took skill and experience to make these distinctions.

The Navy's initial fire-control instruments were designed to reduce human error and increase the effectiveness of human judgment. The tools performed specific functions, tasks that men could do but that machines could do more quickly. The functions that required experienced judgment, like spotting, remained manual. Nevertheless, at best the Navy now had only a piecemeal solution. Different ships applied automated approaches, along with a variety of manual methods, in different ways. Some of this experimentation was useful—the change-of-range projector was one positive result—but the deficiencies of the Navy's approach led to variable, and often inadequate, results.

The model of the target's movements was too simplistic. The range clock assumed a constant range rate, but in most circumstances the range rate continuously changed. The clock could not be corrected fast enough to keep up. In the 1909 gunnery practice, this deficiency was exposed. Both the target and the firing ship were under way, and the results were disappointing. Lieutenant Commander Bristol explained: "It would be better if an instrument could be devised that would give continuously the course and speed of the enemy, and also the range."[23] The Navy needed more sophisticated computing devices.

TOWARD AN INITIAL SYSTEM

Additional fire-control boards followed the one convened in 1905. These reviewed the current state of practice in the fleet, assessed available technology, and made recommendations for improvement. By 1916, an initial version of a standardized system was in place. It harmoniously blended men and machines into a comprehensive whole. Several specific constraints increased the system's complexity and enabled more rapid action of the fire-control team. These included a grammar for communicating information, defined roles for team members, and processes for bringing the guns on target and keeping them there.

Although complexity and specialization increased, the system remained modular, each individual man or tool addressing a specific need. Components could be exchanged for improved mechanisms as new approaches or technologies became available. None of this was accidental; throughout the development of the system, BuOrd retained responsibility for system integration. It maintained an open architecture, allowing the work most prone to human error to be replaced systematically by machines, improving the overall effectiveness of the system.

The heart of the system was the plotting room, a control station in relative safety below decks, protected behind armor. "The plotting room is the clearing house and computing station for main battery fire control data."[24] The plotting room was next to "central," the nerve center for managing communications on board the ship. The plotting room was the fire-control system's "brain." In it, the model representing the movements of the firing ship and the target was created. Indicators displayed the current range-finder range. Plotters tracked ranges and determined range rates. Other instruments tracked the movements of the target and the firing ship. Range clocks predicted future target ranges. Each of these instruments was duplicated, to allow the ship's fire to be divided between targets and to ensure continued function in the event of casualty or damage.

Telephone communications had, in many cases, been replaced by electronic transmission. Ranges were transmitted to the plotting room from range finders through automatic devices. The target bearing was also transmitted automatically. Bearings were sent to the guns by similar means; in the plotting room, the current direction in which the guns were pointing was displayed, allowing officers there to assure themselves that they were engaging the correct target. The potential of the Navy's fire-control system was increasing, and it was coalescing around a basic design that would prove well suited to future expansion.

Plotting and target tracking collectively became the preferred solution to the problem of modeling and predicting the movements of the target. Although time-consuming, these methods provided a detailed record of the target's movements, one that could be visually assessed. Initially, plotting and tracking focused on quickly determining the range rate, for entry into the range clock. Most ships preferred this method to using the range projector. The Mark I and Mark II Plotting Boards recorded observed target range over time; the slope of a line drawn through the plotted ranges gave the range rate. When it was introduced in 1911, the Mark II board, which allowed derivation of the range rate, quickly became the standard approach, but it was insufficient to model the target's movements fully.

An alternative method was to model the target's motion and plot its course. The Navy called this "target tracking." The Mark III and IV Plotting Boards used this technique. They were true-course plots. The speed and course of the firing ship were plotted on the board. Observed ranges and bearings of the target were plotted at regular intervals, creating an overhead view of the motions of both ships. From this perspective, more accurate predictions of the motion of the target—including its course and speed—could be made, allowing the fire-control team to develop a better solution.

With a more comprehensive model, the fire-control system was less dependent on range-finder observations. For a system using the Mark II Plotting Board, accurate measures of range had to be constantly provided. These determined the range rate, which would indicate the future range to the target. A system using target tracking was less reliant on consistent range observations once the model was developed. If "we know the course, speed, and bearing of the target, we may determine the Range Rate, without a rangefinder."[25] This could be very important if smoke or haze interfered with observations of the target and so prevented effective range-finder readings. The challenge with target tracking was that it required accurate measurements of the firing ship's course. Recent technological developments provided a solution.

Elmer Ambrose Sperry was "one of the premier American inventor-engineers of the early twentieth century."[26] In 1908 he filed a patent for a gyrocompass, a mechanical device with a high-speed rotor that sensed the rotation of the Earth and aligned itself with the planet's rotational axis. The gyrocompass was a precision navigational tool that overcame the limitations of traditional magnetic compasses and gave accurate readings of a ship's course. With it, target tracking was possible, and by 1910 the chief of the Bureau of Navigation, Capt. Reginald F. Nicholson, considered the gyrocompass essential to exploit the advances being made in gunnery.

Sperry believed he could build a fire-control system based on target tracking and the gyrocompass. He designed a plotting mechanism called the "battle tracer," a true-course plotting mechanism like the Mark III and IV Plotting Boards but with greater automation. It displayed a "single graphical representation of the field of battle."[27] Sperry augmented his solution with a series of electrical data-transmission systems. In 1915, the Navy tested Sperry's battle tracer on the battleship *New York*. It showed promise but was not pursued. By then the

focus had shifted to alternative solutions that provided greater automation and were less error-prone.

However, part of Sperry's solution was adopted. He had devised
reliable data-transmission systems, driven by electrical signals, that
rapidly communicated information from one station to another. His
system used these to send target-bearing information automatically
from the plotting room to the turrets. Officers in the turrets would
see the specified bearing on a visual indicator. They would bring their
turrets around (that is, "train them") to the correct bearing, a process
called "following the pointer." Back in the plotting room, another set
of Sperry's instruments—turret-train indicators—would show that this
had been done and that the turret was pointing at the target. It was
a marvelously flexible system that augmented control from a central
location and eliminated the need for verbal orders to bring the guns
onto the right bearings.

However, Sperry's system did not eliminate the need to communicate ranges to the guns verbally. His system worked by transmitting
information in a series of "steps." The steps were granular enough for
bearings but not for ranges. Even with this limitation, however, it was
a significant improvement. The system was installed on *Delaware* for
trials in 1909 and, on the basis of the results, adopted. The Bureau of
Ordnance history of World War I described it: "Advancement in a 'follow the pointer in train' system was rapid. The target-bearing system
used before the war was amplified to include a target turret system,
whereby the relative bearing of the target, corrected for deflection, is
transmitted to the turret. This enables the turrets to fire at an invisible
target by simply following a pointer."[28] Similar transmission systems
were introduced in other parts of the system, reducing the amount of
verbal instructions and decreasing the possibility of error. The range
finders in the turrets of *New York* and *Texas*, for example, sent ranges to
the plotting room automatically, "eliminating confusion and mistakes."[29]

Increasing levels of standardization were helping improve the telephonic communications that remained. Standard nomenclature was
developed for different positions involved in the fire-control system.

"Fore Top" denoted the spotting position in the foremast; "Main Top" was the mainmast; "Plotting Room" designated, of course, the plotting room; and "Control Tower" meant the ship's primary control station. This standardization was driven by the periodic reviews and recommendations of fire-control boards. The boards in fact recommended the adoption of a standard vocabulary for communicating fire-control information, but the ships of the Atlantic Fleet continued to experiment.[30]

Electrical signals could do more than transmit data within the system. They could also trigger the firing of the guns from a central location, reducing the possibility that one or more would fire at the wrong time; this was called "director firing," defined by the 1916 fire-control board thus: "Director firing is a method of firing all or part of the guns of a battery, in salvo, from a central point, with one sight; all the guns fired having been set at a predetermined angle of elevation, measured from a standard 'reference' plane."[31] Director firing eliminated the errors resulting from each gun or turret (a turret might mount more than one gun) firing separately. Previously, the fire order had been signaled by a central mechanism, but variability in reaction times meant that some guns fired later than others, increasing the dispersion of the salvo. Larger dispersion made it more difficult for the spotter to determine the MPI and account for control errors. Triggering the fire of the guns at the same instant from a single sight eliminated the problem.

Director firing also reduced the potential for smoke, funnel gas, or water spray to interfere with the view of the target. The director operator, high in the ship, would have a better view of the target than gunners in the turrets. He would also have a good view of the horizon; this was important. The director was effectively a telescopic sight. Inside the sight was a horizontal wire that the operator used as a reference. When the wire was parallel to a reference point—usually the horizon—he pressed the firing key, and all the guns fired simultaneously. For this reason, directors were initially called "directorscopes." They were lightweight sights that could be mounted high in ships. The first directorscope was an improvised modification of a Mark XXII sight on board *Delaware*. In 1914, an improved Mark II version was introduced and began to be installed in topmasts and conning towers of battleships. The battleship *Michigan*, one of the first to receive one, used it during practice in 1915. Her commanding officer described the procedure:

> The [firing] key is pressed when the cross wire of the periscope touches the top of the target on the down roll. This is firing at the middle of the roll when there is the least yaw, and this firing on the down roll gives the best chance of splashing the "shots" in front of the target. It is essential to continue firing under precisely the same conditions as regards (1) the direction of the roll, (2) the cross-wire junction, (3) the amplitude of roll, etc. so as to eliminate variables and help the spotting.[32]

Other ships received similar installations. The chief of BuOrd commented on the progress in his 1915 annual report:

> Director installations have been made on the *Michigan*, *Delaware*, *South Carolina*, *Utah*, *Florida*, *Arkansas*, *Wyoming*, *New York*, and *Texas*. It is proposed to fit this installation on all other turret ships back to and including the *New Jersey* class, and in all ships building. As this system does not interfere in any way with the present gear it is believed to be a valuable adjunct at present, in that it undoubtedly provides a means of obtaining fairly accurate results in very heavy weather, or in smoke, spray, or gases, when the present system would be admittedly unsatisfactory.[33]

The introduction of director firing is notable for several reasons. It marked a significant increase in capability and potential accuracy. It took advantage of the fire-control system's modular design and open architecture; integrating directors into the system required no major changes. It also represented another symmetry break and the increasing level of specialization developing within the system.

Throughout the early stages of the development of the Navy's fire-control system, redundancy and safe-to-fail approaches were primary concerns. Communication systems were duplicated. The new electro-mechanical transmission systems did not replace the telephones that preceded them; telephones were left in place, so that communications could be maintained if the electronic systems failed. Telephone connections were redundant; if individual circuits failed, backups could be used. If the telephones failed entirely, voice tubes were available.

If any specific station was damaged or destroyed, its responsibilities would shift to others. Spotting could be performed from the foretop or maintop; if both were damaged, the conning tower would take over. If the plotting room was damaged—or communications to it were severed—each of the high turrets at the ends of the ship was equipped to take over fire-control responsibilities. The turrets lacked the same facilities but could perform the role in a limited fashion. If communications were severed and the system broke down, turrets had the equipment necessary to control their fire in isolation; when that occurred, the process was called "local control."

Within the plotting room, every mechanism and process was duplicated. A primary plotting board or tracking board was designated; a backup would track the same information, ready to take over immediately if the first failed. Range clocks were duplicated for the same reason. A central switchboard controlled the electronic connections—both for telephones and electrical data—between different stations, allowing connections to be rewired in the event of a casualty. All these provisions ensured that in the event of damage or failure the ship could continue to fight. The officers on the fire-control boards never lost sight of the fact that the primary purpose of their ships was success in combat. They were expected to go into battle, suffer damage, and continue to use the system as long as possible.

With these new developments, the general outline of the Navy's fire-control system was beginning to coalesce. It was based around a model in the plotting room that predicted the motion of the target ship and determined where to aim the guns. Electromechanical transmission systems brought the guns to the correct bearing; verbal instructions set the range; and an electrical signal from a single director fired them at the right moment. Spotters' corrections refined the model of the target's movements and brought the guns onto the target.

The system worked, but its core was flawed. A better model was needed. The model of the target's movements was overly reliant on manual processes, error-prone, and often took too long to develop. The range clock assumed a constant range rate, which rarely was the case. To solve these problems, the Navy would turn to a new, elaborate mechanical device, an analog computer.

THE COMPLETE SYSTEM EMERGES

The competitive system of target practice repeatedly exposed limitations in the fire-control system. Range finders often gave inaccurate initial estimates, leading to erroneous range rates and poor shooting. It took time to correct these errors and bring the salvoes onto the target. Because the exercises were timed—reflecting the need to hit the target quickly in battle—they could end before some ships scored any hits. Fire-control officers faced a lot of pressure. They had to be able to rapidly synthesize many data points (estimates of target range, range rate, spotting corrections) from a variety of sources (range finders, plotting and tracking boards, electronic telephones) to determine how to bring the guns on target. In some practices, they were not up to the task. There was too much information to process and synthesize in too little time.

The Navy needed to augment the system with a device that could gather together all these different sources of information, process them, and build a model of the target's movements in real time. With a more comprehensive model, officers could focus on bringing the guns onto the predicted point and then refining the model based on feedback from spotting, range-finder ranges, and observations of target bearing. Rear Adm. Joseph Strauss, chief of BuOrd, spoke to this goal in his annual report for 1915: "As the fighting ranges increase, the necessity of a simple yet efficient means of keeping the range becomes more pressing, and the bureau has experimental instruments under construction which it is hoped will aid materially in the solution of this problem."[34] He addressed the same theme the next year: "Increased attention is . . . being devoted to the development of instruments that will get and keep the range with the greatest precision possible, having in mind conditions as they will probably exist in battle as indicated by reports of naval engagements in the present war."[35]

Reports from World War I suggested the Navy was behind British and German standards; they were opening fire at 20,000 yards and fighting beyond 15,000. The Navy's 1914 practice firings were only from 10,000 to 12,000 yards.[36] Greater ranges would require better tools. The fire-control board of 1916 was more specific in its recommendations: move away from the Mark II Plotting Board, which was then in general use.

> The rate of change board (Mark II plotting board) . . . provides a sample method of plotting a curve of rate of change, using range finders and spots. With sufficiently good observations the past rate of change can be obtained and used in connection with the sight-bar range while "straddling" for holding the range. Excellent results have thus been obtained on long range target practices. Such practices however, are necessarily restricted, both in rate of change practicable and, more particularly, in changes in the rate of change,—as compared with what may be expected with own ship and target running at high speed and on varying courses,—as they both may do in station keeping and . . . in attempting to evade fire. For these latter conditions, results from the rate of change board are likely to lag too seriously for efficient range keeping.[37]

The board recommended keeping the range automatically with a mechanical "range keeper" that could model the movements of the target and maintain the firing range through a variety of complex maneuvers. The board argued that the system should work in such a way that "changes in range due to own ship's movements may be applied as nearly as automatically as practicable, to the end that the ship may be free to change course and speed without loss of accuracy."[38] Its members thought that true-course plotters could allow for this but that what was needed was a new device, a mechanical, range-keeping computer.

The Ford rangekeeper was the solution. It was the brainchild of Hannibal C. Ford, an extremely talented mechanical engineer who had been introduced to the challenges of fire control by Elmer Sperry. Ford joined Sperry's company in 1909, helping to develop the gyro-compass and becoming the lead engineer for Sperry's battle tracer. In 1915, Ford resigned from Sperry's company and founded the Ford Marine Appliance Corporation, later renamed the Ford Instrument Company. In 1916, Lt. Cdr. F. C. Martin, responsible for the Fire Control Section in BuOrd, began discussing the idea of a rangekeeping device with Ford.[39] These discussions led to Ford's first product, the Navy's Rangekeeper Mark I.[40]

Ford's rangekeeper sought to address two critical problems with the Navy's existing system. The first was that the tracking and plotting mechanisms were manual, slow to develop a solution, and error-prone; their feedback loop took too long. The second problem was that there was no automated means of controlling for the movements of the fir-ing ship; if it turned or maneuvered, the fire-control solution—the range rates that had been developed—had to be recalculated. Ford solved these issues with an automatic calculation mechanism that pro-vided more rapid feedback to the fire-control officer. The rangekeeper reduced his cognitive burden, allowing him to devote more concentra-tion to the model and the corrections necessary to bring the guns onto the target.

The rangekeeper integrated two separate internal models, one for the motion of the firing ship and another for the target. From these models, it continuously generated a series of outputs required by the fire-control system, including the range and deflection (or bearing) settings for the guns. It integrated well into the existing fire-control system, providing a much more accurate model without the need for redesign. The required inputs were readily available (like firing-ship course from the gyrocompass) or already being gathered by the system (like target range and speed). Some of the inputs, like target bearing, could be provided automatically using the data-transmission system. Because of the smoothness with which the rangekeeper integrated into the existing system, plotting devices could continue to serve as a back-up if it failed, and established practices—like spotting—did not have to change.

What did change, and changed significantly, was the way the fire-control officer assessed the accuracy of the model of the target's movements. Ford designed his machine to provide a great deal of feedback about the quality of its internal model. On its face was a graphical representation of the target. This representation built on the approach Reeves and White introduced in the change-of-range projector. A disk representing the target rotated to reflect its estimated course, and a "button" along its length indicated its estimated speed, just as the projector's "pin" had done. Two wires were placed over this representation. One wire indicated the observed range to the target and the other the observed bearing. If the rangekeeper's model was accurate, these two wires would intersect over the target speed "button." If they did not, the operator knew immediately that corrections were necessary; he could get a sense of what they might need to be by which wires were off and by how far.[41]

This level of feedback was possible because Ford's design separated the motion of the firing ship and that of the target. Although similar computing devices were developed in the early years of the twentieth century, Ford's was the only one to maintain this separation.[42] It allowed fire-control officers to check and refine the accuracy of their solutions before opening fire. Previously, spotting was the only real feedback loop in the system. With the rangekeeper, observations of the target provided a constant check of the developing model, allowing it to be enhanced continually and permitting more accurate fire. Ford's decision was likely influenced by his discussions with Martin and his work with Sperry's battle tracer, which also separated the motion of the firing ship and the target. Regardless, the choice was crucial and one of the most valuable features of the rangekeeper.

The value of feedback was reflected in the initial revisions to the instrument. The first models automatically took in target-bearing information from the data-transmission system. This was quickly replaced by a follow-the-pointer mechanism allowing a manual check. The rangekeeper generated its own prediction of target bearing and displayed it on the face of the instrument alongside the observed bearing. If the generated bearing and observed bearing did not agree, the solution could quickly be corrected. A second modification added a graphical plotter that automatically recorded observed ranges. These could be compared with ranges generated by the instrument, giving the operator a quantitative sense of necessary corrections and augmenting the information from the horizontal wire in the instrument's face. Rapid feedback was an integral aspect of the rangekeeper's design and a core reason why the Navy considered the Ford superior to other candidate devices.[43]

The rangekeeper was initially tested on the battleship *Texas* in 1916, and a board was assigned to assess the results. The board's report was very positive; it considered the rangekeeper superior to any other method and recommended installation on every battleship. Production versions started being installed in 1917. The first ships to receive rangekeepers were the most modern battleships. By early 1918, each of the Navy's dreadnoughts had at least one system. By the spring of the same year, eleven of the older predreadnoughts had them as well.

However, the reception in the fleet was not as enthusiastic as might have been expected. Although the rangekeeper offered a dramatic improvement in potential accuracy, the simplistic conditions of gunnery exercises did not always require such a sophisticated tool. BuOrd was compelled to respond to criticism from the fleet and justify its decision to adopt the new device: "The machine was designed to deal with difficult conditions we expect to arise in battle, where changes of course and speed will be frequent and vision poor. It is impossible to reproduce anything well like this in target practice, and, therefore, not an easy matter to get people to realize the importance of taking these conditions into consideration."[44] Experience in World War I and exposure to the rigorous gunnery practices of the RN led to more challenging exercises. Combined with increasing familiarity with the rangekeeper, these helped the fleet embrace its use.

The introduction of the rangekeeper gave the fire-control system a sophisticated brain; self-synchronous data-transmission systems gave it a more effective nervous system. Sperry's systems had two specific limitations. They lacked the precision for transmitting range data, and because they transmitted information in a series of steps from a "zero" level, they had to be periodically synchronized—set back to zero—to ensure alignment. If they became misaligned in battle, the ship would have to revert to telephonic communications. In 1918, BuOrd began looking for a solution that supported automatic synchronization and increased precision.[45] By this time, Cdr. W. R. Van Auken had replaced Lieutenant Commander Martin in the bureau's Fire Control Section. Van Auken discussed the problem with Ford. The bureau's history of World War I describes what happened next:

> When the elevation system was discussed, all thought was expended toward a design using synchronous motors. About January, 1918, Mr. Ford was called into conference by Commander Van Auken and the manufacture of this system was placed in his hands. In May the first unit, the range converter, was accepted. This was modified as required and in September, 1918, the New Mexico obtained the first synchronous follow-the-pointer elevation installation. This Bureau-Ford system is now being installed on all major ships.[46]

The introduction of self-synchronous systems allowed the Navy to reconfigure the transmission of data the same way it did telephonic communications, dramatically increasing the flexibility and safe-to-fail characteristics of the system. Switchboards were expanded to allow the dynamic reconfiguration of data-transmission systems. Through the switchboard, any director could become the primary source of target bearings; if two targets were being engaged, the system could be divided and two directors used simultaneously, each driving a separate rangekeeper. Different turrets could be connected to different directors and rangekeepers, depending on the circumstances. The ability to self-synchronize allowed the system to be reconfigured on the fly. The advantages were so great that self-synchronous systems for elevation and bearing became the standard in new ships and were retrofitted into existing ones.

The ability to reconfigure the system dynamically and cross-connect components created new opportunities. A feature known as the "stable vertical" capitalized on this potential and addressed a major source of human error. Even if the solution developed by the rangekeeper was correct, the accuracy of individual salvoes could vary because of the reaction time of the director operator. He had to fire the guns at the right time in the ship's roll, usually when the horizontal wire of his telescope was parallel to the horizon. If he pressed the firing key too early or too late, the shells would miss the target. If the horizon was obscured, either by smoke or poor visibility, this was much more likely. The stable vertical solved these problems. It was a gyroscopically stabilized artificial horizon that could be used when the actual horizon was obscured. When connected to the fire-control system, the stable vertical could fire the guns automatically when the ship's deck passed through the horizontal plane, eliminating errors due to the director operator's reaction time or view of the horizon.

Introduced on the Navy's *Colorado*-class battleships, the stable vertical increased the accuracy of fire, particularly at longer ranges—where minor errors had a greater influence—and in conditions of poor visibility. Because the fire-control system could be easily reconfigured through the switchboard, it was simple to incorporate the stable vertical into the system and have it fire the guns. The stable vertical was a modular upgrade made possible through the system's open architecture. As older ships were modernized, it was retrofitted into them, and once sufficient experience had been gained, it became the primary indicator of the ship's inclination for fire-control purposes, replacing the eyes of the director operator.

The final ingredient in the Navy's standardized fire-control system was the creation of a specific language for communicating information between and among the various stations. Precise details had to be communicated quickly, clearly, and succinctly over the telephone circuits. Each circuit was a party line, meaning every station connected to the line could hear all the others and transmit information over the circuit to any. On a battleship, there could be as many as twenty-one stations patched into the captain's battle circuit.[47] It was essential to keep communication brief and convey as much information as possible in a short amount of time, as explained by a 1940 manual:

The development of efficient communications is one of the most important problems in the training of a fire control organization. . . . Successful communication requires, first . . . a satisfactory system of telephones and other transmitting instruments, and second, properly trained personnel. . . . The second requirement, however, is not one that can be met by mechanical perfection of instruments, or by prescribing hard and fast rules for personnel. It demands careful indoctrination and training so that every individual is familiar with the problem at least as it concerns his immediate station and those with which he is in communication, and is prepared to act intelligently in any contingency.[48]

The fire-control system required a communication method with a very high signal-to-noise ratio. Existing English-language structures were insufficient to meet the need; the manual continued, "The demand for brevity has resulted in the development of numerous stereotyped phrases and modes of expression. They constitute what may be termed a 'fire control language.'"[49]

Specific rules—representing an increased level of constraint—were developed to guide communications. Numeric values were transmitted by enunciating each digit separately, except in cases when the last two digits were zero, said as "double oh." A range of 13,350 yards, for example, was communicated as "Range one-three-three-five-oh." A range of 29,000 yards was, "Range two-nine-oh-double-oh." Spotting corrections were similarly constrained. "Up" increased the range; "down" decreased it. Deflection corrections were "left" and "right." To prevent confusion between the two, "oh" was always added immediately after the word "right."

This language significantly reduced the length of communications and the time necessary to convey information. Additional rules governed how to address specific stations, how to acknowledge information, and how to transfer responsibilities from one station to another. The development of this language triggered a new level of complexity and standardization within the Navy's fire-control system. It was a new enabling constraint that enhanced the capabilities of the system and broke symmetry with what came before.

IMPLICATIONS OF THE SYSTEM

The Navy's complete fire-control system, as it emerged in the years immediately after World War I and installed on its most modern battleships, the 16-inch-gunned *Colorado* class, was the most sophisticated in the world. The various elements of the system—the Ford rangekeeper, the stable vertical, reconfigurable connections, data-transmission systems, and a standard vocabulary—had come together to form a cohesive whole that dramatically increased the effectiveness of the officers and men responsible for bringing the guns onto the target. This had several important implications for the development of tactical doctrine in the interwar period.

The system enabled the "very rapid postwar development of U.S. naval gunnery," which increasingly emphasized long-range gunfire using aerial spotting.[50] It triggered the development of more sophisticated battle tactics designed to seize the initiative from opponents and keep them off balance. The system also provided a solid foundation for future investment; alone among the world's major navies, the U.S. Navy emerged from World War I satisfied with its fire-control system. This meant that future research and development could focus on enhancing it while other navies struggled to bring their systems up to the new standard.

Wartime experience illustrated that seizing the initiative in a modern naval battle could be decisive. The Navy hoped that it could use aggressive offensive action and accurate long-range gunfire at the start of an engagement to control its pace and gain an advantage over the enemy. The *War Instructions* of 1923 clearly made this point, stressing that victory could best be obtained through the "assumption of the offensive, which confers the advantage of the initiative and enables us to impose our plan on the enemy."[51] By opening fire at extreme range, the Navy hoped to force an enemy formation to maneuver, possibly disrupting its transition from approach to battle formation. This would put the enemy on the defensive and prevent him from executing his plans. Having obtained the initiative from the outset, the Navy expected to be able to fight a decisive battle and secure victory.

A second advantage of firing at long-range was the increased likelihood of scoring a hit on the deck of an enemy ship. This had important implications. First, it increased the probability that a hit would penetrate vital areas—like machinery spaces or magazines—of the target. Second, the chances of a penetrating hit would be the same regardless of the target angle presented by the enemy (the firing ship's relative bearing from the enemy). At closer ranges, hits would strike the hull and be less likely to penetrate at certain angles.

Finally, as Norman Friedman's numerous design studies have shown, the Navy's battleships enjoyed a relatively high level of protection against "plunging fire." Beginning with the ships of the *Nevada* class, authorized in 1911 and designed under the new General Board process, all of the Navy's battleships had featured the "all-or-nothing" armor scheme. Employing only the heaviest armor over the most vital portions of the ship and only light plating elsewhere, "all or nothing" was the first battleship armor scheme specifically intended to protect the ship in combat beyond ten thousand yards. The Navy's twelve most modern battleships featured this scheme. The battleships of other navies had been designed with "incremental" armor schemes, patchworks of varied thicknesses with much less deck protection, designed for battle at significantly shorter ranges.[52]

Long-range fire introduced a challenge for spotting. To make corrections effectively, spotters had to be able to see the impact of shells that missed the target. They had to be able to observe the target's waterline and thereby gauge the distance between the target ship's hull and the splashes of missing shells. At longer ranges, when the target's hull was below the horizon, it was nearly impossible to adjust the fire-control solution accurately. This effectively limited the maximum range of battleship gunfire to between 22,000 and 26,000 yards.[53] The only way to increase this distance was to increase the height of the spotting position. Masts could only be built so high; aircraft proved an ideal solution.

On 17 February 1919, the battleship *Texas* conducted a long-range firing exercise using aerial spotting. Radio was used to relay spotting data back to *Texas,* and observations from the plane proved much more effective than spotting from the masts of the ship. Lt. Cdr. Kenneth Whiting, in testimony before the General Board, estimated the increase in effectiveness to be as large as 200 percent.[54] The Navy embraced aerial spotting as the key to long-range gunfire. Gunnery lectures and war games at the Naval War College reflected assumptions about its effectiveness, and as early as 1922, the Bureau of Aeronautics was advocating increased elevation for battleship guns (to allow firing at longer range) because of the greater accuracy aerial spotting made possible.[55]

The capabilities of the Ford rangekeeper created new tactical possibilities. Because it could accurately model continuously changing range rates, the Navy began to consider using maneuver to gain an advantage in battle. Manual plotting approaches, like the Mark II Plotting Board, depended on keeping a steady course with relatively consistent range rates. This is one reason why opposing lines of battleships tended to settle on parallel courses. With the rangekeeper, the Navy had a system that could model the challenging situation of a target steaming on an opposite course. This was a significant potential advantage.

Beginning in the late 1920s, the Navy began to experiment with the concept of fighting on a course reciprocal to that of the enemy,

TABLE 2. Accuracy of Battleship Gunfire at Long Ranges

Range (Yards)	Percentage of Hits	
	Top Spot	Plane Spot
12,000	12.3	—
14,000	8.9	—
16,000	6.2	—
18,000	4.2	—
20,000	2.6	4.3
22,000	1.5	3.4
24,000	0.7	2.7
26,000	0.1	2.2
28,000	—	1.8
30,000	—	1.5

Source: Capt. W. C. Watts, "Lecture on Gunnery for War College Class of 1923," 22 September 1922, table E, 46, *Strategic*, box 13.

what it called "reverse action." The evidence suggests that the Navy assumed that the more primitive fire-control systems of the most likely opponent—the Imperial Japanese Navy (IJN)—would be unable to deal adequately with the rapidly changing range rates.[56] The enemy would be forced to fight at a disadvantage or to reverse course, a dangerous maneuver in battle. Either way, the Navy expected to gain a tactical advantage.

Immediately after World War I, there was a global emphasis on reducing military expenditures. National governments participated in a treaty system that reduced the sizes of all major navies and restricted the ships they could build. Large wartime budgets evaporated, and critical decisions about how best to invest the limited available funds had to be made. Because the Navy had already developed an effective fire-control system, investment in this area could be kept relatively low. This was a major advantage. The RN, in contrast, had concentrated on a less sophisticated system, the Dryer Table. Substantial investment was made in the development of an entirely new system in the early 1920s. The resulting Admiralty Fire Control Table was extremely capable, but it was large and costly. Insufficient resources were available to install it in all the RN's battleships before World War II.

The U.S. Navy, having an effective fire-control system already in place, could concentrate on incrementally improving it and applying similar approaches to other areas. More advanced versions of the rangekeeper accounted for more variables and improved accuracy. Automatic remote control of guns and turrets eliminated another source of human error. Sophisticated computing devices for antiaircraft fire control were built to solve the same basic problem in three dimensions. The torpedo data computer gave submarines a fire-control system for their torpedoes. These new developments were ready by World War II and had a profound influence on it.

The emergence of the Navy's fire-control system had important and long-running effects. It influenced battle tactics and doctrine; it provided a solid basis for improvement; and it allowed future efforts to focus on new features and functions. Specific characteristics of the system ensured that it could meet future needs effectively; the most important of these was its open architecture. This made it possible for new technologies—like the stable vertical and radar—to be integrated relatively easily, so that the capabilities of the system could be upgraded incrementally. In the language of complexity, the system had significant emergent potential.

CONCLUSION

The development of the Navy's fire-control system offers insight into effective approaches to learning and innovation. One of the most important of these was the system of learning and feedback that focused attention on a specific objective: accurate gunfire, at long range, in battle. Sims created the initial version of that learning system, by introducing standardized approaches and competitive evaluation of ships and gunners. That system became an enabling constraint that fostered improvements as individual officers and men took it upon themselves to refine their skills and achieve better scores. The system of learning and feedback was augmented by the regular fire-control boards that examined current practices and recommended improvements. This incorporated a second level of feedback into the system; it identified the most effective approaches for further exploitation, eliminated the worst deficiencies, and fostered increasing standardization.

BuOrd sat above both of these feedback loops, taking in recommendations from the boards and the fleet and combining them with its own view as to what was possible. It sought new approaches to address deficiencies, often by farming out the invention of new technologies to specialists. The bureau consistently reserved the responsibility of system integration for itself, ensuring that the system met the Navy's needs. Ultimately, the new fire-control system emerged from this interplay of individuals, their organizations, and these cycles of feedback.

The seed of the first innovative step came from Sims, triggered by his interaction with Scott and his system of continuous aim. Sims played the role of the reformer. He recognized the value of the new approach and agitated for its introduction. In this effort, Sims had powerful allies. Without the sponsorship of Rear Admiral Taylor, Sims never would have been appointed inspector of target practice. The connections Sims established with President Theodore Roosevelt also served him well, and they ensured protection for his methods and ideas, even when they disrupted existing approaches and institutions.

This was because Roosevelt and Taylor sought institutional realignment; they pushed the Navy toward a new era of professionalism, where evidence and data would trump anecdote and tradition. This contrasts with the traditional view of Sims as the enlightened radical who pushed for innovation against a tide of fierce resistance.[57] Resistance there certainly was, but Sims did not operate alone. He was the willing foil of the president and more senior officers who wanted to bring about a revolutionary transformation.

Sims played the part well. Not satisfied with continuous aim, he sought to introduce a more radical change—an expectation of continual improvement that would provide the basis for the Navy's advancements in fire control over the next forty years. This was the promise Sims brought when he assumed the role of inspector of target practice in 1902. Upon the introduction of the concept of fire control in 1905, he fulfilled it. Sims proved an able choice and impressed upon a willing generation of like-minded younger officers the need to continually refine and improve their work.

Technical expertise was also required to create the fire-control system. New technologies had to be invented to allow the system to deliver its potential. Sperry's gyrocompass and his data-transmission systems were essential first steps. Ford's rangekeeper was vital and became the heart of the new system, but it would not have been as effective without the self-synchronous transmission systems that came soon after.

The Navy recognized that outside expertise was necessary to create the components of the new system. BuOrd effectively harnessed the skills of Sperry, Ford, and their businesses to build a series of new technologies that made the innovative system possible. As the fire-control system developed, additional firms provided components, including General Electric and Arma. The importance of bringing in outside ideas—either of a technical nature, as in this case, or from some other field—should not be underestimated.

Variability played a key role. After the introduction of the con-straint—Sims' competitive system of target practice—and standard-ized approaches to continuous aim, ships were left to develop their own procedures for improving the accuracy of their fire. The variation in procedures from ship to ship led to multiple, parallel, safe-to-fail experiments as different officers trialed new ideas to enhance their scores. The decentralized climate of experimentation fostered new ideas, such as the range clock and range projector; accelerated overall learning; prevented the Navy from coalescing too rapidly around a single solution; and ultimately led to a more effective system. The fire-control boards tied these lessons together and ensured the whole Navy could learn from them.

Throughout the development of the fire-control system, the Navy remained in control of the overall system and chose to play the role of system integrator. Suppliers like Sperry and Ford contributed to it, but their parts were just components in a broader architecture. Neither vendor could obtain control of the system. That was a critical decision. By maintaining overall responsibility and assuming the role of system architect, BuOrd ensured that the system would perform correctly in battle. A secondary consequence of this decision was the emergence of open architecture; because the Navy contracted for pieces of the solu-tion, the result was loosely coupled through well-defined interfaces. This made it possible to replace the plotting and tracking boards with the rangekeeper quickly and easily. It also made it possible to plug in new technologies, like the stable vertical and the director, as they became available.

The development of the Navy's fire-control system is an excellent case study of how innovation can occur. There are numerous essential ingredients—a new idea, a champion to drive it, and a fertile environ-ment in which the idea can take root. Most case studies stop with a similar list. What the history of the fire-control system illustrates is that more is needed: a system of feedback. Feedback is required to allow the other members of the organization to pursue actively the end goals established by the champion and his sponsors. Without this, the improve-ment efforts will not "scale" and grow throughout the organization;

they will fade when the champion is not there to drive them. If the system can foster learning and experimentation, as the Navy's fire-control exercises did, it will be more effective at identifying ideas that will enhance the initial concept.

Technical expertise is a given when discussing innovation. What the Navy's experience shows, however, is that it is only a narrow aspect of the problem. Technical brilliance must be effectively integrated into a broader system. Ways to use the new technologies must be found; this can entail many challenges, such as new methods of communication, organization, and visualization. To make it all effective, system integration is required, and integration must be achieved with a clear eye to the end goal. For the Navy, this goal was success in battle, and the officers of BuOrd and the fleet focused their work on it; the exercises gave them regular feedback on their progress.

The open architecture was critical. Without the ability to reconfigure the system and improve it incrementally, improved technologies could not have been integrated so rapidly. This would have slowed progress, increased expense, and potentially inhibited innovation. The Navy might have been forced to use less effective solutions longer had the architecture not maintained the emergent potential of the system.

Finally, complexity suggests that the time immediately following a symmetry break can be a turbulent one. The Navy experienced this. The decision was made to move to fire control in 1905, but the existing procedures and equipment were insufficient. The Navy leveraged this uncertainty advantageously by patiently allowing individual experimentation and effective approaches to emerge. The Navy avoided a common problem for organizations pursuing innovation: premature convergence. It did not attempt to identify a "good" approach quickly; instead, it allowed time for an excellent approach to emerge from the collective work of many individuals.

3

PLANS AND DOCTRINE BEFORE WORLD WAR I

> Coordination is made possible by indoctrination
> plus the plan of battle. Concentration is made possible
> by coordination. Effective concentration . . .
> makes victory possible.
>
> —Albert P. Niblack, 1917

At the dawn of the twentieth century, naval tactics focused on coordinating the movements of a fleet in battle. Coordinated movement was critical; without it, ships fought individually and not as a cohesive whole. Just as the Navy improved the capabilities of individual ships through increasingly sophisticated fire-control procedures, so it also developed new approaches to coordinating ships in battle. However, the development of these approaches was hampered by inability to experiment at sea in large-scale maneuvers. At the turn of the last century, the Navy was distributed in small squadrons around the globe. The ships of those squadrons were often further distributed, making tactical exercises with more than handfuls of ships a near impossibility.[1]

Victory over Spain, the increasing size of the fleet, and the rapid pace of naval technology made it more important than ever to determine how best to ensure coordinated action in a modern naval battle.

In 1898, there were four modern battleships in commission; by 1905, there were twelve, and twelve more were under construction. These ships were expected to project American naval power into the Caribbean and across the Pacific; they had to be able to fight as a fleet in battle.

The problem was compounded by the rapid pace of technological change, leading to new ship types and increasing the complexity of modern naval battles. Advances in fire control increased the effective range of ships' guns; turbine engines and oil fuel made them faster; face-hardened armor and new armor schemes made them more survivable; and advances in the design of shells and torpedoes made them more deadly. Radio allowed fleets to coordinate their movements over much greater distances in near real time. New specialized types—scout cruisers, destroyers, submarines, and aircraft—augmented the more traditional battleships and armored cruisers. Modern fleets would move faster, strike harder, and operate over a much greater area than ever before. Naval combat was being revolutionized.

To determine how best to command and coordinate such a fleet in battle, the Navy experimented with a variety of mechanisms. Simulated war games at the Naval War College tested new technologies, explored new techniques, and provided valuable experience for officers. Exercises at sea refined this experience, validating some approaches and rejecting others. The war games and fleet exercises acted as constraints that focused officers on the real problems of coordinated fleet operations. Although the processes involved remained relatively unsophisticated, the Navy, between the turn of the century and the declaration of war with Germany, developed basic frameworks for organizational learning and exposed a cadre of junior officers to the methodologies that would form the basis for institutionalized learning during the interwar period.

MAHAN AND THE ART OF WAR

The most important influence on the Navy's tactical thinking in the late nineteenth century was the concept of "scientific war," which assumed that effective leadership in war was a skill, an art that could be taught through education and practice. This was a relatively new idea at the time, and it broke with the earlier assumption that skill in battle came only through charismatic leadership or native genius.[2] One of the Navy's foremost advocates of scientific war was Rear Adm. Stephen Luce. He believed that there were fundamental principles of war, general in their application, that held for all times and places. This assumption informed his approach as the Naval War College's first president; Luce believed naval officers needed to investigate these principles and learn how to apply them to modern methods of naval warfare.

The principles of war became a central part of the college's curriculum. Officers used research, study, and exercises to approach war scientifically; they familiarized themselves with the principles of war and how they had been applied throughout history. The college's second president, Rear Adm. Alfred Thayer Mahan, built on this approach but subtly altered it. Luce had focused on the scientific nature of war; Mahan stressed its artistry.

Mahan placed more emphasis on the importance of practical knowledge. As Jon Tetsuro Sumida has explained, under Mahan the principles became collectively a starting point that focused historical analysis and study.[3] Mahan firmly believed that command was a skilled art, that to be effective officers had to choose the right principle for the given situation and apply it at the right time. This required experience, analytical thought, and contextual understanding. Mahan succinctly described the process: "It is for the skill of the artist in war rightly to apply the principles and rules in each case."[4]

In Mahan's view, this was the essence of command. He improved the nascent Naval War College curriculum and introduced an analytical approach to history that provided a foundation for the exploration of complex strategic and tactical problems. Officers used historical examples to illustrate how principles had, or had not, been applied; then they developed their own solutions. It was the beginning of a systematic approach to problem solving that emphasized critical thinking, rigorous examination of the facts, and contextually driven application of the "scientific" principles of war. As Sumida explains, "Mahan's approach to the art and science of command, embodied in his strategic and professional arguments, was informed by his recognition that contingency in war precluded mechanistic prescription as the basis of operational decision making. His strategic argument was made through statements of principle and examinations of their application through extended historical narratives, which revealed both variation and exception."[5]

Mahan analyzed the history of war at sea and provided numerous case studies for the application of different principles in different historical contexts. He intended his written works and lectures to be more than just histories; they were to be vehicles for teaching the art of command. The most influential of them were the three volumes of the *Influence of Sea Power* series, in which Mahan not only reinforced his concept of the art of command but argued for the importance of "command of the sea," which he believed was a prerequisite for national greatness.[6] The most effective way to achieve command of the sea, in Mahan's view, was with a fleet of powerful battleships that could confront the enemy's main forces and drive them from the sea.

Mahan's theories took root in the Navy and were embraced by sympathetic politicians, like Theodore Roosevelt. The emphasis on command of the sea helped sustain the momentum of the construction of a modern battle fleet and triggered a broader interest in the development of an oceangoing navy. Mahan's ideas also influenced the Navy's approach to naval tactics; command of the sea required a modern battle fleet, and the Navy had not mastered how to coordinate one in action.

The most generally applicable principle of war appeared to be that of concentration. A concentrated battle fleet could bring all its weight to bear on an opponent in a decisive action. Victory in such a fight would bring command of the sea. Accordingly, the Navy began to investigate the problem of how to concentrate the firepower of a diverse collection of ships in a modern battle fleet. That question was a major focus of experimentation and investigation before the American entry into World War I.

Although Mahan's name has over the course of the past century become synonymous with decisive battle, it is important to recognize that it was command of the sea that he emphasized, not any single means of obtaining it. He knew that objective could be achieved in a variety of ways, including the aggressive use of light forces, blockade, and the seizure of bases. In the right context, these alternative approaches could secure control of the sea without the need for a clash of battle fleets.[7] That subtlety was not lost on the Navy's officers; it underpinned tactical thinking through World War II and influenced plans for a Pacific war. The point that securing command of the sea was more important than winning any individual battle was reinforced in numerous tactical and operational exercises. The Navy began to believe that battles had to fit into an overall strategy if they were to deliver success in war.

STRATEGIC CONTEXT

The geographic position of the United States and prevailing strategic interests also exerted significant influence on the Navy's battle tactics. The large oceans separating the United States from Europe and Asia provided some degree of security from attack, but they also meant that any naval battle was likely to take place far from American bases. The Navy's attention focused on two specific geographic regions, the western Pacific and the western Atlantic.

The western Atlantic was a point of emphasis because of growing interests in the Caribbean and concerns about violations of the Monroe Doctrine. The acquisition of Puerto Rico and establishment of a protectorate over Cuba in 1898 gave the United States a dominant position in the region. However, the numerous islands offered potential launching points for a European incursion into the Western Hemisphere. Germany was considered the most likely enemy, and a contingency plan, War Plan Black, was developed to study and model a German movement into the Caribbean. It anticipated operating the battle fleet from Cuba's Guantanamo Bay; that force would seek out the approaching German fleet, subject it to attritional attacks if possible, and ultimately bring it to action. The war was expected to be decided by a major fleet action in the western Atlantic.

Concerns about the security of the Caribbean increased over the years. In 1901, the Hay-Pauncefote Treaty was signed with Great Britain; it implicitly recognized the primacy of American naval power in the Western Hemisphere. The treaty also freed the United States to proceed with the development of the Panama Canal, which, when completed in 1914, would dramatically shorten the steaming distance between the two coasts. It was to become a centerpiece of Navy strategic planning.

In the Pacific, naval strategy focused on the maintenance of the Open Door Policy in China. The growing power and influence of Japan became a concern, especially after its victories over China in 1895 and Russia in 1905. Japan was poised to dominate the western Pacific region; to study a Pacific campaign against that island nation, the Navy developed War Plan Orange. Plan Orange was similar in its broad outlines to Plan Black but with the Navy operating on the offensive. The fleet would move across the Pacific, making use of faraway bases in the Philippines and Guam, acquired from Spain in 1898. Eventually, it would find and defeat the Japanese battle fleet somewhere in the western Pacific, most likely at a time and place chosen by the IJN.

The great distances involved made Plan Orange much more challenging logistically, but because Plans Orange and Black presented opposite situations—operating on the defensive in one and the offensive in the other—the Navy developed exercises that modeled both potential conflicts simultaneously. One element of the fleet would be the aggressor, steaming into enemy territory and attempting to seize an advanced base. The other would be the defender, seeking to locate the approaching enemy, engage his main body, and defeat it.

The emphasis on these two geographic regions on the opposite sides of the world created difficulties. Before the opening of the Panama Canal, the Navy could concentrate the fleet on one coast or divide it between them, risking defeat in detail. The journey around Cape Horn from New York to San Francisco was 19,000 miles, much too far for mutual support, even with a slow buildup to war. Dividing the fleet was out of the question; it had to remain concentrated. The East Coast, with its much more capable fleet-maintenance facilities, was the logical choice for basing the battle fleet. This also placed it closer to the most likely combat zone, the western Atlantic.

However, the anticipated base at Guantanamo was itself far away from East Coast bases, over 1,300 miles from New York and 1,100 from Norfolk, Virginia. Once assembled in Guantanamo, the battleships of the fleet had to have sufficient steaming endurance remaining to find, fix, and fight an approaching enemy. All this meant that the Navy's battleships had to be designed for long-range cruising: they would have to fight effectively in the western Atlantic and survive the journey across the Pacific. Geographic realities had serious implications for battle tactics.

WAR GAMING

In November 1893, Capt. Henry C. Taylor became president of the Naval War College. He continued the work of Mahan and Luce but departed from the existing curriculum. Taylor introduced Strategic and Tactical Problems that challenged officers to develop solutions to simulated wartime conditions. William McCarty Little, a retired lieutenant on the college's staff, developed the first versions of these war games. Little had studied military simulations for years; under Taylor his war games became an important constraint that encouraged experimentation with new tactical approaches and that improved the ability to assess them.

The primary purpose of the games, or "war problems," was to further the education of officers. They gave practice at applying the principles of war, encouraged critical thinking, and provided training in the art of command. Ronald Spector has described the approach: "Through these methods the graduates of the Naval War College became accustomed to making quick decisions to cope with rapidly changing situations. The war problems, although somewhat unrealistic in nature, were nonetheless invaluable in giving the officer students the 'feel' of war situations and in teaching them the techniques of command."[8]

The use of the term "problem" was deliberate. Officers were confronted with a challenge and were expected to solve it. Once the solutions were ready, the "conference method" was used to critique and discuss proposed solutions openly. These conferences brought officers together in collaborative discussions that encouraged critical analysis, regardless of rank. They built on the work of Mahan; rather than individually determining how best to apply the principles of war, officers began to collaboratively analyze how best to solve problems. They also tested their techniques on each other; unlike games in most other services, the Navy's problems employed opposing teams of officers. This provided valuable practice and helped emphasize the importance of creativity—essential to the art of command—rather than canned solutions.

Before the creation of the Atlantic Fleet in 1907, the Navy's capacity to perform modern fleet exercises and to experiment with new tactical concepts was severely limited. Ships, again, were distributed around the world in squadrons, and although these squadrons occasionally came together for exercises—like those in Caribbean during the winter of 1902–3—such occasions were rare. The North Atlantic Squadron attempted to work closely with the college to test modern tactics but was never able to do so; too many other demands were placed upon the squadron.[9] Modern fleet tactics could only be explored in theory, not with actual ships. Expanding these theories became one of the primary missions of the college's war games.

The 1903 version of the *Rules for the Conduct of the War Games* provided a simple framework. It postulated three generic ship types—battleships, armored cruisers, and protected cruisers—and fairly basic combat rules that emphasized the importance of broadside fire and relatively close range, under six thousand yards. It was a convenient way to work out tactical problems, repeatedly experiment with new concepts, and provide valuable training for officers. They became accustomed to analyzing situations, thinking critically about them, and issuing orders to control ships under their command. At a time when it was impossible to drill and experiment as a large fleet, the Naval War College simulations were beneficial in increasing the competency and skill of officers.[10]

In 1905, the *Rules for the Conduct of the War Games* were revised. The most significant change was explicit emphasis on the game as a *learning* device and the fact that, as such, it could be only as good as the assumptions embedded within it. The *Rules* themselves explained:

> The object of the naval war game is to aid students of strategy and tactics in the comprehension of these subjects. . . . In a war game a most important thing to remember is that the players should not look for victory . . . but for instruction. . . . The correctness of any apparent lesson of a war game is . . . inherently dependent upon the fidelity with which the assumptions represent the actual conditions of war. For several reasons the War College claims no finality for the rules . . . but expects that . . . officers . . . should learn to vary the rules . . . to apply them to new situations.[11]

The college's archival copy of the 1905 *Rules* reflects just such modifications, with new rules to account for increasingly sophisticated combat modeling. The edits included an imposed delay between issuing orders and executing them, a temporary reduction in fire effectiveness when switching from one target to another, and a decrease in accuracy when turning.[12] The changes illustrate how the games became increasingly sophisticated as more experience was gained.

The 1905 *Rules* mark an important symmetry break. They illustrate the beginning of a learning system based on war gaming and simulation. Within this system, learning occurred on two levels. During the war games, officers gained experience applying military principles to varied combat situations. Outside the simulations and using feedback from them, officers continually refined and improved the rules of the games as they gained experience handling ships and formations at sea. The college's system of war games became an enabling constraint that emerged from the assumption that command was an art that could be taught and learned. Over the coming decades, the war game rules would become more elaborate and more realistic, allowing officers to test increasingly sophisticated fleet tactics. The system of war games at the college—like the Navy's gunnery system—promoted continual learning and ever-increasing complexity.

BATTLE PLANS NO. 1 AND NO. 2

Initial versions of the rules reflected faith in the principle of concentration, and unsurprisingly, concentrated gunfire decided the college's early war games. The fleet that could bring more ships into action at the critical moment would win. A contemporary Naval War College analysis described the emerging consensus: "To concentrate in naval tactics is, to bring the units of a force into action in mutual support, and to the greatest possible advantage. Its aim is to bring to bear upon the force of an opponent, or a portion of its force, such a superiority as will insure the initial advantage and reasonably assure a favorable decision."[13]

Analyses of simulated combat led to the development of the "n-square law," which held that the relative power of two naval forces varied with the square of their fighting strengths. If, for example, one force had a fighting strength equal to 80 percent (0.80) of its opponent's, its relative power would be the square of that, or only 64 percent (0.64). Should those two forces engage in combat, the stronger would triumph. After annihilating the weaker, the stronger force would retain 60 percent of its fighting strength. Although not immediately intuitive, the formulas were straightforward. Remaining fighting strength after an engagement was the square root of the difference between the squares of the relative strengths. In this example, 100 percent (1.00) minus 64 percent (0.64) gives 36 percent (0.36). The square root of that is 60 percent (0.60), the remaining strength of the stronger force. Tables illustrating these concepts were published in *Proceedings* and distributed at the Naval War College.[14] They first appeared in Bradley Fiske's prize-winning 1905 essay "American Naval Policy." Fiske's tables emphasized the importance of bringing concentrated firepower to bear, although he was careful to stress that fighting power depended on context and could not be reduced to a single matériel factor.[15]

The n-square law and faith in the power of concentration gave the Navy its most important doctrinal principle: concentration enables victory, dispersion leads to defeat. The challenge for naval officers was how to concentrate the firepower of the fleet in battle. The most critical prerequisite was effective ship handling. Battle tactics in the early years of the twentieth century were as much about coordinated movement as they were about specific plans of action. There were two competing theories in the Navy about how most effectively to coordinate the movements of the battle line: the column formation and the line of bearing.[16] In a column formation, each ship followed in the path of the one ahead. A column had the advantage of simplicity; it could maneuver with a minimum of signals. However, it had weaknesses. A commander positioned in the center of the line so that he could see both ends and coordinate the actions of all ships could easily lose control because he had to rely on slow and uncertain relay of his signals up and down the line. If the commander led the column, he might lose sight of the ships at the rear and fail to issue appropriate orders at a critical moment. In a line-of-bearing formation, the ships would be positioned along a line oriented on a specific point of the compass—the line of bearing—that was not the same as their course. During maneuvers, all the ships would turn together, maintaining their positions along the line of bearing as their courses changed. This formation required greater coordination than the columnar formation and presented greater signaling challenges. The debate between the two approaches would dominate discussions of tactics at the Naval War College in the early years of the century.

Ultimately, the characteristics of the Navy's battleships would determine which approach to take. Because of the strategic requirement to steam great distances, the Navy's battleships were built to carry enough coal, and thereafter oil, to steam to distant locations. Once they got there, they had to have sufficient fighting power—firepower and protection—to win a naval battle. Battleship design was a balance of speed, fighting power, and steaming radius. Although speed was important, the U.S. Navy did not consider it as vital as the other factors, and its battleships were slower than those of other nations.[17]

This in turn presented a danger when steaming in a line, either a column or a line of bearing. An enemy could secure an advantage by concentrating on one end of it. A "flank" attack like this could overwhelm that end of the line before ships at the other could arrive to assist. The most dangerous form of this attack was called "capping the T." It involved sending a line of ships across the path of the enemy and raking his leading ships with broadside fire, to which they could respond only with their bow guns. A formation with a speed advantage could use it to make flank attacks; the Japanese defeated the Russians at Tsushima in May 1905 in just this way.

Countering this danger became the focus of the Navy's initial battle plans. After the Naval War College's 1902 conference, the column formation was chosen as the basis for fleet tactics. It could more easily prevent a flanking maneuver. If the enemy had a speed advantage, the leading ship of the line would gently turn to keep the foremost enemy abeam; the remainder of the formation would follow. By turning inside the enemy, the Navy's battle line would nullify his speed advantage. This scheme of maneuver was called "Battle Plan No. 1."

> Battle Plan No. 1, by requiring the column leader to steer a course determined by his relation to the enemy, relieves the column from rigidity and delay, makes it flexible, and preserves the best presentation of the batteries by a gradual change of course, a condition requisite to the maintenance of uninterrupted and accurate fire. . . . The distinctive feature of Battle Plan No. 1 is this free and automatic movement. . . . Battle Plan No. 1 . . . is . . . a tactical device of great value. . . . In the present state of the science of naval tactics it appears to embody a fundamental principle which requires its habitual employment unless orders are given to the contrary.[18]

The tactical device worked well on the game board but could not solve all the problems presented by slow speed. One of the most troublesome was the American battleships' vulnerability to torpedo attack. Potential enemy battleships had larger torpedo batteries and could use their speed advantage to close and launch a large salvo of torpedoes.[19] Fear of this threat helped reinforce the developing emphasis on gunfire—explored in the previous chapter—and led to an increasing focus on using battleship guns as the primary weapon in battle, to keep the enemy outside torpedo range.

It was some time before Battle Plan No. 1 was tested in the fleet. In early 1907, the Atlantic Fleet experimented with it at sea. Four different maneuvers were held, pitting a faster Blue fleet against a slower Red one. The speed advantage varied from 30 percent to 50 percent. If the two fleets steamed in roughly the same direction, the difference in speed made little difference. However, if the opposing fleets steamed in opposite directions, matters became very dangerous for the slower. On the second day of the exercises, the Red fleet turned about and steamed in the opposite direction, creating a reverse action. This gave the Blue fleet the opportunity to use its speed advantage. It closed and concentrated on Red's rear flank. Results were similar on the fourth day, even though Blue had less of a speed advantage. The report concluded: "The slower fleet should wait until the faster swings into column, and then turn immediately to the same general direction. Once in column parallel to the enemy, the leaders should keep each other abeam."[20]

Further experimentation led to the introduction of Battle Plan No. 2 in 1911. This plan expanded on Battle Plan No. 1 and provided for the division of the battle line into semi-independent squadrons. Instead of the entire line following in the wake of the lead vessel, each squadron would maneuver independently to keep the enemy abreast. The entire fleet would still steam in a rough line, but Battle Plan No. 2 acknowledged that the fleet was getting too large for a single commander to handle. Some delegation was necessary.[21] Both plans were little more than simple constraints that increased the flexibility of the battle fleet. They were rough beginnings that foreshadowed the increasingly complicated plans that would develop during the interwar period.

ESTIMATE OF THE SITUATION

In 1910, the Navy developed a structured approach to problem solving, the "estimate of the situation," and integrated it into the Naval War College curriculum. It was an important constraint that provided a common frame for conceptualizing and discussing approaches to wartime—or simulated wartime—situations. In a 1912 lecture, Cdr. Frank H. Schofield defined the estimate "as a natural method . . . used unconsciously in every day life." It involved assessing a situation, considering difficulties to overcome, analyzing options, and finally, determining a course of action. Until the late 1920s, the estimate had four basic components reflecting these steps: the *mission*, an assessment of *enemy forces*, an evaluation of *own forces*, and finally, the *decision*.[22]

The mission was usually derived from instructions or orders from a superior; however, training revealed the need to review these instructions thoroughly to produce a clear, and common, sense of the mission. "Experience has shown that the statement of a problem to men whose strategic and tactical ideas have not been coordinated by training will result in marked diversity in the statements of the *mission*."[23] Schofield was after "unity of action"—what the German army called *einheit*—and it required training to produce a common conceptual frame among all officers. Without it, different commanders would approach the same problem in different ways, undermining their ability to cooperate toward a common goal.

Once the mission had been identified, officers explored how enemy forces might prevent its accomplishment. They examined the strength of the enemy forces, their disposition, and their probable intentions. The most important aspect of this section was assessing the situation from the enemy's perspective and arriving at his point of view, "to think as he would think of us, to consider all the plans that he would consider and estimate which of those plans would be most injurious to us." A thorough assessment could avoid surprise.[24]

The next step was to examine courses of action available to one's own forces. All avenues that could achieve the mission were to be considered and analyzed. One of these would be chosen, and that would become the decision, the basis of orders to subordinates. Schofield emphasized that it was important to make the decision clear and resolute, so that it would inspire concerted action in subordinates. However, he also noted, the decision should not project a plan so far into the future that it would be overtaken by events. Balance was necessary.

The Naval War College introduced, in this four-step method, a specific problem-solving framework based on facts and analysis, one intended to allow officers to conceptualize and address situations in a common way. Schofield emphasized the "scientific" roots of the idea: "The habit of mind induced by practicing the method of the estimate of the situation is a scientific habit, one that compels action to flow from reason, one that forbids the acceptance of opinion that is based solely on prestige."[25] This process was an important constraint that increased the cohesion of the Navy's officer corps and promoted unity of action; it remained a core part of the Naval War College curriculum through World War II.

EXPERIMENTS IN THE ATLANTIC FLEET

In April 1907, the Atlantic Fleet was formed by President Theodore Roosevelt. Prior to that time, the Navy had lacked an organized battle fleet; instead, it had a collection of geographically distributed squadrons. They could not come together often enough for exercises, and as a result, the Navy lacked real experience operating a large, modern battle fleet. Roosevelt wanted to address this deficiency and at the same time assemble a platform for deliberate experimentation.

The fleet's first commander was Rear Adm. Robley D. Evans. A Civil War hero who had graduated from the Naval Academy in 1864, Evans was extremely familiar with the challenges presented by modern steel ships. He had brought the Navy's first modern seagoing battleship, *Indiana,* into commission in 1895. During the battle of Santiago in 1898, he had commanded the battleship *Iowa* and fired the first shots at the Spanish squadron. As Atlantic Fleet commander, he would help provide a foundation for the Navy's new approach to tactical development by initiating its first major exercise, the voyage of the Great White Fleet.

Evans led the fleet to the West Coast, where he fell ill and was relieved by Rear Adm. Charles S. Sperry. Sperry regularly drilled the fleet in evolutions, tactical formations, and other maneuvers. The long voyage across the Pacific provided ample opportunities for practice and melded the individual ships into a fighting unit. Lt. Cdr. Ridley McLean, the fleet ordnance officer, described these regular exercises:

> Exercises began on leaving San Francisco with . . . individual drill of the crews and fire control parties . . . this was followed by the simplest form of fleet exercise and . . . has become gradually more and more advanced by the introduction of . . . steering from below, signaling from battle stations, telegraphing casualties [simulated

damage] from the flagship, introduction of torpedo attack during the action, substituting the use of blank cartridges for simulated fire, and finally the substitution of .45 caliber sub-caliber practice for blank cartridges, thus permitting actual aiming and firing . . . exactly as if in action.[26]

The increasingly sophisticated exercises involved mock battles between squadrons and simulated night battle practices. These tested the fleet's capabilities—such as the effectiveness of searchlights, fire control, and communications—and gave it vital practice in operating as a unit.

One of the most impressive capabilities the fleet displayed was its endurance. The cruise validated the assumption that the Navy could project power to distant parts of the globe, including the western Pacific, and demonstrated that War Plan Orange was a viable concept. Roosevelt and Sperry sent a clear message to Japan about the Navy's strategic mobility.

FLEET MANEUVERS AND BATTLE TACTICS
After its return to the East Coast in February 1909, the Atlantic Fleet became a laboratory for modern fleet operations. Complex tactics and maneuvers were studied on a large scale for the first time. Contested maneuvers were introduced to challenge officers and men. Although a small number of officers had experienced opposed maneuvers on the game board at the Naval War College, this was the first real opportunity to try them at sea. The method used was very much like the college's war games, and a similar set of rules adjudicated the maneuvers.

Initial versions of the rules were published in 1910 and 1911 in the *Instructions for Battle Plan Exercises*. In 1913, the Atlantic Fleet's commander, Rear Adm. Charles J. Badger, issued the more sophisticated *Rules for Battle Maneuvers*. These emphasized that the game board and fleet exercises complemented each other. The board was best at demonstrating tactical concepts; exercises with the fleet provided practical experience. This mirrored the concepts of Rear Admiral Fiske, the Aide for Operations, and it is likely that Fiske influenced Badger's revision of the rules.[27]

Badger specified the following objectives for fleet exercises, illustrating the importance he placed on practical experience:

- To acquire familiarity with the aspect of a modern sea battleground;
- To give experience in handling, squadrons, divisions, and ships;
- To afford practice in quickly recognizing conditions and changes of conditions and in the appreciation of tactical principles;
- To afford experience in noting and appreciating the actual physical features of wind, spray, smoke, sun, etc., and their influence;
- To afford opportunity for gunnery training and particularly for the exercise of range finder, plotting, and fire-control parties under battle conditions;
- To exercise signal and radio parties.[28]

To help govern the exercises and ensure the rules were applied correctly, each ship appointed an umpire. Umpires kept track of the action and scored the appropriate damage. Dice were used to assess the effects of gun and torpedo fire. Lights and flag signals designated targets. The accuracy of the exercise and its value as a learning tool largely depended upon the umpires' performance.[29]

Plotting increased the effectiveness of exercises as learning tools. Each divisional flagship was expected to maintain a plot of the maneuvers, recording the positions of all ships as accurately as possible every five minutes. This gave staffs valuable practice at plotting and provided an invaluable reference for later analysis. Plots also helped increase situational awareness by giving commanders visual representations of the developing action.

Exercises investigated specific topics; "fast wing" tactics was one of the most common. The Navy lacked battle cruisers, a new ship type introduced by the RN's *Invincible* class, and was curious to understand how they might be used. Battle cruisers combined the firepower of a battleship with high speed but sacrificed protective armor. The Navy explored how these ships might operate using substitute vessels, generally positioning them on the engaged flank ahead of the battle fleet.

These maneuvers tended to reinforce the value of concentration; it was easy for the fast ships to find themselves isolated from the support of their main body and destroyed by enemy fire.[30]

Experimentation was common. Tactical Problem No. 33-13 of 25 July 1913 pitted the fleet's destroyer flotilla, representing a fleet of high-speed battleships, against the fleet's battleships. The destroyers split into three divisions and maneuvered to come into action almost simultaneously. The battleships also split into three divisions, but one of the flank divisions failed to keep the destroyers on the beam and was roughly handled. The commentary on the problem considered the evolution "interesting and instructive as a tactical exercise," in that it "presented several features which had not been previously brought out during fleet maneuvers."[31] Much of this may have been thanks to the commander of the destroyer flotilla, Capt. William S. Sims. He was developing a new approach to command, one described in more detail below.

Other Tactical Problems investigated the effectiveness of destroyers and submarines. Their torpedoes were powerful weapons but had limited range. It was much easier to get close enough to use them under cover of darkness than by day. With practice, destroyers became particularly effective at these tactics. Battleships had difficulty defending themselves against nocturnal destroyer attacks, even when screened by other ships. In one exercise, Sims reported, his destroyers had hit with at least eleven and probably thirteen torpedoes out of eighteen, which struck six different battleships.[32]

The increasing effectiveness of destroyers and submarines illustrated the changing nature of naval tactics. Fighting strength could not be represented by battleships and their heavy guns alone; it would vary depending on circumstances. At night, a squadron of aggressive destroyers might have more relative strength than a division of battleships. In daylight, the conditions would be very different. Regardless, the essential lesson of Fiske's n-square law was validated: fighting strength was a nonlinear function.[33] The Navy began to emphasize coordinated action in battle to maximize striking power:

When all ships work together . . . when each knows that his neighbor knows what he is doing, because they have all been given sound practical methods, then much of the difficulty of handling formations will disappear, and a few simple signals, by flags or by radio, or by both will suffice to handle naval forces. This will require the thorough constant practice, which will produce satisfaction and confidence born of efficiency.[34]

In addition to regular tactical experiments, large-scale annual maneuvers were held in the Atlantic and Caribbean. The most sophisticated of these foreshadowed the Fleet Problems of the 1920s and 1930s. These exercises emphasized coordinating the movements of the whole fleet; although they helped to improve fleet tactics, they were often more effective at pointing out limitations and flaws, such as the inadequacy of scouting methods and the difficulty of coordinating dispersed forces over a large area.

In 1912, Rear Adm. Frank Friday Fletcher assumed command of the Atlantic Fleet's battleship divisions. Building on experience with Battle Plans No. 1 and No. 2, he developed his own plan for battle and described it in a paper, "Tactics of the Battle Line and Signals." In it he argued the merits of maintaining the line perpendicular to the enemy, regardless of the course of individual ships, and justified his view with the need to deliver concentrated firepower.

It matters not what formation the enemy may be, whether in line, column, echelon, or whether he is in pursuit, or in retreat, or on a parallel course. Your line should be kept normal to the bearing of the enemy. Neither does it matter in what formation your line of ships may be. . . . The bearing of the target should be normal to your line. . . . The object of keeping the enemy normal to the line is to have the target at a nearly uniform distance from all the guns of your line which can bear. This position enables you to concentrate the advantage on a part of the enemy, if he commits the error of not holding you normal to his line.[35]

Fletcher's approach was a simple constraint—keep the line perpendicular to the bearing of the enemy—that simplified the signaling necessary for coordinating the movements of ships in battle. They would all turn in unison, but the types of turns and methods of communicating them could be greatly simplified. This method resolved the debate that had existed before the introduction of Battle Plan No. 1. Fletcher's answer to the question of whether to operate in line ahead or on a line of bearing was to do both. His plan allowed the battleships to steam toward or away from the enemy together, while keeping them all in a position from which they could easily engage and concentrate their firepower.

In September 1914, Fletcher assumed command of the Atlantic Fleet and earned the opportunity to test his tactical ideas more broadly. In May 1916, he issued a set of *Battle Instructions* that codified his approach. The *Instructions* continued to emphasize the necessity for concentration, but it was no longer enough to concentrate the guns of the battle fleet against the enemy. The entire fleet needed to concentrate its weapons and operate as a whole. Fletcher's *Instructions* marked the official start of the Navy's emphasis on employing all elements of the fleet together in battle to destroy the enemy.

Fletcher's *Instructions* also reflected the belief that the conditions of battle would be fundamentally unpredictable. Detailed plans could be developed, but the assumptions embedded in them might not survive for long. To help ensure coordinated action during battle, Fletcher intended to issue a battle plan not to specify the actions of individual commanders but to give them sufficient background to understand his intent and act in accordance with it.

A plan of battle will specify the role to be played by each subdivision of the fleet in the situation which the plan is intended to cover; it will fix the direction . . . from which the enemy is to be attacked; the speed of the force; . . . the direction in which the enemy is to be turned or the turn that is to be denied; whether the attack is to be pressed home to short-range or kept at long-range;

whether a quick decision is to be sought for or containing tactics adopted; whether destroyers are to attack the enemy, deny him a certain area, or remain in reserve as a means of giving a coup de grace.[36]

Fletcher's *Instructions* were an important milestone. They marked the beginning of the idea that battle plans would provide the context for coordinated action in battle. Rather than prescribing how various elements of the fleet would act, these plans described the commander's overall intentions and his concept for how different parts of the fleet could best further those objectives. The Navy's battle plans became constraints that helped align the actions of subordinate commanders while permitting them sufficient freedom to determine how best to accomplish their objectives.

Unsurprisingly, Fletcher also emphasized the need to keep the battle line concentrated, reflecting experiences in tactical exercises and war games. A division of enemy forces would be countered by maneuver, not by dividing the battle line.

> Battleships will be kept in one line as long as the enemy's battleships are kept in one formation. No advantage can be gained by dividing our battle line to attack the enemy's line from different points. If, however, the enemy divides his force with a view to attacking either one or both of our flanks a detachment of suitable force from our flanks must operate against his detached forces. Our detached forces, however, will operate only at such distances from our flank as will insure correct maneuvering for gunfire. This disposition maintains our forces on interior lines and enables them to concentrate and take advantage of any tactical errors of the enemy.[37]

Because accurate gunfire relied on visibility, Fletcher's *Instructions* placed significant emphasis on weather conditions, which could limit the effectiveness of spotting and range finding. The deployment course was vital; exercises had shown it could make the difference between accurate fire and wild shooting. Numerous effects had to be considered, including the wind and its influence on funnel exhaust and hot gasses from the guns; the direction of the sea and its effect on the motion of the ship; and the position of the sun.[38]

Fletcher recognized destroyers as legitimate offensive weapons, second only to battleships in importance. In action, they would take station at the van and rear of the battle line. They had two tactical roles. Their primary mission was to attack enemy battleships with torpedoes. Even if unsuccessful, the threat of an attack could force the enemy formation to maneuver and reduce the accuracy of its fire. Destroyers were expected to operate offensively and defensively; if the enemy destroyers made a similar attack, Fletcher expected his to break it up.

Before a general action, destroyers would screen the battle fleet and act as scouts. Although too small to be ideal scouts, they did have a major advantage: if they located the enemy, they could strike immediately with their lethal torpedoes. This allowed them to combine the missions of scouting and attacking, an approach repeatedly practiced in fleet exercises. As the exercises showed, such attacks could be particularly effective at night. Destroyers began to practice the "night search and attack." Honed repeatedly in exercises in the Atlantic Fleet, the night search and attack became a staple of U.S. Navy destroyer doctrine for the next thirty years.

Fletcher devoted considerable attention to avoiding similar attacks by the enemy. When cruising at night, destroyers would separate from the battle line, leaving cruisers to screen it. This separation was intended to prevent friendly fire and ease identification of the enemy; if the cruisers or battleships saw a destroyer, they would assume it was hostile and open fire. Searchlights and star shells would help separate friend from foe in the darkness.

INITIAL STEPS TOWARD A DOCTRINE

While Fletcher was refining his tactics in the Atlantic Fleet, a young lieutenant commander named Dudley W. Knox was studying Mahan's methods at the Naval War College. Knox believed a uniform doctrine of command was essential. In a 1913 article, he emphasized that the existing approach of issuing lengthy orders was not the way to "produce the unity of effort—the concert of action—demanded by modern conditions in a large fleet." Instead, they reduced initiative and fostered "blind obedience."[39] In their place, Knox proposed the development of "common doctrines" that would leverage the initiative and responsibility of subordinates. Although the importance of doctrine had been recognized earlier, little had been done to develop it formally. A 1901 Naval War College memorandum on tactics stated, "The prime essential of the Naval Tactics of today is the mutual understanding and confidence that must exist among the Captains of a fleet."[40] Knox echoed these ideas; he believed doctrine would help align decision making in battle and improve coordination. Knox would soon have an opportunity to demonstrate this approach within the Atlantic Fleet.

Captain Sims, who had done so much to develop the Navy's system of gunnery, completed the Naval War College course in July 1913. Like many other officers at the time, he did not relish his appointment to the college, but after some initial trepidation, he enthusiastically embraced his studies. He met Lieutenant Commander Knox and became attracted to his ideas about doctrine. When the course finished, Sims assumed command of the Atlantic Fleet's Torpedo Flotilla. Knox became his aide; together they turned the flotilla into a laboratory for the development of tactical doctrine.

At first, Sims was reluctant to take his new command. He set certain conditions before he would agree to it. One was a proper flagship, initially the tender *Dixie* and later the light cruiser *Birmingham*; another was an adequate staff. Sims had met several other individuals at the Naval War College who, like Knox, were interested in demonstrating how modern tactical ideas could be integrated with fleet operations. Sims brought them with him to the flotilla. Although these requests would not be unusual today, they were revolutionary at the time. The prior commander of the Torpedo Flotilla had had no staff at all.[41]

Sims specifically intended to use the flotilla to explore modern tactics. He considered it an "exceedingly valuable school for trying out all kinds of maneuvers at small expense."[42] His staff agreed. Besides Knox, there were Cdr. William V. Pratt, who served as Sims' chief of staff, and Lt. John V. Babcock, the operations officer. These men and their colleagues would create the Navy's first effective doctrine for coordinating the actions of ships and men in battle.

One of Sims' first steps was to create a new approach to planning based on the Naval War College's conference method. He held frequent conferences, attended by all commanding officers, as Gerald Wheeler explained:

> To create a flotilla doctrine, Sims inaugurated the use of the conference method. . . . [Sims] recognized that the Navy's hierarchical system would not permit his subordinates to disagree with him . . . or advance their own ideas unless he changed the ground rules. Thus he called for setting aside rank in conference—ideas would be studied on their merits irrespective of origin. Dissent and argument became the rule of the conference until consensus occurred; then all were expected to give complete loyalty to the operating plan and the guiding doctrine.[43]

Within the flotilla, Sims created an environment that emphasized discussion, collaboration, and trust. Before an exercise, his captains would mutually agree on a common approach—a doctrine—to guide them. Wheeler continued: "Every commanding officer would understand the doctrine and its underlying assumptions because he had helped to create it. With this amount of personal investment in a plan, loyalty to it was not difficult to achieve." Captains adhered to the plan because they had helped formulate it; their common understanding of it reduced the need for signals and increased cohesion.[44]

Flotilla doctrine was developed iteratively using the game board on board the flagship and in maneuvers with the fleet. It informed how the flotilla would operate in combat and came to emphasize aggressiveness in destroyer attacks, particularly at night. However, the stress of this work took its toll on Knox; he developed ulcers and collapsed under the strain. Knox recommended the young Lt. Cdr. Ernest J. King take his place. Although King was, he would later recall, "never one of Sims's devoted disciples," he ably served as aide and helped the flotilla refine its doctrine.[45]

Sims described the approach they were taking in his comments on Tactical Problem No. 35-13, held in July 1913: "Previous to the maneuver, two forenoons were spent by the flotilla commander and all destroyer captains in playing the problem on the maneuver board on the *Dixie,* and it is believed that this training was of great benefit to the officers concerned in actually executing the problem on the water."[46] This became the flotilla's standard approach. Maneuvers were rehearsed and discussed in conference before they were executed operationally. An excellent example was the use of custom radio signals in a particularly complicated night search and attack in March 1915. Much depended on the ability of the operators: "As the plan was drawn up by the whole gang in conference, including the radio operators who would have to handle the messages, it was an expression of their confidence in what they could accomplish, and was therefore adopted after being well thrashed out on the game board—the cabin floor."[47] The operators were successful with their custom signals, and the flotilla performed a series of coordinated attacks.

The Torpedo Flotilla developed doctrine from the "bottom up"; Sims encouraged his officers and men to experiment with new ideas and validate them in exercises. He did not impose solutions. The process kept his captains open to possibilities and ensured that they developed plans in line with their capabilities. The flotilla's doctrine became an enabling constraint that fostered self-organization and coordinated distributed action in battle. By 1915, Sims' destroyers had become a potent arm of the battle fleet; their doctrine was codified in the flotilla's *General Service Instructions.* A year later, Admiral Fletcher's 1916 *Battle Instructions* recognized the effectiveness of their doctrine by emphasizing the place of destroyers in naval battle.

A key aspect of that doctrine was aggressive action. "Under Sims, destroyer men adopted an aggressive ethic based on speed, agility, and daring."[48] This aggressiveness relied on individual initiative, and the combination of the two was considered essential for tactical success. Many of the Navy's future leaders—Ernest J. King, Harold Stark, Rufus Zogbaum, Aubrey Fitch, Harris Laning, George Cook, John Newton, William F. Halsey Jr., Franck T. Evans, and Frank Jack Fletcher (nephew of the fleet commander)—were immersed in Sims' laboratory and influenced by the collaborative approach he took toward doctrine. They would bring these ideas with them as they advanced in rank.

The concepts developed in the flotilla became part of the Naval War College curriculum. Commander Pratt, Sims' chief of staff, lectured at the Naval War College before reassignment to the Canal Zone in December 1915. Pratt worked with Lt. Cdr. Harry E. Yarnell to refine the theories developed in the flotilla and bring them to a broader group of officers. Yarnell defined the process: "A doctrine is simply a code of rules upon which we act spontaneously and without order, for the accomplishment of the mission. To be of value the doctrine must be based on correct principles and methods of conducting war. Then it must be instilled by study and actual fleet training into the minds of officers until it becomes almost a reflex action."[49] He stressed the use of war games, conferences, and fleet exercises to develop shared understanding through practice and drill.

The great value of this approach was that it helped ensure coordinated action in battle without the need for direct orders or precise control. Doctrine was the key to unity of action in a modern, diverse, and distributed battle fleet, as Yarnell described: "From skill and doctrine flows the initiative of the subordinate. Give the subordinate a proper understanding of the mission and proper training, and he may be relied upon to act correctly in an emergency when orders or instructions from higher authority are not available."[50] Doctrine augmented the developing emphasis on "unity of action" provided by the estimate of the situation.

The emerging concept of doctrine also integrated well with Fletcher's approach to battle plans. Fletcher's plans provided context and explained objectives, leaving subordinates to act on their own to further the mission. He expected them to adjust to developing circumstances without specific orders. Doctrine gave them a framework for coordinating their actions, by providing a shared context for decision making in furtherance of a common plan.[51] However, most officers still viewed tactics as a discipline involving precise maneuvering rather than shared understanding. It would be years before the fledgling doctrine developed by Sims' flotilla became the Navy's dominant approach to coordinated action in combat.

THE GREAT WAR

World War I provided the Navy valuable experience. The nascent destroyer doctrine developed in the Atlantic Fleet was validated. The new office of the CNO brought increased organizational cohesion; Rear Admiral Benson and his staff brokered differences between civilian authority, Adm. Henry T. Mayo's Atlantic Fleet, and Vice Adm. William S. Sims' theater command. Partnership with the RN during the war provided a unique learning opportunity, exposing the Navy to a wealth of wartime lessons. At the same time, existing assumptions about naval warfare were invalidated. The most pressing enemy was not the German battle line; it was the U-boats.

The Navy's emphasis on strategic mobility—preparations to fight in distant waters from rudimentary bases—made it possible to steam to European waters and quickly join the fight. Cdr. Joseph K. Taussig's 8th Destroyer Division, sent to Queenstown on the west coast of Ireland in May 1917, reported itself ready for operations immediately after arrival, impressing Taussig's RN superiors. Rear Adm. Hugh Rodman's Battleship Division 9—consisting of *New York*, *Delaware*, *Florida*, and *Wyoming*—fought storms across the Atlantic. The ships arrived at Scapa Flow, the British Grand Fleet base, on 7 December 1917 and became the Sixth Battle Squadron of the Grand Fleet. Operations with the Grand Fleet exposed the U.S. Navy to "British signals, radio codes, maneuvering orders, fire-control methods, and battle instructions." The Navy was quick to learn and adopt more effective techniques, such as an improved method of visual signaling and more rigorous gunnery training.[52]

The Grand Fleet coordinated its movements through a sophisticated set of instructions and plans. To keep concentrated, the battleships cruised in a compact formation of parallel columns. In battle, they deployed by turning to form a single line, perpendicular to the bearing of the enemy. The Grand Fleet's light forces—destroyers and cruisers—arranged themselves on the flanks of the battle line, slightly closer to the enemy. From these positions, they protected the flanks from enemy attacks and were ready to close the enemy and attack with torpedoes. After the war, the U.S. Navy adopted nearly identical battle formations, arranged to maximize concentrated firepower.

The Grand Fleet enhanced coordination through effective use of plotting. The U.S. Navy had used plotting to understand fleet exercises better before the war, but the British approach was more sophisticated. It was a deliberate method of increasing situational awareness by creating a visual representation of the tactical situation. At Jutland, Adm. John Jellicoe, who used his plot to control his ships, obtained "a considerable advantage" over his German opponent, Adm. Reinhard Scheer.[53] Service with the Grand Fleet exposed American officers to this approach, and they adopted plotting as a tactical tool. It quickly became a central component of fleet operations, increasing the situational awareness of admirals and squadron commanders.

Sims had been promoted to rear admiral and made president of the Naval War College in January 1917, but by the end of March, he had been ordered to London. His mission was to establish liaison with officers of the RN and prepare for the American entry into the war. Once that occurred, Sims became commander of American Naval Forces in Europe, with a temporary promotion, in May, to vice admiral. It was an ideal opportunity to spread his approach to doctrine. Sims' instructions to his command stressed two core elements. The first was the concept of a mission and general plan to focus the attention of subordinates on critical objectives, promote mutual understanding, and foster individual initiative:

> It is manifestly impossible for the Commander of the operation to give detailed instructions in advance that will cover all emergencies; it is equally impossible for the Commander of an operation to give these instructions on the spot to meet adequately a local situation suddenly developed. Hence the importance of having the immediate Mission and General Plan clearly understood in advance, and the necessity for leaving as wide an area of discretion to subordinates as possible.[54]

The second core element was that very discretion. Sims stressed individual initiative as the way to overcome uncertainty in battle: "No officer should fail to exercise his initiative and judgment in support of the General Plan when confronted by unexpected conditions." Sims expected his doctrine to be "a bond of mutual understanding."[55]

It worked. Sims collaborated with his subordinates and the British to develop effective doctrines for hunting U-boats, combating German raiders, and escorting convoys. These were augmented by war games and shipboard exercises like those he had employed in the Atlantic Fleet. During the war, many more officers—particularly destroyer captains—became familiar with Sims' approach to doctrinal development. Their successes validated his methods.

CONCLUSION

By the time the United States entered World War I in April 1917, a rudimentary framework had emerged. The Naval War College had introduced mechanisms to study the art of war, challenge officers with mock combat, and methodically analyze strategic and tactical problems. Exercises at sea provided real experience handling large formations and coordinating them in simulated battle. Sims had turned the Atlantic Fleet's Torpedo Flotilla into a laboratory for the development of tactics and doctrine, providing a model for continued development. However, the framework was tenuous. A sustained basis for improvement did not yet exist. The Naval War College remained relatively small and exerted limited influence; it was closed during the war and had to be reconstituted after the armistice. The doctrinal approaches Sims championed competed with more traditional forms that emphasized scripted maneuvers and disciplined "tactics."

Wartime experience exposed numerous limitations but also provided an important trigger for new and more sophisticated approaches. Plotting approaches were rudimentary and of small value for tactical decision making; the Grand Fleet showed what was possible, and the Navy emulated its approach. Gunnery exercises were improved and made more challenging. More sophisticated tactical formations, like the Grand Fleet's battle formation, were adopted. The progress made before the war primed the Navy to make the most of the lessons learned from working with the Grand Fleet.

A conceptual framework was emerging that was to inform the development of tactical doctrine. This framework was triggered by the series of constraints the Navy introduced before 1917. The use of history to derive principles of war, the analytical method of the estimate of the situation, the employment of opposed war games, the use of large fleet exercises, and the conference method were all essential ingredients. These were constraints that began to foster the emergence of more sophisticated approaches. In the interwar period, they would allow officers to deliver on Mahan's goal of "asserting judgment rapidly in the face of uncertainty and other difficult conditions."[56] Experience in World War I was the catalyst that allowed these factors to come together and create a sophisticated system of learning.

4

THE INTERWAR LEARNING SYSTEM

We must have the tactical forms to admit of quick change, and the flexibility of mind to use them

—William Cole, 1930

The Navy's experience in World War I marked an inflection point; in the interwar period experimentation with doctrine, systems of exercises, and education at the Naval War College became institutionalized. Doctrine had been an uncertain quantity when William S. Sims began to experiment with it in the Torpedo Flotilla; during the war, it proved its worth as destroyer commanders ably performed convoy escort and antisubmarine duties. The approach to exercises in the Atlantic Fleet became the basis for a system of learning; the Fleet Problems—large war games—exposed officers to the anticipated challenges of war and forced them to learn the art of command. Larger classes at the Naval War College provided broad exposure to war gaming, training in the conference method, and practice using the analytical framework of the estimate of the situation. Regular tactical exercises tested existing doctrinal approaches and encouraged the development of new ones. Individual commands assessed these lessons and created specific doctrines for their own forces. By the start of

World War II, these institutionalized approaches had allowed a sophisticated tactical framework to emerge.

The Navy's approach had two main levels of constraint. The first was the institutionalized framework; this was the regular cycle of tactical exercises (including the Fleet Problems), the work of the Naval War College, and the doctrinal development performed in individual commands. These focused the work of the Navy's officer corps and increased its willingness to try new ideas through consistent evaluation and experimentation. This initial constraint triggered the emergence of a second one that emphasized the development of a shared context for decision making in battle. This second constraint rested on two concepts, the use of a battle plan and common tactical heuristics. With them, the Navy moved beyond the doctrinal principles emphasized by Alfred Thayer Mahan to a more sophisticated approach, while preserving Mahan's emphasis on the importance of context.

Tactical heuristics were a refinement of the Navy's doctrinal principles. The principles had stressed the generic value of a concept—like concentration—but provided no guidance; heuristics channeled actions in specific ways. They were contextual constraints that became part of the Navy's conceptual fabric. Battle plans complemented the heuristics. According to Admiral Fletcher's 1916 *Battle Instructions,* plans became the mechanism for commanders to impress on subordinates their objectives and expectations, what today is called "commander's intent." Initially rather loosely structured, during the interwar period the Navy's approach to battle plans became increasingly sophisticated. By the late 1930s, a complex vocabulary for them was in place, offering unprecedented levels of coordination in battle.

Together, the plans and tactical heuristics combined to give officers a rich, shared context for making decisions in rapidly changing circumstances; they were mutually intertwined contextual constraints that created a more unified approach to combat. As the Navy developed more complex approaches to experimentation in war games and fleet exercises, officers were challenged to increase the sophistication of their tactics. More sophisticated tactics required more complex simulations and problems for experimentation. This interdependent relationship allowed the Navy's system of doctrinal development to build on itself. The result was extremely effective; the tactics developed between the wars were instrumental in the successes the Navy enjoyed in the first year of war in the Pacific and influenced the war-winning doctrines that emerged in 1943.

THE TREATY SYSTEM

The Navy's interwar development was heavily influenced by a series of international disarmament treaties designed to limit the size and cost of navies. Three disarmament conferences resulted in agreements. The first was in Washington in 1922, the second in London in 1930, and the last in London in 1936. Each of these influenced the designs of new ships and the composition of the fleet.

The Washington Conference resulted in a series of treaties that ended the alliance between Britain and Japan, limited naval armaments, and internationalized the Open Door policy toward China.[1] The Five-Power Treaty—often called simply the Washington Treaty of 1922—had the most significant impact on the development of naval doctrine and tactics. It limited new battleships to 35,000-ton displacement and restricted the maximum size of their guns to 16-inch. The Navy was limited to 525,000 tons of capital ships and 135,000 tons of aircraft carriers; Great Britain had the same upper limits, but Japan was restricted to 315,000 tons of capital ships and 81,000 tons of aircraft carriers. More aggressive officers in the IJN considered relegation to secondary status an insult.[2]

These limits codified a 5:5:3 ratio in capital ships between the United States, Great Britain, and Japan. The U.S. Navy considered parity with the RN an acceptable outcome in exchange for the termination of the Anglo-Japanese alliance. Superiority over Japan was necessary if the Pacific Fleet was to have sufficient margin to steam across the ocean and win a decisive battle in the western Pacific. The Navy's calculations assumed that the fleet would lose 10 percent of its fighting strength for every thousand miles it steamed. Since it was roughly three thousand miles from Pearl Harbor to Tokyo, a superiority of 5:3 (that is, 10:6) at the start of the war would allow a ratio of 7:6 once the fleet reached the western Pacific. The Japanese calculations were similar, and their representatives argued for a ratio of at least 10:7. They wanted to fight on at least equal terms in the western Pacific.

Article XIX of the treaty was particularly important. It stated that, with certain exceptions such as Hawaii, island possessions in the Pacific could not be further fortified. This meant that plans to upgrade the defenses of the Philippines and Guam had to be dropped, leaving them extremely vulnerable in the event of war. Article XIX called into question the existing strategy of moving rapidly across the Pacific to relieve the garrisons on those islands before they fell to the Japanese; eventually, new plans were created that assumed a more realistic, methodical advance.[3]

Although battleship construction was limited, the treaty placed no restrictions on ships smaller than ten thousand tons and armed with guns up to 8-inch. This triggered a new building race in these "treaty cruisers." The cruiser race was curtailed by the London Treaty of 1930; it restricted building programs for cruisers too and established overall tonnage limitations—like those in place for capital ships—for smaller combatants. At the insistence of the Japanese, the tonnage ratio between the United States and Japan was set at 10:7. Overall limits on cruiser tonnage were 323,500 tons for the United States and 208,850 tons for Japan. The British were allowed 339,000 tons, because of the obligations of their global empire. Further limitations were placed on the size of battle fleets; the United States and Great Britain agreed to just fifteen capital ships. To preserve the 5:5:3 ratio, the Japanese reduced their fleet to nine.

In 1936, another conference was held in London. The Japanese left the negotiations early and withdrew from the treaty system. The United States, Great Britain, and France signed the resulting agreement. It restricted new battleships to 14-inch guns. An "escalator clause" allowed battleships with 16-inch guns and up to 45,000-tons displacement if Italy or Japan refused to sign the treaty. These restrictions defined the modern fast battleships that were to join the fleet in World War II.

By the start of that conflict, the Navy had three distinct groupings of ships. The oldest were the battleships, destroyers, and submarines built before, during, and right after World War I. The second group included the ships built after the Washington Treaty, the large carriers *Lexington* and *Saratoga*, the small carrier *Ranger*, and the older heavy cruisers. The most modern vessels built under the London treaties comprised the third set. These were the four newest carriers (*Yorktown, Enterprise, Wasp,* and *Hornet*), two modern battleships (*Washington* and *North Carolina*), and the latest cruisers, destroyers, and submarines. The Navy's tactical doctrine had to account for the diversity of these groupings.

SYSTEMATIC EXPERIMENTATION

After World War I, William S. Sims returned to the Naval War College as its president. His first task was to reestablish the institution, which had been closed during the war. He wanted it to become a more influential institution than in the past, to allow a broader pool of officers to benefit from its methods. He asked Secretary of the Navy Josephus Daniels to increase class sizes, augment the staff, and assign higher-ranking officers to head the major departments. Daniels, a firm believer in education, readily agreed. In fact, he examined officer education comprehensively, modifying the Naval Academy curriculum to emphasize logical reasoning and leadership—the "indispensable attributes of an officer"—as well as the technical aspects of the profession.[4]

By the end of 1921, about half of the admirals of the fleet and their chiefs of staff were graduates of the college, a testament to the work of Sims and a reflection of the growing influence of the institution. By selecting Dudley Knox as his chief of staff, Sims made sure that these officers were exposed to the doctrinal approaches pioneered before the war in the Atlantic Fleet. During their tenure, they continued to emphasize war games and the conference method: "War College leadership, faculty, and students all contributed toward creating a climate that encouraged experimentation and learning in a group setting."[5]

In the interwar period, the links between the Naval War College and the fleet—always spotty and haphazard before—were finally institutionalized. The Strategic and Tactical Problems explored at the college were integrated with the development of tactics, doctrine, and war plans. Work at the college fed into the development of exercises and helped to analyze their results. Sims was at the forefront of this effort. He helped ensure that the college could serve as a laboratory for the development of tactics and doctrine, using his time in the Torpedo Flotilla as a basis for his approach.

Sims' vision integrated well with the work of the new CNO, Rear Adm. Robert E. Coontz. Coontz came into the position at a vital time. The Navy was shrinking and demobilizing while simultaneously trying to gather lessons from the war and develop plans for an uncertain future. At the time, OPNAV was staffed with some of the most talented officers in the Navy: Capt. Joseph M. Reeves, Capt. Harry E. Yarnell, Capt. Thomas C. Hart, Cdr. Charles A. Blakely, Cdr. Chester W. Nimitz, and Cdr. Robert L. Ghormley. Coontz and his staff institutionalized a new planning process, a broad learning cycle that integrated war planning in OPNAV, experimentation and learning at the Naval War College, and fleet exercises. The General Board sat outside this cycle but fed into it at various points, influencing the design of ships, the structure of war plans, and the integration of new technologies.

Later CNOs and Naval War College presidents built on this foundation. Adm. Edward W. Eberle, who served as CNO from July 1923 to November 1927 continued using the planning process to "guide, as a whole and toward a common end, all activities of the Navy."[6] William V. Pratt, who had served with Sims in the Torpedo Flotilla and in OPNAV during World War I, became the college's president in September 1925. He restructured the college to make its organization more like that of the fleet. In effect, Pratt created a large extended staff that OPNAV and the CINC could use to explore a variety of questions. This enhanced the effectiveness of the institutionalized planning process and more closely integrated the college with OPNAV and the fleet. Pratt also restructured the college's approach to war gaming. The divisions between strategy and tactics were deliberately blurred, leading to the more realistic and more generic concept of the "operational maneuver." Pratt's changes had a dramatic influence on the preparation for war in the Pacific.

In 1930, Rear Adm. Harris Laning, in his first opening address as president of the Naval War College, described the type of learning system that was emerging there:

We call it the Naval War College, but in reality this institution is more of a laboratory than a college. Here we study only enough to learn the sound principles on which successful warfare is based, the greater part of the time being devoted to actual operations and experiments carried out in chart maneuvers or on the game board. It is through such war games, conducted in miniature, that we can see the whole picture, that the student learns how to apply to actual war situations the principles he has learned through this study.[7]

The college challenged officers and prepared them for high command. They explored problems and solved them using the estimate of the situation. They trialed numerous tactical approaches on the game board and identified better ways to handle the fleet in action. They studied the interrelationship of tactical plans and strategic goals. Conferences discussed potential solutions, and regular critiques identified the most valuable ideas. The Naval War College experience provided officers with a shared conceptual perspective, a common framework within which to think about and solve problems; attendance was "both an education and an indoctrination."[8] Pratt believed it so valuable that when he became CNO in September 1930, he made it a prerequisite for flag rank. Pratt's decision reflected the increasing influence of the college during the interwar period. In January 1924, twenty-five of forty-nine admirals had attended the institution, or roughly 50 percent. By 1930, this had grown to thirty-six of fifty-seven, nearly 65 percent. By June 1941, eighty-three of eighty-four admirals were graduates of the Naval War College.

The institutionalization of OPNAV's planning process and the increased influence of the Naval War College operated collectively as a constraint, increasing the cohesion of the Navy's officer corps and providing high-ranking officers a shared context for assessing situations and exploring alternatives. The college created the mechanisms underpinning the framework: the war games, the conferences, the training in the estimate of the situation, and war planning. These were the lower-level routines that fostered increased cohesion. Although they had been in place for many years, it took the institutionalization of the Naval War College and of the planning process to bring them to the majority of high-ranking officers in the fleet.

The General Board served as a "balance wheel" for this work.[9] Until 1932, the CNO and president of the Naval War College were ex officio members of the board, the CNO serving as its president. Admiral Pratt believed this was a mistake. He felt the board could better serve its function if it could provide independent advice to both the secretary and the CNO. As long as the CNO was the board's president, such a relationship was impossible. In March 1932, Secretary of the Navy Charles F. Adams approved a reorganization based on Pratt's recommendations; the ex officio members were removed, and the board became more independent, further decentralizing the management of the Navy Department and forcing a more collaborative atmosphere. It was exactly what Pratt had desired. He was extremely comfortable with this sort of approach and believed in its value, having been exposed to the conference method early in his career in the Atlantic Fleet's Torpedo Flotilla.

FLEET PROBLEMS

The Navy's Fleet Problems were the culminations of each year's fleet training regimen. Exercises were conducted throughout the year, but the largest and most sophisticated were the Fleet Problems. They drew together all available ships into opposing naval forces that modeled one or more strategic and operational problems. Twenty-one Fleet Problems were held from 1923 to 1940.

The Fleet Problems were made possible by a fleet-wide reorganization in 1922. Immediately after the war, in the spring of 1919, two fleets of about equal size were created, one in the Pacific and one in the Atlantic. This fostered a healthy competition between the two but prevented a uniform approach to planning and training. In 1922, the Atlantic and Pacific Fleets were brought together to form the U.S. Fleet. The Battle Fleet (renamed Battle Force in 1931) and Fleet Base Force were stationed in the Pacific, the Scouting Fleet (renamed Scouting Force in 1931) and Control Force in the Atlantic. The Fleet Problems brought all these forces together.

The Fleet Problems blended the guidance of the CNO with the objectives of the CINC. They checked the assumptions embedded in war plans. They studied the kinds of operational challenges anticipated in wartime: moving as a unit with a "fleet train" of supply ships across a vast distance; seizing an advanced base; locating and engaging an enemy fleet; attacking a fleet with submarines; performing and defending against night searches and attacks; and determining how best to integrate the new carriers and cruisers with the fleet. The Problems had a significant impact on the development of fleet tactics and doctrine.

The Problems were intentionally designed as learning exercises. To prepare for each operation, commanders and their staffs went through the estimate of the situation using the Naval War College method and formulated a plan to achieve specific objectives.[10] During the Problem, both sides leveraged their skills and abilities to accomplish their missions and thwart their opponents. After the exercise, officers gathered for a critique using the conference method. Observations from all levels were shared, helping the Navy derive valuable lessons.

Initially, the Fleet Problems were adjudicated using rules like those employed before the war; they relied heavily on the "professional judgment" of umpires.[11] Variability in their assessments led to inconsistencies and hindered effective learning. In 1930, observers agreed that this method "was unsatisfactory."[12] They recommended a revised system that would create a more uniform approach. An initial version was trialed in 1931 during Fleet Problem XII. Feedback was mixed, but additional improvements led to more satisfactory results in Problem XIII the following year. Vice Adm. William H. Standley noted that the new rules reflected "the dangers and hazards of actual war" and provided "a yardstick by which we can measure our knowledge of general strategic principles, the initiative of the subordinate, the quickness of thought and action, and the soundness of decisions."[13] Further improvements followed, and by 1934, the rules provided detailed instructions on the amount of damage each type of attack would inflict at various ranges. A few years later, die rolls were reintroduced to inject some variability in assessments of damage.[14]

The Fleet Problems led to more sophisticated formations—for cruising, approach, and battle—that balanced the need to concentrate the fleet's power while simultaneously providing the necessary security against surprise attacks. The battle formation merged Rear Admiral Fletcher's concepts with experience gained from the Grand Fleet; the other dispositions were developed through analysis and experimentation at the Naval War College and exercises at sea.

Cruising formations emphasized security. They were used when the position of the enemy was unknown and the chances of contact with his main body slight. Before the interwar period, they were rectangular; during course changes, complex maneuvering by each ship was required to maintain station.[15] Gaps would often develop in the screen, increasing the likelihood of surprise attack. Cdr. Roscoe McFall proposed an alternative. In 1922, during an exercise at the Naval War College, he positioned cruisers and destroyers in concentric circles around the battleships at the center of the formation. This made it much easier for the whole fleet to change direction quickly without intricate maneuvers. It also concentrated antiaircraft fire more effectively. The formation was used in Tactical Problem IV of that year and discussed at length.[16]

Cdr. Chester W. Nimitz, a classmate of McFall, introduced the circular formation to the fleet in 1926, during Fleet Problem V. Nimitz was assistant chief of staff to Adm. Samuel S. Robinson, commander of the Battle Fleet. Robinson commanded the Black Fleet during the Problem and used a circular formation based on Nimitz's recommendation.[17] It worked well and soon became a standard. As carriers joined the fleet, the value of circular formations increased. They proved to be extremely well suited to the frequent course changes required by carrier warfare; to recover and launch planes, carriers had to steam into the wind, which rarely was aligned with the fleet's course.[18]

Once the general location of the enemy had been determined, the fleet shifted into an approach formation. Approach formations were designed to locate the enemy precisely and allow a quick transition to battle formation once contact was made. Scouting forces—generally the new "treaty cruisers"—were positioned ahead of the fleet. Their role was to push back enemy screening forces and make contact with

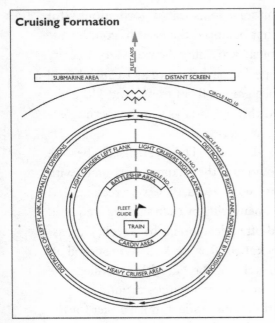

Cruising Formation

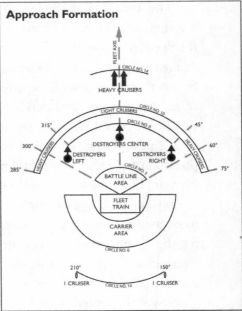

Approach Formation

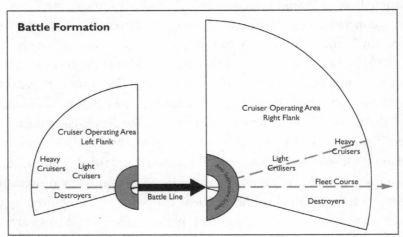

Battle Formation

FIGURE 1. Interwar formations refined in the Fleet Problems: the circular cruising formation, the more concentrated approach formation, and the linear battle formation

the enemy main body. Closer to the battle line were light cruisers and destroyers, placed to screen it and provide warning of approaching enemy forces. More vulnerable ships—the carriers and fleet train— brought up the rear.

For deployment for battle, the fleet commander would choose a specific base course. As Fletcher had emphasized, the deployment course was extremely important. It had to account for the sea state, direction of the sun and wind, and the position of the enemy. The battle line would keep the enemy on the beam so that all guns could bear. The rest of the fleet would shift into battle formation, a concentrated arrangement designed to allow all units to employ their weapons and destroy the enemy. Light forces—cruisers and destroyers—were at the head and rear of the battle line. They had two objectives: to attack the enemy line with torpedoes and break up similar enemy attacks. Carrier planes would secure control of the skies; floatplanes from the battleships would spot their fire. In numerous mock battles in the Fleet Problems, the arrangements were refined and improved.

These new dispositions constituted one of the first and most visible results of the Fleet Problems. Many other improvements followed. The Problems provided a framework that expanded the tactical and doctrinal experimentation introduced in the Atlantic Fleet before World War I. They introduced a series of constraints—systematic preparation of orders, standardized rules for mock combat, and formalized critiques—that enabled effective learning. The framework of the Fleet Problems fostered the development of an effective and flexible tactical doctrine that the Navy would leverage during World War II.

A LEARNING SYSTEM

In the early 1920s, Admiral Sims' approach to doctrinal development became the foundation of a formalized system. Officers who had been exposed to his ideas established a collaborative learning system. They founded schools and used lectures, tabletop problems, and exercises at sea to capitalize on their wartime experience and draw out solutions to the problem of coordinating their ships at sea. The core of the learning system was the force under Rear Adm. Charles Plunkett. Plunkett had been responsible for the success of the Navy's 14-inch railway battery in France during the war and had become commander of the Atlantic Fleet's destroyers in 1919. He had attended the Naval War College and was familiar with its methods. Plunkett's chief of staff, Capt. Harris Laning, had served under Sims in the Torpedo Flotilla and understood the importance of doctrine. Together, they promoted a new, more formal approach to doctrinal development.

Plunkett and Laning created a "School of Doctrine" at Charleston, South Carolina, to investigate how best to incorporate lessons from the war and coordinate ships in battle. Captain Yarnell, who had served under Sims during World War I, continued to actively promote the concept of doctrine by leading many of the efforts of the school. He gave lectures and led committees responsible for the development of standing orders and attack procedures.[19] Yarnell maintained a correspondence with Sims, allowing Yarnell to incorporate the latest thinking from the Naval War College into the work of the school.

In the Pacific Fleet, another veteran of Sims' Torpedo Flotilla introduced a parallel approach. Captain Pratt assumed command of the Pacific Fleet Destroyer Force in November 1920. He and his subordinates—including other former members of the flotilla, like William F. Halsey Jr.—continued to promote an aggressive doctrine. Pratt established a "Destroyer Staff College" at San Diego, California, to facilitate regular experimentation and indoctrination. The college educated the officers of the Pacific Fleet, increasing their familiarity with destroyer tactics.[20]

The Atlantic Fleet's school and Pratt's college regularly exchanged lessons.[21] The name "Staff College" more aptly described their work, so the school at Charleston changed its name and became the Atlantic Fleet's Destroyer Staff College. Cdr. William Victor Tomb, who had been awarded the Navy Cross during the war, commented on its work in 1921. "My first impression . . . upon observing the work done at the Staff College was one of amazement that such excellent tactical maneuvers could be carried on by the Officers of the Destroyer Force of whom only the Force Commander and the Director of the maneuvers were War College graduates."[22]

The colleges were familiarizing a broader pool of officers with the latest techniques and improving their skills. It was part of a conscious effort to ease the transition back to a peacetime footing. Laning and others were worried that the lessons of war would be lost if tactical thinking stagnated. "The more we can fight off this effect [stagnation] by work and study along the lines of our profession, and by an endeavor to embody in our 'War Instructions' the best ideas as developed in past wars, in study, and research, that much easier will be our task when the next war comes. The work at this Staff College is one effort toward that end."[23]

By 1921, enough experience had been gained to codify the lessons in a new tactical manual. It blended experience in the war with experimentation in tabletop problems, fleet exercises, the latest thinking in both destroyer staff colleges and the Naval War College. Capt. C. R. Train chaired the committee that produced the manual; it completed its work in September:

> The final result of the year's work as planned by Captain Laning was . . . a manual of Destroyer Doctrine covering all phases of destroyer activities in war. Although considerable work was done this mission was not finally accomplished until September of this year [1921] when a committee of officers headed by Captain C. R. Train completed the compilation of "Destroyer War Instructions" embodying the work of the Staff College at Charleston, the Destroyer Staff College at San Diego, and other available destroyer practice as developed in the World War. . . . This manual . . . will be . . . tested out on the game board and by actual squadron maneuvers at sea.[24]

The resulting manual, the Atlantic Fleet's 1921 *Destroyer Instructions*, represented a new paradigm, a symmetry break. It was the first Navy manual developed by a deliberately created system of learning. The system seamlessly blended work ashore—in the Destroyer Staff College and the Naval War College—with exercises at sea. The introduction to the manual reinforced this point, noting that the *Instructions* were "based upon the best obtainable experience of our Service preceding and during the recent war, supplemented by considerable subsequent game board and practical experience and trial."[25] It was a comprehensive manual designed to provide guidance to the fleet's destroyers while still preserving independent action for individual ship and squadron commanders. Future doctrinal publications would follow this paradigm.

DECENTRALIZED DOCTRINAL DEVELOPMENT

Plunkett and Pratt developed a more sophisticated approach than those of other commands, but their basic concept became the Navy's standard model for doctrinal development in the immediate interwar period. The *War Instructions* of 1923 codified it.[26] The publication stressed that indoctrination was essential but that its development would be driven by individual commands and not handed down from the fleet level. Doctrine would emerge from the bottom up. Commanders were responsible for developing their own doctrines to reflect the specific strengths and limitations of their forces. This flexible approach allowed the Navy to remain open to new approaches and encouraged creativity among junior commanders.

However, this flexibility also meant that a coherent doctrine for the fleet was lacking. Some officers urged the development of a more common and centralized approach. Lieutenant Commander Knox, in a 1924 lecture at the Naval War College, criticized the Navy for failing to grasp the importance of a comprehensive doctrine. Knox considered doctrine a "basis for harmonious decisions" and argued that it was the only effective way to coordinate the actions of distributed forces in battle: "No plan, however well it may be expressed, can possibly be co-ordinately executed by a large force of vessels . . . unless the squadron, division and ship commanders have the same conceptions of war as their commander-in-chief and are well indoctrinated."[27]

The *War Instructions* deliberately avoided this comprehensive approach. In part, this was a reaction to the Navy's experience in World War I. The Grand Fleet had been guided by its extensive *Battle Orders*. They laid down instructions for virtually every situation, but in voluminous detail that inhibited the initiative of subordinates. As James J. Tritten explains, "These fighting instructions [the Grand Fleet *Battle Orders*] attempted to provide guidance for all eventualities and offered the unit commander very little opportunity for his own initiative."[28] They provided "limited scope" for independent action.[29] To encourage individual initiative and foster contextually driven decision making, the U.S. Navy accordingly refrained from publishing a fleet-wide tactical doctrine. Instead, specific manuals, like the Atlantic Fleet's *Destroyer Instructions*, provided detailed guidance while preserving the initiative of individual commanders. This approach pushed the responsibility for doctrinal development down to lower levels.

That did not mean that doctrine was unimportant. On the contrary, the *War Instructions* stressed its value, emphasizing that victory in battle would be aided by "indoctrination of the forces, so that there may be mutual understanding of the intentions and plans of the commander in chief and so that there may be coordination in the means and methods employed in carrying out the tasks assigned and of the necessary procedure when without orders."[30] This is what Knox wanted to see. However, the *War Instructions* left the details of that doctrine unspecified, allowing it to be flexible and change depending on circumstances. The Navy put doctrinal development in the hands of individual commanders, promoting contextually sensitive doctrines.

This approach had two important results. First, just as it had done with the fire-control system, the Navy avoided prematurely converging on any specific approach. It left its options open, so that as new concepts emerged, doctrines could be rapidly modified to account for them.[31] This was particularly important in the interwar period, which was an era of rapid technological change. The Fleet Problems and tactical exercises provided a framework to test new ideas and new technologies; they became a feedback loop for the Navy's doctrinal methods. Second, the Navy encouraged flexibility and individual initiative within its officer corps. Since doctrinal development was in their hands, junior commanders learned to take responsibility and not seek answers from higher authority. This fostered their creativity and encouraged them to derive solutions for their own specific circumstances.

THE FIRST HEURISTIC: AGGRESSIVE ACTION

The dominant theme of the Navy's doctrinal development in the early interwar period was aggressive action to seize and retain the tactical initiative. The focus was on keeping the enemy off balance—forcing him to be reactive—by controlling the pace of battle. In modern terms, the Navy sought to get "inside the enemy's decision loop"—a loop characterized in the 1950s by Col. John Boyd, U.S. Air Force, as a cycle of *observe, orient, decide, act* (OODA)—and then stay one or two steps ahead. Exercises in the Atlantic Fleet before World War I had demonstrated the value of this concept, and in wartime conferences, Rear Admiral Benson had stressed its importance: "Time is everything, never waste it, keep ahead of it, deny it to the enemy."[32]

Interwar tactical exercises and Fleet Problems frequently illustrated the value of possessing the initiative. Tactical instructions emphasized how aggressive action could seize it; the *Destroyer Instructions* of 1921 warned that "time must not be wasted in endeavoring to attain the most desirable positions from which to attack. It is essential that . . . destroyers, when the tactical situation requires, attack at once and by the most direct route. . . . An effective destroyer attack early in the action will probably assure success in the major action."[33] The *War Instructions* of 1923 reinforced this concept, emphasizing that victory could best be obtained through the "assumption of the offensive, which confers the advantage of the initiative and enables us to impose our plan on the enemy."[34]

Maneuver became the Navy's preferred approach to seizing control of a battle-line action. Before World War I, reverse action—a fight on opposite courses—had resulted in disaster for the slower fleet; during the interwar period, it was embraced as a way to keep the enemy off balance. The Japanese had four—reduced after the London Treaty of 1930 to three—battle cruisers of the *Kongo* class. These ships were expected to operate as a "fast wing" and use their speed to gain position ahead of the American battle line. From there, they could force it to buckle or "cross its *T*." The U.S. Navy had no equivalent, but a reversal of course could negate the threat. As the 1934 *War Instructions* stated:

> If our fleet can induce the enemy to deploy with the greater part
> of its light forces or fast detached wing in its van in one direction
> . . . a deployment by our fleet in the opposite direction should be
> advantageous. . . . This is because it would place the enemy's light
> forces opposite our rear in a position from which they cannot
> make a successful attack, and a reversal of course by the enemy
> fleet will not improve the situation for the enemy unless a redis-
> tribution of light forces could be made.[35]

Reverse action also allowed the Navy to take advantage of the capabilities of the Ford rangekeeper. That device could develop a solution
when fighting on opposite courses, when the range rate would be
changing the fastest. It is uncertain how much was known in the U.S.
Navy about Japanese capabilities, but there is reason to believe that it
expected a reverse action to overtax Japanese fire-control systems.[36]

Aggressive action proved to be particularly important with aircraft
and carrier operations. In Problem X of 1930, the carrier *Lexington* of
the Black Fleet sought out the enemy carrier force and seized control of
the air. Although outnumbered, her planes found and struck both Blue
Fleet carriers, *Saratoga* and *Langley*. With these disabled, the Blue Fleet
was at a significant disadvantage. In his summary report, CINC U.S.
Fleet, Admiral Pratt highlighted the observations of the chief observer:
"The suddenness with which factors of strength can be destroyed and
the completeness of success which may be achieved if tactical advantages are realized and seized in a modern action furnishes ample material for thought and reflection."[37]

The exercises demonstrated that aggressive action early in a battle
could bring a significant, potentially insurmountable, advantage. This
was clear for carrier combat but was equally true in surface action. Gunnery practices reflected the emphasis on aggressive action by rewarding ships that got their guns on target rapidly and scored early hits.
Ships that got on target early but scored fewer hits could achieve higher scores than those that scored more hits but had found the target
late.[38] The Navy was beginning to realize the decisive importance of
"attacking effectively first," a concept coined by the modern naval tac-
tician Capt. Wayne P. Hughes Jr.[39] The emphasis on aggressive action

became part of the Navy's conceptual framework; it was an enabling constraint that informed its approach to combat.

The scout bomber, a concept that culminated in the famous Dauntless SBD, was a natural outgrowth of this emphasis.[40] The scout bomber was a plane that could do in the sky what the Navy's destroyers were doing on the surface: search for the enemy while carrying sufficient ordnance for a decisive attack. The destroyers used torpedoes. The SBD used five-hundred-pound bombs. At the battle of Midway, in June 1942, this concept proved its worth.

With its emerging focus on aggressive action, the Navy moved beyond the principles of war. In their place it was developing a series of tactical heuristics, formative building blocks of a more sophisticated doctrine. Aggressive action to seize the initiative and keep the enemy off balance was the first of these. The Fleet Problems illustrated its importance at the tactical level and demonstrated the influence it could have operationally. Aggressive action could do more than win battles; it could determine the outcome of campaigns. Adm. Frank H. Schofield, CINC U.S. Fleet, in 1932, summarized the developing consensus when he declared, "We are stronger, quicker, and more effective when acting on the offensive than on the defensive."[41] The enemy, forced to react, would be at a disadvantage, leaving the Navy free to exploit its own tactics.

NOT REFIGHTING JUTLAND—WINNING IT

The emphasis on aggressive action became a lens through which the Navy assessed the results of exercises and examined history. This was particularly true for the battle of Jutland, fought on 31 May 1916. The Navy has been criticized for placing too much emphasis on decisive battle in the interwar period, for preparing to "refight" the largest fleet engagement of World War I. These criticisms have their root in a misreading of Mahan. Traditional interpretations view his emphasis on sea control as an argument for decisive battle by large fleets. While he considered this development likely, he also acknowledged many other paths to obtaining a strategic decision.[42] These subtleties underpinned the Navy's beliefs about a future war. It had to be prepared to fight and win a decisive battle but simultaneously explore other means to achieve command of the sea.

The Navy examined Jutland to learn from it, not to emulate it or "refight" it. In 1925, Captain Reeves became the head of the Tactics Department at the Naval War College. He considered the battle of Jutland a useful vehicle for the examination of modern naval tactics. Reeves' detailed critique of the battle stressed the importance of flexibility when applying the principles of war. He argued that it was incorrect to try to apply all principles simultaneously. Only one or two would be most appropriate for a given set of circumstances. The challenge was in selecting the right one or two and determining how to apply them. "In all the many tactical situations . . . which arise before and during an engagement, a commander has two things to do: *First,* select the principle which is vital or of paramount importance in the special situation; *Second,* decide on the method of applying that principle."[43] This contextual approach derived directly from Mahan's ideas.

Reeves also emphasized the importance of acting aggressively and seizing opportunities, not only at the tactical level but also in formulating grand strategy. Holloway H. Frost shared this view. He had entered the Naval War College in 1916 as a young lieutenant and immediately turned his attention to the battle. In cooperation with Lt. Harry E. Yarnell and Capt. Albert P. Niblack, Frost conducted a war game simulating it in September 1916. Sims and Knox traveled to Newport to join them and learn from the exercise. In November, Frost produced an official Naval War College report on the battle.[44]

Frost continued his analysis after the war; his detailed study of Jutland was published in 1936, a year after his death. In it Frost provided a uniquely American perspective. He started by framing the strategic background. Victory over the German fleet would have given the British freedom to move aggressively into the Baltic Sea. Effective communication could have been established with Russia, permitting resupply and closer strategic coordination. Trade between Germany and Scandinavia could have been severed, hindering the movement of vital war material. Finally, Germany would have been forced to shift resources and personnel toward the defense of its coasts, depleting the reserves needed for fighting on both the eastern and western fronts.[45]

Therefore, a decisive British victory at Jutland had the potential to change the course of the war. However, the approach taken by the Grand Fleet's commander, Adm. John R. Jellicoe, showed no understanding of this. His orders and guiding principles emphasized the avoidance of risk and the preservation of his fleet. Decisive action would ensue only if he could be certain of a positive outcome.[46] Harris Laning too had emphasized this point; Jellicoe's defensive posture meant he was "unwilling to pay . . . for the victory which . . . lay in his grasp" despite placing his fleet "in one of the most powerful positions ever obtained."[47]

Frost and Laning both criticized Jellicoe for failing to align his tactical posture with strategic opportunities. This criticism was motivated not by faith in decisive battle but by knowledge of the overall strategic context. Jellicoe would have been justified in taking much greater risks with his ships because victory had the potential to change the war. In the words of Frost, "Jellicoe . . . conducted his fleet ably in accordance with an inherently erroneous conception of naval warfare."[48] Laning felt the British had "lost sight of their primary objective" and failed to act aggressively when the decisive moment came. For Laning, this was "the outstanding lesson of Jutland."[49]

Frost and Laning both noted that Jellicoe's subordinates failed to act with the necessary initiative. They missed opportunities to damage the enemy, failed to report sightings accurately to higher authority, and embraced the risk-averse attitude that, with a few notable exceptions, seemed to dominate the Grand Fleet. They blamed Jellicoe's detailed instructions for dampening the initiative of his subordinates. Laning explained it this way: "The British failed to gain decisive victory . . . because their higher commanders . . . had not prepared themselves and their subordinates to win."[50]

Jutland was a focus for the Navy not because its leaders wanted to refight the battle but because it was an excellent lesson in lost opportunities. The study of Jutland became a tool to reinforce the emerging aspects of the Navy's doctrine. These included the importance of fostering the independence of subordinates, urging them to seize the initiative, and stressing the need to make the most of momentary opportunities that appeared in battle. To achieve a strategic decision through tactical victory, the Navy had to go into battle with the right tactical posture, one that accurately reflected the current strategic situation. This would require great flexibility and determination.

THE SECOND HEURISTIC: QUICK AND EFFECTIVE GUNFIRE

Once a battle was joined, the most effective way for the Navy's surface ships to seize the initiative would be quick and effective gunfire. This led to the Navy's second tactical heuristic: an emphasis on opening fire early, to seize the initiative and put the enemy off balance. In daylight, this meant using the fire-control system to develop an accurate model of the target's movements and opening fire at the maximum possible range. At night, it meant firing immediately upon sighting the enemy. Modeling the target's movements was less important; spotting corrections would bring the guns onto it.

The Navy's fire-control system, based on the Ford rangekeeper, allowed accurate fire at very long ranges even during complicated maneuvers. Chapter 2 describes some implications of this system, including an increasing emphasis on long-range gunfire using aerial spotting. During the interwar period, long-range gunnery became a fundamental aspect of the Navy's surface-warfare doctrine. It was how officers expected to win battles. The *War Instructions* of 1934 stressed the point: "Fire should be opened, normally, at the maximum range at which an effective fire can be delivered under the conditions which exist at the time. The advantage of an initial superiority is so great that every effort should be made to establish early hitting."[51]

The ability of the fleet's battleships to fire accurately at long-range was limited at the start of the interwar period. Only the five most recent battleships—the "Big Five" of the *Colorado* and *Tennessee* classes—could elevate their guns sufficiently to hit beyond 27,000 yards. The older battleships could reach only about 21,000 yards. During the early 1930s, as the older battleships were modernized, gun elevations were increased to create a more homogenous battle line. In his annual report for 1929, CINC U.S. Fleet Adm. Henry A. Wiley remarked on this work: "Turret gun elevations of the *Nevada* and *Oklahoma* are now being increased. . . . [T]his same important work will be done during the modernization of subsequent battleships."[52]

Initially, long-range gunfire was employed only by battleships, but by the mid-1930s, all new surface ships were being given advanced fire-control computers. Powerful motors were developed to control the guns remotely and bring them onto targets. Initially mounted on destroyers, these systems ultimately equipped cruisers and battleships as well. They reduced the potential for human error, increased accuracy, and allowed guns to be brought into action more rapidly, both at long range and in close-range nocturnal encounters. Doctrinal manuals capitalized on these improvements by stressing the need to fire immediately once a target came into range.[53]

Emphasis on the decisive effect of gunfire influenced ship designs, most notably the ten-thousand-ton "treaty" cruisers. The first of these were lightly protected and heavily armed, reflecting the existing emphasis on offensive action. Capt. Frank H. Schofield described current thinking in a 1923 memorandum: "Since the size of cruisers is limited to ten thousand tons, it will probably be necessary in our new designs to forsake nearly all attempt at passive defense of these vessels—armor—in order to have weight available for the full development of speed, steaming radius and gun power. I think it is fundamental that once an American cruiser comes into contact with an enemy cruiser its gun power must be superior to the gun power of that enemy cruiser."[54]

The General Board's designs reflected this concept. In 1923, its preferred cruiser design featured twelve 8-inch guns and no armor. Although other schemes with heavier armor were proposed, the board eventually decided on a design with modest "antidestroyer" armor and ten 8-inch guns; this became the *Salt Lake City* class. The following *Northampton* class was similar. Once complete, the *Northampton*s displaced less than anticipated, and future designs used the difference to provide better armor without sacrificing firepower.

The large, ten-thousand-ton light cruisers of the *Brooklyn* class were an extreme example of the Navy's emphasis on firepower. Although designs with twelve 6-inch guns were being considered, the Japanese announcement that the forthcoming *Mogami* class would be armed with fifteen 6.1-inch guns led the Navy to select a similar layout. The large number of guns made the *Brooklyn*s powerful, but what made them overwhelming was the new semifixed ammunition they fired. Each of the guns could fire between ten and twelve rounds per minute. In sixty seconds, one of these cruisers could fire over 150 shells, enough to overwhelm a destroyer or light cruiser if they could be brought onto the target. The rangekeepers at the core of their fire-control systems made this outcome extremely likely.

By the end of the interwar period, faith in the importance of gunfire had led to a tactical heuristic. Informed by the effectiveness of the fire-control system and the advantage of "attacking effectively first," the Navy's surface forces would seek to win battles by employing rapid, accurate gunfire at the outset of an action. Other approaches began to assume secondary importance.

FIGHTING INSTRUCTIONS AND BATTLE PLANS

In November 1927, the commander of the Battle Fleet, Adm. Louis R. de Steiguer, issued a new tentative (issued for trial, but not official) publication, *Battle Fleet Fighting Instructions*, reflecting the Navy's increasingly sophisticated approach to coordinating a modern fleet in battle. De Steiguer emphasized three critical points. First, the specific flow of battle was uncertain; naval officers had to be prepared to fight effectively despite it. To maximize the potential of the fleet, special prearranged procedures would be used to secure an advantage at the start of an action. Finally, in battle, the entire fleet—all available arms—would engage the enemy simultaneously in a coordinated effort. The *Instructions* stated:

> Because of the impossibility of knowing in advance the particular combinations and situations that will develop in a naval engagement a Commander-in-Chief cannot lay out a plan of battle that will carry with certainty beyond the opening of the main gun action. Nevertheless by adherence to a plan of procedure during the approach and until the Main Bodies are fully engaged, in which . . . a fleet has become skilled by repeated exercises, the fleet

can be brought to a position of such initial advantage . . . that by a quick coordinated attack of all the forces in the fleet with guns, torpedoes, bombs, and mines a decisive victory can be gained.[55]

The *Instructions* introduced a new series of constraints to govern the conduct of the fleet. The "procedures" were rehearsed maneuvers, employed in the approach to battle or in its preliminary phases. Although the whole battle could not be scripted, de Steiguer felt, some maneuvers could be. He expected to use one or more "canned" plans, triggered by a signal, to react to a developing situation and maneuver the fleet into a position of advantage. By introducing the idea of canned plans, de Steiguer took an initial step toward a new vocabulary for coordinating a fleet in battle.

De Steiguer had explicit objectives. He wanted to divide the enemy battle line—most likely the Japanese—and separate its battle cruisers from the battleships. He wanted to maximize the firepower of his ships by taking "full advantage of the gun fire of our own long-range battleships" and moving "quickly through certain gun ranges at which that line is at a disadvantage." Ultimately, de Steiguer wanted to bring the fleet's "full gun power into play simultaneously."[56] Because the fighting strength of the Navy's battle line varied considerably at different ranges, it was important to maneuver effectively. The most modern ships could fire accurately at very long ranges, but most of the battle line was made up of older ships that could only reach, as noted above, about 21,000 yards. To overwhelm the enemy with gunfire, de Steiguer had to get his ships close.

De Steiguer's last objective was more complicated. It deserves to be quoted at length: "To provide the various Task Force Commanders in our fleet with advance information that will enable them to operate their forces as to . . . have them in their proper deployment stations for delivering the final coordinated attack at the decisive instant."[57] The nascent idea contained in Rear Admiral Fletcher's 1916 *Battle Instructions*—that all arms should coordinate in battle—had become a reality. It had been trialed and demonstrated in the Fleet Problems, and now, over a decade later, it was being incorporated into the new, emerging doctrinal framework. The next stage would be a more formal codification of the approach outlined by de Steiguer.

In May 1929, Admiral Pratt became CINC U.S. Fleet. Pratt had been chief of staff to Sims in the Atlantic Fleet Torpedo Flotilla and had participated in the development of the Navy's first effective doctrine. After serving as assistant to the first CNO, Rear Admiral Benson, Pratt had contributed to the development of the Atlantic Fleet's 1921 *Destroyer Instructions*; since then he had held numerous important posts, including command of the Battle Fleet and presidency of the Naval War College. Pratt was in the ideal position to have a lasting impact on the Navy's doctrinal development.

Pratt oversaw the creation of a new manual, *Tentative Fleet Dispositions and Battle Plans*. Issued in 1929, this document encapsulated experience with battle tactics so far. It built on the work of de Steiguer and introduced a formal set of plans for major action, along with vocabulary to communicate them. *Tentative Fleet Dispositions* was one of the most important steps in the evolution of the Navy's surface-warfare doctrine; it was a critical enabling constraint that informed fleet tactics for the next fifteen years. It bridged the tactical concepts developed at the Naval War College at the turn of the century and the doctrine that governed the fleet during World War II.[58]

Each plan took a specific form and was identified by a pair of coded letters and numbers. The first number determined the type of action; *1* for normal action and *2* for reverse. Additional numbers were used for more complex situations, like pursuit and withdrawal. A letter prescribed a specific range band: *E* for extreme range, 27,000 yards and above; *L* for long range, 21,000 to 27,000 yards; *M* for medium range, 17,000 to 21,000 yards; and *C* for close range, 17,000 yards and below. Other letters provided details on the use of supporting forces. The plan's "objective" described what the commander hoped to accomplish. "Assumptions" reflected his assessments and formed the basis of the plan. A "general plan" described how the commander expected the plan to influence the battle. Together these created a guide that increased the cohesion of the fleet. Additional sections described the specific missions of each major subordinate unit.[59]

This structure for battle plans became a new language and grammar, a specific way of creating and communicating plans for battle. It succinctly described the plan, the assumptions behind it, and the mission of subordinate forces. These constraints enabled the development of more sophisticated coordination. Battle Plan 2E, for reverse action at extreme range, is an excellent example of the form.

The boundaries of the four letter-coded range bands corresponded almost exactly with the known capabilities of battleships then in service. The outer limit of the moderate-range band was the maximum effective range of the guns on the Navy's older battleships, and the outer limit of the long-range band corresponded with the maximum range of the 14-inch guns on the majority of Japanese battleships and battle cruisers.[60]

TABLE 3. Battle Plan 2E

Object	Concentration of effort on rear of enemy battle line and denial to enemy detached wing and light forces of opportunity to attack the van of our battle line in order to destroy enemy battle line or force it to maneuver to our advantage.
Assumptions	• That our battleships may not be superior in strength to the total strength of enemy battleships and battle cruisers. • That our battleships capable of firing at extreme ranges are superior in strength to those of the enemy capable of firing at extreme ranges. • That the speed of our battleships is less than that of the enemy battleships. • That the enemy may employ a detached wing of battle cruisers or of battle cruisers and fast battleships. • That the enemy battle line will seek action at long ranges and can close to ranges that are favorable to it. • That our air force has adequate strength to prevent the enemy from denying aircraft spotting to our battleships. • That the enemy has deployed with his detached wing and the majority of his light forces in his van. • That the initiative taken by our battle line will compel the enemy battle line to meet our maneuvers or suffer a gunnery disadvantage. • That high day visibility conditions prevail.
General Plan	To engage the enemy by moving on courses opposite to that of the enemy in order to concentrate effort on rear of enemy battle line and to deny to enemy detached wing and light forces opportunity to attack the van of our battle line.

The Navy enjoyed a marked superiority in the extreme-range band. In 1929, the five battleships of the *Colorado* and *Tennessee* classes represented the most powerful collection of battleships in the world that could reach targets beyond 27,000 yards. As a result, combat at extreme range was considered very advantageous. Extreme-range battle plans concentrated on the use of long-range gunnery to defeat the enemy; light forces would be withheld unless a favorable opportunity presented itself. The enemy was not expected to be able to respond effectively to fire at these maximum ranges.[61]

In the long-range band, however, the Navy was, as de Steiguer had noted, at a significant disadvantage. Before the modernization of the older battleships, only the same five ships could fire effectively at these ranges. Battle in the long-range band was to be a delaying action; it was to be maintained only as long as necessary before closing to moderate distances or retreating to extreme range. Light forces would attack the enemy battle line immediately, to reduce the speed of their ships and allow the Navy's battle line time to increase or decrease the range.[62]

At moderate ranges, the Navy's battle line was superior to any potential enemy. Within this range band, all the Navy's battleships could fire effectively and the enemy would be subjected to their concentrated fire. Light-force attacks could be supported by the primary and, if the range were close enough, secondary guns of the battleships, but light forces were to be withheld unless a favorable opportunity arose or the battle progressed poorly.[63] The heavy guns of the battleships were expected to be decisive.

Close range would be simply an all-out brawl. The extreme lethality of close-range battleship gunfire and the proximity of enemy light forces would lead to a deadly melee. Although the firepower of the entire battle line could be brought to bear on the enemy, hostile cruisers and destroyers would be able to make effective torpedo attacks. To counter them, the Navy's light forces would attack immediately, without orders.[64]

Like de Steiguer's *Instructions*, the new *Tentative Fleet Dispositions* assumed that all arms would concentrate on the enemy simultaneously. The perceived disadvantage of the long-range band increased interest in this approach. In 1932, the Navy's War Plans Division emphasized how aircraft could augment the fleet's firepower: "In view of . . . the reduced [gun] range of certain of our capital ships, and our lack of light cruisers, it should be our constant effort to maintain our present superiority in seaborne aviation, which, to a degree, can compensate."[65] Adm. Harris Laning, writing in 1933, described the need to focus all arms simultaneously on the enemy: "With so many weapons carried on such different types of ships it is apparent that if we are to get the maximum effect of all weapons and make our blow the sum total of the blows of all, there must be perfect coordination between the types carrying them."[66] Coordinated attacks would be performed by all elements of the fleet, including battleships, destroyers, airplanes, submarines, and minelayers. The effectiveness of each individual attack would be increased by making them simultaneously. Such attacks were a recurring feature of the Navy's Fleet Problems and tactical exercises, reinforcing the idea that coordinated action would be the best way to destroy an enemy fleet in battle.[67]

Starting with Fleet Problems X and XI of 1930, the Navy tested and refined the concepts of *Tentative Fleet Dispositions*. Individual commanders used the plans as models for their own specific approaches. For Problem XI, the Black Fleet developed a plan based on reverse action at extreme range. A second Black plan called for a normal action at extreme range. Each of them was like those in the tactical publications, but the second had one significant difference; it employed the battleship *California* as a detached wing. For Problem X, the Black Fleet battle plan called for closing quickly to decisive ranges and concentrating fire on the van of the enemy battle line. The Blue Fleet used the same battle plans for both problems. Aerial spotting would be employed between 25,000 and 29,000 yards, and fire would be concentrated on one flank of the enemy battleships. If aerial spotting was impossible, Blue would close to around 20,000 yards. Once the battle was progressing favorably, the range would be closed to ensure decisive effect: "Battleship ranges will be closed to maximum destructive effect when superiority of hitting is gained."[68]

Problems X and XI demonstrated that the new battle plans represented a significant improvement. Vice Adm. William Cole, who commanded the Blue Fleet in Problem XI, offered the following comment:

> The tactics of the general engagement . . . in Problem XI, as in Problem X, offer the widest field for discussion. . . . The "Tentative Fleet Disposition and Battle Plans, 1930" give to us the greatest single advance in fleet tactics I have known in my years of service in the fleet. It affords to the OTC [officer in tactical command] an extraordinary increase in the flexibility of control from the beginning of tactical scouting through the general engagement. . . . Our greatest danger lies in an inflexible adherence to a conception of the enemy's strength and disposition made even under the best conditions of visibility for tactical surface and air scouting, but made with the fleets separate by forty to sixty thousand yards. We must have the tactical forms to admit of quick change, and the flexibility of mind to use them.[69]

Vice Adm. Lucius Bostwick, commander of the Black Fleet, had similarly positive comments and called for the revision of existing tactical manuals to incorporate the new approaches.[70] In 1934, with the publication of FTP-143, *General Tactical Instructions*, the concepts in *Tentative Fleet Dispositions* were officially codified. The new manual stressed the importance of plans and encouraged officers to create their own based on the new form. Continued testing did not reveal any need for significant changes, and the concepts were published again in 1940 in the revised version of the FTP-188, *General Tactical Instructions*.

The lack of significant changes over this span reflects the success of the basic framework introduced by Admiral Pratt. It was a flexible set of constraints that enabled increased coordination of the fleet in battle. The plans were not prescriptive but collectively a sample vocabulary that promoted concerted action. They represented a symmetry break that enabled a new level of sophistication in the Navy's tactical doctrine. The plans were the Navy's most important tactical development of the interwar period.[71]

MAJOR ACTION AND THE NIGHT SEARCH AND ATTACK

However, as flexible as this framework was, it had a significant limitation; it focused exclusively on "major action"—decisive battles between large fleets. There was no centralized set of plans, no agreed-upon constraints, to help guide commanders who took smaller forces into battle. These "minor actions" were largely neglected. It was a blind spot that would have significant implications during the first year of war.[72]

Admiral Pratt recognized the deficiency and took steps to address it in November 1930, when, as CNO, he introduced the concept of "type" commands. These provided a mechanism for the development of doctrines for each major type of ship: battleships, carriers, cruisers, and destroyers. Each of the various type commands was an administrative organization that took responsibility for training and creating more detailed doctrines for its respective ship type. However, the main emphasis of these doctrines remained major action. They explored the roles that the ships would play in a large battle, dominated by a clash of battle lines. Very little attention was devoted to exploring how best to handle cruisers or destroyers in minor actions.[73]

The only type of minor action that was a standard part of the Navy's doctrinal development in the interwar period was the "night search and attack," first formulated by Sims in the Atlantic Fleet. Experimentation in the interwar period refined and expanded the original concept. Although subordinated to major action—it was almost always conceived as an augmentation of a daylight battle—the night search and attack was an important component of the Navy's tactical doctrine in the years before World War II and had a pervasive influence on the development of the Navy's night-battle doctrine.

For the first decade of the interwar period, the main emphasis in this connection was on the two component elements—the search and the attack. The search was critical; before the enemy could be attacked, he had to be found. During the search, destroyers steamed parallel courses on a long scouting line, perpendicular to the assumed direction of the enemy. Sophisticated search patterns were employed to maximize the chances of sighting the opposing formation. Once the enemy was found, destroyers formed up into attack units; sometimes, a dedicated striking group was held in reserve, ready to attack immediately once the enemy was located.[74]

The division into the Scouting Force and the Battle Force created a degree of specialization; normally, the Scouting Force destroyers performed the night search and attack.[75] In the early 1930s, when the cruisers of the *Salt Lake City* and *Northampton* classes joined the Scouting Force, they worked closely with destroyers in scouting and screening missions. Simultaneously, the fleet was gaining more experience attacking and defending formations at night. These two factors led to an emphasis on penetrating an enemy screen before attacking. This introduced a third, and increasingly important, step to the process: fighting through the enemy screen to establish contact with the main body at the center of the formation.

This new step was introduced in 1931, with a revision of the *Destroyer Tactical Instructions*. They stressed the importance of penetrating the enemy screen to locate definitively the main objective—the capital ships at the center of the formation. If the enemy lacked an adequate screen, this was an easy task; individual destroyers could be used as scouts. However, if the enemy had effective screening forces, destroyers needed to be grouped into units of "penetrative strength" for the scouting phase so that they could fight their way through.[76]

To give the attack units more firepower, cruisers were integrated into them. The initial approach was to place a cruiser behind each destroyer scouting unit. The cruiser would use its guns to blast a path through the enemy screen, which the destroyers would then pass through. As screens became stronger, cruisers were concentrated together and placed at the front of the formation so they could fight their way in: "Should the approach to the enemy main body be covered by a strong distant screen, it may be necessary to penetrate this screen in a concentrated formation before deploying for the attack. In such a situation cruisers detailed to attack [with] the destroyer operations will usually be stationed in advance of the massed destroyers in sufficient concentration to bring superior force to bear on the enemy screening vessels which are likely to be encountered."[77]

By 1937, sophisticated procedures were being developed to coordinate destroyers and cruisers in these operations.[78] The night search and attack now comprised three distinct phases. During the "scouting" phase, the attacking destroyers and cruisers divided into scouting units, searched for the enemy formation, contacted its outer screen, and fought their way past it. Once one or more destroyers located the capital ships at the center of the enemy formation, the "contact scouting" phase began. They continually transmitted contact reports, allowing the other ships to locate the quarry. Finally, in the "attack phase," groups of destroyers closed with the large enemy ships and attacked them with torpedoes.[79]

Depending on the nature of the attack and the formations used, the cruisers either escorted the destroyers into the enemy formation or broke off after creating an opening in the screen. Two specific formations were developed to coordinate a destroyer squadron with one or

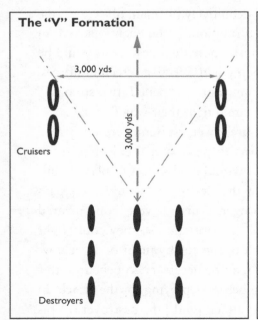
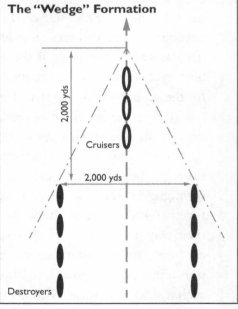

FIGURE 2. Night-search-and-attack formations developed in the 1930s. Both relied on cruiser gunfire to penetrate an enemy screen. The "V" had the cruisers break off after opening a hole for the destroyers to pass through; the "Wedge" was designed to take the attackers through the enemy formation.

more supporting cruisers. The "V" formation divided the cruisers into two roughly equal groups, 1,500 yards off either bow of the lead destroyer and three thousand yards ahead. The destroyers were arranged in a compact formation of three parallel columns astern of the cruisers. The "Wedge" formation placed the cruisers in a single column two thousand yards ahead of destroyers, with the destroyers arranged in two parallel columns, two thousand yards apart. The two formations were used differently. The "Wedge" was intended to take the attackers through the enemy formation; the cruisers engaged the screening vessels with their guns while the destroyers enmeshed the enemy main body in a crossfire of torpedoes. The "V" formation allowed the cruisers to break off after making an opening for the destroyers to pass through.[80]

The Navy practiced the night search and attack extensively. Of the twenty-one nocturnal tactical exercises performed during fiscal year 1938, all simulated a night search and attack on an enemy disposition of battleships.[81] It was a major focus of interwar tactical training. However, although the fleet's destroyers became skilled thereby at maneuvering into position and attacking at night, the exercises contained numerous artificialities that hindered the development of night combat doctrine, such as the use of searchlights to represent gunfire. The most pervasive of these was the underlying assumption that a night search and attack would be integrated with a major fleet action between battle fleets.

This led to a significant change in destroyer tactics during the interwar period. Since an attack on a battle fleet would require penetrating an enemy screen, destroyers focused on using their guns first. This tendency was reinforced by the emerging heuristic emphasizing quick and effective gunfire. Whereas before and immediately after World War I the focus had been on stealthy attacks, with small ships firing torpedoes from obscured positions, by the late 1930s the destroyers were using gunfire to fight their way to firing position. The earlier emphasis on stealth had been abandoned. Torpedoes remained important weapons but no longer weapons of surprise. This was a major and decisive shift; one that, again, had a significant impact during World War II.

THE THIRD HEURISTIC: DECENTRALIZED COMMAND AND CONTROL

In the 1930s, the Navy began deliberate development of a third tactical heuristic, an emphasis on decentralized command and control. This concept had been a core component of the Navy's early experimentation with doctrinal development. During the interwar period, it was systematically embraced. The mock combat of the Fleet Problems repeatedly reinforced the need to rely on the initiative of subordinates if large formations were to be handled effectively.

The foundation of this emphasis was articulated in the 1922 *Destroyer War Instructions*, which gave subordinates discretion to emulate Adm. Horatio Nelson and "turn a blind eye" to certain orders.

> The responsibility for the proper action to be taken always rests with the senior officer immediately present. . . . If, when in actual contact with the enemy, the senior officer of a group, or commanding officer of a ship acting singly, receives an order from higher authority which it is evident may have been given in ignorance of the existing conditions, and which, if obeyed, would result in a definite or partial failure of the general plan, discretion must be used as to obeying the order and an early opportunity taken of reporting the existing conditions.[82]

To create an environment where this was feasible—where officers could use individual judgment and yet cooperatively further the overall objective—the Navy sought to strengthen the ability and effectiveness of officers, but to do so within a standardized framework. The educational system of the Naval War College was a core component of the framework, and starting in 1929, the structure of the estimate of the situation was refined to further foster the initiative of subordinates; it became an American equivalent to the German practice of *Auftragstaktik*, or "mission command."

The essential changes were the introduction to the estimate process of a step directly comparing opposing forces—to make it easier to assess "all factors of strength, such as material, personnel, position, disposition, composition, and, above all, morale"—and an increased emphasis on objectives—the ends, not the means—to create freedom of action for subordinates: "You are cautioned always to state the Courses of Action in terms of what is to be accomplished and not in terms of the operations to accomplish them."[83] Effective instructions created options for subordinates and leveraged their initiative.

The revised approach was beneficial, but it led to a substantial and problematic change in how officers assessed enemy intentions. A focus on determining the "enemy's probable intentions" shifted attention toward the enemy's *most likely* course of action and away from the *most dangerous* ones.[84] This increased the likelihood that officers would assess enemy intentions in terms of the Navy's own capabilities, leading to "mirror imaging." Despite this flaw, the process of generating the estimate continued to be a powerful enabling constraint. It was an analytical approach that encouraged a common approach to framing, analyzing, and solving problems. Ultimately, it resulted in its own supersession—by a new pamphlet, *Sound Military Decision*, which enhanced the process of estimating the situation.

The Fleet Problems were another component of the framework. They gave officers practice in estimating situations, formulating plans, writing orders, relying on subordinates, and operating as they would in wartime. The large and open critiques ensured that all officers got a broad view of the Problem just completed and the way it had been executed, giving them a sense of the way the fleet would operate in wartime and of the parts they were expected to play. In the summary of Fleet Problem XII of 1931, the CNO, Admiral Pratt, emphasized the nature of the Problem as a teaching tool, while stressing the importance of flexibility and individual initiative: "I wish to impress on every officer here, particularly the younger ones, to never attempt to draw out of the plans a canned solution. The purpose of this problem was to teach you to act quickly and to form a clear and concise decision. From this decision evolves a clear and definite plan. . . . You will get a number of valuable lessons but do not accept them as gospel."[85]

The vocabulary of the battle plans was the final component of the Navy's conceptual framework. By giving subordinates insight into the overall objective and explaining their parts, plans made it possible for the whole fleet to coordinate its efforts in battle. But to do so, every officer would have to act on his own initiative, in furtherance of the main objective.

The relatively small size of the officer corps was one reason the Navy was successful at creating a shared conceptual framework. In 1921, there were less than 3,500 line officers on permanent active duty, few enough to allow great familiarity among them. Even fewer officers were in higher command positions, and they quickly learned which subordinates could be trusted with greater responsibility.[86] "The flag list was short enough in the 1920s that any officer on it knew the strengths and weaknesses of those above and below him."[87] This helped create an environment of trust and effective delegation.

The Navy capitalized on this environment and the developing framework by stressing decentralized decision making and individual initiative. The 1934 *War Instructions* reflected this emphasis: "Subordinates should not be given instructions as to the method of accomplishment of their assigned tasks except to the extent necessary to insure coordination of the various task forces."[88] In other words, orders were written to define the "what" and not the "how," leaving subordinates to determine how best to accomplish their objectives.

To provide training in rapid decision making and reinforce the need for tactical flexibility, Adm. David F. Sellers, then CINC U.S. Fleet, eschewed battle plans entirely for Fleet Problem XV of 1934. He wanted to "present to opposing commanders of all ranks a rapidly changing situation over an extended period."[89] The goal was to encourage officers to acknowledge the fluidity of a combat situation and allow them to develop the skills to thrive in it. Sellers explained, "Our tactical training thus far has been based almost entirely on the estimate of a single situation. While this may sometimes be appropriate under some conditions, it is believed that training in making a continuous or running estimate of a situation that is changing from hour to hour is far better preparation for war. War might be likened to a moving picture. As its story unfolds our minds must be alert in following its course."[90]

Sellers believed a "running estimate" more accurately reflected the kind of war that would occur in the Pacific, where the Japanese would attempt to subject the fleet to a continual series of attritional attacks and wear it down before a decisive engagement. Consequently, he stressed the ability of officers to think quickly and continually reassess developing situations for emerging opportunities. The emphasis on rapidly evaluating changing situations persisted long after Sellers introduced it. In 1941, Adm. Husband E. Kimmel stressed it during his training exercises in the Pacific Fleet, noting in his annual report that "emphasis has been placed on rapid estimates of changing situations."[91]

The focus on dynamic reassessments reflected the goals of the Navy's emerging doctrinal framework. Subordinate officers were consistently given latitude to act on their own initiative in furtherance of the battle plan. This had proved to be the most effective approach to coordinating the efforts of a large fleet in battle or during a campaign. It was impossible to exercise direct control of subordinates in such a fluid situation; instead, they had to be granted the freedom to act on their own. The shared conceptual framework aligned their efforts.

In this way, the Navy could harness the creative talents of its officers and create a whole—the loosely coordinated units of the fleet, acting in concert—that was very much more than the sum of its parts. Sellers explained his reasoning in detail in the lead-up to Fleet Problem XV: "Our officer corps is the most intelligent and best educated of any in the world. It is our greatest naval asset today. He [the commander-in-chief, i.e., Admiral Sellers] desires that it be used to maximum advantage in battle. Therefore, he expects that every battle situation shall be judged strictly on its own merits, and not upon instructions printed long before. Decisive, positive, aggressive action suited to the actual situation, must be the guiding idea of every flag and commanding officer.[92]

By the mid-1930s, the necessary structures were in place; individual initiative had become a core aspect of the Navy's tactical doctrine. Just as he ignored battle plans in Fleet Problem XV, Sellers also refused to send detailed instructions to subordinate commands. He relied instead on the shared conceptual framework—the indoctrination—that had developed over the preceding fifteen years. The officer corps was becoming a cohesive unit, tied together and aligned by a series of contextual constraints.

Adm. Ernest J. King, who was to be both COMINCH (CINC U.S. Fleet) and CNO for most of World War II, reflected these concepts in instructions he issued early in 1941, when he assumed command of the Atlantic Fleet: "If subordinates are deprived . . . of that training and experience which will enable them to act 'on their own'—if they do not know, by constant practice, how to exercise 'initiative of the sub-ordinates'—if they are reluctant (afraid) to act because they are accustomed to detailed orders and instructions—if they are not habituated to think, to judge, to decide and to act for themselves in their several echelons of command—we shall be in a sorry case when the time of 'active operations' [war] arrives."[93] By creating a common conceptual framework and consistently emphasizing tactical flexibility and individual initiative, the Navy developed a decentralized approach to command and control that allowed it to exploit effectively the unpredictable nature of war and leverage the skill and experience of its officer corps. This was the third and final interwar tactical heuristic. During the war, the investment in it would reap substantial dividends.

CONCLUSION

By the end of the interwar period, the learning system established by OPNAV, the Naval War College, and the fleet had allowed a sophisticated framework within which tactical doctrine could emerge. The Navy planned to coordinate its forces in the complex environment of a modern naval battle using well-defined plans and a set of tactical heuristics. These leveraged a shared conceptual framework to permit decentralized decision making and rapid action, allowing the Navy to capitalize on fleeting opportunities and maximize the training and education of the officer corps.

Battle plans were deliberately contextual; they reflected the commander's understanding of the prevailing conditions and how best to capitalize on strengths and weaknesses. Initially, they were designed for just the preliminary phase of battle and to frame the commander's intent for his subordinates. They were not expected to anticipate the variety of circumstances that might develop in a fleet action. The introduction of *Tentative Plans* in 1929 transformed the situation. By providing a standardized method for composing and quickly communicating sophisticated plans, the new approach dramatically increased the ability of commanders to coordinate their forces in battle. This was a new level of constraint—effectively, a language for communicating battle plans—that allowed a new level of complexity to emerge.

The Navy's tactical heuristics were also dependent on context but operated very differently; they were part of a shared conceptual framework developed from the principles of war and distilled through experience in tactical exercises and war games. They helped to ensure a common approach to tactical situations by focusing on aggressive offensive action, quick and effective gunfire, and distributed command and control. The heuristics provided a basis for concerted action through a common set of assumptions. They had become, collectively, the core of the Navy's tactical doctrine.

These two major concepts—battle plans and tactical heuristics—were developed together and interwoven; advances in one area stimulated new approaches to the other. As experimentation revealed better ways to develop and communicate plans, the focus of doctrinal principles narrowed into heuristics. As tactical heuristics became more ingrained, the options available for battle plans increased. The two concepts catalyzed each other, increasing the Navy's capability to fight the kind of major action anticipated in a Pacific war.

However, as the focus of tactical planning narrowed and as more emphasis was placed on plans for war in the Pacific, less attention was devoted to minor tactics and independent operations. This had the greatest impact on plans for night combat, which were skewed toward preparation for decisive battle. As a result, over the interwar period, tactics for destroyer combat at night changed dramatically from what had been originally anticipated. Stealthy torpedo attacks under the cover of darkness gave way to close-range brawls dominated by gunfire.

But the negative impacts of the emphasis on major fleet action were more than outweighed by the positive influence of the new tactical frameworks developed during the interwar period. The vocabulary for battle plans and the tactical heuristics reflected a core belief in the importance of flexible and contextually driven decision making. They continually reinforced the need to adjust to changing circumstances. Combined with the emphasis placed on learning, experimentation, and analysis, they allowed the Navy to assess lessons from combat quickly and adjust tactical doctrines to maximize the potential of its ships and men.

5

HEURISTICS AT GUADALCANAL

For us who were there . . .
Guadalcanal is not a name but an emotion.

—Samuel Eliot Morison, 1948

The first year of World War II challenged the Navy's prewar tactical doctrine, exposing its flaws and validating its strengths. Carrier raids and battles—at Coral Sea, Midway, the Eastern Solomons, and Santa Cruz—largely reflected prewar assumptions from the Fleet Problems about the speed and decisiveness of carrier attacks. Surface actions were another matter. Surface actions developed far more quickly than anticipated, particularly at night. Confusion overtook commanders. They were unable to prepare their forces adequately; there was no time to develop task force doctrines and plans. Night surface actions devolved into confused melees, with individual ships fighting on their own. Victory, when it was achieved, in night surface actions came through application of the Navy's core doctrinal heuristics. Quick and effective gunfire, reliance on individual initiative, and aggressive action—even when employed without coordination by individual ships—allowed the Navy to emerge victorious from the Pacific War's first major campaign, the struggle for the island of Guadalcanal.

On 7 December 1941, Japan began the long-anticipated Pacific War with coordinated strikes across that ocean. All eight battleships at Pearl Harbor were damaged; four of them were sunk. Adm. Husband E. Kimmel, CINC Pacific Fleet, had hoped to use those battleships to support an incursion into the Marshall Islands and potentially trigger a major fleet action with the Japanese. In keeping with established tactical ideas, he anticipated defeating them in a medium-range reverse action that exploited the gunnery of his battle line and reduced the effectiveness of enemy battle cruisers and light forces.[1]

After the attack on Pearl Harbor, however, Kimmel was relieved of his command. Secretary of the Navy Frank Knox reorganized the Navy's command structure. The Navy's highest ranking officer would be in Washington, to help coordinate the global conflict. Executive Order 8984 of 18 December 1941 authorized the necessary changes, and two days later, President Franklin D. Roosevelt selected Adm. Ernest J. King for the role. King was an officer of "superlative competence" who brought a wealth of experience to the task. He had commanded destroyers, submarines, and aircraft carriers. Attendance at the Naval War College had given him training for high command, and he had demonstrated his potential in the Atlantic Fleet. King thoroughly embraced the Navy's aggressive tactical and operational doctrines and understood the variety of ways in which those doctrines could be put into effect. In March 1942, his authority expanded when he became the first to hold the offices of COMINCH (i.e., CINC U.S. Fleet) and CNO simultaneously.

Adm. Chester W. Nimitz was chosen to lead and reconstitute the Pacific Fleet. A graduate of the Naval Academy class of 1905, he understood the Navy's talent base, having been head of the Bureau of Navigation. Nimitz had also attended the Naval War College and thoroughly appreciated the importance of aggressive offensive action and operational tempo. He was to temper ably King's strategic vision with inspirational leadership, methodical planning, and determined execution.[2]

Although the United States was on the defensive in the Pacific, King urged Nimitz to be aggressive. Exploiting the lessons of the Fleet Problems, Nimitz used his carriers to raid Japanese positions. In February, individual carriers struck Wake Island and atolls in the Marshalls and Gilberts and attempted to bomb Rabaul. In March, carriers operated in pairs; they attacked the northern coast of New Guinea and, on 18 April, mounted the most famous of the raids, when Army B-25s from the carrier *Hornet* stuck the Japanese mainland.

In early May, carrier raids gave way to fleet actions. Rear Adm. Frank J. Fletcher's Task Force (TF) 17 stopped the Japanese invasion of Port Moresby at the battle of Coral Sea. Less than a month later, the Combined Fleet commander, Adm. Yamamoto Isoroku, initiated his attack on Midway. Nimitz responded by sending two task forces—Rear Admiral Fletcher's TF 17 and Rear Adm. Raymond A. Spruance's TF 16—to ambush the Japanese. Fletcher was in tactical command, but he and Spruance operated independently. Nimitz had been worried about the vulnerability of the carriers and adhered to prewar doctrine that called for separating them, despite wartime experience already gained suggesting they would be safer concentrated.[3] Fletcher and Spruance "flanked" Vice Adm. Nagumo Chuichi's striking force, sinking all four Japanese carriers.

TABLE 4. Carrier Raids and Battles of 1942

Date	Description
27 January	Planned raid on Wake Island—cancelled (*Lexington*)
1 February	Raid on the Marshalls (*Enterprise* and *Yorktown*)
20 February	Planned raid on Rabaul—cancelled (*Lexington*)
24 February	Raid on Wake Island (*Enterprise*)
4 March	Raid on Marcus Island (*Enterprise*)
10 March	Raid on Lae and Salamaua (*Lexington* and *Yorktown*)
18 April	Raid on Japanese mainland (*Hornet* and *Enterprise*)
4–8 May	Battle of Coral Sea (*Lexington* and *Yorktown*)
3–7 June	Battle of Midway (*Yorktown*, *Enterprise*, and *Hornet*)
24–25 August	Battle of Eastern Solomons (*Enterprise* and *Saratoga*)
5 October	Raid on Shortlands (*Hornet*)
25–27 October	Battle of Santa Cruz (*Enterprise* and *Hornet*)

Midway has been called the turning point of the Pacific War. The term is too generous. Prior to Midway, the Japanese had the initiative and so controlled the operational tempo. The defeat wrested it from them but did not transfer it to Nimitz and his Pacific Fleet. Nevertheless, King and Nimitz understood that they had an opportunity. If they could seize the initiative, they could take control of the war in the Pacific. They made their decision as they had been trained—with years of experience in a culture that emphasized aggressive action—and resolved to take the offensive.

On 2 July, King, along with the other Joint Chiefs of Staff (JCS), ordered the start of Operation Watchtower. Its ultimate objective was the base at Rabaul; the first step was the anchorage at the island of Tulagi, in the Solomons. Two days later, aerial reconnaissance observed that the Japanese were building an airfield on the large island of Guadalcanal, across the sound from Tulagi. The airfield became the offensive's preliminary objective. Under the leadership of Vice Adm. Robert L. Ghormley, Nimitz's commander of the South Pacific Area, the 1st Marine Division landed on 7 August. Seizing the airfield the next day, the Marines named it Henderson Field.

Over the next six months, Guadalcanal became the focus of a fierce struggle, as Nimitz's Pacific Fleet and Yamamoto's Combined Fleet fought over the island and its vital airfield. Two carrier battles and five major night surface actions—Savo Island, Cape Esperance, Guadalcanal I and Guadalcanal II (otherwise known as the First and Second Naval Battles of Guadalcanal), and Tassafaronga—were fought. These night battles were the most significant test of the Navy's prewar surface warfare doctrine. The Japanese had developed well-conceived doctrines based on stealth and surprise. The U.S. Navy's plans for "minor" tactics proved inadequate. Its efforts to coordinate task forces at night failed. So many ships were lost off Guadalcanal that sailors called the neighboring body of water "Ironbottom Sound." Victories did eventually come, but thanks only to individual ships, employing doctrinal heuristics developed in the interwar period. Those victories were crucial. Desperate actions by surface ships preserved Henderson Field, assured success in the campaign, and turned the tide of the war in the Pacific.

NIGHT COMBAT IN 1942—GUNNERY, RADARS, AND LITTORAL TERRAIN

The technical characteristics of weapons systems had an important influence on the fighting off Guadalcanal. In the interwar period, the firepower of surface ships had dramatically increased. Improvements in fire control—including more advanced models of the Ford range-keeper—had made gunfire and torpedo salvoes more accurate; advances in fuse and shell technology had made shells deadlier; and new torpedoes had increased lethality. These enhancements combined to make ship combat more intense than ever before. However, the maximum effective range of these weapons was still limited by that of the human eye.

The upper limit of visual range at night off Guadalcanal was almost always within ten thousand yards; often it was within five thousand. At the battle of Savo Island, the Japanese opened fire on the northern group of Allied cruisers at about ten thousand yards, using search-lights. During the decisive portion of Guadalcanal II (sometimes "the Naval Battle of Guadalcanal"), the battleship *Washington* engaged the battleship *Kirishima* at 8,400 yards with the aid of radar ranging and star-shell illumination. At Cape Esperance, the Japanese were sighted at five thousand yards, and fire was opened almost immediately. Guadalcanal I descended into a melee because of the low visibility. The leading ships of the opposing formations first sighted each other at three thousand yards; fire was opened soon thereafter.[4]

The close engagement ranges, combined with the lethality of the ships' weaponry, explain why the combat off Guadalcanal was so furious and deadly. They also illustrate the importance of hitting first. Surprise was decisive in the night surface battles, a better predictor of victory than any other single factor. The other hallmark of these fights was extreme confusion. The Navy had anticipated that night combat might be chaotic. A 1938 doctrinal manual for light cruisers warned that night battle would develop quickly and be fast-paced, with only brief opportunities to score hits on opponents as they appeared out of the darkness. This emphasis found its way into drills and practices, which stressed getting on target extremely quickly. Hitting first was important in daylight action; in night combat, it was decisive.[5]

Night battle practice—scores in which made up a significant per-centage of a ship's individual gunnery merit ranking—reinforced this emphasis by training crews to acquire and engage targets in the short-est possible time. The highest scores went to the ships that got on tar-get the fastest and scored the most hits.[6] The heavy cruiser *Augusta* gave an exceptional performance in March 1937 while flagship of the Asiatic Fleet:

> A total of thirty-eight hits, or 42.2% on run one with the main battery, of which fifteen were early hits obtained in the first six salvoes in three minutes and ten seconds can be considered little short of remarkable. . . . The target diagram of hits shows the high degree of accuracy and consistency in both range and deflection, indicating extreme thoroughness of the director check and bat-tery line-up as well as the accuracy of the fire-control procedure and spotting.[7]

Augusta's ability to get on target quickly was aided by her ranging tech-nique. She fired "a three salvo ranging ladder in 500 yard increments by individual turrets" to determine more accurately the target range. That is, the first salvo would have been fired at a range five hundred yards beyond the estimated range, the second at the estimated range, and the third five hundred yards below that. Spotting from these three salvoes would have provided an accurate target range very quickly. In effect, she used her gun battery as a rangefinder.[8]

Lloyd M. Mustin, a future admiral, served on board *Augusta* dur-ing this time and described how her gunners achieved such impres-sive scores: "I guess there were really two keys to our whole approach of taking a target under fire at night, both much interlaid with each other. One was heavy emphasis on the utmost speed in opening fire . . . [using] an estimated range. . . . [The other was] much more stream-lined internal procedures that [permitted] . . . a minimum of required transmissions back and forth between the Captain on the bridge and the man who had the firing key in his hand."[9] *Augusta*'s approach of using the guns to find the range became standard procedure.[10] Reports of night battle practices stressed that rough estimates of enemy course and speed were all that could be made before opening fire. Hits were to be obtained by firing immediately and correcting the fall of shot; there was no time to develop a model of the target's movements. This was the opposite procedure from that used in daylight, when firing was deliberate, controlled, and based on precise calculation of the target's future position.

Firing without a precise solution would introduce errors. Through experimentation, the Navy discovered that the best way to secure a large number of hits was a "rocking ladder." Once they found the range, Mustin and his contemporaries altered the range up and down in slight increments with each salvo, "rocking" the shells back and forth across the target. The variation in range compensated for errors in the fire-control solution and increased the number of hits. At night, it was extremely easy to believe that shells were on target when in fact they were slightly short or long. Continually rocking the shells back and forth overcame this problem and became the prescribed doctrine for night firing. The results were impressive; Mustin described the target raft after one practice as a "shambles"—it had been "literally shot to pieces."[11] The emphasis on opening fire immediately was well worthwhile; all the night surface actions of the campaign—except for the last one—were to be decided by gunfire.

Radar too played an important role in the night battles of 1942. The Navy's willingness to experiment allowed it to realize quickly the potential of using radio waves to develop a more detailed picture of the surroundings.[12] However, the radars used at Guadalcanal were fairly primitive. Most displays were unsophisticated, and effective procedures to harness the information they provided had yet to be developed. Radar was not yet a transformational technology, but in the right hands, it was an extremely useful tool.

Radar research and development was performed under the auspices of the Navy's technical bureaus. There were two parallel threads. Search radars, designed to provide early warning of approaching ships and planes, were the responsibility of the Bureau of Ships. BuOrd focused on fire-control radars, which could provide range, bearing, and other information necessary to augment fire-control solutions. The Navy's heuristic emphasizing quick and effective gunfire led to the rapid development of the latter.

Search and fire-control radars used similar technology but were employed differently. Search-radar antennas were typically kept rotating so that they could scan the area around the ship. When an unknown echo was observed, the earliest installations—like the SC radars in use in 1942—had to be stopped so that range and bearing could be estimated. When its antenna was stopped, the radar could not search other sectors, increasing the chances that the operator would miss approaching contacts.

Fire-control radars were occasionally used to search like this, but their specialty was specific targets. The open architecture of the fire-control system made it easy to integrate radar into it; there was no need for major modifications to take advantage of radar information. Fire-control radars could augment existing fire-control procedures by providing the range to the target, reducing the need for ranging ladders and allowing the target to be "straddled" more quickly.[13]

The Navy's most modern fire-control radars, the FC (Mark 3) and FD (Mark 4) were used extensively off Guadalcanal. The FC was designed for surface fire control; the FD was similar but configured differently to allow it to be used against airplanes as well as surface ships. Both used lobe switching—alternating transmission in two lobes on either side of the antenna—to improve directional accuracy. Although some ships considered the FC and FD sufficiently accurate for "blind" firing, fire control was most accurate when using radar ranges and visual bearings. This helped ensure that the engagement ranges at Guadalcanal were short.

Initially, the standard radar display was the "A-scope," a two-dimensional view of reflected signals on a specific bearing. The horizontal axis displayed range, while the vertical axis indicated the strength of the reflected signal. If the radar detected nothing, there would be no return, and the display would be dominated by "grass"—low-level noise signals detected by the receiver, akin to "snow" on early television sets.[14] When the radar did detect an object, a vertical spike would appear at the appropriate range. The strength of the signal was indicated by the size of the spike. Strong signals produced a tall vertical "pip"; weaker ones were shorter. If using a search radar, the operator would stop the antenna and note the bearing and range. The nature of the display meant that the radar could either search, scanning for potential contacts, or focus on a single bearing, recording the specific location of a contact. It could not do both simultaneously.

It took effort to translate this information from the display into a picture of potential contacts. Search-radar operators were trained to focus on pips and accurately determine their range and bearing. They were not responsible for tracking the contacts they identified, and the A-scope made it very difficult for them to do so. Instead, they reported a series of ranges and bearings. Other members of the crew took this data and added the necessary context to create situational awareness. On large ships, like carriers and battleships, this was done in a Radar Plot. On smaller ships, it was done in the captain's brain. Both mechanisms were frequently overwhelmed.

On fire-control radars, the focus of the A-scope could be narrowed. Operators could increase the resolution and zoom in on a small area of the display—either five hundred or a thousand yards in range—and see more detail around the target. This allowed them to determine target range very accurately and, if conditions were right, even to observe the splashes of shells. However, this procedure limited their view to a narrow window. If the target slipped outside, it could easily be lost.

Radar signals reflected off land as well as ships, and the peculiar littoral terrain near Guadalcanal made it difficult to identify contacts. Savo Sound is surrounded by three islands. Guadalcanal forms the southern border. To the north, Florida Island hems it in and forms the sheltered anchorage at Tulagi. The southern tip of Florida reaches toward Guadalcanal, forming the eastern entrance to the sound. Reefs segment that entrance into three separate channels: Nggela, Sealark, and Lengo. To the west, the small island of Savo divides the western entrance to the sound into two roughly equal channels. The proximity of land interfered with radar signals, cluttering displays with echoes from the islands and making it difficult or impossible to distinguish targets. This interference was a surprise, and it undermined prewar faith in radar systems. These limitations informed how radar was used and how battles were fought. Radar was not yet the sophisticated technology we think of today; for the first year of war in the Pacific, it was a rudimentary tool that did not seamlessly integrate with existing shipboard information systems. This largely explains why the Navy, despite this powerful new technology, found the battles off Guadalcanal so confusing and difficult.

However, some ships benefitted from much more sophisticated radar installations. One of the most important outcomes of the prewar work with radar was the development of the "plan position indicator," the PPI scope. It was a dramatic improvement over the A-scope and vastly enhanced the ability of operators and their ships to process radar information. The PPI was the brainchild of Dr. Robert Morris Page of the Naval Research Laboratory. Page applied a particularly nautical solution to the problem of radar displays; he took the Navy's established plotting paradigm—the top-down view—and devised a way to present radar information in a similar format. It was the first iteration of the display with which we are all familiar, with the radar in the center surrounded by a bird's-eye view of contacts.

As the radar revolved, potential contacts appeared as pips. Each pip would remain momentarily on the screen, allowing the operator to record the bearing and range without pausing the radar's scanning motion. The strength of the return, giving some estimate of the relative size of the target, was reflected in the size and brightness of the pip. The new display tightly integrated radar information with the mental models of the operators, making it much easier to translate that information into a picture of the surrounding world and increase situational awareness.

The first radar to use the PPI scope was the SG, the Navy's first microwave search radar; later, it became the standard display for all search radars. A few ships that fought near Guadalcanal, including the cruiser *Helena*, destroyer *Fletcher*, and battleships *Washington* and *South Dakota*, were equipped with the SG radar and PPI scope. These ships consistently had better situational awareness in combat, but they lacked an effective means to share that picture with other ships in company.

Rear Adm. Alfred T. Mahan reconceptualized the American naval officer. He believed naval warfare was an art that could be taught, and as president of the Naval War College, he enhanced and improved the school's curriculum, emphasizing contextual analysis and collaborative learning. *Naval History and Heritage Command*

Vice Adm. William S. Sims. As a young officer, he introduced competitive gunnery exercises that led to the creation of the Navy's fire-control system. Before World War I, Sims developed a preliminary doctrine in the Atlantic Fleet's Torpedo Flotilla. After the war, as president of the Naval War College, he helped refine the Navy's learning system. *Naval History and Heritage Command*

Adm. William V. Pratt as Chief of Naval Operations in the early 1930s. Pratt was a talented officer who served with Sims in the Atlantic Fleet's Torpedo Flotilla, was a member of OPNAV during World War I, and developed destroyer doctrine in the early 1920s. His greatest contribution was a new vocabulary issued in 1929 for battle plans. The battle plans gave the fleet "unprecedented flexibility" and were used through World War II. *Naval History and Heritage Command*

Capt. Arleigh Burke, Commander Destroyer Squadron 23 (in profile, left center), reading on the bridge wing of his flagship, the destroyer *Charles Ausburne*. Note the squadron's insignia painted on the bridge wing and the "scoreboard" on the side of the Mark 37 director. Burke was instrumental in developing effective night-combat tactics for destroyers in 1943. *Naval History and Heritage Command*

Adm. Chester W. Nimitz, Commander in Chief Pacific Fleet, shares a beer with Rear Adm. Charles H. McMorris, his chief of staff, during an enlisted men's picnic in September 1943. Nimitz was extremely effective at creating an atmosphere of psychological safety, a talent that comes through in this image. *Naval History and Heritage Command*

Adm. Ernest J. King, Commander in Chief U.S. Fleet and Chief of Naval Operations during World War II. King was one of the most experienced officers in the fleet when he became commander in chief, having served in surface ships, submarines, and aircraft. He was a product of the transformations that had taken place in the Navy Department in the early years of the twentieth century. *National Archives and Records Administration*

Nevada, the first battleship to benefit from the Navy's new ship-design process incorporating the General Board. *Nevada* was the first battleship in the world explicitly designed to fight at ranges over ten thousand yards. *Naval History and Heritage Command*

A gun pointer working the elevating gear of a battleship's 5-inch secondary gun. Note how he can work the gear with his hands while keeping the target within his sight. This was how "continuous aim" was done, the new approach to gunnery introduced by William S. Sims in 1902. *Courtesy of Thomas C. Hone*

Targets for short-range battle practice. These have been hit multiple times by the 14-inch main guns of the battleship *Oklahoma*. Each target has three or four holes, indicative of accurate shooting. The year was 1922. *Official U.S. Navy photograph*

One of the *Colorado*-class battleships fires her guns during long-range battle practice. These ships were part of the interwar "big five"; they could fire accurately at extreme range, beyond 27,000 yards. Note the large, dark cloud created by the gunfire. *Courtesy of Thomas C. Hone*

The foredeck and forward gun of a destroyer in the Atlantic Fleet's Torpedo Flotilla. These vessels were the basis of William S. Sims' experimentation with tactical doctrine before World War I. Note the small size of the ship; this acted as a constraint, increasing the collaborative nature of the flotilla's work. *Courtesy of Thomas C. Hone*

The battleship *Washington* in 1942. Her SG radar is the small dish mounted in front of the fire-control tower. There is an FC radar atop the main gun director at the top of the tower. Beyond it is an SC search radar. An FD radar is mounted on the Mark 37 director in front of the tower. *National Archives and Records Administration*

The cruiser *San Francisco*, flagship at the battles of Cape Esperance and Guadalcanal I, returns to Pearl Harbor in December 1942. Battle damage from her fight with the Japanese battleship *Hiei* is visible, as are the FC radars atop her main-battery directors. *National Archives and Records Administration*

A cruiser fires her 6-inch guns at night. Large flashes like this provided a visible aim point for Japanese torpedoes. Many cruisers were damaged or sunk by torpedoes in the battles of 1942 and mid-1943. *Official U.S. Navy photograph*

The destroyer *Fletcher* in March 1943, anchored off Florida Island. She fought at the battles of Guadalcanal I and Tassafaronga in late 1942. *Fletcher*'s captain, Cdr. William R. Cole, and executive officer, Lt. Cdr. Joseph C. Wylie, worked out the details of one of the Navy's first effective CICs. Fletcher has a full suite of radars: SC atop the mast, SG just below it, and FD on top of the Mark 37 director. *Naval History and Heritage Command*

The battleship *Washington* was Rear Admiral Lee's flagship at the battle of Guadalcanal II. Her 16-inch guns sank the Japanese battleship *Kirishima*. Edwin Hooper helped refine her fire-control procedures. *National Archives and Records Administration*

The battleship *New Jersey* approaches the smoke cloud left by the explosion of *Shonan Maru 15* during Operation Hailstone on 16 February 1944. *New Jersey* sank the auxiliary with her secondary battery. Together with *Iowa*, she formed the core of BatDiv 7; in this operation, they were part of Task Group 50.9. *National Archives and Records Administration*

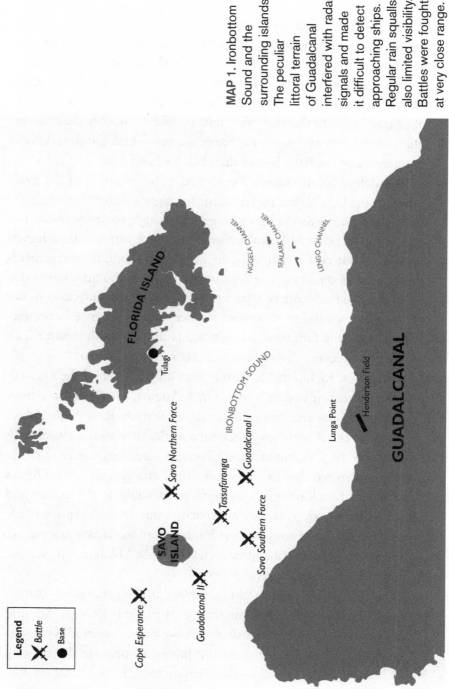

MAP 1. Ironbottom Sound and the surrounding islands. The peculiar littoral terrain of Guadalcanal interfered with radar signals and made it difficult to detect approaching ships. Regular rain squalls also limited visibility. Battles were fought at very close range.

AN EMBARRASSING BEGINNING

The Guadalcanal campaign began with a crushing defeat. The night after the Marines took Henderson Field, a mixed Japanese force of seven cruisers and one destroyer under the command of Vice Adm. Mikawa Gunichi attacked with the intention of wreaking havoc among the Allied transports. In this they were not successful, but they did enter the Allied disposition and sink four heavy cruisers—USS *Quincy*, *Astoria*, *Vincennes*, and the Royal Australian Navy's *Canberra*.

The defeat has frequently been cited as an example of the inadequacy of the U.S. Navy's preparations for night combat. However, the explanation for the defeat lies elsewhere. The single most important factor was the fact that Mikawa achieved complete surprise; he achieved it not once but twice, that same night, in two separate engagements with the Allied screening forces. Surprise in the initial attack was due to a poor Allied estimate of Japanese intentions and failure to consider seriously the possibility of a night surface attack. Surprise in the second resulted from fatigue and command failures. In both instances, an inadequate screening disposition was a contributing factor.

Rear Adm. Richmond K. Turner was commander of the Guadalcanal and Tulagi invasion forces. On 8 August, his ships were busy unloading supplies and repulsing Japanese air raids. Rear Adm. V. A. C. Crutchley of the Royal Navy, seconded at the time to the Royal Australian Navy (RAN), commanded Turner's screening forces. Neither of them anticipated that the Japanese would attack with surface forces later that night. In hindsight, this seems remarkable. Search planes had sighted Mikawa's ships as they approached, and contact reports made their way to the Allied commanders hours before the Japanese attacked. However, neither admiral appreciated the threat Mikawa represented. This failure was due to several factors.

One was the shift that had taken place in the process of estimating the situation. When the contact report made it to Rear Admiral Turner, he followed the established process and considered what was the "most likely" course open to the Japanese. Because the sighting report indicated—incorrectly—that the Japanese force contained two seaplane tenders, Turner assumed that its intention was to establish a seaplane base at Rekata Bay on the island of Santa Isabel, from where they could launch additional attacks on his transport force. The possibility of a night surface attack, the most dangerous course open to the enemy, was ignored.[15]

In arriving at this estimate, Turner correctly followed the existing methodology but drew a critically mistaken conclusion. He did not anticipate that the sighting report might be in error; he also did not entertain alternative, and potentially more threatening, courses of action open to the Japanese. Turner quickly gravitated to the idea of seaplane attacks because of the air raids he had been fighting off; a series of strikes from Rabaul had kept the ships on alert, prevented the timely unloading of supplies, and damaged ships. The transport *George F. Elliott* was on fire and abandoned. The destroyer *Jarvis* had been torpedoed and towed to Tulagi harbor.

The crews of Crutchley's screening vessels, fatigued from fighting off these raids, were now unprepared for a night surface action. When the Japanese opened fire, most of the Allied ships were in reduced conditions of readiness. On *Astoria* and *Vincennes*, only two of three guns in each turret were manned; *Quincy*'s guns were fully manned, but not all the watertight doors were closed. The officers in command of these ships, and most of the others, were resting when the battle started; after waking, they had very little time to familiarize themselves with the developing situation before Japanese shells struck their ships.[16]

A final factor in the surprise was the expectation that the most serious nocturnal threat to the invasion forces was Japanese submarines. Rear Admiral Crutchley had experience fighting German U-boats in the Atlantic and was predisposed to see submarines as the greater threat. His night screening disposition reflected this assumption. He divided his forces into three groups to cover all three major entrances to the sound. The western entrances around Savo Island were guarded by the Northern and Southern Groups, each with three heavy cruisers and two destroyers. Crutchley placed himself in the Southern Group with the RAN cruisers *Australia* and *Canberra* and the American cruiser *Chicago*. Capt. Frederick Riefkohl commanded the Northern Group, with *Vincennes*, *Quincy*, and *Astoria*.[17] An Eastern Group, under Rear

Adm. Norman Scott, patrolled the eastern entrance to the sound with two light cruisers and two destroyers. In all groups, the destroyers operated as an antisubmarine screen.

Crutchley expected to be able to concentrate if Japanese surface forces approached. To ensure he would have time to do so, he placed two radar-picket destroyers outside the entrances around Savo Island. *Blue* and *Ralph Talbot* were equipped with SC radars, and their placement was in line with the Navy's established doctrine, which specified the use of "radar guard ships . . . stationed beyond the outer screen."[18]

The division of forces, however, went against fundamental assumptions of the Navy's tactical doctrine. The Fleet Problems had repeatedly illustrated what resulted from attempting to coordinate dispersed screens at night.[19] Crutchley was unfamiliar with these lessons. The Naval War College's postwar analysis was to criticize his arrangement, noting that each of his groups was inferior to the Japanese forces that were known to be within steaming range. A concentrated attack could deal with each group in succession: "It cannot be determined why he deemed it necessary or desirable to divide his forces."[20] A wartime analysis offered similar criticisms: "The basic concept of the defense of our transports off Guadalcanal 8–9 August was wrong. Our cruisers should have been kept concentrated, and our destroyer scouts . . . should have been projected far enough westward to insure timely and sure warning."[21]

Crutchley compounded the difficulty of coordinating his forces by not issuing a battle plan. He apparently expected to be able to coordinate the dispersed formations in battle himself, using radio signals. This is not surprising, as the RN had developed techniques for distributed formations at night.[22] The American experience was vastly different, and Riefkohl formally objected to the plan. A postbattle analysis concluded: "These instructions may have been adequate for units of the British Navy, but I [i.e., Vice Admiral Ghormley] do not believe the phraseology and the terms used were definite enough to convey to our units a clear cut picture of the underlying conception or the special factors involved in the tactical situation . . . nor did they reflect clearly the Commander's scheme of maneuver or battle plan."[23]

For Crutchley's plan to work, *Blue* and *Ralph Talbot* had to provide early warning of approaching enemy forces. Current Pacific Fleet radar manuals anticipated that their SC radars would be able to detect approaching surface ships at 25,000 yards, long before they came into visual range.[24] However, interference from the surrounding islands prevented them from detecting Mikawa's formation. The Naval War College analysis explained: "Had the optimum . . . radar effectiveness been obtainable, the *Ralph Talbot* might possibly have given a warning about fifteen minutes before an enemy could close to within gun range of the *Vincennes* group from the northward; but 'land interference' denied this degree of radar effectiveness. This analysis is equally applicable to the *Blue*'s radius of patrol from the *Australia* Group."[25] The result was disaster, first for *Canberra* in the Southern Group, and then for *Quincy*, *Astoria*, and *Vincennes*. A series of command failures made Mikawa's victory easier.

The initial mistake was Crutchley's. He had planned to command the screening forces personally from the cruiser *Australia* but was absent when the battle occurred. Rear Admiral Turner had called a conference to discuss the situation, and Crutchley had left the screen to attend, taking *Australia* with him. In his absence, command of the Northern and Southern Groups devolved to Captain Riefkohl. However, Crutchley failed to inform Riefkohl of his absence, and Riefkohl remained ignorant of his additional responsibilities. As a result, when the Japanese struck, the centralized command necessary to ensure coordinated action was absent.[26]

Even if Riefkohl had been informed, he would have found it impossible to coordinate the two groups effectively. He was already overtaxed with the dual responsibilities of commanding the Northern Group as well as *Vincennes* herself. When the Japanese attacked his force, Riefkohl was unable to develop a clear picture of the situation; he initially thought that friendly forces were firing on him. The action overwhelmed Riefkohl: he focused on commanding his own ship and ignored his responsibilities even as a group commander, let alone commander of Crutchley's whole force. *Quincy*, *Astoria*, and *Vincennes* fought the Japanese as individual ships.[27]

The Japanese, although they had previously attacked the Southern Group, were able to surprise Riefkohl and his cruisers because of the dark night, rainsqualls in the area that restricted visibility, and the failure of the Southern Group to provide an adequate warning. In Crutchley's absence, Capt. Howard D. Bode, captain of *Chicago*, was in command of the Southern Group. The Naval War College analysis is particularly critical of Bode's performance, noting that he failed to raise a warning or to command the Southern Group. Bode's "failure to exercise command properly contributed in a large degree to the unfortunate events which were to follow in Iron Bottom Sound."[28]

Cdr. Frank R. Walker, in the destroyer *Patterson*, and Capt. H. B. Farncomb, in *Canberra*, were the only commanding officers of the Southern Group to display awareness of the seriousness of the situation. Farncomb immediately turned *Canberra* to cut off the Japanese approach to the transport area, but a hail of Japanese gunfire killed him and reduced his ship to a flaming wreck. Walker, when the battle began, immediately issued a warning to the entire Allied disposition and then engaged the Japanese. "[He] immediately transmitted via TBS voice radio the following general alarm to the entire task force: 'All ships. Warning! Warning! Three enemy ships inside Savo Island.' By this action . . . he evidenced a thorough appreciation of the urgent necessity of immediately informing . . . all Commanding Officers of vital information concerning the enemy."[29] Although the TBS radio operator on board *Vincennes* heard Walker's warning, it was not passed on to Riefkohl or his executive officer. Shortly thereafter, the Japanese were upon them.

When they attacked Riefkohl's cruisers, the Japanese used guns as the primary weapon and displayed a high level of skill in visually directed gunfire. The first salvo from the flagship, *Chokai*, was five hundred yards short and two hundred yards off in bearing from *Astoria*. *Aoba*'s first salvo, fired at *Quincy*, was similarly off. The inability of the Japanese to get the correct bearing on their first salvoes meant that they had to bring the guns into line before correcting for range, but they did so quickly. *Aoba* hit on her third salvo. *Chokai* hit with her fifth. *Kako*, which had been firing at *Vincennes*, had the right bearing with her first salvo and walked the range up deliberately, hitting with her third. These early hits started fires and made the American ships easier targets.

Even under duress, the potential of radar-directed fire was made clear. The doomed *Vincennes* hit *Kinugasa* with her second salvo, the first that she fired using the radar-indicated range. But Riefkohl's ships reacted too slowly. By the time *Vincennes* scored those hits, she had been hit by shells from *Kako*'s third, fourth, and fifth salvoes. The advantage the Japanese had gained by surprise was impossible to overcome; Riefkohl's cruisers became flaming wrecks.

The setback at Savo Island was a significant defeat. The screening forces were devastated. Turner's transports were left without adequate protection, but they survived. Sinking four cruisers had been enough for Mikawa; he turned back after striking the Northern Group and did not attempt to engage the transports. The next morning, Turner and his men unloaded more vital supplies before heading back to Noumea. Several lessons seemed apparent. The greatest surprise was that radar could not guarantee adequate warning. Commanders lost faith in it.[30] Dispersed formations seemed more dangerous than ever; extremely concentrated dispositions were developed to maximize striking power and prevent defeat in detail. The process of estimating the situation reverted to the earlier methodology, which had focused attention on the most dangerous potential enemy action, not the most likely. These lessons were quickly absorbed in the combat zone because of the emphasis on decentralized doctrinal development.

Arguably, the most important lesson of Savo was that the prewar emphasis on quick and effective gunfire had been valid. Although the Japanese had hit with torpedoes, their gunfire had decided the action, by knocking out control stations, setting their targets ablaze, and damaging machinery.[31] Surprise coupled with rapid gunfire appeared to be the key to victory; in future battles, the Navy's prewar experience would be leveraged successfully.

BALIKPAPAN

One of the reasons the Navy could expect better results was the performance of a collection of old destroyers from the Asiatic Fleet seven months earlier. Four destroyers had successfully attacked Japanese transports anchored in the bay at Balikpapan on the east coast of Borneo on the night of 23–24 January 1942. The attack illustrated how doctrinal development and planning could enhance the fighting power of the Navy's ships in battle.

The destroyers had all worked together before the war in the Asiatic Fleet's Destroyer Squadron 29. Their captains knew each other and were well acquainted with their leader, Cdr. Paul H. Talbot. Through regular practice and drill, a common understanding of what to do in a night battle had been inculcated in them.[32] Talbot enhanced the effectiveness of this indoctrination by providing a model battle plan. Succinct and perfectly clear, Talbot's plan is exactly the sort of order the Navy expected for coordinating ships in battle:

> Primary weapon torpedoes. Primary objective transports. Cruisers as necessary to accomplish mission. Endeavor launch torpedoes at close range before being discovered. . . . Set torpedoes each tube for normal spread. Be prepared to fire single shots if size of target warrants. Will try to avoid action en route. . . . Use own discretion in attacking independently when targets located. When torp[edoe]s are fired close with all guns. Use initiative and determination.[33]

Talbot's message was the foundation of the Navy's first clear victory in the Pacific War. Four transports and a Japanese patrol boat were sunk. Only one of the attacking destroyers was damaged; *John D. Ford* received a superficial hit that started a small fire.[34] Effective indoctrination and planning came together to give the destroyers the maximum opportunity to inflict damage on the Japanese transports. These essential elements of the Navy's doctrine were consistently absent off Guadalcanal.

FLAWS IN THE NAVY'S APPROACH

They were missing because of invalid assumptions about how commanders and their ships would approach combat. The Navy recognized that a decentralized system—in which each commander applied his own judgment to his circumstances—could adequately deal with the complexity of combat. The emphasis on decentralized doctrinal development reflected this, and it made squadron and task force commanders responsible for formulating doctrines and plans to guide their forces in battle. To make the system effective, however, ships had to stay together long enough to absorb a common doctrine and create a shared context for decision making. But the demands of the Guadalcanal campaign and the needs of a two-ocean war combined to destabilize the Navy's fighting units and undermine this process.

Creating a shared context took time and required preparation. Although the fleet had devoted significant attention to preparing for major fleet actions, it had spent very little time preparing for fights between smaller task forces. Individual task force and squadron commanders were expected to fill the gap and develop specific plans for their forces. Off Guadalcanal, they were consistently unable to do so. Forces were repeatedly thrown together piecemeal without the necessary time for indoctrination.[35] The resulting problems are evident throughout the campaign. In the aftermath of the defeat at Savo, Vice Admiral Ghormley cited the lack of time available for indoctrination: "Detailed plans and orders for the Watchtower Operation were of necessity prepared in a short space of time immediately prior to its execution, giving little, if any, opportunity for subordinate commanders to contact commanders of units assigned to them for purposes of indoctrination."[36]

During Guadalcanal I, the lack of an effective doctrine was an acute problem. Rear Adm. Daniel J. Callaghan was given command of a "scratch team" formed from two separate forces the day before the battle. There was no time to indoctrinate the new ships, and because Callaghan had assumed his own post as a task-group commander (TG 67.4) barely two weeks prior to the battle, there was no doctrine even for his own force.[37] Vice Adm. William S. Pye, president of the Naval War College, would note this deficiency in his comments on the action: "It seems . . . that the American force went into this action without any battle plan; without any indoctrination, or understanding between the OTC [Callaghan], and his subordinates; with incomplete information as to existing conditions in possession of subordinates."[38]

At Guadalcanal II, two days later, Rear Adm. Willis A. Lee was in a similar situation. None of his six ships had ever operated together before. His four destroyers were from four different divisions and possessed nothing resembling a common doctrine. The same held true for his two battleships. Lee suffered "from the same lack of practice in teamwork that had plagued Callaghan."[39]

Planning suffered along with indoctrination. Before the war, the Navy assumed the OTC would develop a battle plan that would explain his intentions and the way he expected to fight. It would provide context for the interpretation of task-force doctrine and help align decision making.[40] To prevent confusion, these plans had to be concise and extremely clear. Unfortunately, the same circumstances that undermined the ability of task force commanders to develop common doctrines also inhibited the creation of battle plans. Captains frequently went into battle without the shared context required for effective coordination. Instead of fighting as cohesive units, the Navy's task forces broke apart and fought as individual ships.

The Navy understood that this approach was very costly, but there was no alternative.[41] The battles of Guadalcanal I and II came during the decisive moment of the campaign; Lee and Callaghan were fighting to ensure the survival of Henderson Field, which had become the key to victory. Success or failure depended on their ability to fight their confused collections of ships.

The Navy's performance in the night battles of 1942 was also hindered by prevailing assumptions about how to employ torpedoes. The emphasis on major fleet action limited the Navy's destroyer doctrine and focused destroyer commanders on attacking a well-defended enemy formation at night. In such an attack, torpedoes would be fired at the enemy battleships after the cruisers and destroyers had used their guns to penetrate the screen. This meant that destroyers were trained to preserve their torpedoes and use their guns first. Originally weapons of stealth, the Navy's destroyers had lost the art of using their torpedoes in a surprise attack.[42]

The 1929 *Destroyer Instructions* reflected these prevailing assumptions. Torpedoes were to be used primarily against the "objective," the enemy capital ships. Only a limited number could be expended against other targets: "While the main mission of the attack is to sink the objective [enemy battleships,] . . . it must be remembered that favorable positions for torpedo fire are very seldom gained in night operations, and that every opportunity must be taken to inflict damage on any enemy ships encountered. . . . For this reason, destroyers are authorized to fire one torpedo at any destroyer and two at any cruiser or light cruiser encountered at such close range that there is a practical certainty of hitting."[43] The 1938 version of *Night Search and Attack Operations* reinforced the emphasis on preserving torpedoes for large targets: "While penetrating an enemy screen advantage will be taken of any favorable opportunity to torpedo enemy cruisers. Torpedoes will not normally be used against enemy destroyers."[44]

These assumptions led to simplistic interwar torpedo exercises. Battle Torpedo Practice C was the Navy's standard night-torpedo exercise, designed to simulate an attack on an enemy battleship. It assumed that the target would be slow-moving and that the attack would come after the destroyer division had penetrated the enemy screen. This meant the target would be fully alert to the presence of the attacking destroyers, open fire to repulse them, and thereby reveal its location and provide a convenient point of aim for the destroyer torpedoes. Blinking lights simulated the battleship's gunfire.[45]

While the Navy's gunnery exercises measured how quickly the guns were brought on target and how often they hit, successfully focusing crews on the importance of quick and accurate gunfire, Battle Torpedo Practice C considered only the accuracy of a single torpedo.[46] If the torpedo hit the target, the ship received a perfect score. If it missed, the score was zero. Most destroyers, aided by the blinking lights, managed to hit. The only way they could improve upon their scores was to fire their torpedoes earlier in their attack runs. The artificialities of the exercises and emphasis on major action prevented the development of more sophisticated and effective torpedo tactics. Although there were extensive night exercises before the war, not one of those held in 1938 simulated an encounter like the battles off Guadalcanal, which were to be dominated by fast-moving cruisers and destroyers.[47]

Immediately before the war, more complex exercises with faster targets and more challenging torpedo-fire-control problems were in fact introduced.[48] But they came too late to alter the pervasive beliefs that enemy capital ships were the primary target for destroyer torpedoes and that most attacks would be delivered at close range against slowly maneuvering, well-illuminated targets. Off Guadalcanal, the Navy eschewed the potential of stealthy torpedo attacks and focused instead on gunfire as the dominant weapon.

The IJN approached the problem quite differently. Forced by the interwar naval-limitation treaties to accept a fleet of significantly smaller size, the Japanese had sought to redress the imbalance through technological innovation. The U.S. Navy failed to anticipate this and went to war assuming that Japanese ships and weapons would possess capabilities broadly similar to its own. That the Japanese would develop torpedoes with unprecedented range and striking power was wholly unanticipated.

The Type 93 Mod 2 torpedo, more commonly known as the Long Lance, was the IJN's counter to the large size and fighting power of the American battle line. Introduced in 1936, it was capable of a range of 20,000 meters (21,900 yards) at fifty knots, its highest speed setting. Its warhead weighed 490 kilograms (1,080 pounds). The Navy's contemporary, the Mark 15, had a range of only six thousand yards at forty-five knots; it carried an 825-pound warhead. The better performance of the Japanese torpedo was due to its larger size and the fact that it used pure oxygen as a combustion agent. The Mark 15 used regular air.

The Japanese also developed stealthy tactics that emphasized firing torpedoes before opening fire with their guns. At night, gun flashes created clear aim points. If torpedoes were fired and gunfire held until the torpedoes were among the enemy ships, the targets could be quickly overwhelmed by shells and torpedoes striking simultaneously. The lethality of this tactic was demonstrated at Savo Island.

American naval officers consistently underestimated the range and speed of Japanese torpedoes. They believed that submarines were firing them, not cruisers and destroyers. In the aftermath of Savo Island,

Rear Admiral Turner expressed his belief that heavy cruisers *Vincennes*, *Quincy*, and *Astoria* "ran into [a] submarine and torpedo trap."[49] An intelligence summary issued after Guadalcanal I reflected a similar assumption about Japanese torpedo tactics: "Jap[anese] torpedo attacks are the biggest threat. They appear to succeed in firing well placed torpedo salvoes. They hit from the flank and also the disengaged side. They undoubtedly use destroyers and cruisers as well as submarines well placed in area."[50]

Ignorance regarding the range and accuracy of Japanese torpedoes resulted in tactics that played to their strengths. At the battle of Tassafaronga, Rear Adm. Carleton H. Wright maintained the course and speed of his cruisers while rapidly firing at Japanese destroyers. The cruisers' gun flashes provided excellent points of aim, and their steady course carried them right into a barrage of enemy torpedoes. Two struck Wright's flagship, the heavy cruiser *Minneapolis*; *New Orleans*, *Pensacola*, and *Northampton* were also hit. The Navy failed to recognize the true capabilities of the Long Lance until late 1943, far too late for the Guadalcanal campaign.

THE FIRST SUCCESS

After the Japanese victory at Savo Island, the campaign settled into an attritional struggle. Admiral Yamamoto's complex plan to recapture Guadalcanal was defeated by Rear Admiral Fletcher and the carriers *Saratoga* and *Enterprise* at the battle of the Eastern Solomons on 24 August. *Enterprise*, however, was damaged and had to be withdrawn to Pearl Harbor for repairs. A few days later, *Saratoga* was torpedoed by the submarine *I-26* and also left the theater. On 15 September, *I-19* sank the carrier *Wasp* and damaged the battleship *North Carolina*. For the remainder of September and most of October, *Hornet* was the only carrier available.

The next night surface action was fought on the night of 11–12 October, the battle of Cape Esperance. It was triggered by a major Allied reinforcement effort. The 164th Infantry Regiment of the Americal Division was moving to Guadalcanal. Rear Adm. Norman Scott's TF 64, with four cruisers and five destroyers, provided distant cover. As the Americans approached Guadalcanal, Scott received warning of an approaching Japanese bombardment group. He advanced into Savo Sound, well prepared for the coming action and in fact seeking it. Unlike most commanders at Guadalcanal, Scott had had time to drill and practice with his ships; he had devoted considerable attention to indoctrinating his force and training it for night action. Samuel Eliot Morison was to describe Scott as "ready to accept night action" and intent on being "master of the situation."[51]

To prevent the problems seen at Savo with distributed formations, Scott developed an extremely concentrated one. He cast aside the pre-war training that had focused on the independent operation of destroyers in night search and attack. Instead, he placed destroyers with the cruisers in a line of battle, arguing that the column formation was "most practical for night action."[52] The linear formation appeared to offer several advantages. It would ease command and control, by allowing each ship to keep station by simply conforming to the movements of the ship in front of it. With destroyers at the van and rear of his line, Scott created a "double header" formation that permitted "engaging on either side instantly."[53] He was very concerned about a surprise attack from a disengaged flank. The concentration of the entire force into a single group would prevent defeat in detail, and a compact disposition would avoid the confusion that could lead to "friendly fire."

The possibility of friendly fire had contributed to the confusion at Savo; when Captain Riefkohl first sighted the Japanese, he had mistaken them for friendly ships that were mistaking him, in turn, for the Japanese. After the battle, *Chicago* and the destroyer *Patterson* had briefly fired at each other in a case of mistaken identity. No hits had been scored, but Savo drove home the dangers of friendly fire in a confused night action.[54] Scott's formation was designed to minimize them. As Scott's ships entered Savo Sound, therefore, they were in "line ahead." Three destroyers were in the van, followed by Scott's flagship, the cruiser *San Francisco*, and the cruisers *Boise*, *Salt Lake City*, and *Helena*. The remaining two destroyers followed.

Scott had issued a detailed set of instructions, but it was not a battle plan, and it left out important details. He failed to explain when and how to open fire. That omission would lead to confusion and reduce the effectiveness of Scott's force when the Japanese were most vulnerable. There was also no guidance for destroyer torpedo attacks.[55] The lack of an effective plan combined with a more insidious problem. In action, Scott was unable to process all available information effectively and develop a picture of the battle. He had selected a flagship with effective plotting facilities and communications, but *San Francisco* did not have an SG radar.[56] Other ships in the formation did, but what was lacking—and what the Navy had yet to develop—was a way to process quickly, store, and visualize all the data that came in from radars, sighting reports, and other sources so that decisions could be made rapidly with all the best available information. Scott was left trying to do those tasks in his head, and he lagged mentally behind the developing situation, unable to coordinate his forces effectively.

As the ships of Rear Adm. Goto Aritomo's bombardment group approached, the SG radars on *Helena* and *Boise* located them. *Helena* made her first contact at 2325, at a range of 27,700 yards; her crew tracked the target for fifteen minutes before reporting it. In the meantime, Scott remained unaware of the developing situation. Scott had turned off *San Francisco*'s SC radar, lacking faith in it and fearing the Japanese would be alerted by its transmissions.[57]

At 2330, Scott ordered a reversal of course to keep his ships athwart the main entrance to Savo Sound. The order was executed at 2332. His line turned 180 degrees to a southwesterly course. Because Scott was anxious to retain his advantageous position relative to the nearby islands, he turned the line in two pieces. The cruisers immediately turned to port in succession, by individual column movement; the destroyers behind them followed in their wake. The van destroyers turned independently, tracing a wide path to port that would bring them parallel to the cruiser column on its starboard side. They increased speed to regain their position.

It was then, with the van destroyers off in the darkness to starboard, that *Helena*'s contact report made it to Scott. When he received the report he thought *Helena*'s radar might have picked up the van destroyers and not a hostile force. Uncertain, Scott hesitated and attempted to ascertain the location of the three van destroyers, *Faren-holt*, *Duncan*, and *Laffey*. Scott's inadequate situational awareness cost his force valuable time.

If the approaching danger was unclear to Scott, *Helena*'s fire-control team realized the decisive moment had arrived. Coached onto the target by the SG radar, the spotters could see the lead ships of Goto's force. Although Scott's plan allowed the cruisers to open fire without permission, the details of when they could do so were vague. *Helena*'s commanding officer, Capt. Gilbert C. Hoover, requested permission before opening fire. This would only confuse matters further, as Morison later recounted: "On the voice radio, Captain Hoover broadcast a two-word signal, 'Interrogatory Roger,' which meant 'Request Permission to Open Fire.' It so happened that the code word 'Roger' was employed also to acknowledge receipt of a voice transmission, and on the flag bridge of *San Francisco* Hoover's question was interpreted as a mere request for acknowledgement of a previous message. So Scott answered, 'Roger,' intending to indicate 'Message Received.' But an unqualified 'Roger' also meant 'Commence Firing!'"[58] *Helena* opened up with her main and secondary batteries at 2346. The other ships in the American column followed suit. The initial salvoes found Rear Admiral Goto and the rest of his force completely unprepared. Rapid fire quickly set Goto's flagship, *Aoba*, ablaze and mortally wounded him; the cruiser *Furutaka*, the next ship in column, was crippled, and she hauled out of line. She would sink within the hour.

Had Scott continued firing, the battle might have been an unqualified success, but he hesitated. *Helena*'s opening salvo had come as a shock to him, and still fearing that his own van destroyers were the targets of the onslaught, Scott ordered his ships to cease firing; some, certain of the identity of their targets, did not obey.[59] By the time Scott had satisfied himself that the targets were hostile and had given the order to resume firing, four minutes had elapsed. This brief respite allowed the Japanese to begin to slip away. Scott endeavored to pursue, but the opportunity for a decisive victory was lost.

The lack of a plan for destroyer attack had unfortunate consequences of its own. The van destroyer *Duncan* sighted the approaching

Japanese as she was executing the change of course. In the absence of specific instructions, her captain, Lt. Cdr. Edmund B. Taylor, seized the favorable opportunity and closed to attack with torpedoes. The other destroyers with her, *Laffey* and *Farenholt*, continued through the turn, apparently unaware of the approaching Japanese. *Duncan* attacked alone; while she was between the two forces, she was sunk in a deadly crossfire.[60]

Scott's victory actually suggested that the linear formation was a valid approach to the problems of night combat, but initial appearances were deceptive. Scott was fortunate. He had managed to position his line across the path of the approaching Japanese, allowing him to bring the concentrated firepower of his whole formation to bear. At the moment the American column opened fire, Scott had unknowingly crossed the Japanese *T*. He also caught his opponent unaware; Rear Admiral Goto was completely surprised. In the next major action, Scott's model would be emulated, but under much different circumstances, and its limitations would be exposed.

Despite Scott's victory, the Navy remained unable to control the waters off Guadalcanal. The Japanese continued to send in reinforcements and bombard the beleaguered garrison. Two days after Scott's triumph, on the night of 13–14 October, two Japanese battle cruisers—modernized and reconstructed as fast battleships during the interwar period—bombarded Henderson Field, destroying more than half its planes. The next night, two cruisers executed a similar bombardment, and on the following day, a convoy of Japanese transports started unloading. Some of the remaining planes from the airfield attacked them; to try to keep the airfield in check, more cruisers shelled the airfield the next night.

Admiral Nimitz's assessment of the situation was bleak: It was "critical" and his forces were "unable to control the sea" surrounding Guadalcanal.[61] Nimitz knew a change was needed. After a conference with his staff on 15 October, he decided to relieve Vice Admiral Ghormley. The situation called for more aggressive leadership; Nimitz chose Vice Adm. William F. Halsey Jr. as his new commander in the South Pacific. The next day, Admiral King approved.

If aggressiveness was needed, Halsey was an excellent choice—it was his core characteristic. Halsey had spent his early career in destroyers, first in the Atlantic Fleet under William S. Sims and then the Pacific under William V. Pratt. Those early experiences had taught him the importance of aggressive action and how to use it to seize the initiative. On 18 October, he relieved Ghormley and immediately began to infuse his new command with his characteristic mind-set.

Meanwhile, the campaign was moving to its climax. With their reinforcements in place, the Japanese launched a major effort to take Henderson Field. Admiral Yamamoto supported the attack with powerful naval forces, including four carriers (*Shokaku*, *Zuikaku*, *Zuiho*, and *Junyo*). Rear Adm. Thomas C. Kinkaid, with the carriers *Hornet* and *Enterprise*, fought them at the battle of the Santa Cruz Islands on 26 October. *Hornet* was seriously damaged, abandoned, and sunk, leaving *Enterprise* as the Navy's last operational carrier in the Pacific. The Japanese withdrew, having suffered extensive losses in planes and aircrews. The last carrier battle of 1942 was over.

On Guadalcanal, the soldiers and marines defeated Japanese attacks and successfully defended their perimeter. Unwilling to accept defeat, Admiral Yamamoto resolved to seize the airfield and recapture Guadalcanal in November; he organized another reinforcement convoy. Simultaneously, Halsey accelerated the shipment of supplies to the island. He was determined to end Japanese resistance and bring the campaign to a successful conclusion. These two plans collided in mid-November; the outcome would decide the campaign and determine who would hold the initiative in the Pacific.

"AN INCREDIBLE MELEE"

To cover his reinforcements, Yamamoto planned a massive bombardment to render Henderson Field unserviceable. Vice Adm. Abe Hiroaki, with battleships *Hiei* and *Kirishima*, would deliver it the night of 12–13 November. Meanwhile, Halsey had sent Rear Admiral Turner to Guadalcanal with a large reinforcement and resupply convoy. Turner's ships unloaded on 11 and 12 November, despite periodic interruptions by Japanese air strikes. When Abe's approaching force was sighted on the twelfth, Halsey reacted aggressively and ordered Turner, who was planning to withdraw his transports that evening, to stop them. Turner detached his escorts—a mixed collection of cruisers and destroyers—and ordered them to sweep Savo Sound. They approached Guadalcanal that night under the command of Rear Adm. Daniel J. Callaghan while the transports retired to Noumea.

Callaghan was a gunnery expert and very familiar with the developing campaign. As chief of staff to Vice Admiral Ghormley, he had closely followed the efforts to hold Guadalcanal and control the waters around it. He was also familiar with his flagship, *San Francisco*, having been her commanding officer before the war. As his ships steamed toward Ironbottom Sound, Callaghan formulated a plan for the coming battle. He knew his five cruisers and eight destroyers were no match for Abe's battleships and screening forces. Callaghan also knew that they lacked a common doctrine and were unaware how to fight a night action cohesively. The careful planning that had existed before Cape Esperance was absent.

The decision to have Callaghan lead the force has been criticized, mainly because of his performance in the confused battle that followed. But the choice made sense. Turner was commanding the amphibious force, and Callaghan was slightly senior to Scott, who was also in the task group, on board the light cruiser *Atlanta*. Scott might have been more experienced with night action, but he did not act as decisively at Cape Esperance as Callaghan would at Guadalcanal I.

With a thorough understanding of the Navy's surface-warfare doctrine and knowledge of the context surrounding the battle—that is, the critical need to prevent a bombardment of Henderson Field—it is possible today to give a proper assessment of Callaghan's performance. In Callaghan the Navy had an admiral who would not fail to act aggressively; his actions would echo a prewar light-cruiser manual that had reminded its readers that "great odds have been and will again be overcome by determination and knowledge."[62]

Callaghan's greatest failing was the fact that he did not issue a battle plan to his subordinates. Without a task force doctrine, a plan was the only hope they had of fighting as a unit in battle. Callaghan did not provide one. By reconstructing from the facts available his apparent approach to the battle, it is possible to discern why he never shared the details. That evening, as the ships neared the sound, Callaghan discussed his intentions with the captain of *San Francisco*, Capt. Cassin Young. A young officer overheard them.

> I . . . happened to overhear the Admiral . . . and the Captain . . . talking on the starboard wing of the navigation bridge. The wind carried their voices to me as I paced the deck and I was able to clearly observe the demeanor of each. They were discussing the unannounced fact that there were battleships . . . coming . . . that night and that our little group of cruisers and destroyers were ordered to prevent them at all costs from bombarding Henderson Field and landing reinforcements from the accompanying transports. . . . Captain Cassin Young . . . was in an understandably agitated state, sometimes waving his arms, as he remarked, "but this is suicide." Admiral Dan Callaghan replied, "Yes I know, but we have to do it."[63]

Young had been recognized for his bravery. When the Japanese attacked Pearl Harbor, he had commanded the repair ship *Vestal*, moored alongside the battleship *Arizona*. Young was fighting fires when the salvo of bombs that destroyed *Arizona* fell. Blown overboard by the explosion, Young swam back to *Vestal* through the flaming oil and helped his crew save the ship. He was awarded the Medal of Honor for his efforts. What would cause an officer with Young's mettle to consider a plan suicidal? Callaghan had estimated the situation and, considering the factors of strength and weakness, had found himself at a considerable disadvantage. Abe had two battleships, with a combined sixteen 14-inch guns. These guns could destroy the airfield and wreck any ship that got in their way. The battleships were sure to be screened by a supporting force of destroyers, and likely cruisers as well. Against them, Callaghan could muster just three large cruisers, two small ones, and eight destroyers. He was overmatched.

However, Callaghan knew that under the right circumstances, his force could overpower one of the Japanese battleships. He knew gunnery well, having served as fire-control officer of the battleship *Idaho* and gunnery officer of the battleship *Mississippi* before assuming command of *San Francisco* in May 1941. The fighting-strength comparisons developed by the Naval War College showed that at very close ranges—under ten thousand yards—two of his large cruisers would have a small advantage over one of the Japanese battleships. With three of them, he could secure a decisive advantage, if he could get close enough.

This was apparently Callaghan's concept for the coming battle. He would close the range with his three large cruisers and engage each of the battleships in turn, overwhelming them with gunfire and preventing the bombardment of Henderson Field. It is obvious why Captain

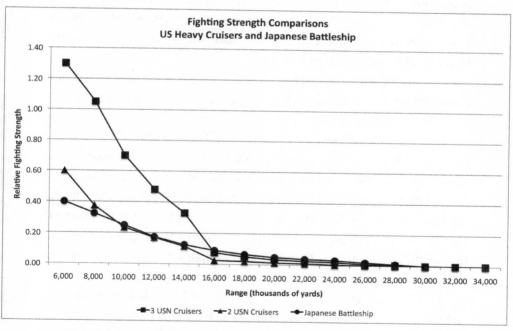

FIGURE 3. Relative fighting strengths of three U.S. Navy cruisers, two U.S. cruisers, and a single Japanese fast battleship as assessed by the Naval War College. Inside 10,000 yards, two U.S. cruisers have a slight advantage. Inside 16,000 yards, three Navy cruisers have an advantage and below 12,000 yards a significant advantage. Rear Admiral Callaghan was familiar with these fighting-strength comparisons.

Young would have considered this suicidal. However feasible Callaghan's plan was in theory, in practice cruisers did not survive close-range engagements with battleships.

There are two likely reasons, then, why Callaghan did not share his plan. First, if Young was objecting to it, other captains would as well. Callaghan would not have wanted to undermine confidence in his own leadership by promulgating a plan that might lead subordinates to question his sanity. Second, since the heart of the plan relied on close-range action by the three large cruisers, Callaghan expected to be able to lead them from the bridge of *San Francisco*; the other ships of the formation could fend for themselves. Although it is impossible to say definitively how Callaghan expected to fight the battle, this explanation is the best fit with what is known or inferable.

Since it had proved effective at Cape Esperance, Callaghan adopted Scott's linear formation, with the cruisers in the center and destroyers at either end of the line. In action reports, it was described as "Battle Formation Baker One" and was broadly similar to Scott's "double header," although Callaghan's line was much longer because of the greater number of ships.[64] The linear formation was expected to ease coordination, prevent friendly fire, and concentrate the fighting strength of Callaghan's ships.

It accomplished none of these things. The long line dispersed the fighting strength of Callaghan's formation. Scott had concentrated his fire because he found himself across the Japanese line of advance; Callaghan ran into Abe's formation head on. Callaghan's ships broke into the Japanese formation one at a time and then fought individual battles once they were inside. Effective control proved impossible in the resulting melee; *San Francisco*, Callaghan's flagship, fired on the next ship ahead in the line, the cruiser *Atlanta*.[65]

To some degree, the chaos might have been deliberate on the American side. Callaghan focused on getting his cruisers inside the large enemy formation and past the two lines of Japanese destroyers screening the enemy battleships. He may have purposefully used his van destroyers to open a path through the Japanese screen. This would have been an inversion of the standard night-search-and-attack tactics, which relied on cruiser gunfire to open a hole in the enemy screen for destroyers. Whether it was deliberate or not, a path was opened.

As the Japanese approached in the early minutes of 13 November, Callaghan's picture of the developing situation was provided by *Helena*'s SG radar, which had made the first contact. Captain Hoover sent frequent contact reports, but they did not give Callaghan an adequate sense of what was happening.[66] Fifteen minutes after *Helena*'s initial contact, the two forces were in visual range. Callaghan could have leveraged *Helena*'s contact reports to gain the advantage of surprise, but he held fire until the Japanese forced the issue: once they sighted the American column, they illuminated the lead ships with searchlights and opened fire. Postbattle analyses would criticize that hesitation.[67]

His formation quickly disintegrated. Japanese shells hit *Atlanta*'s bridge superstructure, starting fires and killing personnel. The head of the American column fragmented as the lead destroyers attempted to launch torpedoes or hauled out of line damaged ones. *San Francisco* mistook the burning *Atlanta* for the enemy and opened fire, killing Rear Admiral Scott and most of his staff.[68] The mistake was quickly realized, and Callaghan gave an order to cease firing.

This order has been the subject of severe criticism and much confusion in studies of the engagement. The difficulty stems from the fact that Callaghan gave the order not only to *San Francisco*'s gunners but to his entire force. A classified information bulletin concluded that "considerable uncertainty and confusion existed" and suggested that withholding fire had been a mistake: "The OTC appears to have entertained fear of own ships firing at each other. Ships with SG radar and good visual sight apparently continued fire because they were confident of [the] enemy character of their targets and they knew if they did not knock the enemy out they would be knocked out."[69] Most commentators, however, have assumed that Callaghan meant the order only for his flagship and not the rest of the force. Given the fury that was raging at the time, this interpretation makes sense. However, when asked by other ships to clarify his intentions, Callaghan clearly indicated he wanted a cease-fire. Why would the admiral order his ships to stop firing in the middle of a deadly night action?

Callaghan was putting his plan into motion. His van destroyers had disrupted the cohesion of the Japanese screen. *San Francisco* led Callaghan's two other large cruisers through the breach and into the heart of the enemy formation; Callaghan told these ships, "We want the big ones."[70] The cruisers could, if they stopped shooting, fade into the darkness and sneak up on the battleships without drawing their fire. Prewar exercises had demonstrated the potential of this tactic by showing how difficult it was to identify attacking ships once they had entered a screened disposition.[71] By withholding fire, Callaghan hoped to get his cruisers close enough to cripple the Japanese battleships.

But only one of the cruisers would reach decisive range. *Portland*, immediately astern of *San Francisco*, lost control when a Japanese torpedo shattered her stern. She spent the rest of the battle steaming in circles, firing at targets of opportunity. *Helena* became distracted by the plethora of targets; she used her rapid-firing 6-inch guns to disable several ships but lost track of the flagship. *San Francisco* closed the enemy flagship alone.

The battle's climactic moment saw the two flagships, the battleship *Hiei* and cruiser *San Francisco*, engage at point-blank range, just 2,200 yards. Young's assessment proved prophetic; he, Callaghan, and all but one member of the admiral's staff were killed when a 6-inch shell from *Hiei*'s secondary battery wrecked *San Francisco*'s signal bridge. But it was not a vain sacrifice. The gunnery of Young's crew was exemplary. *Hiei* was hit repeatedly. *San Francisco*'s 8-inch shells penetrated her steering-gear room and disabled electrical generators. Additional hits—from *Portland*, *San Francisco*, and American destroyers—riddled *Hiei*'s superstructure, wounding Abe and disrupting his control of the Japanese formation. Soon after closing with the enemy battleship, Callaghan's mission was accomplished: the Japanese formation, confused, separated, and lacking cohesion, abandoned its bombardment mission.

Within complex systems, individual actions can have extreme importance, particularly at unstable "bifurcation points," when the outcome is uncertain. As Robert Artigiani has explained, "It is individual human choices, made at instabilities, that determine the structure and form of societies."[72] Callaghan's battle was such a bifurcation point. The American strategic victory at Guadalcanal I resulted from Callaghan's decision to engage decisively at close range. Since he did not have time to develop a common doctrine and chose not to communicate his battle plan, he knew his ships would fight without cohesion. In such a circumstance, the most favorable development would be a confused melee, in which Callaghan and his subordinates could leverage tactical heuristics developed before the war. Callaghan's plan, and the decisiveness with which he executed it, saved Henderson Field. Both he and Scott were awarded posthumously the Medal of Honor.

The Navy was quick to learn from Callaghan's sacrifice. The linear formation was immediately abandoned. It prevented destroyers from operating effectively and reduced overall fighting strength. In prewar exercises, destroyers had used their speed and powerful torpedoes to attack aggressively. By keeping them in column with the cruisers, Callaghan and Scott severely limited their potential. A classified information bulletin issued after Guadalcanal I made this very clear: "This battle formation did not recognize the different types of ships with their different armaments and capabilities. . . . Destroyers are essentially an offensive weapon, particularly at night with their torpedo batteries. Destroyer gunfire at night is secondary to torpedoes. The four destroyers in the rear could have been more effectively employed in the van concentrated with the other destroyers prepared to make a high speed torpedo attack and retirement from the immediate vicinity of the action."[73]

In his own comments on Cape Esperance and Guadalcanal I, Admiral Nimitz echoed these views, stressing the inability of destroyers to attack from the column: "Their disposition in such close proximity to and in a single long column with the cruisers is questionable." He argued that one of the formations for night search and attack "might have made possible a greater application of potential power against the enemy."[74] The failure of the linear formation at Guadalcanal I signaled the abandonment of Scott's experiment. Under exceptional circumstances at Cape Esperance, it had worked well, but it had been inadequate in Callaghan's fight. Future formations would allow destroyer commanders the freedom to practice the techniques they had learned before the war.

NIGHT OF THE BATTLEWAGONS

The battle of Friday the thirteenth forced a pause in Yamamoto's plan. With Henderson Field undamaged, the approaching transports would be exposed to a daylight attack; they returned to the Shortlands. But the pause was brief: a force of cruisers and destroyers under Admiral Mikawa arrived off Guadalcanal that night. Mikawa detached two cruisers to bombard the airfield; they destroyed eighteen planes. The transports resumed their approach.

Halsey knew he had to stop them. He instructed Rear Adm. Thomas C. Kinkaid to detach two battleships and four destroyers from his carrier group to intercept Mikawa's force. Rear Adm. Willis A. Lee was placed in command of this powerful task group; he moved toward Guadalcanal but was too far away to stop Mikawa. Lee spent the day of 14 November trying to avoid being seen and monitoring the developing situation. Meanwhile, aviators from Henderson Field and *Enterprise* found the Japanese transports and attacked throughout the day. Six of the eleven transports were sunk or abandoned; one was damaged and turned back. The remaining four continued toward the island. Ahead of them was Vice Adm. Kondo Nobutake's bombardment group, comprising the battleship *Kirishima*, four cruisers, and nine destroyers. Yamamoto ordered Kondo to shatter the airfield. Kondo's approach was sighted that afternoon. Lee prepared for battle.

Rear Admiral Lee and his battleships were sent into the narrow waters of Ironbottom Sound because Halsey's resources were growing thin. After the battle two nights before, he lacked an effective cruiser-destroyer force, the kind of formation that traditionally would have been used at night. Battleships had proved vulnerable in mock night actions before the war; at close range, smaller ships could overwhelm their control positions with concentrated gunfire. The decision to use battleships this way thus violated existing doctrine; Halsey did it because he knew that the success of the campaign depended on preserving the airfield and that Lee's force was the only one that could do it.

Like Callaghan, Lee had a collection of ships that were unfamiliar with each other and went into battle without a common doctrine. However, Lee had time to develop and communicate an effective battle plan. There was not enough time for a formal operation order; he communicated his intentions by visual means. The plan called for a simple formation. The four destroyers would operate independently ahead of the battleships, not tied to the battle line; they were given freedom to use their initiative. *Washington* and *South Dakota* would follow approximately five thousand yards astern. Destroyers would flush out targets for the battleships. Gunfire would be the decisive weapon; all ships were instructed to open fire as soon as targets presented themselves.[75]

Lee's emphasis on gunfire was natural. He was a gunnery expert and uniquely well suited to handle two of the Navy's most modern and powerful battleships in action. As director of fleet training before the war, Lee had had the opportunity to become intimately familiar with the Navy's night battle practices; he knew the effective techniques. He was also very familiar with radar and understood its principles and limitations even better than the engineers who designed the systems. Lee's knowledge informed the fire-control procedures of his flagship, *Washington*. On this night, his crew would put them to good use.[76]

The Japanese, in three separate formations, came at Lee's ships from different directions. In the early stages of the battle, the guns of Lee's battleships disrupted Japanese coordination, kept them from concentrating or using their combined strength. When the shooting started, one of the Japanese formations was rounding the eastern edge of Savo Island. *Washington* and *South Dakota* were to the south, and from the considerable range of 18,500 yards, they opened fire. They scored no hits but forced the cruiser *Sendai* and two escorting destroyers to retire behind a smoke screen. *Sendai* disappeared from sight and radar screens, and *Washington*'s gunners believed they had sunk their first target.

While *Sendai* was dodging battleship shells, a destroyer detached from her formation earlier rounded the western side of Savo. The *Ayanami* hugged the island's shore, obscuring her from radar screens. Behind her followed cruiser *Nagara* and four destroyers; this was the Japanese screening unit. Lee's destroyers sighted them and engaged. In a fight dominated by Japanese guns and torpedoes, *Preston* and *Walke* were sunk, *Benham* was crippled, and *Gwin* was knocked out of the fight. The battleships opened fire to aid their smaller brethren; as *South Dakota* engaged, she lost electrical power.

The situation worsened. Unable to ascertain her position relative to the flagship, *South Dakota* left the formation and steamed dangerously close to the Japanese forces. Searchlights illuminated her, and *South Dakota* received the concentrated attention of the Japanese force. *Kirishima* and the two heavy cruisers battered *South Dakota*'s superstructure. The battle hung in the balance. Lee's destroyers were crippled or sinking; *South Dakota* was incapacitated; and the Japanese were poised to complete their mission and bombard the airfield.

That was all about to change. Obscured in the darkness beyond *South Dakota* was *Washington*, and her gunners had been developing a fire-control solution on the largest target in the enemy formation. The solution was good. The director was on and tracking. They were ready to open fire. For several moments, Lee hesitated. There was uncertainty about the identity of the target. *Washington*'s SG radar was mounted in front of the fire-control tower and so had a blind spot aft. *South Dakota* had been in that blind spot. Was she still there, or was she the "target" to starboard? Lee, like other admirals in similar situations before him, lacked an effective picture of the situation.

When the Japanese searchlights came on and illuminated *South Dakota*, the uncertainty ended. The hostile nature of target became obvious. Lee gave Cdr. Harvey Walsh, *Washington*'s gunnery officer, the order to open fire. The firing keys on the director closed, *Washington*'s roll leveled out, and nine 16-inch armor-piercing shells left their tubes in a blinding flash. Her action report described the moment: "Fire was opened at 8400 yards and a hit was probably obtained on first salvo and certainly on the second."[77]

The target was *Kirishima*; she withered under *Washington*'s fire. Commander Walsh used visual bearings and a rocking ladder to secure the maximum number of hits. The exact number is uncertain. A postwar report put the number at nine, but more recent research suggests that twenty 16-inch hits were scored.[78] Whatever the number, this was some of the most accurate battleship gunfire ever seen. Lee's familiarity with effective radar-directed gunnery techniques won the battle in seven minutes. Mortally wounded, wrecked, and burning, *Kirishima* veered away and lost steering control.

But Lee was not done. With *Kirishima* sinking, he moved aggressively toward the northwest, drawing the remaining Japanese ships away from *South Dakota* and forcing them to shadow his movements. This aggressive maneuver threatened the Japanese transports. They backtracked to avoid action with the approaching battleship. This is exactly what Lee wanted; it delayed their approach and gave the airmen ashore more time to attack the transports in the morning. Lee's tactical victory had strategic importance. *Washington*'s gunfire had won the battle, guaranteed the survival of Henderson Field, and doomed the Japanese invasion force. The next morning, planes from the airfield repeatedly attacked the delayed transports. The last Japanese effort to retake Guadalcanal disintegrated; victory in the campaign was assured.

WHY DID THE NAVY WIN AT GUADALCANAL?

The Navy won the Guadalcanal campaign because it recognized it for what it was, the decisive struggle of the war. Victory at Guadalcanal meant gaining the strategic initiative and putting the Japanese onto the defensive. King had foreseen this when he committed the Navy to what has been derided as "operation shoestring." Both he and Nimitz realized that even if they were not fully prepared, the time was ripe to move aggressively and attempt to put Yamamoto's Combined Fleet on its heels. In Halsey, they found a local commander who shared their vision.

The campaign must be understood as a whole, a conflict across all dimensions—in the jungles of the island, in the skies above it, and on, as well as below, the seas around it. Each of these spheres bore upon the others, and it was necessary to win in all of them together. Without the work of the Navy's surface forces and the narrow victories they achieved in Ironbottom Sound, defeat would have followed. Those victories were delivered by the Navy's tactical heuristics developed and inculcated before the war.

The most important heuristic was the emphasis on quick and effective gunfire. Off Guadalcanal, gunfire proved devastatingly effective; the close ranges and confused nature of the fighting ensured that gunfire would decide the outcome in each of the four night battles of the decisive phase of the campaign. At Cape Esperance, the rapid fire of

Scott's force set the cruiser *Aoba* ablaze and mortally wounded *Furu-taka*. Callaghan, in his desperate engagement with *Hiei* at Guadalcanal I, used the guns of *San Francisco* and his other cruisers to doom the Japanese flagship. At Guadalcanal II, Lee seized the initiative and disrupted enemy formations with accurate salvos. The battleship *Washington* sank *Kirishima*, prevented the bombardment of Henderson Field, and thwarted Japanese plans. The effective prewar training in night battle practice and integration of radar into fire-control systems meant the Navy was well prepared to win such fights. The techniques developed before the war allowed the Navy to achieve victory despite its inability to indoctrinate forces properly and formulate effective battle plans.

The second important heuristic was the emphasis on aggressive action; it had been a defining characteristic of the Navy's doctrine and now became an essential part of victory in the campaign. Scott, Callaghan, and Lee all sought out the Japanese and aggressively maneuvered their forces to gain advantage and thwart enemy plans. Scott positioned his ships across the entrance to Savo Sound, intending that any approaching formation be subjected to the concentrated fire of his cruisers and destroyers. The battle developed much as he envisioned, preventing the Japanese from mounting an effective response. Callaghan maneuvered his cruisers into Abe's formation, deliberately seeking battle with the enemy flagship at decisive range. Lee, having dispatched the enemy bombardment force, steamed toward the approaching transports, forcing them to delay their approach. All three admirals used maneuver to keep the Japanese off balance and create more favorable circumstances. They also fought with knowledge of the strategic context, recognizing the place of their tactical decisions within the broader campaign.

Decentralized command and control was also beneficial. In one respect, the Navy's emphasis on it was a weakness at Guadalcanal: task force commanders were unable to generate the necessary doctrines and plans to ensure coordination in battle. However, in the confused melees, the emphasis on individual initiative was also a strength. Cdr. Jesse Coward, captain of the destroyer *Sterett*, exemplified this strength during Guadalcanal I when he, despite losing contact with the other ships of the formation, closed with *Hiei* and engaged at close range, firing torpedoes and ten salvoes of 5-inch guns. Three 14-inch hits from the battleship started fires and destroyed one of *Sterett*'s guns, but Coward continued to look for targets.[79]

The Navy's ship captains may have fought these battles individually, but they were well prepared to do so. By aggressively opening fire on targets as they came into view, they did their utmost to damage the enemy and secure an advantage. In the chaotic battles of the Guadalcanal campaign, the Navy's loosely coupled approach to command and control allowed ships to maximize their individual potentials, even if they could not fight as a cohesive team.

DENOUEMENT

The last night surface action of the campaign—the battle of Tassafaronga, fought on the night of 30 November–1 December—introduced a new paradigm. Both sides had learned from the earlier battles and were starting to apply new approaches. The context of the campaign had shifted; the Japanese had paused in their efforts to retake Guadalcanal. They would soon give up entirely. Halsey still acted aggressively to cut off their attempts to resupply the trapped Japanese garrison and sink their ships. When eight destroyers under Rear Adm. Tanaka Raizo approached the island, he moved to stop them.

Prior to the battle Rear Admiral Kinkaid had assessed the lessons from earlier engagements and developed an aggressive plan incorporating them. He instructed his destroyers to press ahead and attack from close range with torpedoes; the lead destroyer would use an SG radar to develop a clear picture of the action and guide the others to the launch point. Cruisers would remain distant, far from the threat of Japanese torpedoes; they would use radar-assisted gunfire as their primary weapon. Like Lee, Kinkaid refused to employ Scott's linear formation.[80]

But Kinkaid was wrong about Japanese torpedoes. He expected them to be similar to the Navy's own. Since ten thousand yards was beyond their effective range but was also the maximum effective range of radar-directed cruiser gunfire at the time, Kinkaid instructed the cruisers to engage from that range. He expected in that way to stay out of "torpedo water" while inflicting maximum damage to the enemy.

Two days before the battle, Rear Adm. Carleton H. Wright replaced Kinkaid. The problem that had plagued earlier battles resurfaced; Wright lacked the time to familiarize himself with his force and indoctrinate them. He had no choice but to go into battle with Kinkaid's plan, and his lack of familiarity with it and with his subordinates would have serious consequences. The classified information bulletin analyzing the battle would remark, "Unfortunately so far this war, it has been necessary to organize task forces quickly with no opportunity for the commander to effect proper indoctrination of his units."[81]

Compounding the problem, two destroyers, *Lamson* and *Lardner*, were attached to Wright's force immediately before the battle. He noted the difficulty they presented: "The *Lamson* (ComDesDiv 9 [i.e., flying the "burgee" pennant of Commander, Destroyer Division 9]) and *Lardner* joined the force under my command in accordance with dispatch orders of the Commander South Pacific Force at about 2100. . . . [I]t was not possible to transmit to these vessels the Operation Plan, Communication Plan, and special instructions under which the Force was operating. The *Lamson* and *Lardner* were therefore directed to join as the rear unit in the formation."[82] The two destroyers were positioned behind the cruisers, where they could do the least harm and stay out of the way.

Wright's lack of familiarity with the plan and his subordinates proved costly. His van destroyers were in position to attack from close range with torpedoes before the firing started. However, when *Fletcher*'s captain, Cdr. William M. Cole, sought permission to do so, Wright refused. In Wright's estimation, the range was too great. Cole had a better picture of the situation and should have fired anyway. By the time he received Wright's permission, the opportunity for a surprise attack had been lost.

Wright's cruisers opened fire moments after Cole released his torpedoes. Tanaka's destroyers had already seen Wright's ships and were setting up their own torpedo attack. Using the gun flashes of the cruisers as aiming points, they demonstrated what a volley of Long Lances could do. *Minneapolis* and *Pensacola* were hit. *New Orleans*' bow was blown off. *Northampton* was sunk. The Japanese destroyer *Takanami*, closest to Wright's column when the shooting started, was hit repeatedly and overwhelmed in the first few minutes.

Wright's crews claimed many more enemy ships sunk, but their gunners had been fooled by the peculiarities of the A-scope. They had focused their scopes on the target, zooming in the presentation to give a more precise picture, and fired as fast as possible. As the Japanese destroyers launched their torpedoes and turned away, their radar echoes were lost in the mass of pips produced by the splashes of the shells landing around them. The gunners continued to track their last known course, following the splashes of their own guns. When they ceased firing, the "targets" disappeared and the gunners assumed they had been sunk. Meanwhile, Tanaka and his remaining ships were escaping.

Although thwarted by inadequate indoctrination and by Japanese skill, Kinkaid's plan was considered sound. It incorporated lessons from prewar night combat exercises and experience in the campaign. The integration of close-range destroyer torpedo attacks and supporting cruiser gunfire derived from the night-search-and-attack doctrine promulgated before the war. The emphasis on radar and radar-directed fire control was a new feature, a synthesis of prewar doctrine and wartime technology. With improvements, Kinkaid's basic plan became the basis for the conduct of future battles.

CONCLUSION

The Navy quickly assessed lessons from the night battles off Guadalcanal and integrated them into new approaches. The emphasis on decentralized doctrinal development and reliance on low-level commanders were key aspects of the process. Three of the most critical challenges were the lack of coordination in battle, the inability of ships and commanders to keep up with and effectively process all available information, and the lack of an effective and coherent vocabulary for communicating in action.

The inability to coordinate effectively in battle was a direct result of the breakdown of the Navy's force structure. Commanders lacked the time to familiarize themselves adequately with their units, indoctrinate them, and produce effective battle plans. The comments of *Secret Information Bulletin No. 5*, part of a series of condensed battle lessons issued by Admiral King, emphasized the cost: "It is unsound and a waste of material to throw forces together just prior to an action with no opportunity for OTC to issue instructions, doctrine, orders, etc. We are paying heavily for this."[83]

Addressing this problem required a new approach. The prewar assumption that commanders would have adequate time to indoctrinate their forces and issue detailed battle plans had proved incorrect. The Navy needed to develop a new paradigm; the prewar work with plans for major actions provided a potential model. In early 1943, Nimitz and his subordinates would solve the problem by applying that model to all types of action, major and minor.

Even though information from radar and other sources could have provided a clear picture of the fighting around them, none of the commanding officers in the Guadalcanal battles—Riefkohl, Scott, Callaghan, Lee, or Wright—were able to develop and maintain a sense of what was really happening. The problem was not a lack of information; the problem was that there was no facility to integrate and process information into an actionable picture. Existing shipboard organizations varied, but they all relied on the captain to take in available information, synthesize it, and determine what to do. In the night battles of 1942, commanders became overwhelmed and confused because they could not keep pace with all the incoming details. The cognitive load was too high.

Nimitz was aware of the problem. In November 1942, he issued a tactical bulletin that ordered all ships to introduce a "Combat Operations Center" to receive, analyze, and evaluate information from all sources.[84] The name was later changed to "Combat Information Center," but the function remained the same. This new organization would offload from the commanding officer or OTC the processing of information, develop a clear picture from it, and supply the information needed to command the ship or formation in battle.

Individual ships too were working on solutions. That same month, the Navy's first effective CIC was trialed during the battle of Guadalcanal I on board the destroyer *Fletcher*. It was an ad-hoc arrangement created by her captain, Commander Cole, and his executive officer, Lt. Cdr. Joseph C. Wylie. Wylie would stand at the edge of the radar room where he could observe the SG display. He formed a picture of the developing action and orally communicated, via sound-powered telephone, relevant information to Cole and the ship's weapons, coaching them onto targets. Wylie would go on to help lead the Navy's formal development of the CIC.

The Navy also lacked a clear and uniform vocabulary for communicating in battle. This problem led to confusion at the start of Cape Esperance, when *Helena* opened fire after receiving an affirmative response to her "Interrogatory Roger." Different meanings for the same signal undermined the ability of ships to coordinate their actions. Signals were revised and the duplication eliminated, increasing clarity.

The campaign for Guadalcanal validated important aspects of the Navy's surface-warfare doctrine and exposed its limitations. The mechanisms designed to achieve concerted action in combat—the development of a shared decision-making framework based on indoctrination and battle plans—did not work. Instead, the Navy had to fall back on its core tactical heuristics: aggressive action, quick and effective gunfire, and individual initiative. In the confused, close-range fighting in Ironbottom Sound, these heuristics were enough to deliver victory. The Navy was able to achieve its strategic aims of preventing Japanese bombardments of Henderson Field at critical moments, ensuring the survival of the garrison and thwarting Japanese reinforcement attempts.

However, these victories were extremely costly. Many officers and men were lost. A good number of them—like Callaghan and Scott—had been in the service a long time and were difficult to replace. Their sacrifice is memorialized at Land's End in San Francisco; the bulwarks of the bridge wings of *San Francisco* stand facing the sea, with holes from the shells and shrapnel of 13 November 1942 still present. A compass rose indicates the great-circle course to Guadalcanal, bearing 253 degrees true. A series of plaques express deep emotions. With the success those men and others earned at Guadalcanal, Nimitz held the initiative in the Pacific. In 1943, he would use it to control the operational tempo and put "unremitting pressure" on the Japanese. New approaches to doctrinal development for small task forces would be an essential component of the offensives he would initiate later that year.

6
THE CIC

There are no rules or doctrine made before a battle
which if rigidly followed will prevent losses in a battle.
Units must be trained for battle, placed in a position
where they will be effective and then aggressively
fought under competent, bold leadership.

—Arleigh Burke, 1943

The night battles off Guadalcanal exposed two serious problems
with the Navy's approach to surface combat. The first was the
assumption that small units—squadrons and task forces—would be
together long enough to develop a sense of cohesion and common level
of indoctrination. The second was the belief that ship and squadron
commanders would be able to quickly make sense of a developing situation and act on the information available to them. Neither of these
held true; the results were predictable. Formations disintegrated, and
captains fought their ships individually. More effective approaches to
doctrinal development were desperately needed.

The challenges would be addressed in two complementary ways.
At the fleet level, a more comprehensive approach to task-force doctrine was developed. That process is the subject of the next chapter.

In the meantime, the problem of indoctrination was eased somewhat by the growing size of the fleet. As additional ships became available, formations became more stable and the need to throw unfamiliar ships together without adequate preparation was reduced. Task-force commanders prepared more thoroughly, guided by established constraints, like the Navy's emphasis on individual initiative and decentralized command and control.

The second major development was the introduction of a new mechanism for managing shipboard information, the Combat Information Center. The CIC was a revolutionary solution to the challenge of making sense of a naval battle. In the fighting off Guadalcanal, this had been at least as serious an issue as inadequate preparation. There was no effective means within the current shipboard organization to rapidly collect and assimilate information from all sources. Radars, TBS radio, and sighting reports could have provided commanders an accurate picture of the battle around them, but existing structures for managing and processing information prevented it. On most ships, captains were overwhelmed by how much data they had to synthesize and how quickly they had to do it. For task-force commanders, the challenge was even more daunting. They had to assess information from all ships in the formation, quickly make sense of the entire battle, and give clear orders. With existing plotting approaches, this was virtually impossible.

The CIC was the solution; it used a series of plots to display all available information in a centralized location. The visualization was assessed by a new command function, the "evaluator," an officer who interpreted the developing situation and presented a clear, actionable picture to the captain or OTC. The CIC introduced new procedures—encapsulated in a series of constraints—that redistributed the cognitive workload.[1] Commanders were free to act more decisively and focus on leading their ships and men. CICs also allowed increased levels of coordination because all captains now had access to a much clearer view of the situation. Ship captains and squadron commanders would take advantage of these new capabilities by developing new approaches to surface action. The Japanese, suffering from the same cognitive challenges but lacking equivalent innovations, would be left behind. But before that transition could occur, Vice Admiral Halsey began his advance in the Solomons.

THE CONTINUING CAMPAIGN IN THE SOLOMONS

The Japanese evacuated their garrison from Guadalcanal in February 1943. By that time, attention had shifted to the area around Kula Gulf. The Japanese had built an airfield on the western tip of New Georgia, at Munda Point, and started another at Vila, across the gulf. Admiral Yamamoto, hoping to blunt Allied blows and ultimately regain the initiative, was strengthening his defensive perimeter. Halsey began attacking these installations from the air in December 1942. In early January, he sent TF 67 under Rear Adm. Warden L. Ainsworth to bombard Munda. Ainsworth "held conferences, studied charts and photographs, and drew up an excellent detailed plan" before striking on 4 January 1943.[2] On 23 January, Ainsworth returned to bombard Vila, igniting "spectacular fires." On both these occasions, specialized radar-equipped PBY floatplanes, the "Black Cats," observed the fall of shot and radioed corrections.

Nimitz was urging Halsey to advance and keep the pressure on the Japanese. During the next eight months, Halsey's forces—redesignated the Third Fleet—fought seven major night surface actions as they advanced up the Solomons. These battles illustrated the gradually improving potential of the CIC, the Navy's increasingly cohesive approach to doctrinal development, and the costs of continuing to underestimate the Japanese.

INTRODUCING THE CIC

Radar was a remarkable new technology, but it could not become revolutionary without systems to realize its full potential. Off Guadalcanal, radar was used in an adaptive manner; it was coupled with existing shipboard functions, like search and fire control. Information from the radars flowed through established organizational structures, limiting its potential and preventing a comprehensive view. A new organization— a centralized processing function—was required to assess all the available information, analyze it, and present it in a distilled form. Only

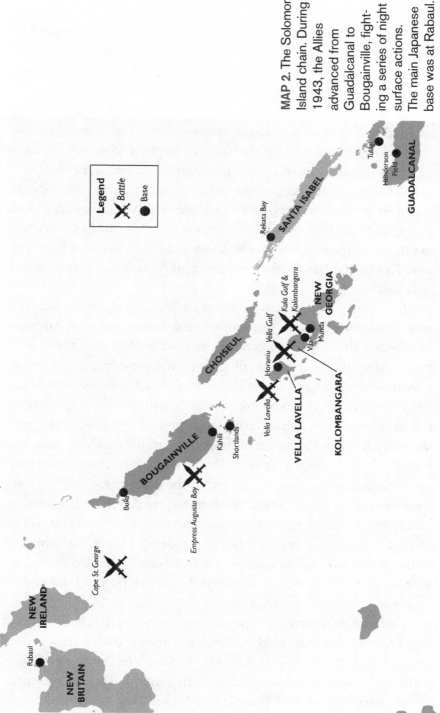

MAP 2. The Solomon Island chain. During 1943, the Allies advanced from Guadalcanal to Bougainville, fighting a series of night surface actions. The main Japanese base was at Rabaul.

Legend

✖ *Battle*

● Base

GUADALCANAL

Tulagi

Henderson Field

SANTA ISABEL

Rekata Bay

CHOISEUL

Kula Gulf & Kolombangara

Vella Gulf

NEW GEORGIA

Munda

Vila

Horaniu

Vella Lavella

VELLA LAVELLA

KOLOMBANGARA

BOUGAINVILLE

Kahili

Shortlands

Buka

Empress Augusta Bay

Cape St. George

NEW IRELAND

Rabaul

NEW BRITAIN

then could the Navy take full advantage of the new technology.[3] This need had not been anticipated before the war, but the fighting off Guadalcanal demonstrated its importance. The quest for a solution would lead to the CIC.

As described in the previous chapter, the Navy's first CIC for surface action was an ad-hoc arrangement—a pragmatic experiment—in the destroyer *Fletcher* during the Naval Battle of Guadalcanal. *Fletcher*'s captain, Commander Cole, placed his executive officer, Lieutenant Commander Wylie, at the edge of the radar room. The arrangements were rudimentary but revolutionary. Together with radar operator Tom Hollyday, Wylie kept track of the developing battle and kept Cole and the ship's weapons supplied with evaluated assessments of the situation. This helped *Fletcher* emerge unscathed from the convoluted melee of Guadalcanal I.

There were two critical elements of Wylie's role that made this arrangement a significant innovation. First, he became the focal point of information from the ship's radars and radios. Wylie was responsible for assessing the information, filtering it, and providing it to Captain Cole in a format that Cole could immediately act upon. Second, Wylie freed Cole of the need to coordinate the activities of the ship's various departments. Wylie, using information from the radars, anticipated the order to open fire and took responsibility for coaching guns and torpedoes onto potential targets. This freed Cole to concentrate fully on commanding the ship; when he gave the order to engage, weapons were already on target. These two features, the centralized evaluation of combat information from various sources and the coordination of shipboard weapons systems in combat, ultimately became the hallmarks of the Navy's CIC. Wylie's actions off Guadalcanal marked the beginning of a revolution that transformed the way shipboard information was processed and disseminated.

Cole and Wylie were not the only ones to recognize the need for a new approach. At Pearl Harbor, Admiral Nimitz and his staff analyzed combat reports and assessed the performance of the Pacific Fleet. They gathered lessons and disseminated them through *Tactical Bulletins*, *Confidential Letters*, and *Confidential Notes*. These were preexisting mechanisms; before the war, the fleet had used them to communicate new procedures. Nimitz and his staff leveraged the existing system and formalized it, regularly communicating new and improved practices as wartime lessons were absorbed.

"Tactical Bulletin 4TB-42," issued in November 1942, ordered all ships to establish a CIC. The bulletin provided a succinct explanation for this substantial change in organization: "Maximum combat efficiency by individual ships and task organizations can best be attained through full utilization of all available sources of combat intelligence." The CIC would receive, assimilate, and evaluate information.[4] What form would this new structure take? Nimitz and his staff did not say.

This was a critically important decision and wholly in line with the Navy's approach of relying on decentralized decision making and individual initiative. Nimitz intentionally left out any specifics about how to staff and structure the CIC. Instead, he leveraged the variability and creativity of his command. In 1942, shipboard organizations were not standardized; captains had the authority to tailor their own. By imposing a high-level constraint, Nimitz triggered a change in behavior, but by allowing the specifics of each CIC implementation to vary, Nimitz harnessed the skill and ability of his subordinates. They developed a variety of alternative approaches, and the best of these formed the basis of further development.

It was a brilliant approach. By allowing individual ships to experiment, Nimitz fostered the development of more effective solutions. 4TB-42 was written to address a specific need, the failure to utilize effectively all available information. However, Wylie had gone farther. He had augmented the ship's command function by advising when and how to engage the enemy; this suggested that the CIC could transform shipboard operations. It was a more radical idea than that outlined in 4TB-42, but by leaving out specifics, Nimitz had put the Pacific Fleet on a path that would lead there. As individual ships took up the challenge and created their own CIC organizations, they would discover the merits of Wylie's concept.

Although they did not specify how the CIC would perform its functions, Nimitz and his staff did indicate what those functions were.

The CIC would maintain master plots of combat information from all sources, as well as a continuous summary of all combat information. That information would be evaluated and disseminated to flag, ship, and fire-control stations; if required, it would also be given to other ships in the formation.[5]

Admiral King too was interested in the problem of shipboard information management. He held a conference in Washington on 8 January 1943 to work through the CIC concept and extend it beyond Nimitz's Pacific Fleet. The most important conclusion of the conference was that "a minimum of four plots should be present: one for navigation, one for air contacts, one for surface contacts, and a spare that might potentially be used for fighter direction."[6] Plots presented the relative position, course, and speed of contacts visibly and conspicuously, allowing officers to assess the developing situation quickly.[7] Wylie had managed without them because he monitored the SG PPI display and tracked potential targets in his head. This approach was limiting; to harness the full potential of the new system, the effort had to be shared across a team.

A destroyer CIC had at least eleven individuals. The *evaluator* oversaw the operation and presented a clear picture to the captain and other shipboard functions; a *CIC talker*, connected to the necessary communication circuits, spoke for him. The *surface-search radar operator* observed the radar display; he communicated with the *surface plot recorder*, who gave the *surface plotter* the information necessary to plot surface contacts. A similar three-man organization recorded aerial contacts. The *TBS recorder* monitored the TBS communication channels and recorded important details; another individual did the same for the task-force warning net. A *sound operator* tracked sonar contacts. The introduction of these new roles was a symmetry break that allowed a more sophisticated approach.

Today, we would consider the CIC a system of "distributed cognition." The visualizations at its heart were a symbolic information system. Each member of the team had a specific, complementary role that distributed the cognitive load and allowed the system to accomplish what Wylie had achieved on board *Fletcher* but with much greater capacity and clarity. The new roles and greater specialization increased the fidelity and capacity of the organization. From the interaction of the members of the CIC team, a radically new potential emerged.

ADAPTIVE TACTICS: JANUARY–JULY 1943

However, in early 1943, the new approaches enabled by the CIC were still in the future. Ships and formation commanders were becoming more effective at using information available from radars and other sources, but tactics changed slowly. They were adaptive, not evolutionary.

The most prominent adaptation was based on lessons from the Guadalcanal campaign. Rear Admiral Kinkaid incorporated them in the plan he developed before the battle of Tassafaronga. While the cruisers remained at about ten thousand yards and employed radar-directed gunfire, the destroyers would close and launch their torpedoes in a simultaneous attack. If all went well, shells and torpedoes would hit the enemy at the same time. In Kinkaid's plan, the prewar emphasis on coordinated attacks with all arms is obvious.

In practice, cruiser gunfire became the primary weapon for night action; destroyer torpedoes were relegated to secondary status. Current doctrinal publications reflected this; a 1943 Pacific Fleet cruiser gunnery manual emphasized that guns would be used "for crippling, stopping, or disabling" enemy ships; if they survived, torpedoes could sink them.[8] Unfortunately, this emphasis prevented the development of more sophisticated tactics and left cruiser formations vulnerable. Accurate gunfire required a relatively steady course; *Light Cruiser Doctrine* of 1939 urged maintaining "the maximum attainable volume of well-directed fire" and avoiding "maneuvers which might adversely affect" that fire.[9]

Cruiser commanders would maneuver but only at intervals and only when obliged by the threat of enemy torpedoes. Since the speed and range of Japanese torpedoes continued to be underestimated, these maneuvers were generally ineffective. As has been seen, Kinkaid had assumed ten thousand yards would be sufficient to keep the cruisers out of range; he was wrong. Ainsworth thought they could reach farther but chose to fight at similar ranges because ten thousand yards was the maximum effective range for spotting with his FC radars.[10] He mitigated the risk by changing course at regular intervals, but he based the timing of his turns on incorrect assumptions about the speed of Japanese torpedoes; they were much faster than he anticipated.

In early 1943, Vice Admiral Halsey had two mixed cruiser-destroyer task forces that employed these tactics. The first was Rear Admiral Ainsworth's. The second was commanded by Rear Adm. A. Stanton "Tip" Merrill. On the night of 5 March 1943, Merrill led his TF 68 into Kula Gulf for another bombardment of Vila. Merrill's force had three light cruisers—*Montpelier*, *Cleveland*, and *Denver*—and three destroyers. During the approach, a scouting PBY reported enemy ships—misidentified as light cruisers—and Merrill prepared for battle. As his ships entered the gulf, the cruisers were in column. The destroyer *Waller*, flagship of Cdr. Arleigh A. Burke's Destroyer Division 43, was six thousand yards ahead; she had been detached from the formation as an advanced picket. *Conway* was two thousand yards ahead of the cruiser column. *Cony* was at the rear, on the port quarter, providing protection against small-boat attacks that might come from New Georgia.

It was a very dark night. Merrill's formation was navigating with its SG radars. Each ship had only one, and using it for navigation "deprived the Task Force Commander and the Commanding Officers of the use of this valuable instrument for searching out enemy surface craft."[11] The ships were using traditional radar plots—they had not yet introduced CICs—and their limited ability to process radar information led to a misidentification. Approaching Japanese ships were initially mistaken for the small island of Sasamboki. The "island" appeared at the right time and on the right bearing, but was nine thousand yards closer than it should have been. It quickly became apparent that the contact was actually two ships.

They were the destroyers *Murasame* and *Minegumo*, approaching on a reciprocal course. When the range had closed to ten thousand yards, Merrill gave the order to open fire. The tactic worked perfectly; the Japanese were completely surprised, and both destroyers were sunk in thirteen minutes. Coordinating with the cruiser gunfire and under supervision from Commander Burke, *Waller* made a successful torpedo attack. Afterward, Merrill and his task force carried out the bombardment mission.

Two of Merrill's three cruisers—*Montpelier* and *Denver*—were equipped with the latest fire-control radar, the FH, or Mark 8. This radar had an innovative display, the B-scope, which made spotting much easier. After the battle, Merrill praised the effectiveness of the Mark 8 and recommended the installation of a second SG radar set in all ships. He spoke directly to the problem the CIC was intended to solve: "The Task Force Commander must know accurately the positions of all his ships. If he doesn't, he must hesitate long enough to establish these positions after contact is made lest he fire on his own forces. If he hesitates he may lose the important advantage of firing first."[12] Merrill had been fortunate to surprise the Japanese destroyers; Ainsworth would not be so lucky.

The ease with which *Murasame* and *Minegumo* were sunk masked the changing nature of Japanese tactics. The Japanese had shifted away from gunfire; instead, they now relied on stealth and their powerful torpedoes. Ainsworth's battle plans, issued on 16 March, incorporated what he believed were the salient lessons to date. They emphasized obtaining an "initial superiority of fire by opening fire first and at ranges beyond sight contact" using radar-directed gunfire and rocking ladders.[13]

Ainsworth's plans inhibited his destroyer captains and failed to use them effectively. Capt. Francis X. McInerney, commander of Destroyer Division 21, screened Ainsworth's cruisers during the fighting in July. McInerney commented on the secondary role assigned to his ships: "The doctrine in [Ainsworth's] Task Force 18 is for the cruisers to open fire first at favorable range in radar control. Then for the destroyers to launch a torpedo attack, if directed by OTC, or at discretion of destroyer commander. . . . The destroyers are not to open with guns (unless taken under fire) until after the cruisers open up."[14]

The flaws in this approach were initially exposed the night of 4 July, when the destroyer *Strong* was lost in Kula Gulf. Several days before, on 30 June, Halsey's forces had seized four separate positions on and around the island of New Georgia. Their objective was to capture Munda.

These attacks triggered another phase of multidimensional combat as both sides sought to dominate the surrounding area. Although shaken by the loss of Admiral Yamamoto in April, the Japanese resolved to hold New Georgia. Halsey's offensive bogged down, and he sent reinforcements to Rice Anchorage inside Kula Gulf on 4 July. Ainsworth's three light cruisers and four destroyers provided cover; they also used the opportunity to bombard Vila and Bairoko Harbor.

The Japanese too sent troops to the area that night. Four destroyers under Rear Adm. Akiyama Teruo were carrying soldiers to Vila. Akiyama's flagship, *Niizuki,* had a prototype radar set that detected Ainsworth's ships as the Japanese destroyers rounded the island of Kolombangara. The Japanese abandoned their reinforcement mission and retired, launching torpedoes—unaimed "browning" shots (fired at a formation generally, rather than specific targets)—into the narrow waters of the gulf.

In the meantime, Ainsworth carried on with the bombardment, ignorant of the danger. He had sent destroyers *Nicholas* and *Strong* ahead to sweep the gulf and identify any targets. They had found nothing, and the bombardments took place as planned. As Ainsworth was turning north to retire, a torpedo hit *Strong.* It had been in the water more than half an hour. Destroyers *Chevalier* and *O'Bannon,* in the rear of Ainsworth's formation, stood by to take off survivors. The rest of his ships retired toward Guadalcanal. The sinking of *Strong* illustrated the remarkable capabilities of Japanese torpedoes, but the lesson was lost. Like his predecessors, Ainsworth assumed that Japanese torpedoes were broadly comparable to American ones and blamed a submarine.

Over the next week, Ainsworth would learn much more about Japanese torpedoes and tactics. If the Navy continued to emphasize the importance of gunfire, the Japanese had developed approaches to counter it. In the battle of Kula Gulf, fought the night of 5 July, just after the loss of *Strong,* four torpedoes hit the light cruiser *Helena* in quick succession and sank her rapidly. At the battle of Kolombangara the night of 12 July, all three of Ainsworth's remaining cruisers—*Honolulu, St. Louis,* and *Leander*—were struck by torpedoes.

The battle of Tassafaronga, the last major action off Guadalcanal, had been the first example of the IJN's new fighting style. Prior to that battle, the Japanese sent heavy ships—heavy cruisers and the occasional battleship—to bombard American installations and sink ships with gunfire. By Tassafaronga, they were limiting their task forces to destroyers and small light cruisers. These ships lacked sustained fighting power, but the Japanese adopted tactics that emphasized their strengths. Upon sighting the enemy, Japanese destroyer commanders would launch a well-aimed torpedo barrage and then turn away, covering their retirement with smoke screens. If circumstances were favorable, and if they could reload their torpedo tubes in time, these aggressive commanders would keep their ships together, return to the battle scene, and launch another volley.

These tactics were very effective against Ainsworth, particularly when the Japanese could mitigate the advantage of American radar. At Kula Gulf, Ainsworth faced Akiyama again. *Niizuki*'s radar allowed early detection of Ainsworth's formation but did not provide sufficient resolution for targeting. *Niizuki* would be sunk in the battle and Akiyama killed. At Kolombangara, Rear Adm. Izaki Shunji employed a radar-detecting device in the light cruiser *Jintsu*. He plotted the approach of Ainsworth's ships for almost two hours before the battle began. These new devices allowed the Japanese to anticipate American attacks and fire their torpedoes once the Americans gave away their position by opening fire. If visibility conditions were good, they could launch their torpedoes even earlier.

Kula Gulf and Kolombangara both took predictable courses. The new Japanese devices detected the presence of American ships. SG radars located the Japanese, and newly established CIC organizations provided an effective picture of the relative positions of the opposing forces. However, once the firing started, actions quickly became confused. Each time, the initial American salvoes overwhelmed the Japanese ship that presented the best radar target. At Kula Gulf, it was *Niizuki*, fatally damaged before she could even launch torpedoes. At Kolombangara, it was *Jintsu*. From then on, firing was largely ineffective; hits were scored but no other ships were sunk.[15] The Japanese quickly recovered, fired their torpedoes, and vanished from sight. In the heat and confusion of battle, they would often disappear from the radar as well.

Unlike Merrill's cruisers, some of which had the latest Mark 8 fire-control radars, Ainsworth's ships were still equipped with the FC and its limited display, the A-scope. Gunners using the A-scope often lost their targets because existing tactics emphasized firing continuously, rather than in salvoes. Each gun would fire as soon as it was ready, without waiting for the others. To spot effectively using the A-scope, the display had to be restricted to a relatively narrow band. Rather than seeing the full spectrum of the radar search, the operator might see just a few thousand yards. Within that narrow band, each shell that hit the water around the target kicked up a splash. The splashes appeared on the radar screen, obscuring the return signal coming from the target. Since there was no pause in firing, it became very difficult to track the target. If it maneuvered, it would often slip outside the narrow band of the display. When the firing ceased and the target was gone, it was invariably considered "sunk."

Ainsworth fell victim to these optimistic reports. He insisted after Kula Gulf that the closest group of Japanese ships had been "practically obliterated by the tremendous volume of fire" of his cruisers.[16] In fact, only *Niizuki* had been lost. Her two consorts had been practically undamaged, and their torpedoes had been in the water less than a minute after the opening salvo. *Helena* presented their best target; she had used up all her flashless powder during the previous night's bombardment and was firing continuously—"a good point of aim for the launching of torpedoes." Four of them struck the cruiser.[17] One was a dud; the other three tore her apart.

This basic pattern was repeated a week later at Kolombangara. Before opening fire, Ainsworth detached Captain McInerney, in command of the van destroyers, to allow his ships to close for a torpedo attack. Rear Admiral Izaki tracked the developing action on board *Jintsu*, taking full advantage of her radar detector and the sharp eyes of her lookouts. He launched a salvo of torpedoes at Ainsworth's cruisers just before McInerney's destroyers could fire theirs and then illuminated the American destroyers with searchlights.

Ainsworth's cruisers opened fire less than a minute later, at the range of ten thousand yards. *Jintsu* was "smothered" by their 6-inch shells. Ainsworth thought he had damaged more: "At the end of five minutes of fire . . . the three leading enemy ships were smoking, burning, and practically dead in the water."[18] Ainsworth reversed course, his standard doctrine for avoiding torpedoes, but they were already among his ships. *Leander* was hit; the destroyers *Radford* and *Jenkins* dodged others.

In the meantime, the unscathed Japanese destroyers regrouped. Under the leadership of Capt. Yoshima Shimai in *Yukikaze*, they had withdrawn to the cover of a rain squall and were busy reloading their torpedo tubes. They completed this in eighteen minutes and then headed toward Ainsworth's cruisers.

After his turn, Ainsworth and *Honolulu*'s CIC lost track of McInerney's ships. They had continued to the west after their torpedo attack and now were heading back, toward the crippled *Leander*. But Ainsworth was ignorant of this. As he turned to pursue the expected enemy cripples, a group of ships appeared at 23,000 yards on the SG radar. He called it a "confusing picture." Not sure if they were McInerney's destroyers, Ainsworth illuminated the contact with star shells; eight minutes after the contact was made, he finally gave the order to open fire. It was too late. Yoshima had executed a perfect torpedo attack. *St. Louis* was hit before she could open fire. *Honolulu* and the destroyer *Gwin* were also torpedoed. Yoshima retired unscathed.

The battle exposed the weaknesses of existing CIC procedures. If *Honolulu*'s CIC had kept track of the van destroyers, Yoshima's approach would have been correctly identified as a threat. Ainsworth's comments in his action report place blame on *Honolulu*'s CIC, its layout and the speed with which it processed information.

The second phase of this engagement is demonstrative proof to this Task Force Commander of the fallacy of placing the CIC below decks where telephone communications with any of the radar operators or DRT plotters would be necessary. In this instance we were not fast enough to keep up with the developments of a very critical situation, even with all the instruments before us. Innumerable times during these night battles the OTC got the immediate information he needed by looking over the radar operator's shoulder [apparently in or near the pilothouse] and directing him to train on a certain contact.[19]

The concerns about speed could be addressed by collocating the radar displays with the plots inside the CIC; this was being done. However, a larger problem was Ainsworth's reliance on his personal view of the PPI rather than on a collective assessment of all available information. A Royal Navy officer who observed Ainsworth's performance in the battle argued that his habit of directing the radar operator where to train was "a contributory cause for the failure to immediately identify the second enemy group [Yoshima's destroyers] as hostile" and that the losses from Japanese torpedoes could be "directly attributed to the reliance on one radar set" rather than an efficient CIC.[20] For commanders to become more confident in their CICs, the men manning them had to become more effective at storing, tracking, and making sense of all available information. More practice was needed with the CIC to perfect it. After Kolombangara, Ainsworth's TF 36.1 had run out of cruisers. His comments after these actions note his superiority of gunfire but also point to the solution the Navy would need to overcome the new Japanese tactics: "It is very evident that we have much to learn from them about effective torpedo fire, especially at night. Just the opposite should be the case inasmuch as our radar control of torpedo fire should give us . . . superiority in handling this essential weapon."[21]

Within a month, American destroyers would demonstrate what was possible. The essential ingredients for a new approach were already in place. Destroyer formations were being kept together longer, allowing them to develop effective tactics and doctrine. They had operated independently from the cruisers in the July battles, giving them practice working as teams with their guns and torpedoes.[22] Most importantly, effective CICs were giving them the ability to coordinate their actions at night. All that was needed was an opportunity to use their torpedoes as the primary weapon.

INSTITUTIONALIZING THE CIC

As ships in the combat zone began to create CICs, they reported on their experiences in action reports and other communications. These were analyzed by Nimitz and his staff, who distributed relevant lessons to the fleet. *Confidential Memorandum 2CM-43* included lessons from Wylie's experience on board *Fletcher*. CINCPAC cited it as "an excellent example . . . of the coordination which should result from a properly organized [CIC]."[23]

The Pacific Fleet's type commands gathered additional lessons and developed processes to exploit them. Rear Adm. Mahlon S. Tisdale became Nimitz's destroyer commander in early 1943. He devoted a significant amount of time and attention to the CIC; installing and manning it was challenging for smaller ships because of their limited space and small crews. Tisdale had seen combat in the battles of the Eastern Solomons, Santa Cruz, and Tassafaronga and was acutely aware of the need for more effective coordination.

Tisdale selected talented junior officers to assist him. Caleb B. Laning focused on the "development of improved communication systems." Wylie's "excellent example" made him an obvious choice; he joined Tisdale's command after Tassafaronga. Laning and Wylie worked together to draft plans for optimal CIC arrangements. They divided it into four parts. Data-capture mechanisms—radar displays and sonar scopes—went aft, and the plots used to make sense of the situation were placed forward. Port and starboard divisions separated aerial contacts from surface and submarine ones.[24]

In June 1943, Tisdale issued a new manual incorporating his staff's preliminary ideas on the CIC. Called *CIC Handbook for Destroyers*, the manual succinctly stated the purpose of the CIC and acknowledged that it was a distinct departure from prior approaches: "The Combat Information Center is . . . an agency for the collection, evaluation and distribution of combat information, and an agency for facilitating the use of that information. It is not . . . merely a radar plot or an antisubmarine plot under a new name." The manual also stressed the important relationship of the CIC to the ship's command function: "The object of the Combat Information Center is to assist the Command in planning a correct course of action, and to assist the Command and weapon-control in execution of that plan." The CIC was expected to "simplify" the work of commanding the ship.[25]

After issuing the *Handbook,* Tisdale sent Wylie back to the combat zone. Wylie established a school on Espiritu Santo, near Halsey's headquarters. The school had a group of instructors fresh from combat; they shared their lessons with newly arriving ships.[26] In concept, Wylie's school was like the destroyer staff colleges created by Rear Admiral Plunkett and Captain Pratt after World War I; it was a way to learn directly from combat experience and help new ships and their officers become familiar with the CIC. Although effective, Wylie's school was an interim solution, a rudimentary beginning for a much more sophisticated system of learning.

Vice Admiral Lee, commander of the Pacific Fleet's battleships, paralleled Tisdale's approach. Lee issued a tentative doctrine for the employment of battleship CICs in June 1944. However, because battleships served different roles and had significantly different capabilities, Lee took a different approach to CIC organization. Tisdale built on Wylie's experience and specified that for destroyers the evaluator should be the executive officer. On board battleships, the executive officer already had a specific and well-defined role; he manned the secondary conning station, ready to assume command in case of damage to the primary. Lee specified that the evaluator on a battleship had to be one of the other officers, but captains had the freedom to pick whomever they felt would be best at the job.[27]

Lee also chose to place the battleship CIC within the battleship's Gunnery Department. There was good reason for this. A battleship's main function in combat was to bring its heavy guns to bear. The new battleships that joined the fleet immediately before and during the war could fire accurately at ranges approaching the maximum radar detection range. This meant that targets could be engaged almost as soon as they were located. For battleships, it was essential that the CIC and the Gunnery Department operate in complete harmony, so that no time was wasted bringing the ship's guns on target.[28]

Lee, Tisdale, and Nimitz all stressed the critical need to rapidly integrate the lessons of combat into tactical doctrine.[29] As experience was gained with the CIC, ships sent back their lessons and assessments for analysis. The lessons were incorporated into bulletins and updated manuals that covered a wide variety of topics, including the layout of the CIC, best practice for the installation of telephone leads, effective lighting to maximize the usefulness of radar displays, and the limitations of search radars.[30]

EVOLUTIONARY TACTICS: JULY–OCTOBER 1943

With Ainsworth's force out of commission, Halsey had just one cruiser-destroyer task force remaining. Rear Admiral Merrill's ships could not be everywhere; alternative means of keeping pressure on the Japanese had to be found. A fortuitous change occurred on 15 July, when Rear Adm. Theodore S. Wilkinson relieved Rear Adm. Richmond K. Turner as commander of TF 31, Halsey's amphibious force. Wilkinson was a former destroyer captain, and he had new ideas about how to fight the Japanese at night. On 19 July, Wilkinson put Commander Burke, then commander of Destroyer Division 44, in charge of TG 31.2 and made him responsible for destroyers in the Solomons. Burke had devoted serious attention to the problem of how best to attack with destroyer torpedoes and had developed new tactics to exploit the capabilities of his ships.

Burke recognized that the most effective way to concentrate the firepower of destroyers at night was to divide them into two divisions. Each would maneuver separately to provide mutual support. While one closed the range for a torpedo attack, the second would remain more distant, ready to open fire immediately if the approach of the first division was detected.[31] Burke's doctrine evoked the "destroyer attack units" used before the war in the night search and attack:

> One division would slip in close, under cover of darkness, launch torpedoes, and duck back out. When the torpedoes hit, and the enemy started shooting at the retiring first division, the second half of the team would suddenly open up from another direction. When the rattled enemy turned towards this new and unexpected attack, the first division would slam back in again. Of course, the

Solomon Islands area was ideally suited to this type of tactic, with the many islands helping prevent radar detection of the second column.[32]

Burke took six destroyers north of Kula Gulf the night of 1–2 August, and was ready to employ his tactics, but his ships failed to make contact with Vice Adm. Samejima Tomoshige's supply run to Vila.[33] On 3 August, Cdr. Frederick Moosbrugger arrived at Tulagi to assume command of TG 31.2. Burke moved on to command Destroyer Squadron 12. Just two days later, Wilkinson, suspecting that the Japanese would make another reinforcement mission on the night of 6 August, ordered Moosbrugger to take his destroyers, sweep Vella Gulf, and "destroy any enemy cruisers, destroyers, or landing barges encountered."[34]

Moosbrugger had little time to prepare for battle. After receiving his orders on the morning of 5 August, he met with his second in command, Cdr. Roger W. Simpson. Simpson introduced Moosbrugger to Burke's tactical concepts. Moosbrugger readily adopted the basic ideas and incorporated them into a specific battle plan for the following evening.[35] Following Burke's doctrine, Moosbrugger divided his ships into two divisions of three; he commanded the first and Simpson the second. Moosbrugger's division had more torpedoes—*Craven* and *Maury* had sixteen and *Dunlap* twelve—while Simpson's ships had each traded a torpedo mount for 40-mm guns, the preferred weapon against barges. The two men adopted a task-force formation that recognized these strengths, with Moosbrugger's division in the lead and Simpson's closer to the shore, where barges (carrying supplies and troops between points ashore) were more likely to be found.

Later that morning, Moosbrugger and Simpson held a conference with all commanding officers to review the plan and go over details. This approach harked back to the original destroyer tactics developed by Admiral Sims almost thirty years before. It was a proven method, and Simpson later credited it for the success that followed: "The complete understanding of all possible situations to be encountered by the Division Commanders and Commanding Officers is largely responsible for the success achieved. Each knew what he was supposed to do and capably carried it out."[36]

But the role of Burke's doctrine should not be diminished. The use of two coordinated divisions and reliance on the torpedo was a breakthrough. Moosbrugger's division made full use of radar and an effective CIC organization to arrive at a favorable launching point, while Simpson's group covered its approach from longer range, ready to open fire immediately. Although divided attack formations had been employed before the war, this was the first time they were used effectively in the Solomons. The plan, which emphasized torpedoes as the "primary weapon," worked perfectly.[37]

The victims were three of Capt. Sugiura Kaju's destroyers, *Hagikaze*, *Arashi*, and *Kawakaze*. *Shigure*, the fourth destroyer in line, barely escaped; a torpedo passed through her rudder without exploding. Unlike Admirals Akiyama and Izaki, Sugiura lacked any early warning devices. He had to rely on the skills of his lookouts, and it was an exceptionally dark night. By the time the lookouts gave warning of Moosbrugger's destroyers, the first salvo of torpedoes was already on the way. Sugiura's formation was destroyed before he could react.

The coordinated attack would have been impossible without the CIC. Lt. Cdr. F. T. Williamson, commanding officer of the destroyer *Craven*, later remarked on the effectiveness of his ship's organization:

> [CIC] functioned smoothly and was able to furnish valuable information to gunnery and torpedo control and . . . the commanding officer in addition to navigating the restricted waters of Gizo Strait. The Executive Officer [acting as the evaluator] was . . . able to identify navigational landmarks, evaluate contacts, disseminate information to control stations, and keep the Captain advised at all times, thereby leaving the Captain free to conn the ship and make necessary decisions without being burdened with countless details.[38]

Although the aggressive use of destroyers had been an essential feature of the Navy's prewar doctrine, numerous factors had prevented their effective employment before Vella Gulf. The lack of time for effective indoctrination, an emphasis on the use of gunfire, and limited formation cohesion had all inhibited the use of destroyer torpedoes. Burke,

Moosbrugger, and Simpson transformed the situation and used the emerging capabilities of the CIC to reintroduce an approach grounded in aggressive prewar concepts.

The victory at Vella Gulf was important for another reason as well. It demonstrated that a resilient officer network was emerging in the combat zone. Officers were sharing lessons better, learning from each other more readily, and refining their skills more rapidly. Stable formations and more regular conferences allowed the collaborative development of new approaches that capitalized on the lessons promulgated by Nimitz and his type commands. Moosbrugger benefitted significantly from this emerging system; he would not have been able to capitalize on Burke's tactical ideas without it.

This was very different from the situation a year before when Rear Admiral Wright assumed command of TF 67 and took it into battle at Tassafaronga. Although Rear Admiral Kinkaid had left a well-considered plan, Wright was unable to make the most of it. He lacked faith in the skills and abilities of his subordinates and hesitated at a critical moment. The increased cohesion in Burke's TG 31.2 prevented a similar failure at Vella Gulf. Moosbrugger and his colleagues were demonstrating how the Navy's learning system could foster the introduction of new methods and techniques without relying on centralized control. The Navy's approach to decentralized doctrinal development was allowing it to adjust to combat lessons faster than the Japanese.[39]

FORMALIZING THE CIC

Following the model of the early interwar period, schools were established to promote and promulgate the new CIC doctrine. One of the most important of these was the Pacific Fleet Radar Center, which started operating in early 1943 at Camp Catlin, just north of Pearl Harbor. Because the CIC introduced a new approach to managing shipboard information, existing training organizations had to be restructured to support the new paradigm. The Radar Center was created to meet this need; its charter was to "centralize administration and furnish proper coordination among all schools which deal with the operation and tactical use of radar."[40] The most sophisticated training was provided at the Fighter Director and Combat Information Center School.

Training at the Fighter Director and Combat Information Center School was rigorous. The curriculum provided the necessary skills and experience to organize and train a CIC combat team; attendees were expected to bring their ships up to the current standard, not just improve their individual performance. It was difficult to get in; the school restricted attendance to those who had demonstrated the necessary ability. It was even more difficult to graduate. Less than 75 percent completed the course, too few to satisfy the demands of the ever-growing fleet.[41]

Cdr. John H. "Jack" Griffin oversaw the school. He adjusted its approach by increasing the flexibility of course offerings. The existing six-week course on CIC indoctrination was broken into three separate courses that could be taken in any order. More advanced courses were augmented with studies of recent action reports. Three additional courses were added for team training; these used mock CICs to exercise actual teams under simulated combat conditions. The more flexible curriculum, combined with the ability to take in a new class every week, expanded the influence of the school and gave the fleet more trained CIC personnel.[42]

Instructors at these schools had experience using the CIC in combat; the curriculum was interactive and stressed the need for continual learning. Students were expected to bring lessons from their own experiences to improve the class content.

> During the period that the Captains and Executive Officers are here at the Training Station, we are going to make an attempt to give you as much instruction in the CIC as possible and, if practicable, supplement it with some instruction in tactics. . . . The purpose of this course is to provide a systematic survey of the entire field [of the CIC] in order to fill up gaps in your previous experience. It is based upon all material we can get and is subject to continuous revision.[43]

Training provided a solid foundation, but CIC procedures were continually refined in the combat zone. Initially, the CIC was used only to assess and evaluate information; it was not integrated into the command function. But as ships gained experience, they discovered the advantages of using the CIC to augment command responsibilities. Eventually, fleet doctrinal publications caught up with this idea, but not before it had already been integrated into shipboard procedures.

The best example was the method developed to fight off night attacks by torpedo planes. Japanese tactics exploited the limitations of search radars and delays in ship command structures. Torpedo planes would orbit just beyond gunnery range, waiting for an opportunity. At the chosen moment, an individual plane would leave the formation and attack without warning. It was difficult to detect the approach of a single plane with the low-resolution search radars, and once an aircraft started its attack run, there were only a few moments before it reached the launch point. Experienced ships quickly learned that there wasn't enough time to relay information to the captain; they had their CICs direct the guns onto the target and give the order to open fire. The CIC became an integral part of the ship's command function.[44]

New manuals and training materials codified the approach in 1944. At the same time, new standards were being established for the organization of the CIC and its internal communications. Sufficient experience had been gained to reduce the variability within the fleet. Nimitz and his staff shifted from an experimental view—which explored alternatives to find the best solution—to an implementation one. They began to standardize CIC processes.

Instructions from CINCPAC and the type commands illustrated this. The CIC was given a standard name; it became simply "Combat" in shipboard communications. Surface contacts were designated with letters, such as "Raid A," "Raid B," to distinguish them from air contacts which were tracked by number, "Raid 1" or "Raid 2."[45] As "raids" broke up into discrete formations, the latter were given additional subscript designators; surface contacts were given a subscript number, such as "Raid A_1" or "Raid A_2." Air contacts were given a letter, "Raid 1_A" and "Raid 1_B." The standardization of vocabulary ensured consistency from ship to ship and made it easier to share information between ships more efficiently. It represented a new level of constraint and a correspondingly increased level of complexity.

To promote the fleet-wide doctrine further, OPNAV began to issue a monthly CIC magazine that covered a variety of topics. Some of the most common were the characteristics of different radars, example layouts of CICs, capabilities of enemy equipment, potential enemy countermeasures, and the use of fire-control radars for spotting and shore bombardment. In contrast to earlier publications, the magazines made effective use of graphics, pictures, and other visual aids to familiarize readers quickly with the content and improve their retention of it.[46]

In the last year of war, the Navy began to integrate the CIC with task-force operations. The CIC had proved its ability to help ships and task groups make sense of their circumstances; large task forces had the same challenges, and task-force commanders began to create integrated CIC networks to enhance their own ability to command their forces. A 1945 tactical manual stated the goal: "It is essential that the CICs in individual ships be interrelated in their specific duties to such an extent that the Task Force's radars and other information gathering sources are integrated into an efficient whole."[47]

The task-force CIC introduced a new level of specialization. Specific CIC-related responsibilities were divided among ships so that tasks could be effectively shared. One ship—generally the flagship—was designated the primary CIC for the entire formation. Other ships were given supporting roles, such as fighter direction, air search, surface search, radar picket duty, interception, and jamming. Depending on the size of the formation and its organization, these responsibilities might be allocated to single ships or to multiple ones. Their reports rolled up to the primary CIC ship, providing a comprehensive picture for the formation commander.

New vocabulary was introduced to allow more effective communication between ships of the task force and "abbreviate the flow of information and orders."[48] Specific terms were identified to communicate radar information more rapidly. An order to "*report*," for example, meant that the designated ship was to provide regular updates regarding the range and bearing of a specific contact; air contacts would be reported on every minute and surface contacts every three minutes. Additional terms were used to share information and transfer responsibilities between ships. Specific radio frequencies were designated for particular types of information, not unlike the dedicated communication circuits within the ships.

This increased level of specialization and the new vocabulary collectively represented another level of contextual constraint. New roles for the individuals operating in the CIC had increased specialization, triggering greater complexity and increasing the ability to process information in a timely manner. Similarly, increasingly specialized roles for ships within task forces created capabilities for the entire formation, allowing its commander to develop a better picture of the combat environment. These approaches were starting to be integrated into the fleet as the war was ending in 1945.

VELLA LAVELLA

The Japanese would achieve one more victory in the Solomons before the Pacific Fleet's revolutionary changes—the CIC and learning system supporting it—fully took hold. The next island confronting Halsey's advance was Kolombangara. The Japanese, anticipating he would move step by step, had reinforced it. To accelerate the advance and keep the Japanese off balance, Nimitz recommended on 11 July 1943 that Halsey bypass Kolombangara and land on Vella Lavella, fifteen miles to the northwest. The forces on Kolombangara could be isolated and left to "wither on the vine."

Rear Admiral Wilkinson was eager to seize the opportunity and bypass Japanese strongpoints. He created a plan to seize Vella Lavella, build an airfield on it, and isolate Kolombangara. On 15 August, a small invasion force landed at Barakoma, on the southeastern side of the island. In response, the Japanese began to evacuate Kolombangara, pulling their forces back to strengthen the defenses of Bougainville, the last major obstacle between Halsey and Rabaul. To support the withdrawal, they decided to establish a staging base at Horaniu, on the northeastern part of Vella Lavella.

On 17 August, Rear Adm. Ijuin Matsuji and his four destroyers escorted a convoy of barges to Horaniu. They were sighted during their approach, and four destroyers under Capt. Thomas J. Ryan were sent to intercept. Ryan tried to emulate Moosbrugger's tactics by withholding fire until after launching his torpedoes, but flares and bombs from

Japanese planes spoiled his surprise. In a running battle, he scored a few 5-inch hits on Ijuin's ships and forced them to retire but was unable to sink enough barges to foil Japanese plans. With the base established, the Japanese prepared for the evacuation of Kolombangara.

Wilkinson tried to interfere. He sent Rear Admiral Merrill's cruiser-destroyer force into the narrow waters on five consecutive nights, starting on 22 September. Consistently harassed by Japanese planes, they found no worthwhile targets. After *Columbia* was nearly torpedoed by a submarine the night of the twenty-sixth, Wilkinson decided to stop risking his cruisers. With the fighter airfield at Barakoma now operational, American planes could patrol the waters off Kolombangara by day and destroyers by night.

For five straight nights starting on 27 September, the Japanese evacuated their garrison. Wilkinson's destroyers intervened on four of those nights, but the barges proved difficult targets, and Rear Admiral Ijuin's destroyers did their best to avoid action. The American blockade was porous; 9,400 men were successfully retrieved from Kolombangara.[49] Ultimately, the last troops remaining were those manning the base at Horaniu. On the night of 6 October, Ijuin came to get them. He had a large force: six destroyers provided cover for three transport destroyers and several smaller craft. Rear Admiral Wilkinson learned of their approach that morning but had limited forces available to intervene. He sent three destroyers under Capt. Frank Walker: *Selfridge*, *Chevalier*, and *O'Bannon*. To make the odds more equal, Wilkinson arranged a rendezvous with three other destroyers diverted from convoy duty, but Walker encountered Ijuin before they could join him.

The night was relatively clear, and Japanese aircraft harassed Walker's destroyers as they approached. The planes misidentified the American forces and gave Ijuin the impression he was facing a mixed cruiser-destroyer force. Assuming he was outgunned, the Japanese admiral approached the engagement cautiously. Walker's attitude was very different. He embraced the Navy's aggressive doctrine and, even though he was outnumbered, closed with his opponent. In his action report, he noted that "the enemy's initial movement indicated a hasty retirement to which I gave chase."[50] One of *Chevalier*'s crew described his feelings: "We were going in . . . though it looked like a suicide mission. Navy skippers were fire-eaters. They wouldn't back down . . . regardless of odds."[51]

Good visibility negated Walker's radar advantage; Ijuin's ships sighted his formation at about 20,000 yards. They set up for a torpedo attack, but having mistaken Walker's ships for cruisers, Ijuin now misjudged the range. SG radars on Walker's ships detected Ijuin's separated formations at 19,500 yards, and CICs tracked them accurately during the approach. Walker intended to engage with gunfire at long range, but Ijuin presented good torpedo targets, so he kept his guns quiet; Walker launched torpedoes when the range reached seven thousand yards. Twenty seconds later, he opened fire. Ijuin quickly followed suit with both guns and torpedoes.

The American gunnery was superior. The destroyer *Yugumo* was the closest target. Under concentrated fire, she lost steering control; a torpedo hit sank her. However, the effectiveness of Japanese torpedoes was undiminished. *Chevalier* was disabled and would later sink; after the hit, the aft part of the ship veered into the path of *O'Bannon*, the next ship astern. Radical maneuvers were not enough to avoid a collision, and *O'Bannon* was out of the battle with severe damage to her bow. *Selfridge* continued the fight alone until Ijuin's second division hit her with a torpedo from long range. The battle ended when Ijuin, notified by friendly planes of the approach of the three additional American destroyers, withdrew. In the confusion after the action, and during the Americans' struggle to keep *O'Bannon* and *Selfridge* afloat, the Japanese successfully evacuated their troops from Vella Lavella.

Although a defeat for the Navy, the battle marked a significant transition. Fatigued by frequent missions to Vella Lavella and Kolombangara, Rear Admiral Ijuin had displayed none of the aggressiveness of his predecessors. In this battle and on earlier nights, he tried to avoid action. Walker, confident in his radars, the CICs that made them effective, and the skills of his team, aggressively sought battle. Wilkinson praised Walker's leadership: "His decision to take advantage of a favorable torpedo opportunity, even though involving a close range engagement with superior numbers, was sound and evidenced his fighting spirit."[52]

The benefits of the resilient officer network were again apparent. Walker had lacked time to familiarize himself with most of his force. He had operated with *Chevalier* and *O'Bannon* only once, the night before the action, and had time for only "one five minute conference" to familiarize himself with these ships and their captains.[53] It was sufficient to ensure effective coordination. Walker considered "the actions and cooperation of these ships . . . most excellent at all times."[54]

Vella Lavella would be the last Japanese victory in surface combat during the war. From this moment forward, the increasing capabilities of the CIC, the greater cohesion of American forces, and the Navy's new tactical approaches would enable a superior level of performance. A month later, during the invasion of Bougainville, these factors would lead to a clear victory.

THE VERGE OF REVOLUTION: NOVEMBER 1943

The ultimate objective envisioned in the plans for Operation Watchtower—the invasion of Guadalcanal—was the base at Rabaul. The Allies were nearing their goal; Gen. Douglas MacArthur was advancing along the coast of New Guinea, and Halsey was continuing to make progress in the Solomons. Instead of assaulting the base directly, the Allies would isolate Rabaul and reduce it through airpower. Halsey was ordered to seize a portion of the large island of Bougainville for airfields that would keep Rabaul under pressure. The spot selected for the invasion was the weakly defended Empress Augusta Bay.

By the eve of the invasion, however, the broader strategic context had begun to shift. After the death of Admiral Yamamoto in April, Adm. Koga Mineichi had been appointed commander in chief of the Combined Fleet. He was convinced of the need to win a decisive battle over the Pacific Fleet in 1943, before the preponderance of American material made such a victory more difficult. Koga held his fleet at Truk, in the Caroline Islands, waiting for Nimitz to begin his anticipated offensive in the Central Pacific. When it had not developed by late October, Koga sent his carrier air groups to Rabaul to fend off Allied advances in the south. Koga's pilots encountered stiff opposition from MacArthur's and Halsey's aviators; the Japanese were unable to disrupt the invasion of Bougainville from the air.

Rear Admiral Merrill's TF 39 figured prominently in the effort to seize Empress Augusta Bay. He had the cruisers *Montpelier*, *Cleveland*, *Columbia*, and *Denver*, along with Destroyer Squadron 23, now commanded by Captain Burke, who had returned to the combat zone. As a prelude to the invasion, Halsey sent Merrill to bombard nearby Japanese airfields on the night of 31 October. Shortly after midnight, the cruisers struck the airfields at Buka and Bonis, at the northern tip of Bougainville. Then they headed south to strike targets in the Shortlands just before the sun came up. Later that day, transports steamed in to Empress Augusta Bay, and the invasion began.

Merrill's cruisers were well suited to these operations. As mentioned earlier, the new Mark 8 radar and its B-scope significantly improved the accuracy of the guns of *Montpelier* and *Denver*. *Cleveland* and *Columbia* were still equipped with FC radars and suffered from the associated limitations. The B-scope gave fire-control spotters something akin to the PPI. It was a dramatic improvement over the A-scope's more limited display. The A-scope was particularly problematic because of the emphasis on continuous fire. The Navy's modern 6-inch cruisers, starting with the ships of the *Brooklyn* class, had been designed to protect the battle fleet from destroyer attack. Their guns had an extremely high rate of fire, and in daylight, the standard procedure was to fire them continuously, as fast as they became available after each round. At night, predictable salvoes had been fired to allow effective observation of the target, but when radar became widely available, the procedure changed. Firing salvoes meant waiting and delay. Since radar permitted continual "observation" of the target, most 6-inch cruisers shifted to continuous fire at night as well. As we have seen, this was problematic; targets were lost among the return echoes from shell splashes, and although cruisers fired hundreds of shells, most of their targets escaped unscathed.

The B-scope offered a solution to the problems encountered with the A-scope. It displayed a top-down view, like the PPI, but instead of being centered on the radar, it was centered on the target. An operator using a B-scope would see his target as a pip in the center of his display, and then around his target the splashes of the shells as smaller pips.

The B-scope was an attempt to provide a perfect and unobstructed spotting view. It was extremely effective.

The cruiser *Montpelier* was Merrill's flagship and one of the first ships equipped with the Mark 8. After she participated in the sinking of *Murasame* and *Minegumo*, Merrill offered the following comments on the system's advantages:

> As soon as the director was trained to the bearing, the enemy ships were picked up on B scan. . . . Both ships were readily distinguishable and the spotter was quickly able to determine his normal target. . . . All splashes gave definite visible evidence on the screen. As suspected, the presence of a target on the screen greatly improved the spotting performance. . . . [A]s a result of this action and subsequent bombardment, the FH [Mark 8] Radar has been definitely established as greatly superior to any other type of fire control radar in the South Pacific Area.[55]

The B-scope was the final major enhancement of the Navy's gunnery system, a marriage of new technology with the traditional spotting approach in an extremely advanced display. It was a dramatic enhancement that integrated perfectly with the existing system, augmenting and at times replacing visual spotting—the outermost feedback loop of the fire-control system. With the B-scope, spotters no longer had to rely on visually observing the target and the splashes around it. They could see all those things clearly enough through the power of their new radar display. As newer, more powerful fire-control radars were produced, they too employed the B-scope.

When word of the landing at Empress Augusta Bay reached Rabaul during the morning of 1 November, Rear Adm. Omori Sentaro was ordered to attack and break up the American amphibious forces. He had a powerful task force, with the heavy cruisers *Myoko* and *Haguro*, light cruisers *Sendai* and *Agano*, and six destroyers. As Omori proceeded toward the bay at high speed, Halsey sent Rear Admiral Merrill's TF 39 to intercept.

Like Callaghan's force a year earlier, Omori's formation was a "scratch team," thrown together with ships that were available. He had little time to develop a plan for his attack. Merrill, in contrast, had developed a specific plan and familiarized his subordinates with it in conference; everyone "knew the method of attack that would be used."[56] The Navy's resilient network was working, while the established organization of Japanese forces was breaking down; this conjunction would have predictable results.

Merrill's plan reflected the fact that Nimitz's impending Central Pacific offensive had first priority for surface combatants, leaving few for the South Pacific. It was important that Merrill preserve his cruisers. Having learned from Rear Admiral Ainsworth's defeats in July, Merrill planned to keep his cruisers "at ranges close to the maximum enemy torpedo range" and make frequent changes of course to minimize their danger.[57]

> As our four cruisers constituted the principal surface strength left in the South Pacific area to cover planned landing operations from night raids by enemy surface forces, the Task Force Commander felt that he should take every precaution against getting these ships torpedoed. In this particular instance he considered it more important that he decisively defeat the enemy, retaining his force in condition to fight again tomorrow night than to annihilate him at the expense of having several of his own cruisers out of action.[58]

This plan would keep the cruisers relatively safe but reduce the effectiveness of their fire. As revolutionary as the Mark 8 radar and B-scope were, they were unable to spot 6-inch gunfire effectively beyond about 18,000 yards, the maximum range at which the radar returns from the shell splashes could be detected. Ships with FC radars were even less well equipped to fire accurately at long range. To compensate, Merrill had them practice radar-controlled shooting at long ranges during the day. He also had his ships fire deliberate salvoes, rather than continuous fire, to make radar spotting more effective. He felt they were accurate enough, but without the ability to correct their fire by spotting, their effectiveness was limited.

To offset this limitation and make the maximum use of his firepower, Merrill built on Burke's work and stressed the aggressive use

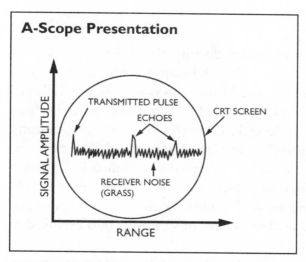

A-Scope Presentation

SIGNAL AMPLITUDE

TRANSMITTED PULSE

ECHOES

CRT SCREEN

RECEIVER NOISE
(GRASS)

RANGE

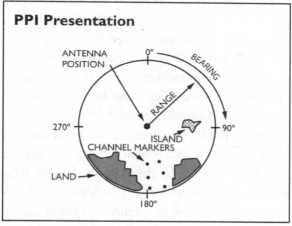

PPI Presentation

ANTENNA
POSITION

0°

BEARING

RANGE

270°

90°

ISLAND

CHANNEL MARKERS

LAND

180°

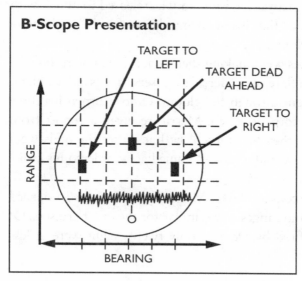

B-Scope Presentation

TARGET TO
LEFT

TARGET DEAD
AHEAD

TARGET TO
RIGHT

RANGE

O

BEARING

FIGURE 4. Radar displays. The A-scope was used with early search and fire-control radars. Starting with the SG, search radars began to use the PPI. With the introduction of the Mark 8, fire-control radars used the B-scope. Both the B-scope and PPI gave vastly superior situational awareness.

of destroyers. He promulgated a doctrine through frequent conferences and tactical exercises. Although he approached the battle area in a line—Burke with Destroyer Division 45 was in the van, followed by the cruisers, and then Cdr. Bernard L. Austin's Destroyer Division 46—Merrill planned to release the destroyers to operate independently. They would use radar to close and launch torpedoes before the cruisers opened fire. He described his doctrinal formulation in his action report: "In furtherance of this doctrine, cruisers are required to hold fire until torpedoes can arrive . . . unless the enemy opens fire or evidences having sighted us. The element of surprise is thus exploited to the fullest."[59]

A second shift had taken place over the preceding year. Gunfire, emphasized as the primary weapon after its success at Guadalcanal, had become secondary. Torpedoes, now recognized as an important weapon of stealth, would be used first. Burke explained the increasing emphasis on surprise attack: "An opportunity for surprise usually comes but once, and advantages of surprise must be taken quickly because opportunities are dissipated rapidly by delay."[60]

Omori approached in three parallel columns. Each flank column had three destroyers led by a light cruiser, *Sendai* to port and *Agano* to starboard. *Myoko* and *Haguro* were in the center. Merrill's flagship, *Montpelier*, initially detected Omori's ships at 34,800 yards. CICs gradually developed the contact into a clear picture of Omori's force and its disposition. Destroyer Division 45 was released to attack with torpedoes; it approached the closest enemy ships—*Sendai*'s column—and launched its attack unseen.

While the torpedoes were making their run, a Japanese reconnaissance plane dropped a flare over Merrill's cruisers. It was a dark night, but *Sendai* sighted them through the gloom. Omori turned his three columns to launch a torpedo salvo. Merrill received a report from *Montpelier*'s CIC that they had turned; he knew that the odds were that Burke's torpedoes would miss and immediately ordered his cruisers to open fire.

Firing ranges were consistent with Merrill's plan. *Montpelier* opened fire at 19,000 yards, and ranges were similar for the other cruisers. Of ninety-seven salvoes fired by *Denver*, only twenty-eight were at less than 20,000 yards.[61] They used salvoes, to avoid the problems of continuous fire and so aid their spotting. As had become typical in night actions, the initial target, the light cruiser *Sendai*, was quickly disabled. Two destroyers astern of her collided trying to avoid being hit. Beyond that success, gunfire proved relatively inaccurate. As Merrill's cruisers shifted their fire to Omori's heavy cruisers, a running gunnery duel developed. The Japanese outgunned Merrill's cruisers and used powerful star shells to illuminate their targets. Both sides maneuvered to throw off enemy fire; Merrill's cruisers made smoke and counter-illuminated with their own star shells to make it harder for the Japanese to observe their fire. With "spots . . . not available for the greater part of the action" and visibility limited, few hits were scored by either side.[62]

Maneuvering to avoid incoming shells, *Myoko* and the destroyer *Hatsukaze* collided; the destroyer was seriously damaged. In the meantime, Commander Austin's Destroyer Division 46 closed to attack. This was the first time these ships had an opportunity to operate together as a unit, and it showed. During Merrill's initial reversal of course, the destroyer *Foote* misinterpreted orders and got out of position. She was hit by one of the Japanese torpedoes. As the remaining three ships closed Omori's heavy cruisers, they masked the fire of Merrill's cruisers. While adjusting their courses, the destroyers *Thatcher* and *Spence* grazed each other; no immediate serious damage was done, but the collision was to have significant consequences.

Austin had been commanding his division from *Spence*'s CIC. The collision brought him to the bridge; it also knocked out the SG PPI display that was in the pilothouse.

Thus "blinded," Austin momentarily lost track of the situation. Two decks below, disoriented by the collision and without Austin's supervision, *Spence*'s CIC evaluator believed the Japanese heavy cruisers were "friendlies." A valuable opportunity to attack them at close range with torpedoes was lost. Instead, Austin's ships closed the crippled *Sendai* and attacked her with torpedoes. After the battle, Austin shifted his flag to *Converse*; her CIC was on the bridge level, allowing him to check more easily on its operations. Omori, with three of his destroyers disabled and *Sendai* crippled, withdrew. Merrill had accomplished his objectives, keeping Omori away from the transports and preserving his cruisers. In the aftermath, Burke's group finished off *Sendai*, and the two American destroyer divisions cooperated to sink the crippled *Hatsukaze*.

The victory would have been impossible without the CIC. It allowed Merrill to operate his force as three separate, coordinated groups. Previously, this would have been inconceivable at night. Merrill's captains recognized its significance; *Denver*'s action report was typical: "This engagement would not have been possible without an active, well trained Combat Information Center. It furnished tactical and gunnery information, coached directors onto targets, and served as a center for handling tactical signals. Target identification, with SC and SG radars both located in CIC, was effective and avoided the necessity of making difficult decisions on several occasions where approaching a target."[63]

Merrill's success was also aided by effective doctrine. He developed, disseminated, and familiarized his subordinates with his intended approach before the battle. Burke cited this as a major factor in the victory and highlighted the faith Merrill had in his subordinates:

> Probably there is no man placed in the responsible position of Task Force Commander who does not desire to hold a check rein. He knows that the subordinates have neither the knowledge nor the information that is available in the flagship. Yet past action in this and other wars indicates that successful actions result from the exercise of initiative by well indoctrinated subordinates. If this be true, the problem resolves itself into teaching the subordinate to react and act in situations similar to the way the Task Force Commander would in the same situations.[64]

By dispersing his ships into three groups, Merrill had concentrated the firepower of destroyers, which had to close in order to use their torpedoes, and of cruisers, which were more effective at distant ranges. Burke continued: "The success of this battle and the complete rout of a Japanese Task Force . . . is due to one man—the Task Force Commander. His success is due not only to good battle plans, sound doctrine and knowledge of his job, but even more to his aggressive spirit, his faith in the ability of his subordinates and the confidence he inspires in both his subordinates and his seniors."[65] Merrill created a shared approach to battle with his doctrine, and the plotting of the CICs created a shared view of it. The two combined to allow Merrill's forces to obtain a dramatically new level of coordination in night battle, out of the question just a year earlier.

However, additional improvements were needed. In the confused action, it had been difficult to distinguish separated groups—particularly Austin's Destroyer Division 46—from enemy forces. For a time, Burke's division had pursued Austin's group, believing it to be hostile. Identification, friend or foe (IFF) equipment had been installed to prevent such misidentification, but it was not working on Austin's ships. Had it been, this miscue would have been avoided. Future actions, like the battles in the Philippines, would benefit from these observations.

Merrill's clear victory—and preservation of his cruisers—was important. More powerful Japanese forces were on their way. When Admiral Koga heard of the landings at Empress Augusta Bay, he sent Vice Adm. Kurita Takeo to Rabaul with seven heavy cruisers of the IJN's Second Fleet. This group could have easily interfered with Halsey's plans and overwhelmed Merrill's cruisers, but a morning raid on 5 November from the carriers *Saratoga* and *Princeton* caught the ships in Rabaul's Simpson Harbor. Kurita's cruisers were damaged and unable to participate in the campaign for Bougainville.

Later that same month, the Navy's increasing capabilities were on display again. During the battle of Cape St. George on the night of 24 November, Captain Burke and Destroyer Squadron 23 intercepted a Japanese reinforcement force under Capt. Kagawa Kiyoto. Burke successfully leveraged indoctrination and the potential of the CIC to employ his signature battle plan, with two destroyer divisions acting separately to provide mutual support and come at the enemy from different directions.

The battle was triggered by Japanese attempts to reinforce Buka, near the northern tip of Bougainville, and evacuate technical aviation personnel from the air base there. Kagawa had five destroyers; three were transports, and two acted as a screen. They had completed their reinforcement mission and were heading back to Rabaul when they ran into Burke's squadron. Burke approached with his division—*Charles*

Ausburne, *Claxton*, and *Dyson*—and launched torpedoes at Kagawa's screening destroyers from six thousand yards, while Commander Austin with *Converse* and *Spence* provided cover. Kagawa sighted Burke's ships just seconds before the torpedoes arrived. Both screening destroyers were hit; *Onami* sank immediately, and *Makinami* was crippled.

Before the torpedoes struck, *Charles Ausburne*'s CIC located the Japanese transport group and Burke pursued them, leaving Austin to finish off the disabled *Makinami*. Maneuvering on a hunch, Burke fortuitously avoided Japanese torpedoes. Over the course of an hour, his ships fired at their fleeing opponents, focusing most of their fire on *Yugiri*, which presented the largest radar target. She slowed and was eventually sunk. Burke called off the pursuit as he neared New Ireland; the other two transport destroyers escaped.

Cape St. George was "almost perfect."[66] Three Japanese destroyers were sunk without any damage to Burke's ships. His victory relied heavily on the CIC and effective indoctrination. As noted in Burke's action report, "CICs performed admirably. At no time was there confusion or lack of knowledge. The battle was conducted better than most drills. The track charts [from different ships] at the end of the battle superimposed one over the other."[67]

Because this was the third consecutive night on which Burke and his squadron had attempted to intercept Japanese ships, he had not had time to discuss his plans with subordinates before the battle. He had been obliged to transmit basic instructions to his squadron via radio. But Burke's squadron had an effective doctrine to fall back on. That doctrine, along with the clear picture developed by the CICs, allowed the ships to operate as a cohesive unit in the face of the enemy. Their success was a clear indication of just how far the Navy had come over the past year.

REVOLUTIONARY TACTICS: OCTOBER 1944

A year later, the impact of the CIC had become even more decisive. The Central Pacific offensive and the battles it triggered will be examined thoroughly in the next chapter, but a brief description of the performance of Capt. Kenmore M. McManes illustrates the transformational nature of the CIC. He and his Destroyer Squadron 24 performed exceptionally at the battle of Surigao Strait the night of 24 October 1944.

Rear Adm. Jesse B. Oldendorf reacted to the approach of a powerful Japanese force by positioning his ships across the top of Surigao Strait, at the entrance to Leyte Gulf, forcing the Japanese to come to him and effectively crossing their *T*. He planned to send destroyer attack groups down the strait to harass the Japanese and attack them with torpedoes. The cruisers and battleships would remain at the top of the strait and engage from medium ranges. McManes' Destroyer Squadron 24 was one of the destroyer attack groups. Like Burke, McManes divided his force into two independent groups and counted on the CICs to prevent friendly fire. McManes was confident in his ships and their CIC organizations. During the battle, he controlled his formation from the CIC of his flagship, *Hutchins*; this gave him an "excellent picture" of the developing situation. He never had any doubt as to the identity of the ships—whether friendly or enemy—in the narrow strait.

Having precise and accurate information, McManes made a series of attacks with his destroyer groups. He sent one in to attack immediately with torpedoes while he took his own farther south to cut off the enemy's retreat. Both groups launched torpedoes using radar before the Japanese sighted them. One hit the battleship *Yamashiro* and slowed her temporarily. McManes' groups opened fire with their guns, and the Japanese became confused. They displayed recognition signals, apparently believing they were victims of friendly fire. Before retiring, McManes fired another salvo of torpedoes, sinking the destroyer *Michishio*. Without any equivalent to the CIC, the Japanese were completely outmatched. McManes observed, "The enemy was not sure where his own forces were. He was completely befuddled."[68]

The other destroyer-attack groups at Surigao performed similarly. They leveraged a clear view of the action to act aggressively and subject the Japanese column to sustained and powerful attacks. In this last great fleet battle, the CIC allowed the Navy's destroyers to attack as Sims had encouraged them to thirty years before. However, they coordinated their efforts far more effectively than Sims would have ever imagined possible, by making full use of the information their radars and CICs provided.

THE IMPORTANCE OF DESTROYERS

Two of the Navy's most revolutionary tactical developments—the surface-oriented CIC and the coordinated use of separated formations at night that it enabled—originated in destroyers. This was not an accident. Destroyers, the smallest of the Navy's major warships, had been a source of doctrinal innovation before, in the Atlantic Fleet prior to World War I. The World War II *Fletcher* class displaced less than 2,500 tons. Most of the *Fletchers*' internal volume was machinery; their decks were crowded with torpedoes, depth charges, 5-inch guns, and antiaircraft weapons. The spaces left for their crews were tiny and crowded.

These narrow spaces and the small size of the ships operated as a constraint. Unlike larger vessels, destroyer crews lacked substantial internal hierarchies or distinct organizational boundaries. Battleships and cruisers had large departments—for gunnery, engineering, navigation, etc.—with clear divisions between them. While the same basic roles existed on destroyers, the boundaries dividing them were more permeable and easier to overcome. The small size of a *Fletcher*'s wardroom (that is, its assigned officers) was more conducive to offering up and trying out new ideas.

All this was essential for the development of the CIC. The CIC was a new approach to command. It integrated existing shipboard functions in new ways and challenged established hierarchies; it created new roles. When Cole and Wylie began their experiments in November 1942, they were introducing a new paradigm. They could do it very quickly on board *Fletcher* because the pool of officers who needed to adjust their behavior and operate in the new model was small. The "retraining" required was limited.

The constrained size of destroyers was also important for the development of Burke's new model of combat. When experimenting with his destroyer division, Burke could develop new methods in his officer conferences more easily because of the relatively small size of his ships. Destroyer captains were fairly junior—a reflection of their command's size—and tended to be more flexible than their seniors. They could more easily reconfigure their mental models and adopt new tactical doctrines that made the most of their ship's capabilities.

Sims had leveraged the same environmental factors when he developed the Navy's initial destroyer doctrine in the Atlantic Fleet's Torpedo Flotilla before World War I. His "band of brothers" was formed out of enthusiastic young officers who were ready to demonstrate their talents. They pushed the limits of their ships and developed an aggressive doctrine emphasizing stealthy night torpedo attacks. They embraced innovative approaches because they were more open to new ideas and less invested in established paradigms.

In the interwar period, the Navy diverged from this approach. The emphasis on major action meant that destroyers practiced set exercises against screened formations. Gunfire became part of the script, and because the flashes of the guns would give away the location of the destroyers in any case, stealthy attacks were abandoned. Burke, using techniques similar to Sims, returned to the emphasis on independent action and, with it, stealth. He was able to make the adjustment quickly because of the specific characteristics of the Navy's destroyers.

These characteristics combined with relatively large numbers to make the destroyer force a mechanism for safe-to-fail experimentation. The Navy could afford to allow officers like Burke, Moosbrugger, McManes, and others to try new approaches in their commands because the impact of any single failure would be limited. Destroyers were not expendable, but of the Navy's major combatants, they were individually the least important, and losses among them were expected, as evidenced by the positive reaction to Walker's defeat at Vella Lavella. The same was not true of larger ships; this gave destroyer commanders a unique degree of freedom to experiment. It was no accident that they were at the forefront of the Navy's doctrinal development throughout the first half of the twentieth century. They were uniquely suited to conceive, try out, and validate new tactical concepts because of their commands' small size and heterogeneous shipboard organization.

CONCLUSION

The introduction of the CIC was a revolutionary approach that allowed the Navy to exploit the potential of new technologies, such as radar, sonar, and TBS VHF radios. It significantly improved coordination in battle by providing officers with a clear tactical picture. Access to that picture offered an unprecedented level of coordination in night combat that—coupled with increasing unit cohesion and accelerated learning through officer networks—allowed the Navy to dominate surface battles in the latter half of World War II.

The CIC emerged from a clear need. Fighting during the first year of war illustrated the problems with internal shipboard communication. Information was available but was not effectively being used. Radar had significant potential, but the limitations of radar displays, inconsistent vocabulary, and restricted facilities for plotting made it difficult to capitalize upon. Nimitz, uncertain of the best approach, chose to establish a high-level constraint and ordered each ship to develop a CIC without providing specifics as to how to do so.

This triggered a broad set of parallel experiments as ships explored how best to solve the problem of organizing and presenting combat information. Variability within the fleet allowed new approaches to emerge; the best were quickly identified, and they formed the basis of initial manuals and training sessions. As more experience was gained with the CIC in combat, additional improvements were introduced and incorporated into school curriculums. Feedback loops between the educational system and the fleet allowed the Navy to learn rapidly from combat experience.

Informal networks developed in the combat zone. Officers used them to share techniques with each other and learn more rapidly than was possible in the more formalized mechanisms established at the fleet level. As formations grew more stable, these networks became more resilient, allowing learning to continue as officers rotated in and out of the combat areas. When officers departed, they took this learning with them and spread it to other areas of the fleet.

Some concepts took time to implement. Ships were still struggling with consistent terminology and language as late as November 1943, as Burke noted: "Most destroyers do not have [an] adequate internal Communication organization. Many failures in destroyers result from the proper authorities not getting the word. These failures frequently occur because of misunderstanding due to the lack of standard phraseology. It is understood that the CIC Training Center is now endeavoring to cure this defect."[69]

Installing CICs in ships not originally designed for them was also a challenge. Compromises were often necessary, and some hindered effectiveness. As Commander Austin learned, separating the CIC from the bridge by two decks made it difficult to assess its effectiveness. Ultimately, the solution would be to command from the CIC, regardless of its location, as McManes did at Surigao Strait.

Despite such challenges, by November 1943 the CIC was one of a series of important changes that allowed the Navy to dominate the Japanese in night battle. The CIC became the "brain" of the Navy's ships. It integrated all available information, evaluated it, and assessed it so that it could be effectively consumed by command functions. As Vice Adm. William S. Pye, the president of the Naval War College, noted, "These devices [radars], together with the development of the CIC, give the OTC advantages not dreamed of a short time ago."[70]

Visualizations—the many plots within the CIC—were this brain's "memory" and allowed it to function as a tool for analysis. Plots gave vital context that could not be provided by the transitory nature of a radar display. Only by recording observations over time could a clear picture be developed; skilled radar operators could do this in their heads for a limited number of contacts but could be easily overwhelmed or distracted in action. By distributing the information, the Navy capitalized on the skills and abilities of a collection of individuals, creating a system that was more effective than any single one of them.

This approach paralleled that taken by the fire-control system; both the CIC and the fire-control system were approaches to distributed cognition. In each, a team of individuals, operating through a defined set of constraints, created a system with capabilities far beyond those of any single person. The CIC redefined shipboard organization, spanning established boundaries and reconfiguring them to enable new, more advanced capabilities. The CIC combined with a resilient network of officers, more coherent formations, and new plans and doctrine to allow a new level of effectiveness in night combat to emerge. Empress Augusta Bay, Cape St. George, and Surigao Strait are emblematic of this key shift.

7

VICTORY IN
THE PACIFIC

The enemy of our games was always Japan, and
the courses [at the Naval War College] were so thorough
that after the start of World War II, nothing that happened
in the Pacific was strange or unexpected.

—Chester W. Nimitz, 1965

After victory in the Guadalcanal campaign, the Allies possessed the initiative in the Pacific. While Vice Adm. William F. Halsey Jr. and Gen. Douglas MacArthur pressured the Japanese with their advance toward Rabaul, Adm. Chester W. Nimitz prepared to assume the offensive with his Pacific Fleet. Lessons from the first year of war were incorporated into new approaches to doctrinal development; these were combined with the new ships joining the fleet to create a much more effective and flexible offensive force. Together, they enabled the Central Pacific offensive, the culmination of decades of planning for war against Japan.

The thrust would take the Pacific Fleet through the Mandates: the Marshall, Caroline, and Mariana Island groups. Both sides had recognized the strategic importance of these islands before the war. They occupied a central position and provided numerous locations for bases that could support further advances. The capture of the mandates was expected to "make available . . . approximately twenty airfields, fifteen seaplane bases, eight submarine bases, and ten fleet anchorages."[1] Accordingly, in June 1943 the JCS directed Nimitz to develop a plan to penetrate the Japanese defensive perimeter; the initial target was the Marshall Islands.

In planning for the offensive, Nimitz and his staff wrestled with the same strategic problem that had bedeviled the Navy for years. They had to determine how to move a large fleet across the Pacific, absorb or avoid Japanese attritional attacks, seize forward bases for further operations, and retain sufficient fighting strength to defeat the IJN's Combined Fleet. These objectives had received a great deal of attention in war games and exercises during the interwar period, but the best way to accomplish them remained uncertain. War experience had not altered the end goal—victory was still expected to come through a blockade of the Japanese home islands—but it had suggested new approaches to achieving it. Prewar plans had assumed an advance by a battle fleet, a battleship-centric formation that, concentrated together with a large fleet train, would move as a unit, seizing objectives along its path. Early in the war, distributed carrier formations had demonstrated an alternative.

Aircraft carriers could apply the principle of concentration in new and different ways. Unlike battleships, which had to steam in compact formations to concentrate their firepower, carriers could attack over much greater distances. They could coordinate strikes while operating independently. The 1 February 1942 raid on distributed targets in the Marshalls by Vice Admiral Halsey's *Enterprise* group and Rear Admiral Fletcher's *Yorktown* group was a prime example. Whereas battleships had to concentrate in space and time, carriers could focus primarily on time alone; they had much more freedom to operate in space. By mid-1943, the Pacific Fleet was experimenting with a fleet organization based on carrier task forces.

The transition from a battleship-centric formation to a network of carrier task forces is generally assumed to have invalidated the strategic and tactical planning carried out before the war. This view is incorrect.

Edward Miller has demonstrated the continuity of the Navy's strategic planning.[2] A similar continuity can be found in the Navy's approach to surface tactics. Although the transition had important implications for tactical doctrine, the basic foundations of that doctrine—the principles and heuristics—remained unchanged. However, the new fleet organization had important ramifications for how those tactical approaches were developed, distributed, and communicated. The need to exploit the flexibility of carrier task forces, along with the failure of prewar methods for developing and disseminating doctrines and plans, required a new approach.

The Navy's Pacific Fleet was the first to synthesize all three elements: the need for a new approach to tactical doctrine, the challenge introduced by fast carrier task forces, and existing prewar doctrinal concepts. These were woven together by new tactical manuals, new fleet organizations, and refined battle plans. Together, they enabled the rapid string of offensives that moved through the Central Pacific, returned American forces to the Philippines, and crushed Japan as a naval power.

THE GRANITE PLAN

The initial campaign plan for the Central Pacific offensive was code-named Granite. It had two major objectives. The first was to sustain "unremitting pressure against Japan." The second was a decisive showdown with "the Japanese Fleet at an early date." Both were important operational goals; together, they formed the basis of the successful campaign.[3]

In early 1943, the relatively slow pace of the offensive in the South Pacific was allowing the Japanese to build a series of defensive positions and regroup after each withdrawal. This made U.S. forward movement costly and difficult. The Japanese were expected to employ the same tactic in the Central Pacific. Prewar experience—and the heuristic emphasizing aggressive action—suggested that the best way to prevent this would be rapid movement at the operational level. If the pace was fast enough, the Pacific Fleet would keep the Japanese off balance and retain the initiative. An effective model for this approach had already been demonstrated; the Japanese had moved so rapidly at the start of the war that they outpaced the ability of the Allies to regroup and establish defensive positions. Nimitz and his planners expected to do the same.

This would be extremely important in the Central Pacific because the Japanese had created a network of mutually supporting bases in the Mandates. Unlike the South Pacific, where the Japanese had to build new bases to hold back Halsey's advance, in the Central Pacific bases were well established. Their networked configuration allowed the Japanese to shuttle planes to threatened areas quickly and contest any incursion. To ensure a successful operation, the Pacific Fleet had to move into the objective area, overwhelm the local defenders, and then fight off Japanese reinforcements. The faster a secure foothold could be established, the more rapidly the next forward movement could occur, and the more successful the offensive would be. Accordingly, Granite emphasized a series of rapid thrusts through the Japanese positions.

The second major objective of Granite was a quick victory over the Japanese fleet. Victory in a major fleet action is commonly assumed to have been a tactical objective of the Pacific Fleet, but the campaign plan illustrates that it was in fact a strategic goal: "All operations will be conducted as to maintain maximum readiness to take advantage of opportunities to bring important enemy naval forces to action." The Japanese fleet was a credible fighting force, and so long as it could sortie and threaten the success of an amphibious operation, it would limit the Pacific Fleet's freedom of maneuver and delay the offensive. Accordingly, Granite assumed that "a major fleet action, although it may delay amphibious operations for a brief period, will greatly accelerate them thereafter."[4] With the IJN defeated, amphibious forces could accelerate their advances toward strategic positions, such as Formosa, the Philippines, or the Ryukyus; from there, planes and ships could interdict Japanese commerce and establish a strangling blockade on the home islands.

However, the old problem of the Orange plans remained: decisive battle could not be forced on the Japanese but had to be fought at a time and place of their choosing. This meant that Nimitz and his subordinates had to be ready for fleet action at any time. Every subsidiary operation plan to Granite—including Galvanic for the invasion of the Gilberts, Flintlock and Catchpole for the Marshalls, Hailstone for Truk, Longhop for the Manus, and Forager for the Marianas—had to account for the possibility of decisive action. Tactical and operational plans were developed to meet this contingency so that the fleet would be ready when the Japanese decided to fight. Their approach was a clear example of complex thinking. Nimitz and his planners focused on their overall goal—the defeat of Japan. Individual operations were designed to bring the Pacific Fleet closer to that objective, but they remained options to be exercised when circumstances were right. The plan was fluid and did not commit itself to detailed outcomes. It retained flexibility to deal with unanticipated challenges and opportunities.

STRUCTURES FOR OPERATIONAL SUCCESS

These two operational goals—to sustain a rapid pace of advance and to be able to fight a decisive action at any time—exerted a significant influence on the fleet. To sustain the fast pace of operations, the striking arm of the fleet would have to operate in forward areas almost continuously. This required a new approach to logistics.[5] It also required a new approach to the development and dissemination of tactical doctrine.

In early 1942, separate carrier task forces had demonstrated their ability to perform simultaneous, coordinated attacks on enemy positions. The more numerous and powerful carrier groups entering the fleet in 1943 would allow this approach to be replicated on a larger scale. However, to maximize their striking power, the carrier task forces had to operate as semiautonomous formations, concentrating on independent, but mutually supporting, objectives. With enough of these formations, any single one could be periodically withdrawn from the forward areas for rest and refitting while the others continued the advance. A modular fleet structure based around carrier task forces would help enable a rapid offensive. However, questions remained. How should a fleet of carrier task forces be organized? How could they come together and fight as a cohesive whole in a major fleet action?

The first problem was how to coordinate multiple carriers within a single task force. The carrier battles of 1942 had given the Navy valuable experience and illustrated the need for improvement, particularly with coordinating multiple carriers in a single formation. The Navy had limited experience with multicarrier task forces. For much of the interwar period, the two large carriers, *Lexington* and *Saratoga*, had been on opposite sides in experiments and exercises. When teamed together, they had operated in independent task groups or had been tied to the battle line.

Technological factors too contributed to the Navy's lack of experience. Before radar and effective fighter direction, carriers were extremely vulnerable. They were repeatedly "disabled" and "sunk" in prewar exercises. The best approach to preserving their fragile flight decks was keeping them hidden. Dispersing carriers into separate strike forces, away from the main body and each other, made them more difficult to locate. Because protecting them once they had been sighted was effectively impossible, dispersal was a logical defensive measure. Accordingly, carrier air groups were dominated by scout and torpedo bombers to maximize their striking power.

Wartime experience and the advance of technology changed the situation. Improved radars to detect incoming strikes and more effective techniques for vectoring fighters to intercept them allowed groups of carriers to pool resources and offer mutual support. The Navy's carrier-task-force doctrine was revised on the basis of this ability and the lessons from the 1942 battles. Single-carrier formations were abandoned; task forces were formed around multiple carriers operating together.[6]

The next problem was working out how to coordinate a collection of these multicarrier formations. It would mean a shift in fleet organization away from a battle fleet and toward a loosely coupled network of fast carrier task forces. The change was significant. The Navy's fleet structure had supported the independent operation of distributed task forces for many years but always under the assumption that there would be a "main body" that contained the bulk of the fleet's strength. The division into carrier task forces was a decentralization that rendered the concept of a "main body" irrelevant.

The shift to a more modular approach gave the Pacific Fleet the flexibility to implement the Granite plan successfully. Carrier task forces could concentrate against multiple targets simultaneously or against a single target without becoming single targets themselves. Using this approach, the fleet could strike into the web of interconnected Japanese bases, overwhelm the defenders over a large area, and support the amphibious forces as they seized an advanced base. However, dispersal was not without risk; carriers were still vulnerable to surface action, and they needed support during their thrusts into the enemy's defensive perimeter. The new fast battleships were ideally suited to provide this support, and they began to be integrated into the carrier task forces.

The dispersal of battleship strength ran counter to the principle of concentration that the Navy had emphasized for decades. It introduced the risk that a single carrier task force might be isolated and destroyed; it also required the carrier task forces to concentrate prior to major fleet action in order to bring the battleships together. Although dispersal enabled the rapid pace of operations, it hindered Granite's second goal, bringing the Japanese fleet to decisive action. To support this contingency, the distributed carrier formations and the ships within them had to be able to come together and form a cohesive force whenever decisive action threatened.

This need was further complicated by the fact that individual ships would join the fleet at uncertain times and in varying states of preparation. They would replace ships that had been damaged in combat or were withdrawing for refits. The carrier task forces allowed great flexibility, but if they were to be effective, the ships that made them up had to be even more flexible. They had to be able to enter the combat zone and immediately become effective components of their new task group, without spending additional time training with their cohorts. This need invalidated the decentralized approach to developing plans and doctrine used before the war; that was discarded with the concept of a fleet that would move through the Pacific as a single, cohesive unit. A new level of cohesion had to emerge to support this more modular structure; a new set of constraints was the key. They would be provided by a new fleetwide tactical manual, *Current Tactical Orders and Doctrine, U.S. Pacific Fleet*, or PAC-10, issued in June 1943.

The genesis of PAC-10 dates to April 1943, when Nimitz created a board to revise the Pacific Fleet Cruising Instructions. The officers of the board were ordered to review current doctrinal publications, examine combat reports, interview officers returning from combat zones, and produce a new set of cruising instructions.[7] In the event, they would exercise their initiative—embracing the Navy's heuristic regarding decentralized doctrinal development—and exceed their mandate. By drawing on operational goals of the coming campaign, existing principles of the Navy's doctrine, and flaws exposed by wartime experience, the board produced a new doctrinal manual for the Pacific Fleet. PAC-10 introduced a more uniform approach to tactical doctrine, one that permitted the interchangeability of ships and task units demanded by the Granite plan.

Although carrier airpower would dominate the coming offensive, Nimitz chose three surface officers for the board and just one aviator. The senior member, Rear Adm. Robert M. Griffin, was an experienced surface ship commander. He left the board before it completed its work and went to command Battleship Division 3. Capt. Roscoe F. Good became senior member with Griffin's departure. Later in the war, he would command the battleship *Washington*. Capt. E. M. Crouch replaced Griffin. As commander of Destroyer Division 57, Crouch had survived the initial Japanese offensives in the South Pacific. The aviator was Capt. Apollo Soucek, who had set aviation records before the war and had been executive officer of the carrier *Hornet* at the time of her loss. The result of their labors would be the most important tactical manual produced by the wartime Navy.

PAC-10 provided what the Navy had been missing: a common set of tactical concepts for the cooperation of small forces and detached units in battle. It ended the relative neglect of minor tactics and granted them the same detailed treatment that major actions had received for over a decade. The coded system of letters and numbers used for major actions—as conceived by Admiral Pratt in 1929—was reused and expanded for the coordination small task forces. Pratt's concepts, informed by his lengthy experience, were the seed of the Navy's successful wartime doctrine.[8]

PAC-10 created a new cognitive framework, a new grammar for formulating and communicating battle plans, that changed how the fleet went about developing tactics and doctrine. It was also a major new set of constraints. The new vocabulary allowed ships and squadrons to move around the fleet freely, while retaining coordination and cohesion. The predefined plans removed the need for individual unit commanders to compose their own; instead of communicating lengthy plans, they could simply transmit, for example, "1E3."[9]

PAC-10 also provided a new set of compact formations, developed specifically for combat with small task forces. They merged wartime experience and prewar doctrine to give the fleet greater flexibility. Formation A-2 was a modified version of the interwar battle formation with light forces distributed in the van and rear. The other formations concentrated light forces in the van and were based on tactical orders originally promulgated in January 1943 by Rear Adm. Willis A. Lee, commander of the Pacific Fleet's battleships.[10] Formations A-1 and A-4 were intended for daylight action. Formations A-3 and A-5 were designed for night combat; they employed mixed cruiser-destroyer attack units, arranged in the prewar "V" or "Wedge" formations.[11]

With PAC-10 in place, new ships could familiarize themselves with its contents as they prepared to join the fleet, and because PAC-10 applied to all task forces in all Pacific combat zones, it was possible for ships to move from group to group or theater to theater without needing lengthy instructions from their new commanders. The importance of this was stressed in the manual's introduction: "PAC-10 is intended . . . to obviate [the] necessity for . . . special instructions under ordinary circumstances and to minimize them in extraordinary circumstances. The ultimate aim is to obtain essential uniformity without unacceptable sacrifice of flexibility. It must be possible for forces composed of diverse types, and indoctrinated under different task force commanders, to join at sea on short notice for concerted action against the enemy without exchanging a mass of special instructions."[12]

Successors to PAC-10 built upon the foundation provided by the original. In February 1944, the U.S. Fleet staff followed the lead of its Pacific arm and issued *Current Tactical Orders and Doctrine, U.S. Fleet*, USF-10A. USF-10A built directly upon PAC-10; format, structure, and the majority of contents were unchanged from the Pacific Fleet's

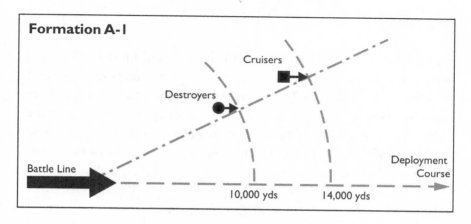

Formation A-1

Cruisers

Destroyers

Battle Line

Deployment Course

10,000 yds   14,000 yds

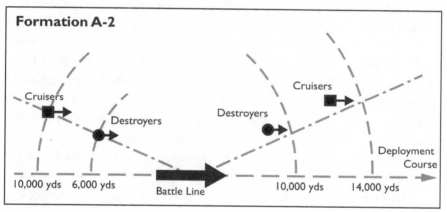

Formation A-2

Cruisers

Destroyers

Cruisers

Destroyers

Deployment Course

10,000 yds   6,000 yds   Battle Line   10,000 yds   14,000 yds

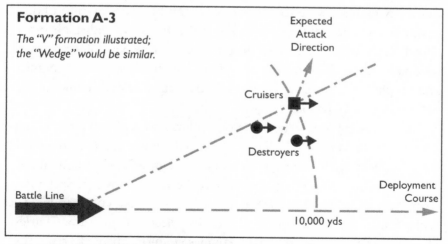

Formation A-3

*The "V" formation illustrated;
the "Wedge" would be similar.*

Expected Attack Direction

Cruisers

Destroyers

Battle Line

Deployment Course

10,000 yds

FIGURE 5. Formations from PAC-10. A-1 was for daylight action with small task groups. If sufficient light forces were present, they could be employed on both flanks as in A-2. A-3 was for night action and employed the "V" or "Wedge."

publication. A revised version, USF-10B, followed in May 1945 and introduced additional wartime lessons. These manuals incorporated effective elements of the Navy's prewar doctrine and improved them using wartime experience. The new consistency of tactical doctrine enhanced the flexibility of the fleet, enabled the modularity required by carrier-centric task forces, and helped ensure the success of the offensive in the Central Pacific.[13]

THE START OF THE OFFENSIVE

Although the JCS directive ordered the seizure of the Marshalls, Nimitz considered a thrust directly into the Mandates too dangerous. Too little was known about Japanese positions in the islands. After Japan had withdrawn from the League of Nations in 1935, travel to them had been restricted. "No foreign ship was allowed to enter their harbors or lagoons, no foreign national to take passage thither on a Japanese ship, no foreign warship to make a courtesy visit."[14] This secrecy had concealed the increasing militarization of the Mandates, and although Nimitz's planners anticipated strong defenses, they were uncertain what to expect.

The lack of intelligence could be addressed through aerial reconnaissance—and experience had demonstrated the value of doing it—but the Marshalls were too far away for land-based planes to photograph them. The nearest was 1,100 miles from Guadalcanal; other Allied bases were even more distant. An intermediate objective was needed if the assault into the Mandates was to be successful. Nimitz and his planners chose the Gilbert Island group. The code name for the operation was Galvanic.

A new command structure would plan and undertake the initial assault. On 15 March 1943, the Central Pacific Force had been renamed the Fifth Fleet. By 5 August, it was large enough to need a commander, and Nimitz chose his chief of staff, Vice Adm. Raymond A. Spruance. Rear Adm. Charles A. Pownall became his carrier commander. To replace Spruance as chief of staff, Nimitz selected Rear Adm. Charles H. McMorris, who had thwarted Japanese reinforcement efforts in the battle of the Komandorski Islands. These admirals and their staffs would plan the offensive. They were assisted by Vice Adm. John H. "Jack"

Towers, Commander Air Force Pacific Fleet, and his chief of staff, Capt. Forrest Sherman; they helped formulate new approaches to organizing multicarrier task forces.

To help test these approaches and gain experience operating the new carriers, Nimitz initiated a series of raids. They explored how to operate multicarrier formations effectively and integrate ships using PAC-10. On 1 September, Rear Admiral Pownall attacked Marcus Island—2,700 miles from Pearl Harbor but only a thousand from Japan—with the carriers *Yorktown* and *Essex*, the light carrier *Independence*, and the battleship *Indiana*. On 18 and 19 September, Pownall struck the Gilberts with the carrier *Lexington* and the light carriers *Princeton* and *Belleau Wood*. They raided Tarawa and Makin, the main objectives of Galvanic. Planes from *Lexington* took low-altitude photos of Tarawa, collecting valuable details that would assist planning for the assault.

While Pownall struck Tarawa, Admiral Nimitz held a conference at Pearl Harbor with Spruance, Towers, McMorris, and Sherman to discuss future operations. They agreed that another carrier strike should be planned before the invasion of the Gilberts, to give more practice with multicarrier formations. Rear Adm. Alfred E. Montgomery would lead the strike as commander of TF 14; his objective was Wake Island.

Montgomery had three large carriers (*Essex*, *Yorktown*, and *Lexington*) and three light carriers (*Cowpens*, *Independence*, and *Belleau Wood*). It was the Navy's largest concentration of carrier power to date. His chief of staff, Capt. H. S. Duckworth, planned the operation. The two of them experimented with a variety of different formations, as described by Clark G. Reynolds: "Montgomery would vary his cruising dispositions between a single task group of six carriers, two groups of three carriers each, and three groups of two carriers each."[15] Montgomery attacked Wake over two days, 5 and 6 October. Six separate strikes were launched, and according to Captain Duckworth, "Virtually all the techniques of ship handling for a multicarrier force which were later used successfully had their origins in this operation."[16] The experimentation with different cruising dispositions validated the basic concepts behind multicarrier formations and worked out the details of how to employ them.

TABLE 5. Battleship and Carrier Dispositions for Galvanic

Formation	Commander	Carriers	Battleships
TG 50.1 Interceptor Carrier Group	Rear Adm. Charles A. Pownall	*Yorktown, Lexington, Cowpens* (CVL)	*South Dakota, Alabama, Washington*
TG 50.2 Northern Carrier Group	Rear Adm. Arthur W. Radford	*Enterprise, Belleau Wood* (CVL), *Monterey* (CVL)	*Massachusetts, North Carolina, Indiana*
TF 52 Northern Attack Force	Rear Adm. Richmond K. Turner	*Liscome Bay* (CVE), *Coral Sea* (CVE), *Corregidor* (CVE)	*New Mexico, Idaho, Mississippi, Pennsylvania**
TG 50.3 Southern Carrier Group	Rear Adm. Alfred E. Montgomery	*Essex, Bunker Hill, Independence* (CVL)	None
TF 53 Southern Attack Force	Rear Adm. H. W. Hill	*Sangamon* (CVE), *Suwannee* (CVE), *Chenango* (CVE), *Barnes* (CVE), *Nassau* (CVE)	*Tennessee, Maryland, Colorado*
TG 50.4 Relief Carrier Group	Rear Adm. Frederick C. Sherman	*Saratoga, Princeton* (CVL)	None

*The battleship *Pennsylvania* was Rear Admiral Turner's flagship and unlikely to participate in a fleet action.

By November, Spruance's Fifth Fleet was ready to begin the offensive. It would seize three atolls in the Gilberts—Tarawa, Makin, and Abemama—to dominate the island group and provide airfields from which to reconnoiter and attack the Marshalls. Although long-range bombers and reconnaissance aircraft could reach the Gilberts, the extreme range forced Spruance to provide direct air support for the invasion forces with his fast carriers. This severely limited their freedom of maneuver. In prewar exercises, combat forces caught supporting amphibious assaults had been damaged by attritional raids and defeated by major attacks. At the battle of Savo Island, the Japanese had reinforced these lessons by decimating the Allied covering force. Japanese responses in the Central Pacific were expected to be even more powerful. Minor raids could be handled by the invasion forces, using PAC-10 as a guide, but a major response would be a serious threat.[17]

Spruance's Galvanic plan accounted for this possibility. Simultaneous attacks against Tarawa and Makin would divide his forces; the best defense against the threat of attack during an amphibious operation was to quickly overwhelm the objectives and gain the freedom to maneuver. This also satisfied the desire to obtain a rapid operational tempo. The main objectives would be seized simultaneously: Tarawa by the Southern Attack Force and Makin by the Northern. The atolls were expected to be occupied before the Japanese could mount a major response.[18]

The concern about a major action was well founded. Admiral Koga, commander in chief of the Combined Fleet, correctly anticipated that the Pacific Fleet would begin its offensive in late 1943. He believed it was essential to win a decisive victory over the Americans immediately, before they achieved overwhelming material superiority. He concentrated his forces at Truk in the Caroline Islands, ready to counter any thrust toward the Mandates. When Pownall raided into the Gilberts on 18 September, Koga immediately sent Vice Adm. Ozawa Jizaburo's Third Fleet forward to Eniwetok. Ozawa was ready to contest any amphibious landing, with his three carriers, two battleships, and eight heavy cruisers. Koga remained at Truk with the rest of the Combined Fleet to await developments. When by 25 September the anticipated attack had not developed, Ozawa returned to Truk. Koga's response to the raid on Wake was even more aggressive. Although he did not advance during the strikes on 5 and 6 October, radio intercepts suggested to the Japanese that another attack was being planned. The bulk of the Combined Fleet sortied on 17 October. Koga took his six battleships, three carriers, and eight cruisers first to Eniwetok and then to a point 250 miles south of Wake Island. Failing to find the Americans, Koga returned to Truk on 26 October.

Nimitz, who had anticipated these moves, estimated Koga could oppose Galvanic with ten battleships, seven aircraft carriers, and supporting cruisers and destroyers.[19] Although this overstated the Combined Fleet's strength, the expectation that Koga would fight was correct. Spruance's instructions stressed the need for preparation: "Current Intelligence indicates the presence of the major portion of the Japanese Fleet in the Truk area. . . . [W]e must be prepared at all times during Galvanic for a fleet engagement."[20]

Over one hundred miles separated Tarawa and Makin; unless Spruance had timely warning of a Japanese approach, the forces covering the assaults would be too far apart for mutual support. Spruance was extremely apprehensive that a powerful attack would fall on a portion of his force and defeat it in detail. Makin was the closer of the two islands to the Marshalls and much more vulnerable. Spruance expected air searches to give him adequate warning and allow time to concentrate the Fifth Fleet. But if weather patterns were unfavorable, storm systems could prevent aerial searches in the direction of the Mandates; Spruance considered delaying the attack on Makin if such circumstances developed.

Even if they did not, the forces around Makin would have to be ready to defend themselves. Spruance placed significantly more firepower in his northern groups. The old battleships in the Northern Attack Force, *Idaho, Mississippi,* and *New Mexico,* had been modified in the interwar period and were the most powerful ships of their vintage available. All six fast battleships supporting the operation were near Makin, evenly divided between the Northern Carrier Group, which provided direct support to the Makin assault, and the Interceptor Carrier Group. This group was under the direct command of Rear Admiral Pownall; its objective was to intercept Japanese aerial attacks and provide early warning of approaching enemy forces. Spruance urged these carrier groups to remain concentrated: "Carrier Task Groups which are screened by fast battleships and are supporting the attack on Makin and covering our northern flank will . . . be operated in as close tactical support as possible of each other and the combatant units of the Northern Attack Force."[21]

If the Japanese sought battle, the nine battleships in the northern forces could separate from their task groups and unite to form a powerful battle line under Rear Admiral Lee. But this is not how Spruance wanted to fight. He wanted a margin of superiority, and so his battle plan called for the entire Central Pacific Force to unite against any major Japanese move. Three old battleships and additional ships supporting the landing at Tarawa would join the forces around Makin, giving Spruance a battle fleet of twelve battleships, nine heavy cruisers, three light cruisers, and twenty-eight destroyers.[22] He emphasized the importance of destroying the Japanese fleet: "If . . . a major portion of the Japanese Fleet were to attempt to interfere with Galvanic, it is obvious that the defeat of the enemy fleet would at once become paramount. Without having inflicted such a defeat on the enemy, we would be unable to proceed with the capture and development of Makin, Tarawa, and Apamama [sic]. The destruction of a considerable portion of Japanese naval strength would . . . go far toward winning the war."[23]

But the major fleet action that both sides anticipated did not materialize. In late October, in response to the threat developing on his southern flank as Vice Admiral Halsey and General MacArthur advanced, Koga reinforced the bastion of Rabaul. He sent his carrier squadrons, along with most of his cruiser forces. Nimitz's rapid operational tempo was already delivering results. Frequent raids had the Japanese guessing where the next blow would fall, and pressured on two fronts, they had now reinforced their southern flank. When Spruance moved into the Gilberts, stripped of its air squadrons and cruiser scouts, there was little the Combined Fleet could do.

Spruance's plan worked well. The coordinated actions of the dispersed carrier groups suppressed Japanese airfields and prevented them from effectively interfering with the operation. Pownall's Interceptor Group attacked Jaluit and Mili in the southern Marshalls the day before the landings and suppressed nearby Japanese positions over the next four days. Twice Pownall's forces intercepted Japanese planes heading to the Gilberts, spoiling their attacks.

Rear Adm. Arthur W. Radford's Northern Carrier Group struck Makin on 19 and 20 November and then stood by the assault forces, fighting off the raids that got past Pownall's Interceptor Group. Rear Admiral Montgomery's Southern Carrier Group initiated operations with a strike on Rabaul on 11 November. Thereafter, it stood by the Southern Attack Force, striking Tarawa on 18, 19, and 20 November. On the evening of 20 November, a flight of Japanese torpedo bombers slipped through the layered defenses; the light carrier *Independence* was hit, badly damaged, and forced to withdraw.

Spruance's fourth carrier group was the Relief Carrier Group, commanded by Rear Adm. Frederick C. Sherman (not to be confused with Capt. Forrest Sherman on Vice Admiral Towers' staff). As mentioned in the previous chapter, this group assisted Halsey's advance with strikes on Rabaul between 1 and 11 November, damaging Japanese cruiser forces and supporting the campaign to seize Bougainville. During the landings in the Gilberts, Sherman's carrier group suppressed the Japanese airfield on Nauru, preventing planes based there from interfering in the operation.

Galvanic's main objectives were secured quickly. Makin was taken fairly easily and declared secure on the morning of 23 November. Later that same day, the difficult struggle for the island of Betio in Tarawa atoll ended. Both islands were quickly developed into air bases. Tarawa was operating fighters by 1 December and heavy bombers later that month. Makin's sandy soil prevented heavy bombers from using its airfield, but fighters and medium bombers started operating from there on 21 December. Both fields would support the next advance, into the Marshalls.

FLINTLOCK AND THE MARSHALLS

With the success of Galvanic, attention shifted to the Marshalls. The important question was how best to continue the rapid pace of the offensive and quickly neutralize Japanese positions in the island group. An airfield that could support bombers was an essential initial objective; there were airfields that could support bombers on Wotje and Maloelap, in the eastern portion of the Marshalls. A phased approach, breaking the capture of the Marshalls into eastern and western operations, was considered and endorsed by the JCS. Nimitz and his planners rejected this idea; they did not want to allow the Japanese to retain a foothold, fearing the offensive would degenerate into an attritional struggle as the fighting in the Solomons had.

As plans for the Marshalls were refined, mixed task forces raided Japanese positions; PAC-10 helped facilitate these minor operations, which involved a rapid reshuffling of ships.[24] Lee's fast battleships moved to the South Pacific with the carriers *Bunker Hill* and *Monterey*. The battleships bombarded Nauru on 8 December. The carriers, under the command of Rear Admiral Sherman, supported Halsey's operations against Rabaul. They struck Kavieng on Christmas Day, New Year's, and again on 4 January.

In the meantime, Pownall led a reconfigured TF 50, with two carrier groups and the remaining carriers, into the heart of the Marshalls. It attacked Kwajalein the morning of 4 December. A second strike had been planned—and aerial photos showed the undamaged bombers that could have been destroyed—but Pownall called it off. An afternoon strike hit Wotje before the carriers withdrew. Later that night, the bombers that had been spared on Kwajalein found Pownall's force; a torpedo hit *Lexington*, wrecking her steering gear. The crew was fortunate to save the ship.

TF 50's raid, however, had collected valuable intelligence. Low-altitude photographs of Kwajalein revealed an unexpectedly large airstrip, one that could support U.S. bombers. This made the centrally located atoll a perfect objective for the planned invasion. The raid also confirmed a lesson. Rear Admiral Pownall, who had behaved erratically during the raids in September, had now demonstrated that he lacked the necessary aggressiveness to command the fast carrier forces. A second raid could have wrecked the Japanese bombers and saved *Lexington* from damage. After holding a conference with Towers, McMorris, and Forrest Sherman, Nimitz relieved Pownall and replaced him with Rear Adm. Marc A. Mitscher, an experienced naval aviator who had commanded the carrier *Hornet* at the battle of Midway and land-based air forces in the Solomons under Halsey.

Forrest Sherman was promoted to rear admiral and became Nimitz's assistant chief of staff for plans. When Sherman saw the photographs from the raid on Kwajalein, he recommended seizing the atoll. Wotje and Maloelap would be bypassed and the Japanese forces there left, again, to "wither on the vine." In a December conference, however, Vice Admiral Spruance and Rear Admiral Turner objected; they preferred a more incremental advance: a thrust to Kwajalein was directly into the heart of the Japanese defensive system, and enemy air bases would be on all sides. Nimitz, recognizing the need to maintain the operational tempo, overrode them.[25]

TABLE 6. Battleship and Carrier Dispositions for Flintlock

Formation	Commander	Carriers	Battleships
TG 58.1 Carrier Task Group 1	Rear Adm. John W. Reeves	*Enterprise, Yorktown, Belleau* Wood (CVL)	*Washington, Massachusetts, Indiana*
TG 58.2 Carrier Task Group 2	Rear Adm. Alfred E. Montgomery	*Essex, Intrepid, Cabot* (CVL)	*South Dakota, North Carolina, Alabama*
TF 58.3 Carrier Task Group 3	Rear Adm. Frederick C. Sherman	*Bunker Hill, Monterey* (CVL), *Cowpens* (CVL)	*Iowa, New Jersey*
TF 58.4 Carrier Task Group 4	Rear Adm. Samuel P. Ginder	*Saratoga, Princeton* (CVL), *Langley* (CVL)	
TF 52 Southern Attack Force	Rear Adm. Richmond K. Turner	*Manila Bay* (CVE), *Coral Sea* (CVE), *Corregidor* (CVE)	*Idaho, Pennsylvania, New Mexico, Mississippi*
TF 53 Northern Attack Force	Rear Adm. Richard L. Conolly	*Sangamon* (CVE), *Suwannee* (CVE), *Chenango* (CVE)	*Tennessee, Colorado, Maryland*

Plans for Flintlock, the operation to capture the Marshalls, were quickly finalized. Kwajalein, which was indeed the centerpiece of the Japanese defensive position, became the main objective. Four attack forces were required. Two would strike Kwajalein: a northern force would assault the twin islands of Roi-Namur, while the southern would capture Kwajalein Island, on the southern end of the atoll. The third force would occupy undefended Majuro Atoll, to give the fleet a local anchorage and act as an operational reserve. A fourth amphibious force would be held ready to assist in the capture of Kwajalein; if not needed, it would be used later for Operation Catchpole, the assault on Eniwetok.

The fast carrier task forces were now designated TF 58. As in Galvanic, they had to provide direct support for the assault forces, but the approach of pinning a carrier task force to a physical objective had been criticized and discarded. It restricted the task force's ability to maneuver, one of its most effective defense mechanisms. The flexibility afforded by the division of the fleet into carrier task forces allowed an alternative, and Mitscher would operate his carriers offensively in the Marshalls, rotating them between objectives to support landings and neutralize Japanese air bases.[26]

Two carrier groups would always be near the main objective at Kwajalein Atoll, close enough together that they could concentrate quickly for mutual support. Three different carrier groups rotated through this position. On 29 January, Rear Admiral Montgomery's TG 58.2 and Rear Adm. Frederick C. Sherman's TG 58.3 attacked Kwajalein. The next day, Rear Adm. John W. Reeves' TG 58.1 replaced Sherman's task group; the latter moved to Eniwetok, farther to the west and closer to Truk. These relative positions were held until Sherman retired to fuel on 3 February.

The use of Frederick Sherman's TG 58.3 as the advanced guard was deliberate. It contained the two newest battleships, *Iowa* and *New Jersey*. The fastest and most powerful in the fleet, these two battleships formed Battleship Division (BatDiv) 7. Their high speed, over thirty-two knots, allowed them to keep pace with the fast carriers when they went to maximum speed. With BatDiv 7, TG 58.3 could outfight any enemy surface forces it could not outrun. If a major Japanese counterattack ensued, Sherman would fall back on the forces at Kwajalein. The remaining six fast battleships were divided evenly between TGs 58.1 and 58.2.

Major action was anticipated. Spruance's battle plan for Flintlock once again called for the concentration of all fifteen available battleships, new and old, into a single battle line. Supporting units would be drawn from both the invasion fleet and the carrier groups. To guide the fleet in battle, Spruance planned to employ major action plans from *General Tactical Instructions*, FTP-188, the 1940 revision of the prewar manual that had contained Pratt's major action plans. These provided a mutual frame of reference with minimum signaling. If necessary, Spruance would develop his own battle plans and distribute them by signal. Rear Admiral Lee would command the battle line.[27]

The anticipated Japanese response never came. Majuro, Roi-Namur, and Kwajalein were all seized without interference from Japanese surface units. The reserve force sailed to Eniwetok, initiating Operation Catchpole. Vice Admiral Spruance set his sights on the Combined Fleet.

CATCHPOLE AND HAILSTONE

Aerial reconnaissance of Truk showed that major elements of the Japanese fleet were in the Carolines. A powerful attack was planned to cover the landings at Eniwetok by neutralizing Truk and destroying any forces encountered; this was Operation Hailstone. It was more than just a raid. It was a deliberate attempt to destroy a large portion of the Combined Fleet. Six fast battleships—all of those involved in the operation—were concentrated into Frederick Sherman's TG 58.3, ready to deploy quickly and engage the enemy. The old battleships and the amphibious forces were left behind.

By the time of the initial air strikes on 17 February 1944, the Japanese had withdrawn their heavy units, but a large amount of shipping was discovered in the lagoon and was attacked from the air. When a group of Japanese light forces attempted to escape, Spruance gave chase with a surface striking force, TG 50.9. BatDiv 7, with *Iowa* and *New Jersey*, formed the core of the force. Two heavy cruisers and four destroyers were attached in support. It was the first employment of the new battleship division in a role to which it would often be assigned—pursuit and destruction of enemy ships. The high speed of these battleships made them especially well suited for it. They destroyed four Japanese ships; a lone destroyer escaped.[28]

The creation and detachment of ad hoc units like this, assembling ships that had no opportunity to train together extensively, had produced unfortunate results fifteen months before off Guadalcanal.[29] Now,

TABLE 7. Battleship and Carrier Dispositions for Hailstone

Formation	Commander	Carriers	Battleships
TG 58.1 Carrier Task Group 1	Rear Adm. John W. Reeves	*Enterprise, Yorktown, Belleau Wood* (CVL)	
TG 58.2 Carrier Task Group 2	Rear Adm. Alfred E. Montgomery	*Essex, Intrepid, Cabot* (CVL)	
TF 58.3 Carrier Task Group 3	Rear Adm. Frederick C. Sherman	*Bunker Hill, Monterey* (CVL), *Cowpens* (CVL)	*North Carolina, Iowa, New Jersey, Massachusetts, South Dakota, Alabama*

PAC-10, and the recent issuance of USF-10A, offered the opportunity to form units on the spot while retaining a significant degree of cohesion. Tactical commanders now had the flexibility to seize opportunities presented by the rapid operational tempo.

The ships of TG 50.9 were not the only ones waiting to strike Japanese "cripples." Ten submarines were prowling the waters around Truk in concert with the carrier strikes. On 16 February, *Skate* sighted and torpedoed the cruiser *Agano* and sank her. The submarine's place in the decisive battle had been found. In future operations, they would be positioned strategically by commanders ashore to provide distant reconnaissance and attack targets of opportunity.

Additional carrier raids followed Hailstone's success. After the withdrawal of Japanese fleet units from the Carolines, Spruance was free to range deeper into the Japanese defensive system. On 23 February 1944, two carrier groups from Mitscher's TF 58 struck Japanese air bases in the Marianas. Montgomery's TG 58.2 attacked Guam and Saipan; Frederick Sherman's TG 58.3 struck Tinian and Rota. These strikes were coordinated with submarines, which sank merchant ships that attempted to flee and rescued downed aviators.

Spruance penetrated even farther the next month. On the last two days of March and the first day of April, the Fifth Fleet hit Palau and Yap in the western Carolines. Palau had become an anchorage for the Japanese fleet after Hailstone, and Spruance, anticipating another opportunity for decisive action, attacked it in force; he had three carrier task groups, with five carriers, six light carriers, and six fast battleships. No major enemy surface forces were encountered, but several small ships and many planes were destroyed. The rapid pace of operations was keeping pressure on the Japanese.

DESECRATE II

The Fifth Fleet's attack into the Carolines was part of a larger operation. It was a preliminary strike in support of General MacArthur's advance on the northern coast of New Guinea. He was planning to invade Hollandia and seize the Japanese base complex between Tamahmerah and Humboldt Bays. Its capture would provide the Southwest

Pacific Force an ideal position from which to support further advances along the northern coast of the island. The JCS ordered Nimitz's carriers to support the operation; their participation was code-named Desecrate II.

In preparing for the operations, Nimitz kept the primary objectives of Granite in mind. The strike on Palau—like the attack on Truk—was a deliberate attempt to destroy major units of the Japanese fleet. Since the fast carriers failed to engage them, he had to be prepared for them to interfere with the coming operation. On 23 March during a meeting with MacArthur in Brisbane, Nimitz emphasized the Navy's priorities. He made it clear that if the Japanese came out to fight, their fleet would become the primary objective of the fast carrier force. Newly promoted Vice Admiral Mitscher's orders to TF 58 reflected this emphasis: "This force will destroy or contain enemy naval forces attempting to interfere with the seizure of Hollandia; will, without prejudice to the foregoing task, neutralize enemy airfields in the Hollandia–Wakde area by repeated air strikes by carrier air groups and by surface ship bombardment."[30] Spruance and the Central Pacific Force's amphibious elements remained behind, preparing for the invasion of the Marianas.

The strikes began on 21 April, and the landings took place the next day. Mitscher used three carrier task groups. Rear Adm. Joseph J. "Jocko" Clark commanded TG 58.1. Clark had no battleships; his group ranged to the west and attacked Japanese airfields at Wakde, Sawar, and Sarmi. Rear Admiral Montgomery's TG 58.2, with the two fast battleships of BatDiv 7, supported the landings in Humboldt Bay, and Rear Admiral Reeves' TG 58.3, with four other fast battleships, covered the landings in Tamahmerah Bay. This arrangement positioned the bulk of Mitscher's surface striking power in the center, facilitating concentration if the Japanese appeared in force.

Surface-action plans were developed for a variety of contingencies. Mitscher, like Spruance, called for the concentration of a powerful battle fleet in his major action plan. The six battleships, with ten heavy cruisers, three light cruisers, and twenty-two destroyers, were to concentrate under Vice Admiral Lee; Clark's carrier group, TG 58.1, would operate in direct support, under Lee's command. In battle, Lee expected to leverage plans and dispositions from FTP-188 and USF-10A. The remaining two carrier groups, stripped of the bulk of their escorts, would remain under Mitscher's control and operate in distant support.[31]

Two additional plans were developed in case the Japanese challenged with smaller forces. One teamed Lee's six battleships with two destroyer squadrons. The other was a pursuit force built around BatDiv 7, very similar to TG 50.9, which had been used during the raid on Truk. This time, the two fast battleships were teamed with two heavy cruisers and seven destroyers. Their preferred battle plan was "1E2," which called for an engagement on parallel courses at extreme range, with light forces on both flanks operating defensively.[32] Little resistance was encountered, and the Japanese fleet refused battle. On 29 and 30 April, on the way back to the new fleet anchorages in the Marshalls, Mitscher raided Truk. His cruisers bombarded Sawatan Island, and the battleships shelled Ponape. These strikes effectively ended the usefulness of Truk as a base for the Japanese, eliminating a major hub of their defensive network.

VICTORIES AT THE PHILIPPINE SEA AND LEYTE

By June 1944, the Japanese defensive perimeter was shrinking. Bases in the outer Mandates—in the Marshalls and Carolines—had been seized or neutralized by the rapid advance of the Fifth Fleet. The major base at Rabaul had been rendered untenable; and the Allies were rapidly

TABLE 8. Battleship and Carrier Dispositions for Desecrate II

Formation	Commander	Carriers	Battleships
TG 58.1 Carrier Task Group 1	Rear Adm. Joseph J. Clark	*Hornet*, *Belleau Wood* (CVL), *Cowpens* (CVL), *Bataan* (CVL)	
TG 58.2 Carrier Task Group 2	Rear Adm. Alfred E. Montgomery	*Bunker Hill*, *Yorktown*, *Monterey* (CVL), *Cabot* (CVL)	*Iowa*, *New Jersey*
TF 58.3 Carrier Task Group 3	Rear Adm. John W. Reeves	*Enterprise*, *Lexington*, *Princeton* (CVL), *Langley* (CVL)	*North Carolina*, *Massachusetts*, *South Dakota*, *Alabama*

advancing along the northern coast of New Guinea. It had seemed the Japanese were content to let their defensive perimeter crumble without risking major fleet units, but this was about to change.

The third major offensive undertaken by Spruance's force was the seizure of the Marianas. Operation Forager envisioned the recapture of Guam and the occupation of Saipan and Tinian. Saipan would be attacked first, on 15 June; landings on Guam were initially scheduled for three days later. The assault on Tinian would follow, but the specific date remained flexible. Because the capture of the Marshalls and Carolines had not produced a fleet action, the "prevailing opinion . . . was that the Japanese navy would not fight for the Marianas."[33]

Nevertheless, Spruance had to be prepared; his battle plan for the Marianas was little different from those of earlier operations. Spruance expected to concentrate all his battleships into one formation, seven old ones from the amphibious forces and seven fast ones from the carrier groups, for a total of fourteen. Concentration still guided the employment of the fast battleships; Spruance ordered TGs 58.2 and 58.3, to which they were assigned, to operate in "close tactical support of each other" so that they could rapidly respond if the Japanese sought a surface action.[34]

An increasing availability of escort carriers allowed the primary focus of the fast carriers to become the suppression of enemy air bases, not direct air support for the invasion. The plan called for the carriers to start their attacks three days before the landings, but this date was advanced because of the "large estimated strength of enemy aircraft in the Marianas."[35] On June 11, planes from Mitscher's TF 58 struck Japanese positions on Saipan, Tinian, Guam, Rota, and Pagan. These attacks continued for the next two days.

The carriers operated in four task groups. Clark's TG 58.1 attacked Guam. The other three struck Saipan and Tinian. The fast battleships were kept concentrated. Montgomery's TG 58.2 contained the two high-speed battleships of BatDiv 7; the other five fast battleships were in Reeves' TG 58.3. Rear Adm. William K. Harrill's TG 58.4 and Clark's task group were supported by cruisers. The night before the landings, these two groups were sent north to attack the islands of Chichi Jima and Iwo Jima. The others, and their battleships, remained in the area, covering the landing beaches and assault forces.

In the meantime, the Japanese had resolved to contest the landings. On 12 June, after receiving word of the strikes in the Marianas, the new commander in chief of the Combined Fleet, Adm. Toyoda Soemu, issued orders to start Operation *A-Go*, his plan for decisive battle. A powerful fleet assembled under the command of Vice Admiral Ozawa. It included nine carriers, five battleships, and eleven heavy cruisers. His forces approached the Marianas in two main groups. Ozawa, the carriers, and three battleships left their base at Tawi Tawi in the southern Philippines and sailed through San Bernardino Strait. A second force under Vice Adm. Ugaki Matome, with the large battleships *Yamato* and *Musashi*, came north from Batjan in the Moluccas and rendezvoused with Ozawa in the Philippine Sea.

Spruance received word of these movements from submarines and realized that a major action was possible if the Japanese continued to approach; he endeavored to seize the opportunity.[36] During the night of 14–15 June, he ordered Clark's 58.1 and Harrill's 58.4 to cut short their attacks on the Jimas and return for a rendezvous near Saipan on 18 June. On 16 June, he postponed the invasion of Guam and held a conference with Vice Admiral Turner, commander of the invasion force. The two developed a plan of action to deal with the approaching threat.

Two aspects of the developing situation presented challenges for Spruance. The battle for Saipan, still going on, limited his mobility; he had anticipated the Japanese would attack while he was tied to the invasion forces. The fact that they were approaching in two distinct groups was more problematic. Spruance's plan anticipated that the Japanese might have two formations, a carrier group and an advanced guard, but within supporting distance.[37] The sightings so far suggested instead two independent formations. Spruance became concerned about what this might mean.

It was not an unusual Japanese tactic, but it surprised Spruance. The Navy's approach to battle emphasized concentration and maximized offensive power. Japanese tactics were different; they used multiple distributed formations and feints. One task group would act as a

TABLE 9. Battleship and Carrier Dispositions for Forager

Formation	Commander	Carriers	Battleships
TG 58.1 Carrier Task Group 1	Rear Adm. Joseph J. Clark	*Hornet, Yorktown, Belleau Wood* (CVL), *Bataan* (CVL)	
TG 58.2 Carrier Task Group 2	Rear Adm. Alfred E. Montgomery	*Bunker Hill, Wasp, Monterey* (CVL), *Cabot* (CVL)	*Iowa, New Jersey*
TF 58.3 Carrier Task Group 3	Rear Adm. John W. Reeves	*Enterprise, Lexington, San Jacinto* (CVL), *Princeton* (CVL)	*South Dakota, Alabama, Indiana, North Carolina, Washington*
TF 58.4 Carrier Task Group 4	Rear Adm. William K. Harrill	*Essex, Cowpens* (CVL), *Langley* (CVL)	
TF 52 Northern Attack Force	Vice Adm. Richmond K. Turner	*Fanshaw Bay* (CVE), *Midway* (CVE), *White Plains* (CVE), *Kalinin Bay* (CVE), *Kitkun Bay* (CVE), *Gambier Bay* (CVE)	*Tennessee, California, Maryland, Colorado*
TF 53 Southern Attack Force	Rear Adm. Richard L. Conolly	*Sangamon* (CVE), *Suwannee* (CVE), *Chenago* (CVE), *Corregidor* (CVE), *Coral Sea* (CVE)	*Pennsylvania, Idaho, New Mexico*

diversionary force. When the Americans attacked it, the Japanese striking force would come at them from another direction.[38] The Japanese in their doctrinal manuals referred to this as "flanking."

To counter the distributed Japanese formations, Spruance abandoned his standing battle plan. He did not concentrate the entire Fifth Fleet. Instead, Spruance and Turner strengthened TF 58 with five heavy cruisers, three light cruisers, and twenty-one destroyers, detached from the invasion forces. The old battleships, three cruisers, and five destroyers were formed into a blocking force and sent west of Saipan. The plan had two advantages. The blocking force provided close cover for the

Saipan beachhead, and TF 58 retained its high speed by not merging with the slower old battleships. This ability to exchange ships rapidly between task groups, again, was possible thanks to the standardized doctrines in PAC-10 and USF-10A. The speed of the fast carrier task forces allowed Spruance to move rapidly; the flexibility of fleet doctrine allowed him to treat his ships interchangeably. The largest reconfiguration of his forces was yet to come.

On 17 June, in preparation for a surface action, Rear Admiral Mitscher recommended detaching the battleships from the carrier task groups and placing them into a separate formation. That would prevent the inevitable confusion if the battleships and their escorts had to form a separate group in the middle of an air battle. Spruance concurred; the resulting TG 58.7 was placed under command of Vice Admiral Lee. It contained all the fast battleships, four heavy cruisers, and thirteen destroyers.[39] Spruance then issued a new battle plan. It called for airstrikes to disable the enemy carriers and surface action by the battle line: "Our air will knock out enemy carriers . . . then will attack enemy battleships and cruisers to slow or disable them. TG 58.7 will destroy enemy fleet either by fleet action if enemy elects to fight or by sinking slowed or crippled ships if enemy retreats."[40]

The rendezvous with TGs 58.1 and 58.4 was planned for 18 June. Early that morning, an additional submarine contact suggested the Japanese were close enough for a surface action that night. Mitscher asked Lee if he desired a night action. Lee declined emphatically: "Do not, repeat, do not believe we should seek night engagement."[41]

Lee's response reflected his own experience and the limited training of his command. He had fought a night action off Guadalcanal and knew how quickly they could degenerate into melees. Formed on the spot from four different task groups, Lee's formation could operate together in daylight by virtue of the common doctrines of USF-10A, but it was not prepared for the additional confusion of night action. Lee's comments after his earlier battle provide clues to his state of mind: "Our battleships are neither designed nor armed for close range night actions with enemy light forces. A few minutes['] intense fire . . . from secondary battery guns can, and did, render one of our new battleships deaf, dumb, blind and impotent through destruction of radar, radio and fire control circuits."[42] That battleship had been *South Dakota*. Although Lee had won that battle, he wanted to avoid repeating those risks.

Soon after Lee responded, Spruance too recommended against night action.[43] He did not want to get too far away from Saipan and was waiting to concentrate all the carrier groups; TGs 58.1 and 58.4 had not yet rejoined. Spruance was also concerned about a "diversionary attack" on the flank. This phrase has usually been interpreted as a reference to a Japanese force slipping around to the south and attacking the invasion beaches, but that is unlikely.[44] From captured planning material, Spruance had become aware of the diversionary nature of Japanese tactics. He had seen translated documents and plans that described flanking attacks as strikes against an opposing carrier force after that force's attack planes had been committed to another, less important target.[45]

That is what had happened to the Japanese at the battle of Midway. Their carriers had been struck by surprise from an unanticipated direction while they were preoccupied with attacking Midway Island. Spruance concluded the Japanese hoped now to do the same. He knew that this type of flanking had been better suited to the early part of the war, when aircraft carriers had been capable of only fragile pulses of offensive power. It was less effective in mid-1944, when increased numbers of fighters and effective means of intercepting incoming strikes allowed carriers to fend off attacks. This explains Spruance's preference to remain concentrated and wait until the Japanese had shown their hand before striking in force. He had confidence that he could accept an initial Japanese blow before retaliating.[46]

Spruance's emphasis on concentration continued to influence the developing action. He did not accept Mitscher's recommendation to detach TG 58.1 to cut off Ozawa's escape route to the home islands. When a direction-finding fix from Pearl Harbor on 18 June placed the Japanese formation approximately 350 miles to the west, Mitscher recommended closing at night to launch a morning strike and get the battleships into position. Spruance again refused; this time he *was* worried about the possibility of an "end run."[47] With that decision, the chance for a decisive fleet action was lost, but the sides would exchange blows.

Ozawa formed his battle disposition early on the morning of 19 June. He placed his main surface striking force, with four battleships, three light carriers, and nine heavy cruisers under Vice Admiral Kurita, in the lead. One hundred miles to the rear were his two main carrier groups. Ozawa commanded Carrier Division 1, with *Taiho*, *Shokaku*, and *Zuikaku*; Rear Adm. Joshima Takaji had *Junyo*, *Hiyo*, and *Ryuho* in Carrier Division 2. Joshima also had a fifth battleship, *Nagato*.

Placing Kurita's force in the van—at the front of the formation—served two purposes. Because it would be closer to the American carriers, it was expected to be the main focus of their strikes; this would free Ozawa to make "flank" attacks with relative impunity. Also, the floatplanes of Kurita's battleships and cruisers would search for the American task forces, providing the "eyes" for Ozawa's strike planes. Soon after the battle disposition was formed, these floatplanes took to the air. They sighted parts of TGs 58.4 and 58.7.

Ozawa, intending to use the airfields on Guam and Rota to refuel and rearm his planes, launched the floatplanes at long range, ranges at which Mitscher could not respond. Over the course of the day, four large raids came at the American task groups. Most were intercepted long before they could make attack runs on Spruance's ships. The declining quality of Japanese aviators combined with effective fighter direction techniques to turn the battle of the Philippine Sea into a lopsided fight. Ozawa's losses in planes and pilots were tremendous; Navy fighter pilots dubbed it "The Great Marianas Turkey Shoot." Unable to sustain the attacks, Ozawa turned toward Japan and began to withdraw. Spruance pursued and, on the evening of the next day, launched a long-range strike that sank the carrier *Hiyo*. Spruance again refused to operate detached task forces.[48] The outcome of the battle was not decisive, even when the successes of the submarines were considered.

Before the action, Vice Adm. Charles A. Lockwood, commander of the Pacific Fleet's submarines, had stationed four of his boats in a square surrounding the area in which he believed Ozawa would operate. On 19 June, two of them found targets. *Albacore* sighted and torpedoed

Ozawa's flagship, *Taiho*, just after she had completed launching her first strike; eight hours later, she sank from explosions triggered by gasoline fumes. In the interim, three torpedoes from *Cavella* sank the carrier *Shokaku*. The Japanese were soundly defeated at Philippine Sea, but many of their fleet units, including most of the carriers and all the battleships, withdrew to fight again. The first phase of the decisive naval battle of the Pacific War, the carrier duel, was over.

In the summer of 1944, to keep up the rapid pace of operations in the Pacific, Admiral Nimitz introduced a second command for his Central Pacific Force, parallel to that of Spruance. The two commanders and their respective staffs would alternate command of the same forces, one commander conducting an operation while the other planned the next, allowing less time between offensives and increasing the pressure on the Japanese. Vice Admiral Halsey, commander of the Third Fleet and victor in the Solomons, was selected to be Spruance's counterpart. When under Halsey's command, the ships of the Central Pacific would be designated the Third Fleet; when Spruance led them, they would again become the Fifth Fleet.

Halsey took Mitscher and the fast carriers, now TF 38, on a series of raids in September 1944. They struck the Palaus, Mindanao, and the Visayas, covering the invasions of Morotai, the Palaus, and Ulithi. The lack of resistance convinced Halsey that the existing timetable for landings in the Philippines could be accelerated. Within a matter of days, the JCS had approved a revised plan.

The invasion of Leyte, code-named King II, differed from previous large amphibious operations. The unity of command that had existed in Galvanic, Flintlock, and Forager was absent. The Central Pacific and South Pacific offensives would meet in the southern Philippines, and King II used forces from both theaters. Command was divided between the two, hindering the effectiveness of the operation and leading to confusion during the battles that ensued.[49] Halsey's Third Fleet retained the fast carriers, but the Central Pacific Force's amphibious units, including the old battleships and escort carriers, were transferred to the Seventh Fleet, under command of Vice Admiral Kinkaid. Kinkaid led the amphibious assault and was subordinate to General MacArthur.

As in Forager, the fast carriers suppressed Japanese air bases, but Halsey was freed of many of the burdens his predecessor had faced at the Philippine Sea. Without the old battleships and amphibious forces under his command, Halsey could develop plans that fully leveraged the mobility of his task forces. He was also free to seek out the Japanese; Nimitz's plan for the operation stressed that "in case opportunity for destruction of major portion of enemy fleet offers or can be created, such destruction becomes the primary task."[50]

Third Fleet battle plans stressed the importance of this objective. They differed from those used by the Fifth Fleet in two important respects. Halsey ignored the old battleships in his tactical planning and focused on a battle line composed of only fast battleships. This increased his flexibility because his surface forces could operate within the carrier formations. Halsey planned to leverage this to employ a well-developed prewar technique.

He planned a coordinated attack, with carrier aircraft and battleship gunfire hitting the enemy nearly simultaneously at dawn. Halsey assumed that his four carrier groups, far superior to what the Japanese could muster at this stage of the war, would either win the opening carrier duel or sight the enemy too late in the day for strike operations. In either case, Halsey would approach at night. Along the way, the carrier forces would reorganize. Battleships, cruisers, and supporting destroyers would leave their respective task groups and form TF 34, a battle formation under the command of Vice Admiral Lee. TF 34 would position itself about seventy miles ahead of the carriers. As morning approached, planes would ready and launch. The coordinated movements of the fleet were designed to bring the attacking planes and the battleships within range of the enemy at the same time.[51]

> Particular effort . . . will be made to gain a position from which a predawn carrier strike may be launched concurrently with the release of fast heavy striking force from a favorable attack position. Development of a favorable tactical situation . . . will be effected by dispatching TF 34 and carrier air groups to attack the enemy. The approach will be so conducted as to give TF 34 an opportunity to strike from a favorable position and so coordinate its offensive efforts with those of carrier air groups.[52]

Halsey considered this the "optimum plan for decisive action." It would collect nearly all the striking power of TF 38 into one decisive pulse and overwhelm the Japanese. Halsey had revived the prewar coordinated attack.

The main landings took place on 20 October, with two of Halsey's carrier groups providing direct support. Vice Adm. John S. McCain's TG 38.1 and Rear Adm. Ralph Davidson's TG 38.4 attacked targets on Leyte and suppressed airfields on Mindanao and the western Visayas. The two other carrier groups, Rear Adm. Gerald F. Bogan's TG 38.2 and Rear Admiral Sherman's TG 38.3 remained concentrated farther north, scouting for potential threats from the direction of Japan and Formosa. Halsey kept all the battleships together; TG 38.2 had BatDiv 7, again with *Iowa* and *New Jersey*. Sherman had four battleships in TG 38.3.[53]

The possibility that the Japanese would commit significant naval forces to defend the Philippines was not seriously considered in Third or Seventh Fleet plans. This was a mistake; in the summer of 1944, the Japanese had created a series of plans, code-named *Sho-Go* (Victory). The southernmost of these, *Sho-1*, covered the defense of the Philippines. Alerted by preliminary landings around Leyte, the Japanese Imperial General Headquarters made the decision to implement *Sho-1* on 18 October. Two days later, Vice Adm. Kuaska Ryunosuke, chief of staff to Admiral Toyoda, issued the final plans to units of the Combined Fleet.[54] These orders triggered the series of fights that together formed the battle of Leyte Gulf.

The Japanese moved toward Leyte in four groups. Admiral Kurita's 1st Diversionary Attack Force divided in two. His 1st and 2nd sections, led by Kurita himself, would transit San Bernardino Strait. Kurita's 3rd section, commanded by Vice Adm. Nishimura Shoji, was ordered to pass through Surigao Strait. Kurita planned to reunite with Nishimura in Leyte Gulf early on the morning of 25 October and destroy the invasion forces. The third Japanese group, the 2nd Diversionary Attack Force, under Vice Adm. Shima Kiyohide, would come through Surigao Strait behind Nishimura. Between them, these attack forces had seven battleships, sixteen cruisers, and twenty-three destroyers.

TABLE 10. Battleship and Carrier Dispositions for King II

Formation	Commander	Carriers	Battleships
TG 38.1 Carrier Task Group 1	Vice Adm. John S. McCain	*Hornet, Wasp, Cowpens* (CVL), *Monterey* (CVL)	
TG 38.2 Carrier Task Group 2	Rear Adm. Gerald F. Bogan	*Bunker Hill, Intrepid, Independence* (CVL), *Cabot* (CVL)	*Iowa, New Jersey*
TF 38.3 Carrier Task Group 3	Rear Adm. Frederick C. Sherman	*Essex, Lexington, Langley* (CVL), *Princeton* (CVL)	*South Dakota, Alabama, Massachusetts, Washington*
TF 58.4 Carrier Task Group 4	Rear Adm. Ralph Davidson	*Enterprise, Franklin, Belleau Wood* (CVL), *San Jacinto* (CVL)	(After 22 October) *Washington, Alabama*

The last Japanese group, commanded by Admiral Ozawa, was a decoy. Ozawa took the Combined Fleet's remaining carriers south from Japan and with them hoped to draw the Third Fleet's covering forces north, away from Leyte Gulf. Ozawa had four carriers, two battleship-carriers, three cruisers, and nine destroyers. Halsey, still confident that the Japanese would not seek battle, was preoccupied with preparations for the Third Fleet's next major operation, an attack against the Japanese home islands.[55] On 22 October, he sent Davidson's TG 38.4 and McCain's TG 38.1 to the fleet base at Ulithi to refuel and rearm. Before detaching them, he took two battleships—*Washington* and *Alabama*—from Sherman's TG 38.3 and transferred them to TG 38.4. Two task groups and just four fast battleships remained in the area.

The same day, Kurita's 1st and 2nd sections left their anchorage at Brunei Bay on the north coast of Borneo. Submarines again provided early warning of Japanese moves. Kurita's ships were sighted and attacked by the submarines *Dace* and *Darter* on the morning of 23 October while transiting Palawan Passage. Three heavy cruisers were hit: *Atago* and *Maya* were sunk; *Takao* was damaged and forced to retire.

Halsey and Kinkaid received these sightings and additional information from long-range air searches; they became convinced that the Japanese were moving toward the Philippines in force. Halsey quickly realized his dispositions were inadequate and recalled Davidson's task group and its two battleships. He did not recall McCain's. McCain had more planes available than Davidson, but Halsey considered the two battleships more important.[56]

Halsey disposed his forces to allow effective aerial searches to the west and provide warning of the Japanese approach. TG 38.3 was farthest to the north, east of Polillo Island. He placed Bogan's TG 38.2 with BatDiv 7 in the center, off San Bernardino Strait, and TG 38.4 in the south, east of Samar. This arrangement dispersed Halsey's battleship strength—each task group had just two battleships—but allowed him to cover the major passages through the archipelago. With BatDiv 7 in the center, Bogan's task group could quickly concentrate on either flank.

On 24 October, Kurita and Nishimura were sighted by Halsey's carriers. Nishimura was attacked by Davidson's TG 38.4; two ships were slightly damaged. Since Kurita had a much more powerful force, Halsey left Nishimura to Kinkaid and moved quickly to consolidate his battleship strength. Davidson was ordered north; all three carrier groups concentrated off San Bernardino Strait. Halsey's reshuffling of his ships and task groups, like Spruance's at Philippine Sea, was made possible by the new doctrinal concepts. He was initially dispersed to suppress Japanese airfields and locate approaching Japanese forces. Once the greatest threat was identified, Halsey rapidly concentrated and prepared for battle.

As the three carrier task groups moved to concentrate, they launched strikes against Kurita's formation. Over the course of several hours, repeated air attacks sank the battleship *Musashi* and damaged several other ships. In the early afternoon, Kurita turned back, seeking relief from the onslaught. In the meantime, Halsey had issued a preparatory battle order in expectation of Kurita's force exiting the strait. TGs 38.2 and 38.4 were close enough to concentrate; the plan combined BatDiv 7 with the battleships *Washington* and *Alabama* from TG 38.4. The four battleships would form a surface striking unit with five cruisers and ten destroyers. Vice Admiral Lee would command the resulting formation, designated TF 34.[57] TG 38.3 was too distant, and its battleships were not included. Halsey planned to make do with the forces immediately on hand.

He did not implement the plan. Scouting reports indicated Kurita was heavily damaged and withdrawing. Intelligence available to Halsey suggested that Japanese forces in the area of the home islands were stronger than they actually were, and this led to the conclusion that the most serious threat would come from the north.[58] In the afternoon, planes from Sherman's TG 38.3 found that threat: they sighted Ozawa's Main Body. Halsey considered his alternatives: "[The option of] leaving TF 34 to block San Bernardino Straits . . . was rejected; the potential strength of the Northern Forces [Ozawa] was too great to leave unmolested, and requiring TF 34 to engage the Center Force [Kurita] while at the same time exposed to attack by land-based and carrier-based air attack was not sound. This alternative spread our strength and risked unprofitable damage in detail."[59]

That evening, Halsey moved north with all his forces to pursue Ozawa.[60] Along the way, he put his battle plan in motion. The fleet slowed as the six battleships, seven cruisers, and eighteen destroyers separated themselves from the carrier groups and formed TF 34. TG 38.2 became the battle-line carrier group; it would provide direct support to Lee's surface forces. Mitscher expected contact to be made at 0430, but estimates of the Japanese position were incorrect. The first airstrike from the carriers hit Ozawa long before TF 34 could come into action. Coordinated attacks would have to wait until the battleships were in position.

Halsey ran out of time. As TF 34 approached the Japanese, urgent messages were received from Kinkaid. Escort carriers on his northern flank were engaged in a running battle with Kurita's 1st and 2nd sections. The remains of the 1st Striking Force had reversed course, passed through San Bernardino Strait, and were moving toward the landing beaches. Halsey sent TF 34, minus four cruisers and nine destroyers, south to assist. TG 38.2 followed in support.[61]

The four cruisers and nine destroyers detached from TF 34 continued north and formed a surface striking force. They attacked Japanese ships damaged by the carrier strikes, finishing off carrier *Chiyoda* and sinking destroyer *Hatsuzuki* after a running gun battle. Ozawa's other carriers, *Zuikaku*, *Zuiho*, and *Chitose*, were sunk by planes from TF 38. The submarine *Jallao*, coached to the scene by Vice Admiral Lockwood, sank the light cruiser *Tama*, previously damaged by air attack. Demoralized and broken, Ozawa's force retreated.

In the meantime, Nishimura's 3rd section had been virtually annihilated in Surigao Strait. Although Kinkaid had not anticipated that the Japanese would seek major action, his Seventh Fleet was well prepared. His plan called for Rear Admiral Oldendorf's Fire Support Group, designated TG 77.2, and Rear Adm. Russell S. Berkey's Close Covering Group, TG 77.3, to combine in the face of strong enemy opposition. Oldendorf had all six of the old battleships supporting Leyte under his command, along with escorting cruisers and destroyers; he and his ships had been part of the Fifth Fleet's offensives in the Central Pacific. Berkey's group was part of the multinational Seventh Fleet.[62] USF-10A was perfect in situations like these when disparate task groups would come together for battle; Oldendorf put it to good use.

By noon on 24 October, Kinkaid had realized that the Japanese were seeking major action and ordered Oldendorf to prepare for a night battle in Surigao Strait and to take Berkey's TG 77.3 in support. Oldendorf began to formulate a plan. He called Berkey and his battle-line commander, Rear Adm. George L. Weyler, together for a conference. They met in Oldendorf's flagship, where he familiarized them with the details.

Because the primary mission of Oldendorf's battleships was to provide gunfire support for the landings, they were loaded mainly with bombardment ammunition. They had few armor-piercing shells suitable for damaging enemy battleships. To compensate for this, Oldendorf planned to fight at medium ranges, where the battleships could fire more accurately and make the most of their limited armor-piercing ammunition. To help ensure the destruction of Nishimura's forces, Oldendorf planned destroyer torpedo attacks that were to occur simultaneously with the gunfire of his cruisers and battleships. The destroyers would approach the Japanese from both sides of the strait, using the backdrop of the surrounding islands to mask their approach and increase their chances of achieving surprise. Their CICs were expected to allow them to coordinate in the darkness.[63]

After the conference, Oldendorf signaled his battle plan to the six battleships, eight cruisers, and twenty-one destroyers of his force. The battle plan called for disposition A-2 from USF-10A, intended for the employment of task forces like this one. A-2 placed the battle line in the center and light forces at either flank. This was an efficient arrangement for the confined waters at the head of the strait, and it maximized the effectiveness of Oldendorf's gunfire.

The plan worked to perfection, including one small addition. Five picket destroyers from TG 79.11 commanded by Capt. Jesse G. Coward were the first to attack. Coward had joined Oldendorf on his own initiative, displaying the aggressiveness inherent in the Navy's doctrine. Coward engaged in the kind of preliminary night search and attack the Navy had planned for decades, attacking with two groups. He took *Remey*, *McGowan*, and *Melvin* down the eastern side of the strait while Cdr. Richard H. Phillips led *McDermut* and *Monssen* down the western side.[64]

During Coward's approach, *McGowan*'s CIC obtained a radar contact at a range of eighteen miles. Within a few minutes, the contact resolved into a column. Nishimura had his four destroyers in the van; the battleships *Yamashiro* and *Fuso* followed. The cruiser *Mogami* was in the rear. As Coward's ships closed, lookouts on the destroyer *Shigure* sighted them. The Japanese sent searchlight beams into the darkness but failed to locate the three destroyers. Two minutes later, lookouts on *Melvin* sighted Nishimura's column, most likely aided by the searchlight beams. Range was just shy of 13,000 yards, long for Coward's torpedoes.

He had lost contact with Phillips' group, so there was no longer an opportunity for a coordinated attack. However, he could still surprise the Japanese if he launched his torpedoes quickly. Coward did so and then turned away, ordering his ships to make smoke to cover their retirement. The range had dropped to nine thousand yards. A searchlight fixed on *Remey*, and the Japanese immediately opened fire, but they scored no hits. Coward's ships were soon out of danger.

Nishimura must have thought that Coward had been driven off before he could launch torpedoes or that his ships were phantoms, because he took no evasive action. It was a critical mistake. *Fuso* was hit by at least one torpedo, and the old battleship sheered out of line. The hit most likely started a fire in her central magazine spaces. Within half an hour, she exploded and broke in two.

At about the time *Fuso* was torpedoed, the Japanese sighted Phillips' ships and opened fire. He held fire to prevent the Japanese from using his gun flashes as a point of aim and closed to launch torpedoes. This time Nishimura maneuvered to avoid the torpedoes, but the evasive action brought his ships directly into their paths. Three of the four Japanese destroyers were put out of action. *Yamagumo* blew up. *Michishio* was crippled and left dead in the water. *Asagumo*'s bow was blown off; she reversed course and retired down the strait. One torpedo hit *Yamashiro*, but she continued without incident.

Rear Admiral Berkey noticed that Coward's destroyers had met little resistance. Berkey seized the opportunity and sent the destroyers of the left flank in to attack earlier than planned.[65] These were the ships led by Captain McManes; their attack—and McManes' able use of his CIC to coordinate his forces—was briefly described in the previous chapter. McManes scored another torpedo hit on *Yamashiro* and sank the damaged *Michishio*.

The final destroyer attack came from the ships on Oldendorf's right flank, Capt. Roland N. Smoot's Destroyer Squadron 56. Smoot divided his destroyers into three attack groups. His group went directly at the Japanese; the other two attacked from either flank. The flank attacks scored no hits. Nishimura turned to bring his broadsides parallel to the American battle line and avoided their torpedoes. Smoot pressed his attack and scored at least one more torpedo hit on *Yamashiro*.

With the Japanese less than 16,000 yards from his flagship, Oldendorf opened fire, first with his cruisers on either flank and then with the battleships. *West Virginia*, at the head of the battle line, was the first battleship to engage. She had repeatedly won gunnery competitions before the war. At Surigao, she was just as accurate. Raised and rebuilt after

Pearl Harbor, *West Virginia* was equipped with the most modern equipment, including the Mark 8 radar and B-scope. With an effective fire-control solution in place at 30,000 yards, she refined it as *Yamashiro* closed.[66] Myron J. Smith's history of the battleship recounts her initial salvos.

> Aboard cruiser *Louisville*, Admiral Oldendorf heard her huge projectiles passing above, sounding "like a train of box cars passing over a high trestle." Suddenly, the admiral and the men up and down the American line had the satisfaction of seeing a tremendous eruption on the horizon. The *West Virginia*'s shot had found the forecastle of the *Yamashiro*. Aboard the "WeeVee," Captain [Herbert V.] Wiley chuckled as Fire Control Officer Commander Robert Crawford, Jr., cheered and exulted. The skipper watched the second salvo depart and "saw explosions when it landed," explosions that crushed the enemy's great pagoda tower like a sand castle.[67]

Tennessee and *California*, also equipped with the Mark 8 fire-control radar, joined in soon after. The other battleships, still relying on the older FC radar, had difficulty locating the target. It made no difference; *Yamashiro* was crippled and sinking. Nishimura's attempt to penetrate Leyte Gulf had failed. *Shigure* and the badly damaged *Mogami* were all that survived. Following in Nishimura's wake, Shima's cruisers "fired ineffective torpedoes at ghosts to the north" and quickly withdrew.[68]

Soon thereafter, Kurita's force reappeared off Samar, within visual range of Kinkaid's escort carriers. A desperate fight ensued, with both Halsey and Kinkaid mustering powerful forces to counter the threat. Kinkaid ordered Oldendorf to send a battleship division, a heavy-cruiser division, and supporting destroyers to assist the carriers. Oldendorf sent the three battleships that had the most armor-piercing ammunition remaining, all four of his heavy cruisers, and twenty destroyers.[69]

None of these forces would arrive in time. Task Group 77.4, commanded by Rear Adm. Thomas L. Sprague, bore the brunt of Kurita's attacks. The small task group was divided into three task units, known as "Taffies." Each had several escort carriers with destroyers and destroyer escorts to screen them. Kurita sighted Taffy 3 and mistook it for part of TF 38; he ordered a general attack. Sprague's screening forces acted in accordance with the Navy's tactical heuristics and attacked aggressively, even though they were badly outgunned. Cdr. Ernest E. Evans' destroyer *Johnston* was nearest to the Japanese and the first to make an attack. She engaged the leading enemy ships—Kurita's cruisers—with guns and torpedoes, hitting Kumano and knocking her out of the fight. The destroyers *Hoel* and *Heerman* joined in; together, the three destroyers closed with the enemy battleships. *Hoel* was the first to be sunk. *Johnston* survived a little longer.

The destroyer escorts—designed for antisubmarine work, armed with few torpedoes, and unpracticed at torpedo attacks—followed them. *Samuel B. Roberts, John C. Butler, Dennis,* and *Raymond* attacked with torpedoes, made smoke, and did their best to help the destroyers shield the escort carriers from Kurita's attack. *Samuel B. Roberts* was lost, but together Sprague's small ships and the desperate attacks of his planes succeeded in delaying, confusing, and disrupting the Japanese formation. The escort carrier *Gambier Bay* was sunk, but in exchange, Kurita lost two heavy cruisers, *Chokai* and *Chikuma,* to aerial bombs and torpedoes. A third, *Suzuya,* had been mortally wounded. The Taffies had put up a good fight. Kurita broke off the pursuit and paused to regroup his forces.

Halsey's TF 34 and TG 38.2 were steaming south to join the fight, but they would not find Kurita. Not long after noon on 25 October, Kurita turned to the north and headed back toward San Bernardino Strait. When he became aware of these moves, Halsey ordered TG 34.5, a pursuit force formed around BatDiv 7, to separate from TF 34 and go after the retreating enemy.[70]

The pursuit force contained two battleships, three cruisers, and eight destroyers under the command of Rear Adm. Oscar C. Badger. Halsey's intention was for Badger to employ battle disposition A-1 from USF-10A, with all light forces concentrated in the van. TF 34.5 would use battle plan "1L1," an action on parallel courses at long range, with light forces on the offensive.[71] Badger arrived too late to engage Kurita but, in the darkness, found the destroyer *Nowaki,* which had remained to pick up survivors, and sank her. The battle of Leyte Gulf was over.

Japanese efforts to contest the landings in the Philippines and Marianas had led to the decisive battle that both navies had anticipated before the war. Although the expected clash of battle lines did not occur, the outcome was decisive. The remaining Japanese surface forces lacked the fuel and strength necessary to challenge further offensives; the Combined Fleet had become a hollow shell.

FINAL OPERATIONS

After the battle of Leyte Gulf, the Navy's fast carriers were free to support additional offensive moves and strike deeper into the Japanese Empire. Vice Admiral McCain relieved Vice Admiral Mitscher as commander of TF 38 on 30 October; Mitscher began to plan future operations with Spruance. McCain and Halsey supported General MacArthur's invasion of Mindoro—code-named Musketeer III—in December 1944 and his landings on Luzon in January, striking targets in the Philippines, Formosa, and the Ryukyus.

Halsey took the Third Fleet into the South China Sea, hoping to find remnants of the Japanese battle fleet in Camranh Bay. On 12 January, a surface striking group based around BatDiv 7 was sent toward the anchorage; Rear Admiral Bogan's TG 38.2 provided close support. No surface action occurred because the Japanese had already moved south to Lingga Roads. After additional strikes on Formosa, Hong Kong, Hainan, Canton, and Okinawa, the fast carriers returned to Ulithi.

TABLE 11. Battleship and Carrier Dispositions for Musketeer III

Formation	Commander	Carriers	Battleships
TG 38.1 Carrier Task Group 1	Rear Adm. Alfred E. Montgomery	*Yorktown, Wasp, Cowpens* (CVL), *Monterey* (CVL)	*Alabama, Massachusetts*
TG 38.2 Carrier Task Group 2	Rear Adm. Gerald F. Bogan	*Lexington, Hancock, Hornet, Independence* (CVL), *Cabot* (CVL)	*Iowa, New Jersey, Wisconsin*
TF 38.3 Carrier Task Group 3	Rear Adm. Frederick C. Sherman	*Essex, Ticonderoga, Langley* (CVL), *San Jacinto* (CVL)	*North Carolina, South Dakota, Washington*

Spruance and Mitscher took command of the Fifth Fleet and TF 58, respectively, on 26 January. In mid-February, they supported the invasion of Iwo Jima with attacks on the Japanese home islands. On 1 March, they struck Okinawa and conducted photographic reconnaissance. Operation Iceberg, the campaign for Okinawa, began later that month with raids on Kyushu and targets in the Inland Sea. For the next four months, the fast carriers supported the invasion forces, intercepting Japanese raids and suppressing airfields on Kyushu and Shikoku. Ten large kamikaze attacks—*Kikusui* operations—took place between 6 April and 22 June, taxing the abilities of the fleet's CICs. Although many of the suicide planes got through, Okinawa was secured by 22 June.

After the capture of Okinawa, Halsey resumed command. He took TF 38 close to Japan and attacked the home islands. Carrier strikes and battleship bombardments "supplemented B-29 [bomber] raids with hard blows against industrial targets and basic war industries."[72] These missions brought the battleships within range of Japanese suicide boats. Airborne radars helped detect them. During a bombardment mission in July 1945, for example, the ships of BatDiv 7 were supported by a pair

TABLE 12. Battleship and Carrier Dispositions for Strikes on Japan

Formation	Commander	Carriers	Battleships
TG 58.1 Carrier Task Group 1	Rear Adm. Joseph J. Clark	*Hornet, Wasp, Bennington, Belleau Wood* (CVL)	*Indiana, Massachusetts*
TG 58.2 Carrier Task Group 2	Rear Adm. Ralph Davidson	*Lexington, Hancock, San Jacinto* (CVL)	*Wisconsin, Missouri*
TF 58.3 Carrier Task Group 3	Rear Adm. Frederick C. Sherman	*Essex, Bunker Hill, Cowpens* (CVL)	*South Dakota, New Jersey, Alaska* (CB)
TF 58.4 Carrier Task Group 4	Rear Adm. Arthur W. Radford	*Yorktown, Randolph, Langley* (CVL), *Cabot* (CVL)	*North Carolina, Washington*
TF 58.5 Night Carrier Group	Rear Adm. Matthias B. Gardner	*Enterprise, Saratoga*	

of radar-equipped TBM Avengers; acting as pickets, they could detect small craft much earlier than could the ship-based search sets. Project Cadillac was an expanded version of the same basic idea; specially modified planes with powerful radars were built to fly over the fleet. Their radars would be connected to the CICs in the ships below, augmenting the fleet's surveillance capabilities. The war ended before these planes could be put into service.[73]

A DISCUSSION OF ASYMMETRY

The Japanese countered American material dominance with an asymmetric approach, the suicide tactics of the kamikaze. Although suicide boats and torpedoes were also used, the most effective suicide vehicle was the airplane. Japanese pilots turned their aircraft into guided missiles, driving them into Allied ships. Kamikaze attacks offered the potential for achieving significantly more damage with fewer planes and less-skilled pilots. They struck battleships, several carriers—*Essex* on 25 November 1944, *Ticonderoga* on 21 January 1945, *Hancock* on 1 April, *Enterprise* on 11 April and again on 14 May, and *Bunker Hill* on 11 May—and many smaller ships. Kamikaze tactics were a response to an earlier asymmetry, the new approaches developed by the Pacific Fleet during the first two years of the war.

These developments are not generally considered asymmetric, but that is only because they have not been studied with sufficient depth and understanding. The development of the CIC permitted a radically new approach to coordinating ships in combat by allowing them to develop a common understanding of the tactical situation. The introduction of PAC-10 enabled the interchangeability of ships and task forces that was so important to the rapid operational tempo that broke the Japanese defensive perimeter in 1944. Both the CIC and PAC-10 were transformational; they changed the nature of tactics and operations. If we consider the approaches the Navy planned to employ in 1941—the decentralized development of plans and doctrine in small units and the movement of a large, consolidated battle fleet across the Pacific as a single main body—the methods of 1944 were radically new. They were asymmetric.

The Japanese had developed defensive methods that were well suited to counter the Navy's prewar approaches. During the campaign for Guadalcanal, the Japanese stalled the American advance and held back the Navy's carrier forces. It was not sufficient to win an outright victory, but it was enough to force a lengthy and taxing campaign. This was important for Japanese strategy. If the advance of the Pacific Fleet could be delayed and the Navy's forces worn down, peace on favorable terms, or even outright victory, could be achieved. The networked defensive system of the Mandates, with its web of naval and air bases, was designed to cripple a large battle fleet. The Japanese would likely have done very well if Nimitz had used the doctrines and plans of 1942.

However, Nimitz and his staff used a broad base of experience to develop a new, asymmetric approach. They leveraged prewar experience with detached carrier task groups; they integrated wartime lessons from carriers and surface forces; they experimented with the new carriers joining the fleet; and they framed all these concepts with the tactical heuristics emphasizing aggressive action and the importance of seizing the initiative. What emerged was a radically new approach based on interchangeable ships, modular task forces, and mobile carrier groups. The Pacific Fleet would not advance as a monolith; it would attack as a distributed network. This allowed the carrier groups to penetrate the Japanese defensive perimeter, overwhelm the defenses of a whole island group, and isolate it from reinforcements. When surface action threatened, the distributed network consolidated its surface forces into a powerful battle line. Otherwise, the striking power was distributed over a wide area, to suppress as many Japanese airfields as possible.

The networked approach allowed the Pacific Fleet to advance much more rapidly than anticipated. Instead of taking time out to rest and refuel, the modular structure of the carrier task groups, combined with forward replenishment support from the service squadrons, allowed Nimitz's forces to maintain a nearly constant forward presence. Individual ships and task groups left the combat zone for rest and refitting, but the Fast Carrier Task Force sustained a rapid pace of advance, the "unremitting pressure" called for in the Granite campaign plan.

The new approach demonstrated the ability of the Pacific Fleet's doctrine to evolve. Additional changes, introduced in response to the increasing threat of suicide planes, further demonstrated this ability. For the Musketeer operation, Vice Admiral McCain concentrated TF 38 into three task groups. This provided a greater concentration of anti-aircraft firepower, enhancing the ability of each group to withstand kamikaze attacks. The composition of carrier air groups changed; previously, less than half of the planes carried were fighters. By December 1944, over two-thirds of the air groups were fighters. This allowed stronger combat air patrols and increased the chances of intercepting suicide planes. It also meant that the fast carriers could keep fighter patrols flying over enemy airfields continually during daylight, destroying planes as they attempted to take off or land. Specific carriers—like the old *Enterprise* and *Saratoga*—were designated for night operations. The use of radar picket destroyers expanded the area over which any one carrier group could operate; picket destroyers could detect incoming strikes and vector fighters to attack them long before they reached the carriers.

In response to the kamikaze threat, task force commanders tried new ideas, demonstrating the potential of the Navy's doctrine to continue to experiment and evolve. In the language of complexity, they were expanding the "phase space" to identify new opportunities. This continued investigation illustrates the capacity the Navy had developed to identify and exploit new ideas. That capacity allowed the Pacific Fleet to overcome the threat represented by the kamikaze.

CONCLUSION

The success of the Central Pacific offensive was made possible by a new approach to naval warfare. Rather than attacking as one centralized fleet, the Pacific Fleet operated as a series of modular task forces, swapping ships, task groups, and commanders freely to build a networked system that could sustain a powerful offensive and overwhelm Japanese resistance.

The most important ingredient in the emergence of this new approach was the shift in how the Pacific Fleet developed and disseminated tactical doctrine introduced by PAC-10 in the summer of 1943. This was a new constraint—a more uniform approach to tactical doctrine—that increased cohesion. Increased cohesion allowed the adoption of a modular approach to ships and task groups, permitting the effective employment of a distributed collection of fast carrier task forces. The new level of cohesion ensured that when task forces came together in the face of enemy surface threats, they could act as a unit. It also rectified the shortcomings of prewar doctrinal development by relieving task force commanders of the burden of creating specific battle plans and doctrines for their forces, something they had been unable to do effectively during the fighting off Guadalcanal.

Prewar concepts were essential to the successful approach embedded in PAC-10. The prewar major action plans, first issued by Admiral Pratt in *Tentative Fleet Dispositions and Battle Plans* in 1929 and reissued in FTP-134 and FTP-188, introduced a new vocabulary for coordinating forces in battle. PAC-10 expanded upon this vocabulary, providing the Navy with a new set of plans applicable to smaller actions and modular task groups.

Wartime lessons and experimentation were also essential. Without the difficulties experienced during the Guadalcanal campaign, the flaws in prewar approaches to plans, doctrine, and information processing would not have been exposed. These revelations led Nimitz to revise his approaches and seek alternatives, resulting in the CIC, PAC-10, and new approaches to coordinating multiple carriers in battle.

Driving all these improvements was the pressure to initiate a successful campaign in the Central Pacific that would win the war. Nimitz and his planners, urged on by Admiral King, embraced the concepts promoted by Admiral Mahan. Strategic victory was the primary goal. Tactical approaches—concerning the defeat of the Japanese fleet—were a means to that end but not an end in themselves. This is why such emphasis was placed on a rapid offensive; the best way to ensure success was to keep the Japanese off balance and limit their ability to react.

The synthesis of prewar principles and wartime lessons in PAC-10 and the follow-on USF-10A benefitted lower-level commanders, who consistently relied upon the new plans. The way Lee and Oldendorf leveraged the new manuals to ensure cooperation and common under-standing has already been described. Other surface commanders, includ-ing Admiral Badger, Admiral Weyler, Rear Adm. John F. Shafroth, and Rear Adm. Robert C. Giffen, employed them the same way.[74] Their use became pervasive.

This was essential. Because the standard operational formations were the fast carrier groups, surface force commanders could not assume they would be able to concentrate all ships of their battle formations for practice or indoctrination. Coordinated action could only be ensured through specific common doctrines provided at the fleet level or above. PAC-10 provided just this; it was a new level of constraint that, once integrated with the fleet's operations, enabled significantly increased flexibility.

However, the Navy's approach was not without its flaws. The greatest of these was the failure to anticipate Japanese responses to the increasing size and power of the Navy's carrier forces. The Japanese addressed the problem in several ways, two of which are relevant here. The first was continued emphasis on a potential equalizer that had been an important part of their surface-warfare doctrine for years—night battle. The second was the use of divided dispositions and dis-persed formations.

The Navy did not deal with either of these effectively. This was par-ticularly true of night combat. Existing doctrinal principles, reinforced by prewar exercises and wartime lessons, stressed that night action was undesirable and dangerous for powerful surface units. Concentrated formations of light forces could win minor battles at night, but major actions were to be fought in daylight. On the night of 18 June at the Philippine Sea, Spruance and Lee showed no desire to challenge these principles and thus missed an opportunity to force the Japanese into battle. Four months later, Oldendorf's ad hoc task force achieved over-whelming victory at Surigao Strait, illustrating what might have been.

A second principle solidly entrenched in the Navy's tactical doc-trine was concentration. Concentration was considered essential to the effectiveness of a battle fleet. Prewar plans assumed that the Japanese would also emphasize concentration and that major actions would be fought between massed formations. The Japanese use of dispersed task groups in the carrier battles of 1942 should have challenged this assumption, but it did not. No major action plans were developed to counter dispersed enemy formations, even though by 1944 the Navy had sufficient strength to consider the possibility of dividing into multiple task forces and simultaneously fighting two battles.

This conservative approach, driven by the fear of defeat in detail, limited opportunities when the Japanese gave battle. At the Philippine Sea, Spruance repeatedly insisted on remaining concentrated and refused to leverage the mobility and flexibility of his forces. This allowed the Japanese to strike the first blow and permitted them to withdraw once their attacks had failed. Halsey faced a perfect opportunity to finish off the Combined Fleet at Leyte; a judicious division of forces would have allowed him to defeat both Kurita and Ozawa on 25 October, but Halsey did not seriously consider divided action.[75] This was unfortunate. The flexibility of interchangeable carrier-centric forces was leveraged effectively at the operational level; it would not have taken a great deal of creativity to have used it at the tactical level as well, but the Navy's emphasis on the principle of concentration had become such a pervasive aspect of the existing conceptual fabric that Halsey and Spruance were unable to do so.

The lesson was learned, but too late. In his analysis of the October fighting, Vice Adm. George D. Murray, Commander Air Force, Pacific Fleet, wrote: "Concentration, though usually sound, may sometimes be pursued too far, with diminishing returns. The ability to divide forces cleverly, as developed by the enemy, and to 'unconcentrate' quickly, may often be an advantage."[76] The failure to recognize and adapt to these Japanese approaches prevented Spruance and Halsey from crushing the Combined Fleet in a single decisive blow. But ultimately it made no difference. The battle of Leyte Gulf effectively destroyed Japan as a naval power.

Victory was won not just by success in battle but through a sustained campaign. The Central Pacific offensive is an illuminating example of the benefits of prioritizing strategic, operational, and tactical goals appropriately, as Mahan had emphasized. The main strategic objective, the defeat of Japan, was paramount. It was achieved by a sustained offensive through the Japanese defensive perimeter. This offensive had two subsidiary goals: a rapid operational tempo and the defeat of the Japanese fleet.

Airplanes and airpower, particularly the Pacific Fleet's carriers but also its land-based air forces, were essential to securing the first of these goals. The modular fast carrier task forces were collectively the engine that drove the fast pace of operations, suppressing Japanese positions, destroying planes and ships, and enabling amphibious landings. A quick review of the tables in this chapter shows just how modular they were, with specific ships moving from one task group to another, commanders swapping between operations, and the whole force reconfiguring as new lessons were absorbed.

By late 1944, the Pacific Fleet had become a loosely coupled network that could integrate new components—new ships, task groups, and tactical concepts—quickly and effectively. This allowed it to sustain the fast pace of operations, rapidly absorb combat lessons, and reconfigure in the face of new challenges. It was a fleet unlike any the world had ever seen before.

It was a complex adaptive system, coupled together by a series of constraints—the mechanisms of the CIC, the doctrines introduced in PAC-10, and tactical heuristics developed in the interwar period—that outpaced its opponent in several important ways. The networked Pacific Fleet could advance more rapidly than the Japanese anticipated. It could learn faster, through resilient networks of officers and established educational systems. In battle, the use of the CIC provided a common view of the action that allowed more decentralized—and therefore more rapid—decision making. Victory in the Pacific came through the fortuitous combination of these factors, each of which can be best understood through the lens of complexity.

EPILOGUE
THE COST OF WAR

Efforts to attain and maintain a satisfactory state
of battle efficiency throughout the year have been adversely
affected by an unstable personnel situation.

—Claude C. Bloch, 1939

In the mid-1930s, the Navy began to grow rapidly. Initially, the growth was part of President Franklin D. Roosevelt's New Deal, but later it was driven by the perceived need to defend the Western Hemisphere from the deteriorating situation in Europe. As World War II approached, a series of appropriations bills allowed construction, first to the limits of the Washington and London Treaties, and then far beyond. Rapid growth changed the structure and shape of the Navy, altering the conditions that had allowed the institution to innovate effectively in the years since the Spanish-American War.

During World War II, the Navy's growth accelerated. Hundreds of ships were commissioned and thousands of men enlisted; to speed their integration, the fleet deliberately reduced the variability of its practices. The focus of learning shifted to emphasizing the perfection of established patterns, not identifying new—potentially better—ones. It was a transition away from *exploration* and toward *exploitation*. By war's end, the factors that had supported the Navy's sustained period of innovation had largely been eliminated, replaced with standardized processes.

A TWO-OCEAN NAVY

The desire for readiness in the 1930s was spurred by memories of how unprepared the nation had been for World War I; Adm. Harold R. Stark, CNO from August 1939 to March 1942, summarized the focus of the Roosevelt administration as the world marched toward war: "Navies cannot be improvised. For the most part wars are fought and won or lost with the navies as they exist at the outbreak of hostilities."[1] Stark worked with the administration and congressional leaders to ensure that the United States was well positioned by the time war came.

Democrat Carl Vinson of Georgia, chairman of the House Naval Affairs Committee, spearheaded the large appropriations bills that triggered the Navy's rapid growth. The Vinson-Trammell Act of March 1934, cosponsored by Democratic senator Park Trammell of Florida, authorized the Navy to build to treaty limits. Adm. William H. Standley considered the passage of this law his most important achievement as CNO (July 1933–January 1937); he made a radio broadcast to help ensure its passage.

The Naval Act of May 1938, also known as the Second Vinson Act, followed. It increased the size of the fleet by 20 percent and authorized three additional battleships, two carriers, twenty auxiliaries, and numerous smaller ships.[2] In his congressional testimony, Adm. William D. Leahy (CNO, January 1937–August 1939) made it clear that these additional ships would help the Navy provide security for American territory and interests but they would be insufficient to project power effectively in a hostile world. For that, additional appropriations were necessary.

They came quickly; the termination of the treaty system and the outbreak of war spurred Congress to action. The Third Vinson Act came in June 1940; it increased tonnage by 11 percent and authorized three new carriers, more cruisers, and additional submarines. France fell to Germany later that same month, and Congress immediately saw the need for a much larger force. In July 1940, the Two Ocean Navy

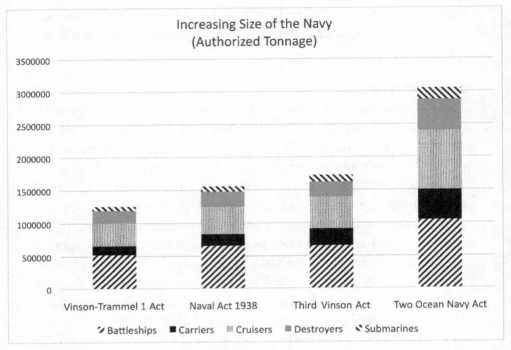

FIGURE 6. Authorized tonnage resulting from naval appropriations leading up to World War II

Act was passed. It authorized an entire fleet for each ocean, increasing the size of the Navy by 70 percent. The act was "designed to give the Navy complete freedom of action against any opposition."[3] These authorizations provided the backbone of the fleet that won World War II.

The officer corps struggled to keep pace with the growing size of the fleet. On 30 May 1934, there were 5,790 officers in commission. By June 1938, this number had increased but only to 6,565. The effective doubling of the fleet over the next two years triggered more rapid increases. By July 1940, the number of officers had grown to 13,162. By the end of December 1941, it had more than doubled; 38,601 officers were in commission. In less than a decade, the number of officers had increased by an order of magnitude.[4]

The number of sailors was also increasing, but in the years before the war, there were not enough of them to fully man all the new ships and adequately prepare for combat operations. Ships were given "allowances" of men, often far less than the "complements" they were expected to have in wartime. Adm. James O. Richardson, CINC from July 1940 to February 1941, commented on these differences, along with the rapid increase in allowances:

> On July 1, 1940, the allowance of men for the heavy cruiser *India-napolis* (CA-35) was 588 men. The complement was 685 men. On July 5, 1940, the CNO increased this allowance by 11 percent, or 68 men, to a total of 656. . . . [O]n September 28, 1940, the CNO increased by 184 men the allowance over the July 1 allowance to 772, or a 31 percent increase. . . . [O]n October 4, 1940, the CNO indicated that the allowance of the *Indianapolis* was to be further increased on July 1, 1941 to 876 or 49 percent greater than the allowance had been a year previously.[5]

For wartime service, the numbers were even larger; large cruisers like *Indianapolis* regularly had crews of over a thousand officers and men, nearly double the number they had been allocated in 1940.

After the Pearl Harbor attack, the Navy grew even more rapidly. By the end of the first year of war, the number of officers had tripled to 118,038. By mid-1944, it had doubled again, and by the end of the war, 325,074 officers in commission. The growth among enlisted ranks was similar, from 144,824 in July 1940 to 3,009,380 by the end of the war.[6] The rapid influx of so many new officers and men changed the Navy's educational systems and altered its culture.

Although the rapid growth immediately before the war reduced the Navy's collective skill and experience, established learning systems were sufficient to train the new officers and men. The Navy was not forced to modify prewar approaches to inculcate them with tactical plans and doctrines. However, because of the increasing number of ships and lack of sailors to man them fully, tactical proficiency decreased and exercises became more rote. Despite this decreased level of readiness, the new officers and men performed well in the first year of war. They succeeded in wresting the initiative from the Japanese by the end of 1942, a testament to the Navy's prewar educational systems and tactical approaches.

The situation later during the war was different. The prewar approaches were inadequate to train and prepare so many additional officers and men. Established routines had to be set aside in favor of more standardized processes. These undermined the effectiveness of the Navy's learning systems and reduced the fleet's ability to innovate. During World War II, the Navy crossed a threshold; out of necessity, experimentation was limited in favor of exploiting proven approaches.

By the end of the war, the Navy had been fundamentally altered by this change in emphasis. Constraints that had fostered experimentation and self-organization became overly rigid. Variability was deliberately limited; ships focused on implementing the "staff solution" rather than on discovering their own methods. This was a necessary consequence of the Navy's rapid growth and the need to maintain cohesion, both from the stresses of scaling and the challenges of war. However, it had dramatic consequences for the Navy's ability to learn and foster innovation. The circumstances that allowed the Navy to innovate rapidly between the Spanish-American War and World War II were temporary; they were sacrificed to meet the needs of the global war.

VARIABILITY AND CONSTRAINTS

The maintenance of local variations—from ship to ship and command to command—was a key ingredient of the Navy's prewar approach. These variations helped to foster innovation because individual officers and men approached problems in slightly different ways. The fleet was, in effect, constantly conducting multiple parallel experiments, rapidly learning from them, and discovering new techniques. Adm. Chester W. Nimitz exploited the fleet's variability effectively when he ordered the ships of his command to develop CICs. The rapid identification of new approaches for managing shipboard information would not have been possible without the fleet's inherent variability; a centralized solution would have taken longer to develop and would not have been as effective so quickly.

The fleet could leverage variability in the interwar period because its officers were relatively few in number and had been immersed in the Navy's culture and ethos. They had a shared mental frame that operated as a set of enabling constraints. It was based on common approaches, like reliance on individual initiative, the conference method, and the estimate of the situation. The rapid influx of reserve officers immediately before and during the war broke this paradigm. The new officers had not been through the Naval Academy, had not been exposed to the Navy's traditions, and did not share the same mind-set. They were unconstrained. There was no time to allow them to absorb the Navy's established culture in the traditional way. They had to become very effective, very quickly.

In response, the Navy altered its approach. The informal constraints employed before the war that slowly indoctrinated officers were reinforced and augmented by detailed instructions. In the years before World War II, officers were trained in principles and theories. It was their responsibility to know how to apply them to specific situations. This was the secret ingredient that enabled variability; human judgment informed the application of knowledge, and because each officer differed slightly, each ship had a different routine. In wartime, the situation changed. Officers were given specific instructions; they were told how to do things. Variability was sacrificed to allow the fleet to grow and absorb new officers and men very rapidly.

Decreasing variability and increasing standardization occurred in many important contexts. One of the most visible was in published materials. Before the war, Navy manuals relied heavily on theory, presenting the underlying principles of the subject matter. Officers and men were expected to use these concepts to develop their own routines. The manuals were guides, not specific instructions.[7] Wartime manuals placed significantly more emphasis on practical problem solving. Texts were shortened by eliminating the complexity of the underlying concepts and placing emphasis on real-life examples. Equations were replaced by pictures and "how to" descriptions. The new manuals represented a shift in the Navy's educational approach and signaled a change from *enabling* constraints to *top-down* ones that limited variability within the fleet.[8]

This shift was particularly notable in postwar tactical manuals. Although the rapid pace of the fighting prevented a thorough revision of tactical instructions during the war, in the immediate postwar period wartime experience was compiled into a new series of manuals. The comprehensive, single-volume format of USF-10B was discarded; numerous additions to the core of PAC-10 over the course of the war had made the document large and unwieldy. A series of new volumes were issued in 1946 and 1947; Admiral Nimitz, now CNO, oversaw their creation. They were USF-2, *General Tactical Instructions*; USF-4, *Carrier Task Force Tactical Instructions*; USF-5, *Surface Action and Tactics*; and USF-15, *CIC Instructions*.[9]

The new manuals retained effective doctrinal concepts and presented tactics for units large and small. The range bands and battle plans first introduced by Adm. William V. Pratt in 1929's *Tentative Fleet Dispositions* were reissued in USF-5. Coordinated attacks were still recommended and considered effective. The problems of combat with small units, the minor tactics first seriously addressed by PAC-10, formed a large part of the new surface warfare manual. However, the flexibility of earlier publications was reduced or eliminated; the postwar manuals were codifications of the most effective wartime practices. The lessons of war had been analyzed, integrated, and incorporated into a more rigid doctrinal framework. Principles were gone; specific practices took their place.

USF-2, for example, contained a section in the chapter on "General Fighting Instructions" presenting "noteworthy tactical procedures" demonstrated by the war; it highlighted the battles of Empress Augusta Bay and Surigao Strait. Stress was placed on the importance of developing an effective plan and doctrine, detecting the enemy early, and adapting to changing circumstances. Plotting was considered particularly important: "[a continual plot of own forces] is one of the most essential methods of facilitating recognition. It is vital in a surface action, particularly at night, in avoiding a melee. More damage could have been done the enemy in World War II, had greater proficiency been attained in this respect."[10] Other well-established concepts received emphasis, including the need for aggressive action, coordinated attacks, and initiative on the part of subordinates.

The new manuals also included lessons from less successful engagements. Although not identified by name, the battle of Kolombangara was featured in USF-5 and was used to illustrate the challenge posed by an "unknown reinforcement group."[11] The manual's authors were unaware that Rear Admiral Ainsworth's cruisers had been struck not by a reinforcement force but by Captain Yoshima's destroyers, which had reloaded their torpedo tubes and returned to the action. However, this lack of detail did not undermine the main point, which was that some opponents, like the Japanese, would be much more comfortable operating in distributed task groups.

Throughout these new manuals, guidance took a very different form than in prewar instructions. Prewar manuals assumed officers would bring a significant amount of their own experience and judgment to unforeseen situations. Principles and heuristics were stressed; specific instructions were avoided. Postwar manuals were much more succinct and direct; the "correct" lessons were known and could now be prescribed. Although combat was still a chaotic domain, full of uncertainty, less was left to the judgment of individual officers. The plans in the manuals went from being guides—flexible foundations that could be reconfigured depending on circumstances—to scripted instructions. Postwar publications emphasized specific solutions and placed much less importance on the need for adaptability.

USF-2's "General Fighting Instructions" illustrated the change. Initially, it included language about the inability of the manual to cover "all circumstances," but later revisions removed this phrasing and instead made it clear the new procedures were "the very basis of . . . tactical arrangements [and] . . . methods of operating."[12] Similarly detailed instructions were provided in USF-5.[13] The manuals no longer contained generic guidance; they had become specific instructions. The Navy's tactical doctrine had gone from emphasizing the inherent variability of ships and formations to a much more standardized approach, a direct result of the Navy's wartime growth.

A similar shift occurred in the way new ships were brought into commission. Traditionally, when a new ship was nearing completion the captain and his staff worked closely with the shipyard, naval constructors, and representatives from the technical bureaus to finalize the configuration of the vessel. Captains had a great deal of leeway to make alterations to improve the ship's capabilities. They and their sub-ordinates determined the processes and procedures that would govern the new ship. Over the course of the war, the variability of this approach and the reliance on human judgment were replaced by standardized procedures.

James O. Richardson, when he took command of the new cruiser *Augusta* in January 1931, succinctly explained the Navy's traditional approach to his assembled officers and men: "Today we take over a new ship of the Navy just delivered by the builders. Now she is an inanimate thing, without life, without spirit, without record and without reputation; what she becomes depends upon us."[14] How this was done—how life was brought to a ship—was described by Edwin B. Hooper, who graduated from the Naval Academy in 1931. After service on the cruiser *Pensacola*, he helped bring the new destroyer *Cushing* into commission in 1936. Hooper served as her damage control officer and later recalled that it "required a tremendous amount of organization, because they didn't have damage control books in those days. You had to do it all yourself, tracing out all the pipes and fittings, and marking them, and organizing."[15]

In other words, Hooper was responsible for understanding the underlying theories and principles of damage control and applying them to his new ship. There were no established procedures to rely upon; he had to develop them. These procedures were extremely important; they would determine how able the destroyer would be to sustain damage, stay afloat, and keep fighting. It was a tremendous amount of responsibility for a young officer, but Hooper was up to the challenge. In November 1942, the procedures he developed helped *Cushing* stay afloat for hours despite severe damage; they saved dozens of lives.

In 1941, Hooper had a similar experience when he helped bring the new battleship *Washington* into commission. He served as her first fire-control officer and would recall the experience in his oral history: "Here again, a new type ship, new equipment, the most up-to-date fire control. You had not only to organize things, I played a large part in that, but even formulated your own procedures to handle this new equipment."[16] Hooper noticed that *Washington*'s initial salvoes were consistently short and suspected a systemic error. He recommended a "calibration exercise" to check his hypothesis. A cruiser steamed parallel to the battleship at known ranges and the guns were fired toward it with a bearing offset, so that they would miss. A camera party on board the cruiser photographed the splashes and determined the actual distance the shells had traveled. "As a result," Hooper concluded, "we did find that we had systemic errors and then knew what arbitrary corrections were needed."[17] When Rear Adm. Willis A. Lee, commander of the Pacific Fleet's battleships, discovered this practice, he made it standard procedure, so that the hitting range of initial salvoes was definitively known.

Hooper also made several internal changes to improve situational awareness and the effectiveness of fire-control practices. He set up repeaters for the search radars, fire-control radars, and other instruments in a variety of places on board *Washington*. One SG repeater was placed in the flag plot so that Rear Admiral Lee could keep an eye on the display. Another set of displays was placed in the admiral's emergency cabin. Lee gave up those quarters so that they could be used as a rudimentary CIC. Hooper installed another set of displays in the fire-control tower, allowing him to keep tabs on the information they provided.[18] When the new Mark 8 fire-control radars were installed, their displays were initially placed in the main battery directors. Hooper changed this configuration and brought the displays down some ten decks to the plotting room, to ensure effective control from that position. He also designed a servomechanism that allowed the radar to follow an output from the rangekeeper and automatically track the target.[19] As with the calibration exercise, these configurations ultimately became standard practice.

In earlier decades, Admiral Stark, like Hooper, had developed his own processes and procedures. When he was executive officer of the battleships *North Dakota* and *West Virginia* in the 1920s, Stark held regular exercises to stimulate problem solving. He worked with each department head to develop a series of simulated casualties. Each casualty was recorded in an envelope: "The man at each local station, whether turret officer, captain, hospital corpsman, shaft alley watch, or what not, would open his envelope at the time designated and would write thereon how he handled the casualty it contained." At the end of the exercise, Stark brought the participants together and held a conference. "At this conference, I started at the top of my list—read the casualty and then requested the person . . . who was responsible for taking care of it, to state exactly what he had done. This was thrown open for a free for all discussion and then the decision was made right there as to how the casualty should be taken care of in the future."[20] Stark used this mechanism as a weekly feedback cycle, enhancing the proficiency of the men on board his ships.

Such processes were not common to all ships; a ship's culture reflected the personalities of its senior officers. Some ships became important incubators for future talent. In October 1933, Chester Nimitz became captain of the cruiser *Augusta*; she joined the Asiatic Fleet as flagship of Adm. Frank B. Upham, who had served with Admiral Dewey at Manila Bay. Lloyd M. Mustin was one of her younger officers; so was Joseph C. Wylie. Wylie and Mustin—both future admirals—rotated through different departments during their time on board *Augusta*. Each of them spent six months in engineering, six months in gunnery, six months in communications, and so on, learning the details of every aspect of shipboard command as a young officer.[21] This exposure served Wylie particularly well a decade later, when he prototyped the CIC on board the destroyer *Fletcher* in November 1942. Mustin was a gunnery expert and helped *Augusta* become one of the most accurately shooting ships in the fleet. In his mind, the cruiser benefitted from "the Nimitz touch," a combination of effective delegation, creative experimentation, and confident leadership.[22]

Wylie became captain of the new destroyer *Ault* in the spring of 1944. He immediately sought something that would make her unique, as he would recall in his oral history: "One of the problems of putting a new ship into commission is that of creating an identity for the crew. By that time all the destroyers had Coca Cola machines and even, beginning with our squadron, ice cream machines. How to make *Ault* unique?" Wylie settled on slot machines that he obtained from a New Jersey district attorney "to illustrate the evils of gambling." After the ship left Pearl Harbor for the combat zone, Wylie placed the machines in the crew's mess. The money they accumulated bought a collection of Christmas presents; at Christmas dinner in 1944, every man on board received a present.[23]

By this time, the process of bringing new ships into the fleet was changing. The options for creating new shipboard procedures were becoming more limited as the Navy increasingly emphasized standardization. In 1944, Edwin Hooper left *Washington* and helped bring the new battle cruiser *Alaska* into commission. He later recalled the new approach and the increasingly restrictive atmosphere in his oral history: "The fitting out period [of *Alaska*] was somewhat as I'd experienced in putting the USS *Cushing* and USS *Washington* in commission. However, there seemed to be less of a tendency to want to get the advice of the ship's officers on the part of the people who were assigned to the ship's construction."[24]

To illustrate the difference, Hooper cited a specific incident. He tried to have a clear vertical plot installed in *Alaska*'s CIC, like the one he had become accustomed to on board *Washington*. He valued how it allowed a quick assessment of the situation from multiple angles, as opposed to a horizontal plot, which could only be seen if you were close to it. Hooper could not convince the project officer at the shipyard to install a vertical plot, a change that would have been straightforward just three years before. There was now a standard process, and project officers were following it; captains and their officers had less authority to customize their vessels to their own needs.

These changes were also reflected in the shakedown period, when the crew familiarized itself with its new ship. Hooper had used this time on board *Cushing* to develop damage-control procedures. On board *Washington*, he had spent it introducing the "calibration exercise." His experience was different on board *Alaska*: "There was now what was known as a Training Command," a group that helped inexperienced officers bring their ships into commission by following standardized procedures. Hooper did not think he, or the other more senior officers on board the larger ships, needed the same assistance.[25]

These experiences illustrated the Navy's changing approach. Before the war, there was no "Training Command." Bringing new ships into commission had been the responsibility of the commanding officer and his subordinates. They formulated the procedures, developed the processes, and created the ship's culture by placing their personal stamps on their commands. The war, and the rapid influx of new officers and men, necessitated standardized approaches that eliminated this variability and with it the nuances that helped make the Navy a diverse learning environment.

INTERWAR RESILIENCY

Although the wartime transition to standardized procedures and reduced variability represented a new paradigm, it was not a new phenomenon. There were moments during the interwar period when training approaches became rigid and inhibited the Navy's ability to learn. In most cases, the Navy's learning system overcame them through effective use of feedback and realistic exercises. However, there were a few exceptions.

The scripted approach to practicing destroyer night torpedo attacks was one. Because the exercises assumed that such attacks would be delivered as parts of major fleet actions, they modeled unrealistic conditions and failed to emphasize the importance of stealth. As a result, officers were unprepared for the fast-paced night battles that took place off Guadalcanal in late 1942. Prewar techniques—the emphasis on individual initiative and low-level tactical planning in conferences—overcame these limitations, and by mid-1943, the situation had completely changed.

A similar problem developed with the Navy's gunnery practices in the interwar period. After World War I, the learning system established by William S. Sims became less effective. Crews focused on competition and began to ignore the importance of continual improvement. The CINC, Adm. Henry A. Wiley, remarked on the problem in 1929: "In the past, efforts to improve gunnery exercises have sometimes failed. . . . For years after the war, gunnery was in a rut, principally because of the restrictions of competition."[26]

But Wiley and his subordinates extricated the Navy from this rut. They leveraged feedback loops in the Navy's learning system and revised gunnery practices to increase their effectiveness. The modified constraints improved overall results and reduced the unanticipated behavior that inhibited learning. The following year, the new CINC, Admiral Pratt, proudly reported on the progress of the new approach: "The gunnery school established in the Battle Fleet is considered to be one of the biggest steps in gunnery training in recent years. This was the first year and many lessons were learned. . . . For the coming year . . . when instructors are more experienced, a marked improvement should be shown."[27] The revised approaches gave "excellent results," and by the eve of World War II, the Navy's gunnery performance was very good. In the surface battles of the Guadalcanal campaign, it was the key to victory.

In cases like these, the interwar learning system worked. Regular feedback and honest assessments altered constraints, and these constraints—gunnery competitions, tactical exercises, Fleet Problems, and the like—fostered self-organization and experimentation. Effective practices emerged within the fleet and were identified through multiple levels of feedback, such as informal shipboard meetings, conferences after Fleet Problems, and General Board hearings. This process continually improved the tactical effectiveness of the entire fleet.

World War II and the accelerated growth required by that global conflict disrupted this system far more than had periodic interwar stagnation. The influx of so many new officers and men fundamentally changed the Navy's approach to the development of tactical doctrine. In the interwar period, emergent potential was fostered by the variability between ships and squadrons. Increasingly standardized procedures—a reaction to the fleet's rapid growth—eliminated that variability and with it an essential ingredient of the Navy's innovative process.

SERVICE CRITICISMS

Most criticisms of the Navy's performance in early World War II have ignored the value of that variability and the influence it had on the fighting. Capt. William Outerson, who graduated from the Naval Academy in 1932 and served in World War II, was scathing in his criticism. In 1981, he summarized his opinions in *Proceedings*:

With few shining exceptions, the performance of our senior naval commanders in the early years of World War II was dismal. Even so, I know of no case in which any but the highest motives of courage and devotion to duty can be attributed to their actions. In many instances, senior officers hazarded their lives and in some cases lost them. My comments are directed at the system which was responsible for their poor performance, not at the officers concerned. My sole purpose is to bring into the light a weakness that ought to be corrected.[28]

Outerson directly criticized the prewar approach. He believed prewar exercises were "set ritual" that "did little to prepare us for our wartime activities." In his mind, the fleet was unready for war: "The lesson to be learned, is that, because of this lack of adequate preparation for our senior officers, we lost a large number of ships and men that under different circumstances might have made all the difference between final victory and final defeat."[29]

Capt. Wayne P. Hughes Jr., who has written extensively on the development of naval tactics and doctrine, offered a similar critique, suggesting that the Navy "was slow to learn" and that "the pace of battles [in the Solomons] overwhelmed" American officers. In his seminal work, *Fleet Tactics*, Hughes wrote that even after the battle of Tassafaronga the "tactical lessons still slipped through American fingers."[30]

Capt. Russell S. Crenshaw Jr. fought in the Solomons. He was gunnery officer of the destroyer *Maury* and witness to the battle of Tassafaronga. In his mind, the Navy's senior commanders were to blame:

The American admirals did not maneuver their ships with confidence and skill in the dark, although it is hard to understand why, since the ships under their command performed intricate maneuvers every night in normal task force cruising. They also concentrated more on controlling the weapons of their ships than they did on placing the ships into positions where those weapons could be most effectively used—a habit that interfered with the efficient use of both guns and torpedoes in all of the [Guadalcanal] ... battles except Lee's.[31]

These are valuable criticisms that reflect two important facts. The first is the increasing ossification of the Navy's approaches in the years before World War II. As the fleet grew, constraints tightened, flexibility diminished, and learning slowed. This was triggered by the rapidly increasing size of the fleet and the resulting lack of crewmen. With their smaller complements, ships' drill became overly simplified, experimentation decreased, and new approaches became more difficult to identify. The criticisms of Outerson, Crenshaw, and others who cite ritualistic exercises reflect this reality.

Hughes' critique is more detailed; it is informed by rigorous analysis as well as personal experience. He looked back at the Navy of 1942 and criticized its ability to learn. His perspective is valid, but it ignores an important subtlety described in the previous chapters. Hughes graduated from the Naval Academy in 1952 and entered the fleet after the changes triggered by World War II. By that time, the variability inherent in the Navy's tactical doctrine—which informed the rapid pace of learning in the interwar period and early World War II—was gone. Standardized approaches were in place. This was a very different context than that of 1942.

In 1942, there was no standard doctrine. Tactics varied between and among task groups. Although it seems that the Navy was not learning between the battles off Guadalcanal, it was. Lessons were being integrated rapidly and doctrine revised after every action. It appears otherwise because the lessons were filtered through established tactical heuristics that emphasized gunfire and subordinated torpedo tactics. This was "wrong" from Hughes' vantage point, because by the time he joined the fleet, the "right" lessons had already been learned. In 1942, the Navy had yet to gain that knowledge.

The Navy's success in World War II was enabled by the rapidity with which officers learned from their experience. Although learning slowed in the final years of peace, it accelerated rapidly during the war. The pace of learning was driven by the variability inherent in the Navy's tactical doctrine; variability allowed experimentation and the rapid exploitation of new techniques. That variability also led to the failures Outerson, Crenshaw, Hughes, and others have cited. Their criticisms have missed the nature of the Navy's broader system and the way it operated. Their focus on specific tactical flaws has been too narrow; they have missed the forest for the trees. The rapid pace of learning and the Navy's early tactical mistakes go together. Commanders learned from previous battles, developed the best approaches that they could, and inevitably made mistakes. That process was an inherent part of the Navy's learning system. Without those mistakes, the Navy would have been unable to evolve its doctrine so much faster than the Japanese did theirs.

CONCLUSION

The specific circumstances that fostered and enabled the Navy's rapid pace of innovation between the Spanish-American War and the end of World War II were temporary. The constraints that governed the Navy's experimentation tightened in the years leading up to the attack on Pearl Harbor. The increasing size of the fleet, the rapid influx of new officers and men, and insufficient manning all slowed the rate of learning. However, it was the massive wartime growth that finally disrupted the Navy's learning system.

Rapid growth fundamentally changed the Navy. The constraints that had fostered experimentation and innovation were repurposed. Prewar exercises had deliberately enabled the development of new approaches; by the end of the war, they focused on reinforcing established solutions. Doing things properly and following the standard procedure had replaced experimenting to find the best approach. Standardized processes reduced variability, inhibited the Navy's ability to experiment in parallel, and ultimately slowed the pace of learning. By 1945, the Navy's learning system, as it had existed before the war, was no more.

CONCLUSION

The navy will resemble a vast and efficient organism,
all the parts leagued together by a common
understanding and a common purpose.

—Bradley A. Fiske, 1916

Between the end of the Spanish-American War and the close of
World War II, the Navy developed a sophisticated learning system
that triggered the emergence of an extremely effective tactical doctrine.
Repeated innovations—the fire-control system, new approaches to
developing and disseminating battle plans, tactical heuristics, and the
enabling structure of PAC-10—sprang from this learning system and
led to increasing levels of coordination and flexibility in battle. These
innovations, along with the systems that led to them, were an essential
part of victory in the Pacific in World War II.

In the first two years of the war, this learning system—and the innovation it fostered—allowed the Navy to evolve its tactical doctrine
rapidly. The ability to exploit lessons from combat and transform them
into new tactics, plans, and force structures was decisive. It helped the
Navy overcome initial Japanese advantages and maintain a faster rate
of learning. The Japanese were unable to keep pace. By late 1943, the

Navy's increasingly sophisticated tactics largely assured success in surface action, and the Japanese adopted increasingly desperate measures.

However, the pressures of global war required unprecedented growth. The Navy grew by two orders of magnitude; to support the influx of so many new officers and men, the Navy was forced to alter the structures that supported the learning system. By the end of World War II, the environment that had fostered such rapid innovation had largely disappeared. This work has endeavored to explain how it came into existence and suggest how it might be re-created.

RECONFIGURING THE NAVY

The insurgents of the nineteenth century—men like Stephen B. Luce, Alfred T. Mahan, and Henry C. Taylor—set out to change the Navy. They wanted to transform it into a modern, professional institution. Chapter 1 described their efforts. Although the insurgents had a vision of what success would look like, transformation of the Navy Department did not adhere to a grand design; as we have seen, it was the product of a complex interaction between individuals and the systems they created. The first, and arguably most important, step in this process was the creation of a new concept of what it meant to be a naval officer.

The initial wave of insurgents recognized that in order to reconfigure the Navy, they had to redefine the nature of their profession and create a new place for the naval officer in American society. This was the principal objective of Mahan's pursuit of a new strategic theory of naval warfare. The significance of his strategic thought is well documented. Unfortunately, the main impression we have been left with over the past century is that Mahan emphasized decisive battle above all else. Most commentators, interpreting his view of sea control too narrowly, have described victory in a clash of battle fleets as Mahan's vision for strategic success. But this interpretation is based on a misconception, and the emphasis it has received obscures Mahan's true impact on the Navy's strategic thought.

Mahan's primary focus was not decisive battle. It was something far more radical. Mahan sought to redefine fundamentally what it meant to be an American naval officer. This objective informed his rigorous study of history and analytical pursuit of fundamental principles of war. He believed that naval strategy was an art—a skill that could be developed and refined through practice—one that required the application of a specialized body of knowledge. Stephen B. Luce agreed with this concept and pushed for the Naval War College so that the Navy would have a professional institution to develop and refine that art.

Mahan harnessed the college's full potential and used it to support his reconceptualization of the naval officer. The first step was to create a new body of knowledge, a uniquely American view of naval strategy, based on the idea that there were foundational principles of naval warfare. Students at the college became familiar with these principles through rigorous study of historical conflict, war games (simulations), and sophisticated exercises. Officers practiced the new art of naval warfare and honed their skills in a variety of hypothetical situations. They learned the importance of applying the principles of war contextually and became motivated to learn more about their emerging profession.

The result was a new conception of American naval leadership, one based on the belief that military command was a sophisticated art. Practice was required to develop and refine the associated skills. Mahan argued that officers needed to think about their role critically, reassess it as circumstances changed, and lead men through a variety of unanticipated situations. As Jon T. Sumida has emphasized, Mahan did not believe in a rigid application of a codified doctrine:

> What he [Mahan] wrote about the contingent nature of war, the value of real experience, and his repeated explicit warnings against the dangers of mechanistic application of rules should be sufficient proof of his genuine appreciation of the artistic dimension of the executive function and the inherent incompleteness of formal pedagogy. It is possible to read Mahan piecemeal and without regard for his naval professional pedagogical intentions and come to the conclusion that he was a rigid doctrinaire. That is a widely held view, but it is faulty and unjust.[1]

Flexibility, enabled by deep experiential knowledge, was at the core of Mahan's redefinition of the naval officer. During his time at the Naval

War College, he stressed these ideas and laid the foundation for a new approach that began to take hold in the late nineteenth century.

It marked a distinct break from earlier tradition. Although it affected the broader society less significantly, the transition paralleled the changes that took place at the dawn of what Karl Jaspers has termed the "Axial Age." Shmuel N. Eisenstadt describes the dawn of the Axial Age succinctly, contrasting the difference between the "mundane order," the world that each of us can see and feel, with the "transcendental," the otherworldly aspirations at the center of this transition:

> In the first millennium before the Christian era a revolution took place in the realm of ideas and their institutional base which had irreversible effects. . . . The revolution or series of revolutions . . . have to do with the emergence, conceptualization and institutionalization of a basic tension between the transcendental and mundane orders. This revolutionary process took place in several major civilizations including Ancient Israel, Ancient Greece, early Christianity, Zoroastrian Iran, early Imperial China, and in the Hindu and Buddhist civilizations.[2]

By positing an external, transcendental source of wisdom, knowledge, and morals, these ancient thinkers redefined the world and their own places within it. This created new possibilities. In the space between that "transcendental order" and the real world, new bodies of knowledge began to emerge. Eisenstadt continues: "The institutionalization of the perceived tension between the transcendental and the mundane orders tends to create the corresponding definition of different worlds of knowledge—be they philosophy, religions, metaphysics, 'science' or the like. Such definitions transformed different types of *ad hoc* moral reflection and classificatory schematization into second-order worlds of knowledge. This step constitutes the starting point of the history of mankind." The Axial Age was a major transition; it was a symmetry break that "transformed the shape of human societies," altered "the dynamics of history," and modified our beliefs about humanity's place in the world.[3]

Mahan's writing and teaching had a similar impact on the Navy. By positing a set of fundamental principles of naval strategy, Mahan created a theory of naval warfare that paralleled the transcendental ideas of the Axial Age. In the gap between that theory and day-to-day practice, Mahan positioned his new body of specialized knowledge. The American naval officer became responsible for interpreting that knowledge. His role was to bridge the gap by proficiently assessing diverse situations, correctly applying the principles of naval warfare to them, and bringing strategy to life.

To put it another way, Navy officers became the high priests of Mahan's new religion, his modern, American conceptualization of the art of naval warfare. This fundamentally changed the dominant paradigm. The role of high-ranking naval officers was transformed from that of the squadron leaders of the nineteenth century—commanders of small collections of ships—to the admirals of the twentieth, who coordinated fleets on a global scale. By effectively presenting this new role to their civilian masters, these admirals helped transform the world and their places within it, ultimately becoming the architects of modern sea power.

The second step in transforming the Navy into a modern, professional institution was to change the role it played in the American republic. Mahan's new strategic theories suggested that maritime power could become a natural extension of the nation's "manifest destiny." The ability of the United States to expand geographically was limited, but the nation could continue to grow its influence through the application of naval power.

These ideas found fertile ground in the immediate aftermath of the Spanish-American War. They had already struck a chord with several influential politicians, foremost among them Theodore Roosevelt. Roosevelt's presidency initiated the creation of a large, modern Navy and led to the establishment of the Atlantic Fleet in 1907. As discussed in chapter 3, that was a seminal moment in the development of tactics and doctrine. By providing the Navy with its first standing fleet, Roosevelt created a laboratory for officers to investigate, refine, and adapt the theories being developed at the Naval War College.

Henry J. Hendrix stresses the importance of President Roosevelt in his history of American naval diplomacy: "The rise of American naval power at the crossover point between the nineteenth and twentieth centuries was not an automatic outcome of history's flow; it represented the concerted efforts of a small group of individuals, most notably Alfred T. Mahan, Henry Cabot Lodge, and Theodore Roosevelt."[4] Both Roosevelt and Lodge believed that a large and powerful Navy was essential to establish the United States as the dominant power in the Western Hemisphere.

William Howard Taft, Roosevelt's successor, joined them in this belief. The twelve years of their combined administrations saw a series of important changes. The first twelve of the Navy's modern "dreadnought" battleships were laid down during this period, two each in the years 1906, 1907, 1909, 1910, 1911, and 1912, providing the basis for a powerful battle fleet. As described in chapter 2, that fleet benefitted from the processes introduced by William S. Sims when he became inspector of target practice in 1902. Also, as we saw in chapter 1, the last two of those battleships—*Nevada* and *Oklahoma*—represented a significant improvement over their predecessors because of the Newport Conference of 1908 and the changes it triggered in the process of ship design.

Although Woodrow Wilson's Navy secretary came into office skeptical of the new naval profession, Josephus Daniels ultimately became one of its most important supporters. Chapter 1 described his diligence in working to replace the existing promotion system and develop mechanisms to reward the talent and skill of younger officers. In 1916, promotion by selection became the new standard. Although initially resistant, Daniels also worked to expand the authority of OPNAV. These changes were tied to a very large building program that, had it been completed, would have created the largest navy in the world. Under Wilson and Daniels, the Navy became the shield of liberty, protecting the American experiment from the war raging in Europe. Most of the ships authorized in 1916 were never finished, but the concept of the Navy as the first line of defense remained. The transformative dream of the insurgents had been fulfilled.

THE NAVY'S LEARNING SYSTEM

Once the foundation for a modern, professional institution had been established, Navy officers started to explore how to harness its full potential. They developed new methods of fighting and winning at sea. Their efforts led to a learning system that triggered the emergence of a sophisticated tactical doctrine. The preceding chapters have described this system in detail and illustrated how it grew from the interrelated efforts of many actors. The uncompromising reformer William S. Sims, the diligent planner William V. Pratt, the empowering leader Chester W. Nimitz, the irascible Ernest J. King, the aggressive William F. Halsey, and the studiously calm Raymond A. Spruance all approached tactics and doctrine slightly differently. But each helped move the Navy forward.

Complex systems lack a supreme guiding hand. There is no master engineer behind the scenes; results that in hindsight seem planned emerge from the interaction of individuals and their environment. Biological and physical systems have been shown to develop increasingly complex relationships in this way, which is why François Jacob (see the prologue) used the term *bricolage* to describe the process. Human systems, like the old Navy Department, operate through the same fundamental principles. If the prior chapters have presented the illusion of an overarching plan, it is a symptom of our very human desire to believe that complexity requires logical design. We naturally assume that increasingly sophisticated systems must be something more than an emergent property of our collective interactions and the constraints that govern our behavior. They are not. Constraints are the engine that drive innovation, and in the Navy's case, constraints were instrumental to producing an increasingly sophisticated tactical doctrine. The constraints can be effectively divided into three different categories: motivations, means, and mechanisms.

MOTIVATIONS—OFFICERS DRIVEN TO LEARN

Motivation was triggered by Mahan's new body of knowledge; it emphasized professional education, historical examples, and contextual analysis. In the emerging paradigm, officers were expected to refine and improve their skills continually so that they had an increasingly broad basis of experiential knowledge to apply in battle. Because the practice of naval warfare was a skilled art, officers had to develop expertise in all relevant subjects. At first, this included naval tactics and strategy, the traditional arts of seamanship, and leadership.

Effective leadership was embedded in Mahan's new definition of the naval officer. He believed officers had to forge the men under their command into a "great machine" that could overcome the "tumult and probable horrors of a modern naval action."[5] In 1879, he described these attributes in an essay in *Proceedings*. Mahan considered "moral power" the ultimate prerequisite, underpinning the qualities of leadership, fearlessness, self-reliance, initiative, and bravery.[6] Mahan envisioned the commanding officer as the agency—the brain—behind the "machine" that harnessed the fighting strength of a ship and her men. The moral fiber of that machine was singularly important; it provided the basis for effective leadership.

Although Mahan used the term "machine" to describe his concept of a fighting ship and the men within it, it is clear from Bradley A. Fiske's expansion of the idea that the word is too limiting. What Mahan, Fiske, and their contemporaries had in mind was not a mechanical orientation but an organic one. For them, the Navy and each ship within it was a "directable organism."[7] As Fiske wrote in 1916: "The organization [of the fleet] will resemble a veritable organism: all the various organs fulfilling separately yet accurately their allotted functions; all the fire-control parties, all the gun crews, all the torpedo crews, all the engineer forces properly organized and drilled; all the hulls of the vessels, all the guns, all the torpedoes, all the multifarious engines, machines, and instruments in good material condition and adjusted for use."[8] The role of the naval officer was to be the intelligent decision-making authority within this living system that coupled men and machinery.

This biological metaphor was strongly influenced by the theories of Social Darwinism. Naval officers, familiar with modern, "scientific" concepts, accepted the idea that competition and "survival of the fittest" applied to human organizations—corporations, nations, and navies— as well as biological species. This motivated them to improve themselves and continually to refine and enhance the work of the fleet. For them, competition promoted continual improvement, and war was the ultimate test.

Biological metaphors had two important consequences. First, Fiske's description of the fleet as a living organism provided an effective mental model for the inherent complexity in a modern navy. Like an organism, the U.S. Navy was made up of many loosely interconnected components that had to align and work together to achieve a common goal. Second, Social Darwinism suggested that relentless competition was the engine of progress. To survive, the Navy had to improve constantly, and each officer had to do his part.

As described in chapter 1, a major shift in officer education took place in 1899, when the Engineering Corps and line officers were integrated. This broadened the relevant scope of knowledge. From then on, naval officers were expected to become familiar with the scientific principles underpinning modern naval machinery. This was revolutionary; it meant that the emerging emphasis on continuing education became intertwined with the principles of scientific inquiry and fact-based investigation. Naval officers began to learn methodically through experimentation. Sims augmented Mahan's conceptualization of what it meant to be a naval officer and highlighted the core aspects of this new approach in his speech to the graduating class of the Naval War College in 1921:

> I think it is apparent that . . . we seek . . . a combination of logical ability and military character—the ability to reach sound conclusions from established facts, and the character to accept, adopt, and fight for these conclusions against any material or spiritual forces. . . . A navy to be successful must be guided not only by men of ability but by men of an intellectual honesty that is proof against personal ambition or any other influences whatsoever.[9]

Sims' speech reflected the increasing emphasis on facts and reason triggered by the merging of the line officers and the Engineering Corps. Officers increased their ability to frame problems, learn from exercises, and evaluate the effectiveness of existing approaches by logically assessing potential alternatives and making fact-based decisions.

As chapter 1 discussed, Secretary Daniels motivated them further by replacing the archaic promotion system with one that rewarded skill and ability. Young officers quickly learned that improving their knowledge offered the potential for more rapid promotion. They also learned that failure to develop the requisite knowledge and expertise meant an early retirement. Adm. James O. Richardson noted that "20 to 30 percent of those remaining in each Naval Academy class" did not advance between each of the major grades, creating in the rest an "urgent desire to become thoroughly qualified in all aspects . . . of the naval profession."[10]

Ernest J. King's career reflected these important shifts. King graduated from the Naval Academy in 1901, in the midst of these revolutionary changes. He worked hard to secure promotion. Before World War I, King was captain of the destroyers *Terry* and *Cassin*, part of the Atlantic Fleet Torpedo Flotilla, and he became Sims' aide. During the war, he served on the staff of the Atlantic Fleet commander, Adm. Henry T. Mayo. In the 1920s, King commanded a submarine division, directing the salvage of *S-51*, which accidentally sank in 1925. The next year, Congress passed a law that all commanders of carriers and aircraft tenders had to be naval aviators. King accepted an offer to command the tender *Wright* and earned his wings at the naval air station at Pensacola, Florida. He was forty-eight years old and the only captain in his class. In 1930, King became commander of the new carrier *Lexington*. In 1932, he attended the Naval War College; the following year, he became chief of the Bureau of Aeronautics. King later rejoined the fleet as Commander, Aircraft, Battle Force. In December 1940, he became commander of the Patrol Force, later redesignated the Atlantic Fleet.

By the time of his appointment as commander in chief of the U.S. Fleet in December 1941, King was one of the most experienced and knowledgeable officers in the Navy. He had continuously expanded his skills by serving in numerous diverse roles. But if he is arguably the best example of the Navy's increased emphasis on learning and education, he is not the only one. Many of King's contemporaries had similarly diverse and challenging careers before they advanced to flag rank. They were motivated by the changes introduced in the late nineteenth century and early twentieth.

MEANS—COLLABORATIVE KNOWLEDGE SHARING

Collaborative knowledge sharing was the primary mechanism for learning the Navy's art of war. Mahan's emphasis on naval strategy as an art reflected his belief that naval warfare was fundamentally complex. To be effective, officers had to apply their knowledge of strategic principles contextually and tailor them to every new, unique situation. Mahan structured the Naval War College curriculum to develop this knowledge through collaborative learning. Discussions, conferences, and cooperation expanded individual perspective and fostered broad contextual understanding of strategic and tactical problems.

As more officers became familiar with these techniques, the influence of the collaborative learning grew. Conferences instilled the habits of working together, learning from each other, and solving complex problems through open discussion. Officers quickly recognized that they could develop effective solutions more rapidly by sharing diverse perspectives. Boards were regularly created to investigate specific problems and provide recommendations. Conferences were held to review lessons, develop tactics and plans, and discuss the results of exercises. The best approaches were identified through interactive sessions that harnessed the value of collaboration, consultation, and open discussion. They became the Navy's preferred mechanism for developing tactical doctrine.

As described in chapter 2, boards helped improve the design of the fire-control system. Boards also made recommendations on new ship designs; they consulted on fleet tactics and doctrine; and they triggered the development of revised manuals like PAC-10. The systematic use of boards allowed the Navy to draw out effective ideas from within the organization, to capitalize on the skill and knowledge of officers, and to introduce new ideas in a relatively informal manner that skirted normal bureaucratic processes. The boards constituted an important method for discovering lessons from experimentation within the fleet. The General Board, introduced in 1900, was based on this model. Its work brought a new level of cohesion to the Navy's plans, operations, and tactics; the introduction of the General Board was one of the reasons the Navy was able maintain a sustained pace of innovation throughout this period.

Conferences were similar, but they were more open-ended than boards. Conferences collaboratively developed and refined ideas, such as lessons from the Fleet Problems or plans for an upcoming tactical exercise. As described in chapter 3, Sims set the example in the Atlantic Fleet's Torpedo Flotilla; Pratt, Laning, and Yarnell built on his approach. After the war, conferences became a standard approach for developing new doctrines—like the 1921 *Destroyer Instructions*—and identifying lessons.

Arleigh Burke leveraged this body of experience when he and his captains developed new destroyer tactics in the South Pacific during 1943. He wasn't unique in holding conferences in combat theaters. Rear Adm. Willis A. Lee brought knowledgeable officers together to help improve the fire control of the Pacific Fleet's battleships, as Edwin B. Hooper recalled: "The Admiral was extremely interested in radar, and . . . he would assemble gunnery and radar officers, those who he felt were technically qualified to discuss the subject."[11] Lloyd Mustin participated in one of these conferences when *Washington* arrived in the South Pacific in September 1942. Mustin was assistant gunnery officer of the light cruiser *Atlanta* and had developed an effective technique for rapidly bringing her 5-inch guns onto attacking enemy planes. Mustin visited the battleship, gave her officers a sense of what combat was like, and described his new technique.[12]

This collaborative atmosphere extended beyond formal boards and conferences. It was a core element of the Navy's learning system. Hooper joined the cruiser *Pensacola* in 1931 as a young ensign, and many years later, in his oral history, he would remark on the trusting environment he found: "In those days, we did not have many officers in the wardroom. The climate there was exceedingly good. I received much good advice from my seniors and within a week or two was studying strategy and tactics and foreign affairs. And, rather than merely reporting the meaning of a signal to the captain or officer of the deck, I would indicate what it meant in terms of fleet maneuvers— where we should go in a new disposition and so forth."[13] *Pensacola*'s wardroom fostered learning, and Hooper, like many of his contemporaries, was encouraged to develop and grow by more senior officers.

Collaborative environments like these became part of the Navy's informal structure and helped accelerate organizational learning. In her research, Amy Edmondson has described the impact they can have: "For a team to discover gaps in its plans and make changes accordingly, team members must test assumptions and discuss differences of opinion openly rather than privately or outside the group. I refer to this set of activities as learning behavior, as it is through them that learning is enacted at the group level." Edmondson has shown that effective organizational learning is promoted by psychological safety, "a shared belief that the team is safe for interpersonal risk taking." This is a form of trust; it should not be confused with the absence of disagreement or with "group think." Psychological safety is what enables differences of opinion to emerge and alternative perspectives to be entertained. It is the "confidence that the team will not embarrass, reject, or punish someone for speaking up" and sharing his or her view.[14] The ability to discuss ideas collaboratively and create an environment safe for learning makes teams more effective. In the years before World War I, the Navy fostered a learning environment; during the interwar period, that environment was maintained, creating fertile ground for new ideas and dissenting opinions.

Certain officers were particularly effective in this milieu; one was Raymond A. Spruance. When he taught tactics at the Naval War College, between 1935 and 1937, his "primary contribution was to set an atmosphere in which both students and instructors were free to express their opinions, to innovate, and to experiment."[15] Chester W. Nimitz was another. The officers who served with Nimitz later remembered him as an effective and disciplined leader who helped foster collaborative decision making.

Joseph C. Wylie served under Nimitz on the cruiser *Augusta* in the early 1930s. In September 1944, the squadron of which Wylie's destroyer was a part arrived at Pearl Harbor. He and a fellow captain took the opportunity to visit the admiral. Wyle described the impromptu briefing they received: "When we got to the office there, he [Nimitz] had the map on the wall, and he started talking about what we were going to do. This included finishing off the Philippines, Iwo

Jima, Okinawa, and the assaults on Kyushu and Honshu. He didn't even tell us not to mention this. Of course, these were the deepest-held secrets of the Pacific War. He just *knew* we'd never tell anybody."[16] Admiral Nimitz's willingness to share these details and to welcome low-level commanders in for a briefing reflects the nature of his leadership style and the importance he placed on fostering a collaborative environment. Although particularly invested in this style of leadership, Nimitz was not unique in that. His approach was a natural development of the work done over decades by individual officers like Mahan, Sims, Pratt, and Spruance to cultivate a learning system.

Without the benefit of modern theories of complexity, the Navy's officers inherently recognized the value of interactive learning and frequently used boards, conferences, and other informal mechanisms. Mahan's view of naval strategy as an art, with its emphasis on the contextual application of underlying principles, necessitated an approach that could rapidly leverage diverse perspectives and expose new ideas. The conference method as developed at the Naval War College was a reaction to this need; the Navy's boards addressed the same goal but with a slightly different organizational approach. Both techniques allowed the Navy to identify and act upon valuable lessons. They were an essential element of the learning system that enabled success in World War II.

MECHANISMS—CONSTRAINTS FOR CONTINUOUS IMPROVEMENT

The regular series of exercises embodied the Navy's mechanism for promoting continuous improvement. Before World War I, gunnery exercises had led to a system of feedback—a competitive environment in which successful techniques were identified and celebrated—that fostered learning. In the interwar period, the approach was expanded. Gunnery practices, engineering competitions, tactical exercises, and the Fleet Problems pitted officers and their ships against each other, driving them to find new and better ways of addressing the challenges of war. These exercises focused attention on developing and refining creative solutions, fostered emergence of new approaches, and harnessed the ingenuity of officers and men. They were important constraints that improved the effectiveness of the fleet.

The best officers used these competitions to motivate their subordinates to new records of achievement. Lloyd Mustin recalled the influence that gunnery practices had on him and his shipmates on board the cruiser *Augusta* in the early 1930s:

> We may have been second [in competition scores] among all the heavy cruisers, but we ensigns certainly had a profound indoctrination in the most meticulous preparatory efforts to be sure that when you did come on the line, when . . . it came time to say "Commence firing," you had left no stone unturned in making sure that you were ready, fully ready, because if you were not in any respect, if you failed to fire any shots because of a casualty to a gun or had other mischances, all of these degraded your score directly and showed permanently in writing on the record of the ship printed and distributed throughout the length and breadth of the Navy, and . . . it reflected . . . in your own fitness report and elsewhere, and you just left no stone unturned.[17]

The competitive system of exercises motivated Mustin and his contemporaries to become intimately familiar with their equipment and how use it. In gunnery competitions, they developed routines that aligned with what the Navy desired: rapid, accurate gunfire at the outset of an action to damage the enemy and secure the initiative.

Similar competitive exercises governed other aspects of fleet training. Admiral Richardson was to remark on their influence in the decade before World War II:

> During these ten years, a very effective competition was held throughout each year between individual ships, and between individual aircraft units for the improvement of the technical proficiency of each ship and aircraft of the Fleet. The details of the competition varied from type to type of ship or aircraft and from

year to year, but covered the skills in airmanship, gunnery, communications, engineering, and damage control. Officers' reputations were made or lost, and selection to higher rank influenced by the capabilities which commands or ship departments or units displayed in the various competitions.[18]

As chapter 4 has described, the largest and most complex exercises were the Fleet Problems. The results of these operational exercises were treated very seriously and could determine officers' future prospects. Vice Adm. Louis Nulton was an excellent example. Commander of the Battle Fleet and second in seniority only to Adm. William V. Pratt, Nulton was made acting CINC U.S. Fleet when Pratt attended the London Naval Conference in 1930. Later that year, Nulton commanded the Blue fleet in Fleet Problem X. He kept his carriers, the modern *Saratoga* and the smaller *Langley*, close to his battle line and operated them defensively. They were surprised by planes from the Black fleet and knocked out of action; without aerial support, Nulton's battleships were harassed and damaged by Black's planes in the ensuing fleet action. Pratt, in his critique of the Problem, asserted that Nulton's failure was "his conservative and defensive employment of airpower."[19] Although next in line to be CINC, Nulton was instead given the First Naval District and reverted in rank to rear admiral. His poor performance in Fleet Problem X effectively ended his career.

A similarly poor performance was given by Rear Adm. George C. Day, commander of the Orange fleet during Fleet Problem VIII of 1928. Day had the mission of locating the Blue fleet as it sailed from San Francisco and then hindering its arrival at Pearl Harbor. Adm. Louis R. de Steiguer commanded the Blue fleet. Day had faster ships but failed to use them effectively; he made inaccurate assumptions about the Blue fleet's capabilities and was embarrassed when de Steiguer arrived at Pearl Harbor undetected and ahead of schedule. In the critique, the CINC, Henry A. Wiley, highlighted Day's mistakes, including his failure to take advantage of his fleet's speed, his vague wording of orders, and poor placement of his patrol lines. "In sum, Day had made numerous errors of judgment, compounding them by making vague suggestions to several of his subordinates when he ought to have issued orders."[20] This poor performance marked the end of Day's shipboard command. He became president of the Board of Inspection and Survey and retired in 1935.

Other officers were able to capitalize on the opportunity presented by these large exercises to illustrate their future potential. Joseph M. Reeves was an extremely talented officer who rose to prominence through innovative use of carrier airpower. In Fleet Problem VII of 1927, he conducted a raid on the Panama Canal from the experimental carrier *Langley*. The raid itself was small, but to mount it, the little carrier launched twenty planes in ten minutes, an unprecedented feat. *Langley*'s fighters overwhelmed the defending aircraft, allowing Reeves' bombers to make their runs unopposed and "damage" the locks at Miraflores. In 1929, during Fleet Problem IX, Reeves reprised this performance with the large carrier *Saratoga*. He convinced Admiral Pratt, commander of the Black fleet and his superior for the exercise, to allow *Saratoga* to operate offensively in an independent task force. The carrier steamed toward the canal at high speed and made a dawn strike against the locks. Although battleships of the Blue fleet intercepted *Saratoga* in the early morning as she launched her planes and "sank" her, the raid was a stunning success, presaging the hit-and-run attacks the Navy would make in World War II. Reeves' performance enhanced his "standing within the upper echelons of the Navy" and opened the gates to high command.[21] When Pratt became CNO in September 1930, he helped Reeves advance. In June 1933, Reeves was promoted to commander of the Battle Force, and in February 1934, he became CINC, the highest shipboard command.

Ernest J. King too demonstrated his potential in the Fleet Problems. During Fleet Problem XII in 1931, he was captain of the carrier *Lexington* and commanded one of the Blue fleet's fast carrier task forces under Reeves. During the Problem, King displayed his characteristic aggressiveness, sailing *Lexington* close to the enemy forces and repeatedly striking from the air. King ensured his carrier's survival by employing a standing combat air patrol, an innovation at the time. The next year, during Fleet Problem XIII, King convinced Vice Adm. Arthur R. Willard, his Black fleet commander, that *Lexington* and her air squadrons could gain control of the air if they operated independently in a fast carrier task force. While the Blue fleet's *Saratoga* attacked one of Willard's scouting lines, King and his task force moved in. In the mock attack that followed, *Saratoga* was judged "heavily damaged" by *Lexington*'s planes. King secured control of the air, drawing praise from the CINC, Adm. Frank H. Schofield.[22] By 1938, King would be Commander, Aircraft, Battle Force and a vice admiral.

Craig Felker accurately summarizes the impact the Fleet Problems and the broader system of exercises had on the Navy's officer corps in the interwar years:

> The Fleet Problems offered invaluable learning opportunities for naval officers. Planners developed exercises incorporating actual naval vessels in an operational setting. The scenarios they fashioned became increasingly sophisticated and complex. Senior officers developed strategic plans, put them into action at sea, and experienced success or failure. Subordinate commanders not only gained insight into the thinking of senior navy leadership but also compared those thoughts with actual experiences. Finally, junior officers who attended the postexercise critiques were exposed to dimensions of naval warfare hidden from them in their watch stations or on the bridge or in the cockpit. The officers who fought in World War II were not accidents of history, nor were they a new generation of Young Turks. Much of their behavior in actual combat was conditioned by experiences gained from nearly two decades of practice.[23]

Practice in the Fleet Problems fostered a whole series of new approaches. Tactical exercises led to more effective techniques for coordinating cruisers and destroyers in night combat. Patrol bombers became effective scouts through practice and regular employment. New techniques for underway refueling were tested and refined. The capabilities of submarines were explored, illustrating their limitations in set-piece battles but setting the stage for their impressive wartime successes as commerce raiders and forward scouts. Most notably, the Fleet Problems were vital for the development of independent, high-speed carrier task forces. This practice and the learning that came with it were results of a deliberate decision to introduce a competitive system of exercises. The exercises were an essential component of the Navy's learning system; they were constraints that motivated continual learning, fostered the development of new tactics, and helped evaluate them at sea. They provided valuable experience that would be leveraged in World War II.

MASTERY—THE LEARNING SYSTEM AT WAR

The Navy's learning system was most valuable in the critical year of 1942, when Admiral Nimitz and his subordinates faced an extremely complex problem. The battle fleet had been heavily damaged at Pearl Harbor, the IJN was proving more capable than had been expected, and numerous flaws in the Navy's tactical doctrine had been exposed. Those flaws could not be addressed by the application of established methods. New ones had to be devised. Nimitz recognized the nature of the problem. He resisted the temptation simply to impose practices that had worked under peacetime conditions. Instead, Nimitz gave his subordinates high-level direction, framing the problem, establishing constraints, and then allowing flag officers, task force commanders, and captains throughout the Pacific Fleet to self-organize around potential solutions. When effective approaches emerged, he moved quickly to exploit them, leading to the CIC and PAC-10.

The rapid wartime learning cycles were triggered by Admiral King's insistence that the Pacific Fleet take the offensive. King recognized the importance of seizing the initiative from the Japanese at the earliest possible moment. He knew that by taking the offensive the Pacific Fleet would achieve two objectives. First, it would control the pace of operations and force the Japanese to react. Second, it would leverage the learning system, rapidly absorb lessons from combat, and refine its techniques. King was confident that his officers, imbued with the emphasis already placed on continuous learning, would evolve their doctrine faster than the Japanese would theirs. He embraced the ideas that Col. John Boyd would later describe as the "OODA loop" and knew the Navy could leverage them at the organizational level. The invasion of Guadalcanal initiated a decisive struggle that allowed Nimitz and his Pacific Fleet to test prewar doctrine, identify its flaws, and develop new approaches to surface tactics.

Nimitz ensured a rapid pace of learning through two supporting mechanisms. The Pacific Fleet regularly rotated experienced officers out of combat so that they could share their lessons with other parts of the Navy. This approach was instrumental to the creation of PAC-10. The existence of dual chains of command built upon the practice of officer rotation and helped distribute lessons. The operational chain of command went through fleet and task-force commanders, like Vice Adm. William F. Halsey at Third Fleet and Vice Adm. Raymond A. Spruance at Fifth Fleet. Operational commands focused on combat operations; they determined how best to organize for the next battle or conduct the next invasion. The type commands, such as Vice Adm. Mahlon S. Tisdale's for destroyers and Vice Adm. Willis A. Lee's for battleships, reviewed operational procedures and continually improved them.[24] Without type commands, the CIC concept would not have been identified and promoted so quickly. The division of effort between the two was logical and fostered rapid learning throughout the fleet.

The use of dual chains of command also allowed operational commands to swap in and out of task organizations without disrupting the fleet's cohesion. The Pacific Fleet's *Command History* noted these benefits: "Operational commands . . . and their task force designations, changed with bewildering frequency. This, indeed, was their strength. The dual system of operational and administrative chains of command allowed for the maintenance of administrative matters under a relatively stable organization, while at the same time, the ships, troop units, or air squadrons could be combined into whatever groupings and whatever chains of command the needs of the combat situation required, under the system of task organization."[25] By using constraints to foster emergence of new solutions, rotating officers out of combat areas, and leveraging the dual command structure, Admiral Nimitz and his subordinates quickly harnessed the initial lessons of the war and transformed how the Pacific Fleet developed tactical doctrine. These concepts were crucial to victory in the Pacific.

BROADER IMPLICATIONS OF THE NAVY'S EXPERIENCE

The Navy developed an effective learning system in the early decades of the twentieth century and sustained it through most of World War II. This learning system fostered repeated innovations and had significant consequences for the war in the Pacific. The Navy's experience suggests that sustained innovation can be fostered by a complex interplay of multiple factors.

First, enabling constraints are crucial to the development of new and innovative approaches. The interaction of individuals and the constraints that channel their behavior can lead to emergence and innovation. The previous chapters have described four specific innovations in the Navy's surface-warfare doctrine. The first was the new fire-control system, refined in the years before the American entry into World War I. The second was the development of a coherent tactical doctrine, emphasizing heuristics and battle plans for major fleet action. The CIC was the third; it was an entirely new paradigm for shipboard command and information management, based on distributed cognition. Finally, the introduction of PAC-10 and its new approach to task-force doctrine enabled the Pacific Fleet's rapid offensive against Japan.

Although officers had the authority to impose solutions in each of these cases, they refrained from doing so. Instead, they fostered innovation by introducing a series of constraints and gathering honest feedback about potential solutions. Their approach was consistently effective and suggests something fundamental about the nature of innovation. Innovative solutions cannot be imposed or planned. They must be allowed to emerge—by fostering creativity with enabling constraints and harnessing new ideas through feedback mechanisms. In the first five decades of the twentieth century, the Navy was so familiar with this approach that it became a regular occurrence.

This basic pattern was employed:

- Identify the problem (e.g., the need to hit at greater ranges)
- Establish the constraints (e.g., the system of competitive target practice)

- Encourage parallel experimentation (e.g., the different plotting and tracking solutions)
- Exploit the best-fitting solution that emerges (e.g., the Ford rangekeeper).

The use of the term *best-fitting* in the last bullet is deliberate. No solution will be optimal, but some will work better than others. For example, Vice Admiral Tisdale and his destroyer command believed that the best officer to serve as the CIC evaluator was the executive officer. Vice Admiral Lee required his battleships to choose a different individual, as the executive officer was needed in a battleship's secondary conning station. The best fit always has the potential to vary with context.

Sensitivity to context is also important to innovation. When Mahan developed his new concept of what it meant to be a naval officer, he stressed the importance of contextually applying the principles of strategy. For Mahan, leadership meant developing sufficient diversity of experience to be able to understand the subtle differences between various situations. The officers who learned these techniques became adept at developing unique solutions for their individual circumstances. This meant that the Navy actively maintained a high degree of local variability. Different ships created different cultures and environments; practices and techniques varied from one to the other; and officers took approaches with them as they moved from ship to ship.

This variability allowed the Navy to preserve a high degree of evolvability. Because there were no standard practices, and because effective practices could move through informal networks from one ship or command to another, the Navy leveraged local variations advantageously. In practice, local variation meant multiple parallel experiments, leading to new ideas and fostering more effective approaches. The previous chapters have highlighted numerous examples of this variability and illustrated how it helped drive innovation.

The obvious lesson is that innovation can be fostered through an effective balance of low-level variability and enabling constraints. The variability allows more rapid *exploration* of potential options and faster identification of effective methods. Enabling constraints focus the experimentation and provide a feedback mechanism. Biology employs a similar approach. Genetic replication is an imperfect process that introduces variation; each individual is, in essence, an experiment that could potentially lead to a new species, one better fitted to the environment.

Standardized procedures, in contrast, inhibit this kind of rapid, parallel learning. Standardization is effective once the best solution has been identified and the primary challenge has become *exploitation*. Over the course of World War II, the Navy was eventually forced by the rapid expansion of the fleet to take this approach. Variability was stifled to limit risk and loss. The result was predictable. Standardization inhibited learning and experimentation; new, and potentially more effective, approaches became more difficult to identify.

The necessity of balancing *exploration* and *exploitation* for effective organizational learning has been described by James March; he concludes that though organizations can raise their average performance in the short term by investing in exploitation, exploration is essential for long-term success, especially in circumstances where success comes through competition. Exploration increases variability and the likelihood of poor performance, but at the same time, it increases the chances that a new, innovative approach will be discovered. In a competitive environment like warfare, exploration is extremely important.[26] Discovery of a new technique may be the difference between victory and defeat. The Navy's experience in World War II—along with the variability inherent in its surface-warfare doctrine—illustrates the reality of these ideas; effective *exploration* was essential to success in the Pacific.

How can we ensure that the parallel experimentation triggered by variability is focused on the desired outcomes? The Navy aligned its efforts through the effective use of constraints—the systems of exercises discussed in detail above—and by identifying an overarching goal—triumph in a transpacific war against the empire of Japan. After the Russo-Japanese War, Japan was considered a potential adversary. During the interwar period, defeat of the IJN became the Navy's primary focus. That emphasis exerted a decisive influence on the Navy's plans and operations; the anticipation of war with Japan was the backdrop against which the system of learning developed.

Innovation is fostered by the interplay of these mechanisms. Constraints drive self-organization and exploration; they foster the emergence of new ideas. Variation preserves evolvability and allows the rapid investigation of parallel alternatives. An overarching goal focuses these efforts and aligns the experimentation with the objectives of the organization.

In adopting these approaches, the Navy of a century ago was ahead of its time. Today's leading organizational theories stress the same basic ideas. In *Embracing Complexity: Strategic Perspectives for an Age of Turbulence*, Jean G. Boulton, Peter M. Allen, and Cliff Bowman describe these concepts in detail and examine how they have been effectively applied to international development.[27] Jurgen Appelo is an author and popular speaker who has demonstrated how these approaches can increase the effectiveness of software-development organizations.[28] In a variety of different formats, Niels Pflaeging has presented the advantages of management techniques that decentralize control, create greater contextual sensitivity, and harness the creative energies of individuals.[29] Dave Snowden's Cynefin Framework provides a valuable model to enhance organizational decision making through leveraging complexity.[30] Agile software techniques, including Scrum, Kanban, and Extreme Programming, are designed to exploit these ideas and foster the creativity of teams. The great innovation introduced by Agile is the recognition that software development is a social activity; quality does not result from easily quantified variables—like lines of code or complexity—but from less tangible ones, like personal relationships, connections with peers in other departments, and the level of psychological safety.[31] The Navy benefitted from these same ideas; its success illustrates their value. They are broadly applicable to challenges of the past, the present, and the future.

They are also particularly relevant to today's Navy. A "Strategic Readiness Review" issued by Secretary of the Navy Richard V. Spencer on 11 December 2017 stressed the importance of developing a "Learning Culture" to "facilitate rapid, informed decisions" and avoid costly accidents. Fortunately, as this work has shown, the Navy has experience creating such a culture; by fostering self-organization, leveraging constraints, and establishing clear goals, it ought to be able to do so again. However, as the "Strategic Readiness Review" explained, decades of subordinating learning and self-organization to "short-term operational effectiveness" has had serious long-term consequences. Significant effort will be required to make the Navy a learning organization once more.[32]

COMPARATIVE ESSAY—THE IJN AND RN

As we have seen, several important factors came together to create the U.S. Navy's learning system. That system and the rapid pace of innovation that it fostered emerged from a specific set of circumstances. Those historical constraints allowed the Navy to avoid the difficulties that hindered learning in the other great naval powers of the time, Great Britain's Royal Navy and the Imperial Japanese Navy. These differences reinforce the lessons described above and offer a broader perspective on the nature of innovation.

When America entered World War I in 1917, the Navy was doctrinally immature. It had not developed a cohesive theory for how to coordinate forces in a modern fleet action. Existing approaches relied on simplistic plans and contextual applications of the principles of war. The Atlantic Fleet, formed just a decade before, had begun to experiment with modern fleet operations, but the Navy's tactical effectiveness was limited by a lack of experience. There was, however, benefit in this; the Navy remained open to many possible approaches and was willing to evaluate them experimentally. For the Navy, there was no "correct" way to handle in battle a large, modern fleet composed of many diverse ship types. Different approaches could be evaluated with a relatively open mind.

The evidence suggests that the RN's experience was very different. By the start of World War I, the RN had been the world's preeminent naval force for over a century, since its victory at the battle of Trafalgar in 1805. The RN was large, well funded, and better positioned than any other navy to experiment with new technologies. No other navy in the world could realistically challenge the RN's position. It capitalized on these advantages at the turn of the century to lead the dreadnought revolution—the series of international battleship-building programs ushered in by the commissioning of HMS *Dreadnought*, the world's first all-big-gun capital ship. However, maintaining that position restricted the RN's flexibility and inhibited its ability to experiment with new tactical approaches. Evolvability was limited by the need to remain preeminent. This affected the development of new tactics, just when the primary motive technology for naval power was changing from sail to steam.

There appear to have been two significant results. One was the failure to develop mechanisms that honestly assessed the effectiveness of tactical plans and doctrine. This does not mean that tactics did not change; they certainly did. The period immediately before World War I saw several different approaches to battle tactics emerge in the RN.[33] What was missing was an effective methodology for testing and evaluating those ideas in light of experience. The second, potentially related, was that the initiative of subordinates was stifled. What Andrew Gordon has called "the long shadow of Trafalgar" appears to have restricted the RN's ability to effectively explore strategic planning, the challenges of handling ships in combat, and the delegation of authority. If this is correct, it would largely explain the tactical timidity that prevented the RN's officers from successful exploiting the opportunities that arose during the battle of Jutland.[34]

The U.S. Navy, in contrast, was unencumbered by its prior victories. Although battles had been won in the Spanish-American War, they were not climactic triumphs. Instead, they fostered an increased level of anxiety and motivation for improvement. It was clear that although American ships had fought well enough to defeat their Spanish opponents, they had not been handled effectively, they had not fired accurately, and they had not fought as cohesive units. The Navy had to learn how to fight a modern naval battle; because it lacked experience, it was forced to experiment. The creation of the Atlantic Fleet, the introduction of the fire-control system, and nascent doctrinal approaches developed in the Torpedo Flotilla all resulted from the need to develop new theories and methods for how to fight and win at sea.

The IJN dealt with different constraints. While the U.S. Navy was introducing new gunnery practices and trying to improve its performance, the IJN was enjoying its newfound status as the dominant navy in the western Pacific. The Russo-Japanese War effectively ended with victory at Tsushima in 1905. Rather than using it as a vehicle for identifying flaws and potential improvements, the Japanese saw Tsushima as a model for how victories against larger and more powerful opponents could be won. As tensions increased with the United States, the Japanese built on their recent success and modeled their plans on the concept of a decisive fleet action. Predisposition toward decisive battle led the IJN to misinterpret the writings of Alfred T. Mahan. As described in chapter 2, in the United States Mahan's ideas fostered an emphasis on contextual analysis. In the IJN, Mahan was considered the preeminent prophet of decisive battle. The victory at Tsushima appeared to validate his theories.[35]

During the interwar period, the concept of decisive fleet action became the IJN's singular focus. In a war with the United States, victory would come through a climactic clash of battle fleets. In the 1920s, the IJN expected that battle to take place close to Japan after it subjected the U.S. fleet to a series of crippling attacks by light forces, submarines, and airplanes on the fleet's way across the Pacific. As time went on, the target location for the battle shifted farther east and earlier in time. After withdrawing from the treaty system, the IJN increased in size and strength. Its officers considered fighting the U.S. Navy on more even terms and closer to American bases.[36] This concept culminated with the attack on Pearl Harbor. It was conceived as a knockout blow that would shatter the Pacific Fleet and keep the United States out of the war long enough to consolidate the occupation of the Philippines, the Dutch East Indies, and Indochina. But the IJN had absorbed the wrong lesson. Instead of embracing Mahan's emphasis on principles and the subtle contextual understanding required to apply them flexibly, the Japanese had focused on the importance of a singular victory, based on their triumph at Tsushima.

The evidence also suggests that the IJN was hindered by its inability to create sufficient psychological safety for effective learning.

Although Japanese officers did learn and apply lessons from combat, their knowledge was channeled and restricted. The dignity of the institution—the potential loss of face that might come from being wrong—took precedence over the acquisition of new knowledge. The most glaring example is arguably the deletion from the First Air Fleet's action report on the battle of Midway of a critical log entry indicating that Adm. Nagumo Chuichi's staff did not expect enemy carriers to be encountered the day of the battle.[37] They wrote their mistakes out of the record, inhibiting their collective ability to learn. Capt. Hara Tameichi later provided another example. He was incredulous at the refusal of his superiors to leverage his skill and experience as a destroyer captain to improve combat tactics in 1943.[38] It was more important to keep the skilled captain at sea and fighting than it was to harness his knowledge for the improvement of the entire fleet. The contrast with Joseph C. Wylie, who was brought back to Pearl Harbor to train his peers in the development and use of the CIC, is stark and illuminating.

The experience of these other navies suggests that the U.S. Navy's innovative learning system was a fortunate outcome of specific circumstances and the actions of individuals who capitalized on them. The Navy had never fought a major fleet action and had no other model—aside from the heroic performance of individual captains in earlier wars—to build upon; doctrinal development started with a relatively clean slate. These favorable circumstances did not exist in the IJN or the RN. Each of them had developed a clear history, a set of foundational concepts that provided the basis for existing tactical doctrine. This limited their focus and overly constrained their efforts at a time when technology was changing rapidly. The Navy remained more open to new possibilities; it had greater emergent potential. This helps explain its greater ability to innovate in the early decades of the twentieth century.

SUMMARY

This work has introduced several key themes that are applicable to all types of human organizations. Examining the Navy's doctrinal evolution during the first half of the twentieth century from the perspective of a complex adaptive system has helped illustrate how constraints can trigger symmetry breaks and the emergence of yet more complex techniques. Constraints can be used to foster a learning approach that maintains a high degree of evolvability and emergent potential.

Emergent potential was critical to the Navy during World War II. It was the evolvability of the Navy's tactical doctrine—its ability to change and develop new combat heuristics—that ultimately enabled its rapid success in the Pacific. This proved far more important than the effectiveness of the Navy's doctrine on the eve of war, which was limited by the inadequate attention paid to minor actions. These limitations were quickly exposed in the Solomons. However, the Navy rapidly learned from these experiences, addressed deficiencies, and evolved new patterns that proved far more effective than anything the Japanese conceived.

Evolvability had been maintained through the interwar period by a series of constraints—the Fleet Problems, tactical exercises, and planning cycles—that contained feedback loops. The Navy leveraged these to revise and refine its approach continually. New patterns were introduced that enabled more complex approaches, including new fleet dispositions, new battle plans, and more sophisticated techniques for fire control. Openness to new ideas allowed the rapid integration of radar and other technologies. A willingness to experiment triggered new tactical formations and more sophisticated approaches to night combat. Although there were setbacks, a sustained pace of learning was maintained throughout the interwar period.

The Navy's learning system was triggered by paradigm shifts that redefined what it meant to be a naval officer and fundamentally altered how the Navy went about preparing for war. The tumultuous period of the late nineteenth century, as officers who had spent their formative years in wooden ships came to grips with the challenge of the new steel Navy, created a new outlook. Spurred on by insurgents like Luce, Taylor, and Sims, the Navy transitioned from a traditional organization to a modern, professional one. After the integration of the line officers and the Engineering Corps in 1899, the Navy's officers had to combine learning, critical thinking, and analysis with an emphasis on experimentation and scientific knowledge. The products of this reorientation were the men who achieved victory in the Pacific: King, Nimitz, Spruance, Halsey, Mitscher, Lee, and their peers.

The Navy's experience has several important implications. It suggests that innovations are rarely singular events. Instead, they are more likely to be triggered by an environment that is conducive to the sustained emergence of new, radical ideas. Innovation can therefore be most effectively fostered by creating such an environment, rather than by trying to trigger a specific technique—innovation emerges from a broad system of learning. In the Navy's case, variability was an essential part of the learning system. Because practices and approaches varied throughout the fleet, it was possible to conduct multiple parallel experiments, each intended to solve the same basic problem. This happened repeatedly during the early twentieth century. The two best examples are the development of the Navy's fire-control system and the introduction of the CIC. In each case, different ships implemented different approaches, allowing the Navy to compare a variety of potential solutions simultaneously.

But this variability came at a price. It meant that when war came, multiple parallel experiments would be performed in combat. Not all of them would be successful, and the resulting failures have been the subject of harsh—and deserved—criticism. However, without the possibility of failure, evolvability would not have been preserved. Those early setbacks were essential to ensuring later success. Without such inherent variability, the Navy's doctrine would not have evolved so rapidly during the war. Learning in military organizations often comes at a price; the Navy's surface-warfare doctrine absorbed costly lessons in late 1942 and early 1943 so that it could dominate for the rest of the war. The stage for that triumph had been set years before, when the Navy transformed itself from a traditional institution to a modern, professional organization. An "insurgent spirit" led that transformation, established the constraints of the learning system, and fostered victory in World War II.

NOTES

Preface

1. Edward L. Beach, *The United States Navy: 200 Years* (New York: Henry Holt, 1986); Clark G. Reynolds, *The Fast Carriers: The Forging of an Air Navy* (Annapolis, Md.: Naval Institute Press, 1992); Reynolds, *Admiral John H. Towers: The Struggle for Naval Air Supremacy* (Annapolis, Md.: Naval Institute Press, 1991); Robert L. O'Connell, *Sacred Vessels: The Cult of the Battleship and the Rise of the U.S. Navy* (New York: Oxford University Press, 1993); James D. Hornfischer, *The Last Stand of the Tin Can Sailors: The Extraordinary World War II Story of the U.S. Navy's Finest Hour* (New York: Bantam Books, 2009); Jeff Reardon, "Breaking the U.S. Navy's 'Gun Club' Mentality in the South Pacific," *Journal of Military History* 75, no. 2 (April 2011).

Prologue

1. Thomas C. Hone, Norman Friedman, and Mark D. Mandeles, *American and British Aircraft Carrier Development, 1919–1941* (Annapolis, Md.: Naval Institute Press, 2009); Williamson Murray and Allan R. Millett, eds., *Military Innovation in the Interwar Period* (Cambridge, U.K.: Cambridge University Press, 1996); Mark Allen Campbell, *The Influence of Air Power upon the Evolution of Battle Doctrine in the U.S. Navy, 1922–1941* (master's thesis, University of Massachusetts, 1992); Reynolds, *Fast Carriers*; Reynolds, *Admiral John H. Towers*.

2. Walter Licht, *Industrializing America: The Nineteenth Century* (Baltimore, Md.: Johns Hopkins University Press, 1995), 192.

3. Adam N. Stulberg and Michael D. Salomone, *Managing Defense Trans-* . *formation* (Burlington, Vt.: Ashgate, 2007); Barry R. Posen, *The Sources of Military Doctrine: France, Britain, and Germany between the World Wars* (Ithaca, N.Y.: Cornell University Press, 1984).

4. Pierre-Simon Laplace provided the foundation for this inductive approach based on probabilities. See Marquis Pierre-Simon de Laplace, *Probabilities,* trans. Frederick Wilson Truscott and Frederick Lincoln Emory (London: John Wiley & Sons, 1902).

5. The "Great Man" theory is an excellent example. Although Herbert Spencer challenged its dominance in the mid-nineteenth century, the basic idea still holds sway, particularly in histories of innovation that rely on "mavericks" and "zealots." See Terry C. Pierce, *Warfighting and Disruptive Technologies: Designing Innovation* (New York: Frank Cass, 2004), 116–20. For Spencer's critique, see Robert L. Carneiro, "Herbert Spencer as an Anthropologist," *Journal of Libertarian Studies 5,* no. 2 (Spring 1981): 153–210.

6. Jean G. Boulton, Peter M. Allen, and Cliff Bowman, *Embracing Complexity: Strategic Perspectives for an Age of Turbulence* (Oxford, U.K.: Oxford University Press, 2015), 29; Peter M. Allen, "Modeling Evolution and Creativity in Complex Systems," *World Futures, the Journal of Evolution 34,* nos. 1–2 (June 1992): 105–24; Joanna Macy, *Mutual Causality in Buddhism and General Systems Theory* (Albany: State University of New York, 1991).

7. François Jacob, *The Possible and the Actual* (Seattle: University of Washington Press, 1982), 31.

8. The following section draws from research across several fields, including Matteo Mossio, Leonardo Bich, and Alvaro Moreno, "Emergence, Closure and Inter-Level Causation in Biological Systems," *Erkenntnis* (2013); Alicia Juarrero, *Dynamics in Action: Intentional Behavior as a Complex System* (Cambridge, Mass.: MIT Press, 1999); and Daniel R. Brooks and E. O. Wiley, *Evolution as Entropy: Toward a Unified Theory of Biology,* 2nd ed. (Chicago: University of Chicago Press, 1988).

9. Juarrero, *Dynamics in Action,* 133.

10. Ibid., 138.

11. Dave Snowden first made this analogy for me.

12. Rong Li and Bruce Bowerman, "Symmetry Breaking in Biology," *Cold Spring Harbor Perspectives in Biology 2,* no. 3 (March 2010), doi:10.1101 /cshperspect.a003475 (21 July 2014).

13. Juarrero, *Dynamics in Action,* 140.

14. Mossio et al., "Emergence, Closure and Inter-Level Causation," 12.

15. Jacob, *Possible and Actual,* 34.

16. Marc Kirschner and John Gerhart, "Evolvability," *Proceedings of the National Academy of Sciences of the United States of America* 95.15 (1998): 8420–27, doi: 10.1073/pnas.95.15.8420 (15 August 2016).
17. Brooks and Wiley, *Evolution as Entropy*, 76.
18. Boulton et al., *Embracing Complexity*, 101–2.
19. This is similar to, but more generically applicable than, the concept of "anti-fragile." See Nassim Nicholas Taleb, *Anti-Fragile: Things That Gain from Disorder (Incerto)* (New York: Random House, 2014).
20. I am indebted to Robert Artigiani and Alicia Juarrero for this analogy.
21. For additional details, see Keith B. Bickel, *Mars Learning: The Marine Corps' Development of Small Wars Doctrine, 1915–1940* (Boulder, Colo.: Westview, 2001); and Posen, *Sources of Military Doctrine*.
22. *Tentative War Instructions and Battle Doctrine, Light Cruisers, 1938*, 1, *U.S. Navy and Related Operational, Tactical, and Instructional Publications* [hereafter *OpPub*], box 109, entry 337, Record Group [hereafter RG] 38, Records of the Office of the Chief of Naval Operations, National Archives, Washington, D.C.
23. It is a common view that militaries "hedge against uncertainty" by adopting prescriptive approaches. See Stulberg and Salomone, *Managing Defense Transformation*, 13.
24. Daniel Kahneman, *Thinking Fast and Slow* (New York: Farrar, Straus, and Giroux), 98.
25. Maj. Blair S. Williams, U.S. Army, "Heuristics and Biases in Military Decision Making," *Military Review* (September–October 2010): 40–52.
26. For an analysis of a "static" view of doctrine, see Col. T. N. Dupuy, U.S. Army, *Understanding War: History and Theory of Combat* (New York: Paragon House, 1987).

Chapter 1. A Professional Officer Corps

1. Rear Adm. Stephen B. Luce (Ret.), "On the Relations between the U.S. Naval War College and the Line Officers of the U.S. Navy," U.S. Naval Institute *Proceedings* 37, no. 3 (September 1911), 793–94.
2. Frederick Winslow Taylor, *The Principles of Scientific Management* (New York: Harper and Brothers, 1911), iv.
3. Jon Tetsuro Sumida, *Inventing Grand Strategy and Teaching Command: The Classic Works of Alfred Thayer Mahan Reconsidered* (Washington, D.C.: Woodrow Wilson Center Press, 1997), 6.
4. Bradley A. Fiske, *The Navy as a Fighting Machine* (Repr.: Annapolis, Md.: Naval Institute Press, 1988), 200.
5. Frederick Jackson Turner, "The Significance of the Frontier," in *Rereading Frederick Jackson Turner: The Significance of the Frontier in American History and Other Essays by Frederick Turner*, ed. John Mack Faragher (New Haven, Conn.: Yale University Press, 1998), 53.

6. Ibid., 59.

7. Donald Chisholm, *Waiting for Dead Men's Shoes: Origins and Development of the U.S. Navy's Officer Personnel System, 1793–1941* (Stanford, Calif.: Stanford University Press, 2001), 420.

8. Quoted in ibid., 419.

9. Ibid.

10. Ibid., 437–592.

11. Paolo E. Coletta, ed., *American Secretaries of the Navy*, vol. 2, *1913–1972* (Annapolis, Md.: Naval Institute Press, 1980), xiv.

12. Capt. A. P. Cooke, "Naval Reorganization," U.S. Naval Institute *Proceedings* 12, no. 4 (1886): 491–526.

13. Ronald Spector, *Professors of War: The Naval War College and the Development of the Naval Profession* (Newport, R.I.: Naval War College Press, 1977), 15.

14. Paolo E. Coletta, ed., *American Secretaries of the Navy*, vol. 1, *1775–1913* (Annapolis, Md.: Naval Institute Press, 1980), 431–32.

15. Ibid., 435.

16. Coletta, *American Secretaries of the Navy*, 2:437; Mark L. Hayes, "War Plans and Preparations and Their Impact on U.S. Naval Operations in the Spanish-American War," http://www.history.navy.mil/research/library /online-reading-room/title-list-alphabetically/s/spanish-american-war -war-plans-and-impact-on-u-s-navy.html (29 November 2015).

17. Rear Adm. Henry C. Taylor, quoted in "Naval Administration: Selected Documents on Navy Department Organization, 1915–1940" (Washington, D.C.: Department of the Navy, 1940), I-2.

18. Capt. Asa Walker, "Memorandum on a Naval General Staff, U.S. Naval War College, 1900," box 70, RG 8, Intelligence and Technical Archives, Naval War College Archives, Newport, R.I. [hereafter *Intelligence*].

19. Ibid., 5.

20. Capt. H. C. Taylor, "Memorandum on General Staff for the U.S. Navy," U.S. Naval Institute *Proceedings* 26, no. 3 (1900).

21. Charles Oscar Paullin, *Paullin's History of Naval Administration: 1775–1911* (Annapolis, Md.: U.S. Naval Institute, 1968; repr. 2012), 458.

22. Ibid., 459; Chisholm, *Waiting for Dead Men's Shoes*, 447.

23. Quoted in Paullin, *History of Naval Administration*, 460.

24. Chisholm, *Waiting for Dead Men's Shoes*, 447–66.

25. Paullin, *History of Naval Administration*, 461.

26. Ibid., 463.

27. "Annual Report of the Secretary of the Navy" (1909), in *Annual Reports of the Navy Department* (Washington, D.C.: Government Printing Office, 1902–1921) [hereafter *Annual Reports (year)*], 27.

28. Chisholm, *Waiting for Dead Men's Shoes*, 535; "Report of the Paymaster General of the Navy, Chief of the Bureau of Supplies and Accounts," *Annual Reports 1911*, 364.

29. Norbert Elias, *The Genesis of the Naval Profession* (Dublin: University College Dublin Press, 2007), 112.

30. Henry J. Hendrix, *Theodore Roosevelt's Naval Diplomacy: The U.S. Navy and the Birth of the American Century* (Annapolis, Md.: Naval Institute Press, 2009), 36.

31. Coletta, *American Secretaries of the Navy*, 1:470.

32. Norman Friedman, *U.S. Battleships: An Illustrated Design History* (Annapolis, Md.: Naval Institute Press, 1985), 7.

33. Henry Reuterdahl, "The Needs of Our Navy," *McClure's Magazine* (January 1908).

34. Friedman, *U.S. Battleships*, 80–81.

35. Hendrix, *Theodore Roosevelt's Naval Diplomacy*, 148.

36. The Royal Navy did not develop a similarly inclusive design process until after World War I. See Norman Friedman, *The British Battleship 1906–1946* (Annapolis, Md.: Naval Institute Press, 2015), 203.

37. Quoted in Coletta, *American Secretaries of the Navy*, 1:490.

38. Ibid., 491.

39. "Annual Report of the Secretary of the Navy," *Annual Reports 1909*, 7.

40. Ibid., 5.

41. Ibid., 8–9.

42. Bradley A. Fiske, *From Midshipman to Rear Admiral* (New York: Century, 1919), quoted in Coletta, *American Secretaries of the Navy*, 2:538.

43. Rear Adm. Julius Augustus Furer, *Administration of the Navy Department in World War II* (Washington, D.C.: Naval History Division, 1959), 109.

44. Ibid.

45. Quoted in Chisholm, *Waiting for Dead Men's Shoes*, 497.

46. Ibid., 503–11.

47. Quoted in ibid., 513.

48. Ibid., 519–22.

49. "Annual Report of the Secretary of the Navy," *Annual Reports 1909*, 25.

50. Ibid.

51. Chisholm, *Waiting for Dead Men's Shoes*, 538.

52. Bradley A. Fiske, "The Naval Profession," U.S. Naval Institute *Proceedings* 33, no. 2 (April 1907): 517–28.

53. Quoted in Chisholm, *Waiting for Dead Men's Shoes*, 558.

54. Ibid., 559–60.

55. Ibid., 561–69; Coletta, *American Secretaries of the Navy*, 2:532.

56. "Report of the Secretary of the Navy," *Annual Reports 1915*, 22.

57. "Report of the Bureau of Navigation," *Annual Reports 1915*, 183.
58. Chisholm, *Waiting for Dead Men's Shoes*, 573–87.
59. Paullin, *History of Naval Administration*, 470.
60. Ibid., 467–68; "Annual Report of the Secretary of the Navy," *Annual Reports 1913*, 5.
61. "Annual Report of the Secretary of the Navy," *Annual Reports 1913*, 6.
62. Ibid.
63. Ibid., 29; "Report of the Bureau of Navigation," *Annual Reports 1915*, 192; "Report of the Secretary of the Navy," *Annual Reports 1915*, 20.
64. Coletta, *American Secretaries of the Navy*, 2:528.
65. See Thomas C. Hone and Trent Hone, *Battle Line: The United States Navy, 1919–1939* (Annapolis, Md.: Naval Institute Press, 2006), 39–40.
66. "Report of the Secretary of the Navy," *Annual Reports 1915*, 188.
67. Gerald E. Wheeler, *Admiral William Veazie Pratt, U.S. Navy: A Sailor's Life* (Washington, D.C.: Naval History Division, Department of the Navy, 1974), 31.
68. Elting E. Morison, *Admiral Sims and the Modern American Navy* (Boston: Houghton Mifflin, 1942).

Chapter 2. The Gunnery System

1. Jim Leeke, *Manila and Santiago: The New Steel Navy in the Spanish American War* (Annapolis, Md.: Naval Institute Press, 2009), 153; Morison, *Admiral Sims*, 194.
2. While the Royal Navy's Admiralty Fire Control Tables provided similar levels of accuracy, they lacked the open architecture and elegant merging of man and machine. They were also far more difficult to produce and install.
3. Norman Friedman, *Naval Firepower: Battleship Guns and Gunnery in the Dreadnought Era* (Annapolis, Md.: Naval Institute Press, 2008), 18.
4. Morison, *Admiral Sims*, 105.
5. "Lecture on Fire Control," 27–28 August 1906, 7–8, box 39, *Intelligence*.
6. Ibid.; Christopher C. Wright, "Questions on the Effectiveness of U.S. Navy Battleship Gunnery, Part II," *Warship International* 41, no. 3 (2004) [hereafter "Battleship Gunnery, Part II"]: 289–313.
7. "Annual Report of the Secretary of the Navy," *Annual Reports 1908*, 19.
8. New tools helped. The Morris Tube and Dotters allowed more frequent practice and increased scores. See "Report of the Chief of the Bureau of Ordnance," *Annual Reports 1906*, 511.
9. Morison, *Admiral Sims*, 146.
10. "Lecture on Fire Control."
11. "Report of the Chief of the Bureau of Ordnance," *Annual Reports 1907*, 465.

12. Christopher C. Wright, "Questions on the Effectiveness of U.S. Navy Battleship Gunnery," *Warship International* 41, no. 1 (2004) [hereafter "Battleship Gunnery, Part I"]: 54–78; "Letter to Lieut. Comdr. T. T. Craven from Commander W. V. Pratt, 14 July 1912," box 96, *Intelligence*.

13. "Report of the Secretary of the Navy," *Annual Reports 1916*, 23

14. "Report of Autumn Target Practice 1905," quoted in Wright, "Battleship Gunnery, Part I."

15. "Report of Behavior of Personnel and Material, U.S.S. *Vermont*, Battle Practice, Manila Bay, November 1908," box 45, *Intelligence*.

16. Other navies developed similar devices around this time. The Royal Navy's equivalent was the Dumaresq. Reeves and White's design was unique in that it separated the motions of the target and of the firing ship into two separate elements. See Friedman, *Naval Firepower*; and Wright, "Battleship Gunnery, Part I."

17. Quoted in Wright, "Battleship Gunnery, Part I."

18. Lt. Cdr. Yates Sterling, "The Nation's Defense—The Offensive Fleet: How Shall We Prepare It for Battle," U.S. Naval Institute *Proceedings* 34, no. 2 (June 1908), 407n2.

19. "Change of Range Projector, 22 May 1908," box 96, *Intelligence*.

20. "Report of Autumn Target Practice 1905," quoted in Wright, "Battleship Gunnery, Part I."

21. Lt. Cdr. Ernest E. Herrmann, *Exterior Ballistics* (Annapolis, Md.: U.S. Naval Institute, 1935), 243–44.

22. Ibid., 243.

23. "Lecture on Fire Control."

24. *Fire Control Notes, 1940, for U.S. Naval Reserve* (Washington, D.C.: Government Printing Office, 1941), 37.

25. Ibid., 100.

26. David A. Mindell, *Between Human and Machine: Feedback, Control, and Computing before Cybernetics* (Baltimore, Md.: Johns Hopkins University Press, 2002), 24.

27. Ibid., 31.

28. *Navy Ordnance Activities, World War, 1917–1918* (Washington, D.C.: Government Printing Office, 1920), 156.

29. "Report of the Chief of the Bureau of Ordnance," *Annual Reports 1914*, 238.

30. "Report of Fire Control Board," 4 February 1916, 3, *Fleet Training Division Records* [hereafter *Training*].

31. Ibid., 47.

32. "The Use of Director Control in Target Practice by the Michigan, Commanding Officer, U.S.S. *Michigan*," 19 June 1915, box 39, *Intelligence*.

33. "Report of the Chief of the Bureau of Ordnance," *Annual Reports 1915,* 299.
34. Ibid., 308.
35. "Report of the Chief of the Bureau of Ordnance," *Annual Reports 1916,* 294.
36. "Battle Practice Discussion, 13 May 1915," box 96, *Intelligence.*
37. "Report of Fire Control Board," 28.
38. Ibid., 5–6.
39. *Navy Ordnance Activities,* 156.
40. A. Ben Clymer, "The Mechanical Analog Computers of Hannibal Ford and William Newell," *IEEE Annals of the History of Computing* 15, no. 2 (1993).
41. U.S. Navy, *Notes on Fire Control, 1933,* FTP-135 (Washington, D.C.: Government Printing Office, 1933), chap. 7.
42. Friedman, *Naval Firepower,* 182.
43. FTP-135, chap. 7; Wright, "Battleship Gunnery, Part II"; Wright, "Battleship Gunnery, Part I."
44. Quoted in Wright, "Battleship Gunnery, Part II."
45. "Report on Director System," 9 March 1918, box 1, *Training.*
46. *Navy Ordnance Activities,* 157.
47. *Fire Control Notes,* 42.
48. Ibid., 41.
49. Ibid., 42.
50. Friedman, *U.S. Battleships,* 173.
51. U.S. Navy, *War Instructions, 1923,* WPL-7, 90, box 5, *Strategic Plans Division Records* [hereafter *Strategic*].
52. Friedman, *U.S. Battleships,* 101–2.
53. Norman Friedman, *U.S. Naval Weapons* (Annapolis, Md.: Naval Institute Press, 1985), 37–38. The spotting tops on the Navy's battleships were 120 feet above the water; in perfect visibility, the observed horizon was 23,500 yards away.
54. Thomas Wildenberg, "In Support of the Battle Line: Gunnery's Influence on the Development of Carrier Aviation in the U.S. Navy," *Journal of Military History* 65, no. 3 (July 2001): 700.
55. Friedman, *U.S. Battleships,* 191.
56. Friedman, *Naval Firepower,* 227–35.
57. Elting E. Morison, *Men, Machines, and Modern Times* (Cambridge, Mass.: MIT Press, 1966), 17–44.

Chapter 3. Plans and Doctrine before World War I

1. For the associated challenges and the effective work done, see James C. Rentfrow, *Home Squadron: The U.S. Navy on the North Atlantic Station* (Annapolis, Md.: Naval Institute Press, 2014).

2. Spector, *Professors of War*, 15–17.

3. Sumida, *Inventing Grand Strategy*, 105.

4. Mahan, *Naval Strategy Compared and Contrasted with the Principles and Practice of Military Operations on Land* (Boston: Little, Brown, 1911), 299–300, quoted in ibid., 71.

5. Sumida, *Inventing Grand Strategy*, 103–4.

6. A. T. Mahan, *The Influence of Sea Power upon History, 1660–1783* (repr.: New York: Dover, 1987); A. T. Mahan, *The Influence of Sea Power upon the French Revolution and Empire, 1793–1812* (London: Sampson, Low, Marston, 1892); Craig C. Felker, *Testing American Sea Power: U.S. Navy Strategic Exercises, 1923–1940* (College Station: Texas A&M University Press, 2007), 11.

7. Sumida, *Inventing Grand Strategy*, 75.

8. Spector, *Professors of War*, 73.

9. Ibid., 30–36. Important work was done in the late nineteenth century. The Navy's North Atlantic Squadron developed "a protean concept of multiship operations" but not "a fleet warfighting capability." See Rentfrow, *Home Squadron*.

10. *Rules for the Conduct of the War Games* (Newport, R.I.: Naval War College, 1903).

11. *Rules for the Conduct of the War Games* (Newport, R.I.: Naval War College, 1905).

12. Ibid.

13. "Introduction, and Consideration of Battle Plan No. 1, 1916," box 93, *Intelligence*.

14. Cdr. Bradley A. Fiske, "American Naval Policy," U.S. Naval Institute *Proceedings* 31, no. 1 (March 1905): 1–80.

15. Fiske, *Navy as a Fighting Machine*, 335.

16. "Conference on Naval Tactics, 12 August 1901," box 106, *Intelligence*.

17. "GB No. 420," 17 October 1903, box 60, *General Board Records* [hereafter *GB*].

18. "Battle Plan No. 1 as amended and Modified for Trial in the Fleet, June 1906," box 108, *Intelligence*.

19. "Report of the Tactical Committee, 1903," box 106, *Intelligence*.

20. "Battle Plan No. 1, 1907, Report of Davis Board," 6 March 1907, box 46, *GB*.

21. "Battle Plan No. 2," 8 December 1911, box 46, *GB*.

22. "Estimate of the Situation, Lecture Delivered by Commander Frank H. Schofield," June 1912, Naval History and Heritage Command Library, Washington, D.C.

23. Ibid. [emphasis in original].

24. Ibid.

25. Ibid.

26. "Report on Gunnery Training for Battle in the Atlantic Fleet, May to October 1908," box 39, *Intelligence*.

27. See, for example, Fiske, *Navy as a Fighting Machine*, 136–37, 180–81.

28. "Addendum to 'Rules for Battle Maneuvers, 1913,' Fleet Order 29-14," 12 September 1914, box 93, *Intelligence*.

29. "Rules for Battle Maneuvers, 1913, United States Atlantic Fleet," 12 May 1913, box 93, *Intelligence*.

30. "Result of Battle Maneuvers, July 1913, U.S. Atlantic Fleet," box 93, *Intelligence*; "Results of Battle Maneuvers, June 1913, U.S. Atlantic Fleet," box 93, *Intelligence*.

31. "Result of Battle Maneuvers, July 1913."

32. "Letters from Flotilla Commander, Torpedo Flotilla, Atlantic Fleet on Attacks by Flotilla against the Battleship Fleet Protected by Double Screen, March 1915," 1, box 42, *Intelligence*.

33. Fiske, *Navy as a Fighting Machine*, 276, 335.

34. "Admiral Fletcher's Tactics of the Battle Line, 1916," box 93, *Intelligence*.

35. Ibid., 2–3.

36. "Discussion on Tactical Principles, U.S. Naval War College, 12–17 June 1916," 4, box 107, *Intelligence*.

37. "Battle Instructions, United States Atlantic Fleet," 27 May 1916, box 48, *GB*.

38. The term *weather gage* was used in this context. Although the term originated in the age of sail, it was still important in the early twentieth century. See Adm. Harris Laning, *An Admiral's Yarn* (Newport, R.I.: Naval War College Press, 1999), app. II, 441.

39. Lt. Cdr. Dudley W. Knox, "Trained Initiative and Unity of Action: The True Bases of Military Efficiency," U.S. Naval Institute *Proceedings* 39, no. 1 (March 1913).

40. "Naval War College, Course of 1901, Naval Tactics," box 106, *Intelligence*.

41. Morison, *Admiral Sims*, 293n2.

42. Quoted in ibid., 292.

43. Wheeler, *Admiral William Veazie Pratt*, 74.

44. Ibid.

45. Ernest J. King with Walter Muir Whitehill, *Fleet Admiral King: A Naval Record* (New York: W. W. Norton, 1952), 90–92, quoted in David Kohnen, "The U.S. Navy Won the Battle of Jutland," *Naval War College Review* 69, no. 4 (Autumn 2016): 122–45.

46. "Result of Battle Maneuvers, July 1913."

47. "Letters from Flotilla Commander," 4.

48. Thomas Hughes, "Learning to Fight: Bill Halsey and the Early American Destroyer Force," *Journal of Military History* 77, no. 1 (January 2013): 71–90.

49. "Naval Tactics," 30 May 1915, box 107, *Intelligence*.

50. Ibid.

51. "A Study in Fleet Tactics: A Proposed Battle Doctrine, 25 June 1917," box 107, *Intelligence*.

52. Jerry W. Jones, *U.S. Battleship Operations in World War I* (Annapolis, Md.: Naval Institute Press, 1998), 25, 29, 82–87.

53. Norman Friedman, *Network Centric Warfare: How Navies Learned to Fight Smarter through Three World Wars* (Annapolis, Md.: Naval Institute Press, 2009), 39.

54. *Doctrine and General Instructions, Force Instructions No. 25*, U.S. Naval Forces Operating in European Waters, London, England, 16 August 1918, box 107, *OpPub*.

55. Ibid., 3–4.

56. Sumida, *Inventing Grand Strategy*, 117.

Chapter 4. The Interwar Learning System

1. The three treaties were as follows: The Nine-Power Treaty between the United States, Great Britain, Japan, France, Italy, Belgium, the Netherlands, Portugal, and China, which internationalized the Open Door; the Four-Power Treaty between the United States, Great Britain, France, and Japan, which replaced the Anglo-Japanese Treaty; and the Five-Power Treaty between the United States, Great Britain, Japan, France, and Italy, which limited naval armaments.

2. Sadao Asada, *From Mahan to Pearl Harbor: The Imperial Japanese Navy and the United States* (Annapolis, Md.: Naval Institute Press, 2006).

3. Edward S. Miller, *War Plan Orange: The U.S. Strategy to Defeat Japan, 1897–1945* (Annapolis, Md.: Naval Institute Press, 1991).

4. "Report and Recommendations of a Board Appointed by the Bureau of Navigation Regarding the Instruction and Training of Line Officers," U.S. Naval Institute *Proceedings* 46, no. 8 (August 1920).

5. John M. Lillard, *Playing War: Wargaming and U.S. Navy Preparations for World War II* (Lincoln, Neb.: Potomac Books, 2016), 41.

6. "A Discussion of the War Plans, U.S. Navy and the Cooperation and Coordination Necessary for Their Preparation," 3, box 21, *Training*.

7. Laning, *Admiral's Yarn*, app. I, 399.

8. Gerald E. Wheeler, *Kinkaid of the Seventh Fleet: A Biography of Admiral Thomas C. Kinkaid, U.S. Navy* (Washington, D.C.: Naval Historical Center, 1995), 55.

9. Wheeler, *Admiral William Veazie Pratt*, 323.
10. "Strategic Problem, 1923, Report on, Commander in Chief, Battle Fleet," 5 March 1923, box 55, *Intelligence*.
11. "System for Damage Penalties in Fleet Problems," 17 July 1930, quoted in Campbell, *Influence of Air Power*, 129.
12. Campbell, *Influence of Air Power*, 130.
13. "United States Fleet—Problem XIII—1932, Report of the Commander-in-Chief United States Fleet," quoted in ibid., 133.
14. "Change no. 10 to USF-10," 9 May 1936, box 270, *World War II Command File* [hereafter *WWII*]; "Change no. 12 to USF-10," 24 January 1938, ibid.
15. *General Tactical Instructions, United States Navy*, FTP-45, 1924, box 106, *WWII*.
16. Friedman, *Network Centric Warfare*, 44n10.
17. Albert A. Nofi, *To Train the Fleet for War: The U.S. Navy Fleet Problems, 1923–1940* (Newport, R.I.: Naval War College Press, 2010), 74.
18. FTP-45; *Current Tactical Orders, United States Fleet*, USF-10, 1934, box 270, *WWII*; Campbell, *Influence of Air Power*, 83–88.
19. "School of Doctrine—Committees, 12 November 1920, Destroyer Squadrons One and Nine, U.S. Atlantic Fleet," box 55, *Intelligence*.
20. Wheeler, *Admiral William Veazie Pratt*, 158–62.
21. "School of Doctrine, Destroyer Force, Atlantic Fleet, 5 January 1920, Problem no. 9," box 55, *Intelligence*.
22. "Suggestions for Improving the Staff College Course, Commander W. V. Tomb," 29 April 1921, box 55, *Intelligence*.
23. "The Destroyer Staff College," 20 October 1921, box 55, *Intelligence*.
24. Ibid.
25. *Destroyer Instructions*, U.S. Atlantic Fleet, 23 November 1921, box 107, *OpPub*.
26. WPL-7.
27. "The Role of Doctrine in Naval Warfare, Naval War College, Newport, RI," 19 May 1924, 13, box 32, *Strategic*.
28. James J. Tritten, *Doctrine and Fleet Tactics in the Royal Navy* (Norfolk, Va.: Naval Doctrine Command, 1994), 20–21.
29. John Brooks, *The Battle of Jutland* (Cambridge, U.K.: Cambridge University Press, 2016), 97–130.
30. WPL-7, 90.
31. The Navy maintained a larger "possibility space" by keeping options open; this is often described as a "cloud of possibilities." See Allen, "Modeling Evolution and Creativity," 105–24; and Robert Artigiani, "Leadership and Uncertainty: Complexity and the Lessons of History," *Futures* 37 (2005): 585–603.

32. "Doctrine (Conference), Navy Department, Washington, DC," 1 December 1917, 3, box 55, *Intelligence.*

33. *Destroyer Instructions,* U.S. Atlantic Fleet, 24.

34. WPL-7, 90.

35. *War Instructions, United States Navy,* FTP-143, 1934, 108, box 108, *WWII; General Tactical Instructions, United States Navy,* FTP-188, 1940, 14-10 through 14-15, box 108, *WWII.*

36. Personal correspondence from Norman Friedman. The Japanese planned to fight on parallel courses; see David C. Evans and Mark R. Peattie, *Kaigun: Strategy, Tactics, and Technology in the Imperial Japanese Navy, 1887–1941* (Annapolis, Md.: Naval Institute Press, 1997).

37. "Report of Fleet Problem Ten," 7 May 1930, 65, roll 13, *Records Relating to United States Navy Fleet Problems I to XXIII, 1923–1941* [hereafter *Records*].

38. W. J. Jurens, "The Evolution of Battleship Gunnery in the U.S. Navy, 1920–1945," *Warship International* 28, no. 3 (1991): 246.

39. Capt. Wayne P. Hughes Jr. (Ret.), *Fleet Tactics: Theory and Practice* (Annapolis, Md.: Naval Institute Press, 1986).

40. "Report of Fleet Problem Ten," 65.

41. "United States Fleet Problem XIII, 1932, Report of the Commander-in-Chief United States Fleet," 23 May 1932, 30, roll 14, *Records.*

42. Sumida, *Inventing Grand Strategy.*

43. Capt. J. M. Reeves, "The Battle of Jutland, Lecture Delivered at the Army War College 1925," May 1925, box 10, *Strategic.*

44. Kohnen, "U.S. Navy Won the Battle of Jutland," 134–35.

45. Cdr. Holloway H. Frost, *The Battle of Jutland* (Annapolis, Md.: U.S. Naval Institute, 1936), 108–10.

46. Ibid., 114.

47. Capt. Harris Laning, "Major Tactics at Jutland," March 1923, 17, box 17, *Publications.*

48. Frost, *Battle of Jutland,* 517.

49. Laning, "Major Tactics at Jutland," 18–19.

50. Ibid., 25. These basic criticisms have been echoed in more recent analyses. See Andrew Gordon, *The Rules of the Game: Jutland and British Naval Command* (Annapolis, Md.: Naval Institute Press, 1996).

51. FTP-143, 87.

52. "Annual Report of the Commander-in-Chief, United States Fleet for the period 1 July 1928 to 21 May 1929," 21 May 1929, 9, box 256, *WWII.*

53. "Gunnery Doctrine and Standard Fire Control Procedures for Destroyers, Destroyer Tactical Bulletin No. 2-38," 2, box 129, *U.S. Navy Technical Publications* [hereafter *TechPub*].

54. "Some Effects of the Washington Conference on American Naval Strategy," 24 October 1923, 4, box 11, *Strategic.*
55. "Battle Fleet Fighting Instructions," 17 November 1927, box 108, *OpPub.*
56. Ibid., 1–2.
57. Ibid., 2.
58. *Tentative Fleet Dispositions and Battle Plans, United States Fleet, 1930,* introduction, box 108, *OpPub.*
59. Ibid.
60. The Navy initially estimated the maximum range of the Japanese battleships to be 27,000 yards; see "Class of 1926, Joint Problem No. I, Blue Statement of Problem and Staff Solution," Numerical Comparison of Forces, box 14, *Strategic.* By 1935, the estimate had increased to 29,000 yards; see "Operations Problem III-1935-SR, Orange, Estimate of the Situation by Orange Commander-in-Chief, Solution by a Member of the Staff," 10, box 21, *Strategic.* Both estimates were too low. The Japanese had increased the effective range of their battleship guns and intended to open fire at extreme range; see Evans and Peattie, *Kaigun,* 250–63.
61. FTP-143, 106. This assumption was incorrect. See note above.
62. Ibid.; FTP-188, 14-3, 14-4.
63. FTP-143, 106.
64. FTP-188, 14-6 through 14-15.
65. "Budget 1932, Estimate of the Situation and Base Development Program," in "Annual Estimates of the Chief of Naval Operations," Office of the Secretary of the Navy, 22, *Confidential Correspondence.*
66. Laning, *Admiral's Yarn,* app. II, 414.
67. See Trent Hone, "The Evolution of Fleet Tactical Doctrine in the U.S. Navy, 1922–1941," *Journal of Military History* 67, no. 4 (October 2003): 1107–48; and Hone and Hone, *Battle Line,* 86–87.
68. "United States Fleet Problem XI, 1930, Report of the Commander in Chief United States Fleet," 14 July 1930, 9, 61–62, roll 13, *Records;* "Report of Fleet Problem Ten," 8, 22.
69. "United States Fleet Problem XI, 1930," 65.
70. Ibid., 65–66.
71. See Hone, "Evolution of Fleet Tactical Doctrine."
72. This is particularly true of the Naval War College. See Lillard, *Playing War,* 49.
73. "Current Tactical Orders for Destroyers, Destroyer Tactical Bulletin, No. 3-39, Commander Destroyers, Battle Force," 1939, box 130, *TechPub;* "Tactical Bulletin, Cruisers, Scouting Force, U.S. Fleet, January 1941," 15, box 22, *OpPub.*
74. *Destroyer Instructions,* U.S. Atlantic Fleet, 36–37.

75. *Destroyer Tactical Instructions, United States Navy,* FTP-88, 1929, box 37, *TechPub;* "Tactical Employment Destroyers, U.S. Fleet, 1932," 26, box 67, *OpPub.*

76. "Revision of Destroyer Tactical Instructions," 3 December 1931, box 40, *Intelligence.*

77. "Tactical Employment Destroyers, U.S. Fleet, 1932," 30.

78. Many details in the published night-search-and-attack doctrine appeared in Fleet Problem XVIII of 1937. See "Light Forces, WHITE Fleet, Operation Plan no. 6–37," 1 April 1937, roll 22, *Records;* "Night Search and Attack Operations, Destroyer Tactical Bulletin no. 5-38," Commander Destroyers Battle Force, 1938, box 129, *TechPub;* "Night Search and Attack, DTP 2-40," Commander Destroyers Battle Force, 1940, box 130, *TechPub;* and "Light Forces in Night Search and Attack," 24 December 1941, box 250, *WWII.*

79. "Light Forces in Night Search and Attack."

80. Ibid., 8–9; "Tactical Bulletin, Cruisers, Scouting Force, U.S. Fleet, January 1941."

81. "Compendium of Tactical Exercises Conducted during Fiscal Year 1938, Destroyer Tactical Bulletin No. 4-38," Commander Destroyers Battle Force, VI-2 through VI-63, box 129, *TechPub.*

82. U.S. Navy, *Destroyer War Instructions,* WPL-6 (Washington, D.C.: Government Printing Office, 1922), 4.

83. *The Estimate of the Situation, Plans and Orders,* U.S. Naval War College, Department of Operations, Newport, R.I., 1932, Naval Historical Center Library.

84. *Sound Military Decision, including the Estimate of the Situation and the Formulation of Directives* (Newport, R.I.: Naval War College, 1938), 77–78.

85. "United States Fleet Problem XII, 1931, Report of the Commander in Chief United States Fleet," 50, roll 13, *Records.*

86. "Annual Report of the Secretary of the Navy," *Annual Reports for 1921,* 25.

87. Wheeler, *Admiral William Veazie Pratt,* 421.

88. FTP-143, 84.

89. "Annual Report of the Commander-in-Chief, United States Fleet for the Period 1 July, 1933 to 30 June, 1934," 11, box 256, *WWII.*

90. Ibid.

91. "Annual Report of the Commander-in-Chief, United States Pacific Fleet for the Period 1 July 1940 to 30 June 1941," 3, box 229, *WWII.*

92. "Fleet Problem XV, May 1934," 13, roll 16, *Records.*

93. Thomas B. Buell, *Master of Sea Power: A Biography of Fleet Admiral Ernest J. King* (Boston: Little, Brown, 1980), app. I, 493.

Chapter 5. Heuristics at Guadalcanal

1. Hone, "Evolution of Fleet Tactical Doctrine in the U.S. Navy, 1922–1941."
2. Samuel Eliot Morison, *History of the United States Naval Operations in World War II* (Boston: Little, Brown, 1984), 3:256–57.
3. John B. Lundstrom, *Black Shoe Carrier Admiral: Frank Jack Fletcher at Coral Sea, Midway, and Guadalcanal* (Annapolis, Md.: Naval Institute Press, 2006), 228.
4. Richard W. Bates, *The Battle of Savo Island, August 9th, 1942, Strategical and Tactical Analysis, Part 1* (Newport, R.I.: Naval War College for Bureau of Naval Personnel, 1950), 152; "Action Report, Night of November 14–15, 1942, U.S.S. *Washington,* 27 November 1942," 10, box 1501, *World War II Action and Operational Reports,* RG 38, Records of the Office of the Chief of Naval Operations, National Archives, Washington, D.C. [hereafter *Action*]; and Morison, *History,* 5:157, 241. A star shell is a powerful flare, fired from a naval gun and set to burst beyond the target, backlighting it. After bursting, the flare descends slowly on a parachute.
5. *Tentative War Instructions and Battle Doctrine, Light Cruisers, 1938:* "Light Cruiser Doctrine, Light Cruiser Tactical Bulletin No. 2-39," 28 April 1939, 14, box 29, *OpPub.*
6. For battleships it was 20 percent. See "Proposed Orders for Gunnery Exercises, 1931–1932, Chief of Naval Operations," 28 January 1931, *Records of the Bureau of Ordnance* [hereafter *BuOrd*], box 124, RG 74, National Archives, Washington, D.C.
7. "U.S.S. *Augusta* Night Battle Practice, 1936–1937—Comment on," Commander-in-Chief, Asiatic Fleet, 11 June 1937, 1, box 195, *Training.*
8. Ibid., 1. Although the record does not say whether *Augusta* used an increasing or decreasing ladder, given the emphasis on decreasing (or "down") ladders in *Night Battle Practices,* it is likely that a decreasing ladder was used.
9. Vice Adm. Lloyd M. Mustin, *The Reminiscences of Vice Admiral Lloyd M. Mustin,* interview by John T. Mason Jr. (Annapolis, Md.: U.S. Naval Institute, 2003), 237–38.
10. "Special Night Battle Practice, Commander Destroyer Squadron One," 3 September 1941, box 307, *Training.*
11. Mustin, *Reminiscences,* 239.
12. "Fire Control Possibilities of Radio Micro Rays, Bureau of Engineering," 10 October 1933, box 213, *BuOrd.*
13. "Heavy Cruisers Night Battle Practice, 1940–1941, Comments on, Commander Cruisers, Scouting Force," 6 March 1941, 2, box 307, *Training.*
14. David L. Boslaugh, *When Computers Went to Sea: The Digitization of the United States Navy* (Los Alamitos, Calif.: IEEE Computer Society, 1999), 14.

15. Bates, *Savo Island,* 86–87.
16. *The Battles of Savo Island, 9 August 1942, and the Eastern Solomons, 23–25 August 1942, Combat Narrative* (Washington, D.C.: Naval Historical Center, 1994).
17. "Special Instructions to SCREENING GROUP and Vessels Temporarily Assigned, V. Crutchley," box 71, *Action;* Bates, *Savo Island,* 55–56. Riefkohl objected to Crutchley's dispersed disposition because of the increased risk of friendly fire; see Bates, *Savo Island,* 59, 288–89.
18. "Special Instructions to SCREENING GROUP"; "Radar Doctrine, U.S. Pacific Fleet," 31 December 1941, 2, *WWII.*
19. "Fleet Problem Sixteen, Report of Commander-in-Chief, United States Fleet," 15 September 1935, 26, *Records,* Dispersed attack formations were another matter; see "Report of Fleet Problem XV," 1 June 1934, roll 16, *Records.*
20. Bates, *Savo Island,* 60.
21. *Secret Information Bulletin No. 2, Battle Experience Solomon Islands Actions, August and September 1942, including Bombardment of Kiska, 7 August 1942,* United States Fleet, Headquarters of the Commander in Chief, 11-1, Manuscript Collection 207 [hereafter MC 207], box 1.
22. "Special Instructions to SCREENING GROUP." Crutchley may have been comfortable with two separate cruiser groups because of the RN's training in divisional tactics; see Jon Tetsuro Sumida, "'The Best Laid Plans': The Development of British Battle-Fleet Tactics, 1919–1942," *International History Review* 14, no. 4 (November 1992): 681–700.
23. "Cruiser Action off Savo Island on the Night of August 8–9, 1942, the Commander South Pacific Area," 17 October 1942, 3, box 71, *Action.*
24. "Radar Doctrine, U.S. Pacific Fleet," 1.
25. Bates, *Savo Island,* 58–59.
26. Ibid., 355. Crutchley may have been influenced by the British Admiralty's opinion that the Japanese were "not good night fighters"; see Ministry of Defense (Navy), *War with Japan,* vol. 3, *The Campaigns in the Solomons and New Guinea* (London: Her Majesty's Stationery Office, 1995), 53.
27. Bates, *Savo Island,* 144, 168–203.
28. Ibid., 130.
29. TBS was a very-high-frequency radio circuit; ibid., 137.
30. James W. Grace, *The Naval Battle of Guadalcanal* (Annapolis, Md.: Naval Institute Press, 1999), 49–50.
31. See Trent Hone, "'Give Them Hell!': The U.S. Navy's Night Combat Doctrine and the Campaign for Guadalcanal," *War in History* (April 2006, 13, no. 2): 171–99.
32. Marc D. Bernstein, "Tin Cans Raid Balikpapan," U.S. Naval Institute *Proceedings* 129, no. 4 (April 2003), 81.

33. U.S. Navy, Office of Naval Intelligence, *The Java Sea Campaign*, Combat Narrative, 1943, http://www.history.navy.mil/research/library/online-reading-room/title-list-alphabetically/j/java-sea-campaign.html (4 August 2015).

34. Morison, *History,* 2:290.

35. Many histories have misinterpreted this idea to mean that the Navy lacked a night-combat doctrine. Rather, what was missing was a specific task-force doctrine. See "Comments on the Battle of Guadalcanal, Nov. 11–15, 1942, the President, Naval War College," ser. 2238, 9 June 1943 (copy provided by Wayne Hughes), 4; and Eric Hammel, *Guadalcanal: Decision at Sea, the Naval Battle of Guadalcanal, November 13–15, 1942* (New York: Crown, 1988), 11–25.

36. "Cruiser Action off Savo Island," 4.

37. Callaghan assumed his post on 30 October; see Grace, *Naval Battle of Guadalcanal,* 13.

38. "Comments on the Battle of Guadalcanal," 2.

39. *The Battle of Guadalcanal, 11–15 November 1942,* Combat Narrative (Washington, D.C.: Naval Historical Center, Department of the Navy, 1994), 61; Morison, *History,* 5:270–71.

40. *Current Tactical Orders, United States Fleet,* USF-10, 1941, 32, box 270, *WWII.*

41. FTP-88 cautioned that "tactical groups, such as divisions and sections, should not be broken up in forming the task organization."

42. "Night Division Battle Practice, Commander Destroyer Division Sixty-One," 14 April 1937, 3, box 195, *Training;* FTP-143, 44.

43. FTP-88.

44. "Night Search and Attack Operations, Destroyer Tactical Bulletin No. 5-38, Commander Destroyers, Battle Force," 1938, box 129, *TechPub.*

45. "Night Division Battle Practice and Battle Torpedo Practice 'C'—Summary, Commander Destroyers, Battle Force," 29 July 1940, box 276, *Training;* "Night Division Battle Practice 1938–39—Destroyers, Battle Force—Summarized Comments on, Commander Destroyers Battle Force," 23 March 1939, 12, box 224, *Training.*

46. "Night Division Battle Practice 1938–39—Destroyers, Battle Force—Summarized Comments on," 11; "Night Division Battle Practice and Battle Torpedo Practice 'C,' 1940–41, Destroyer Flotilla One—Summarized Comments, Commander Destroyer Flotilla One," 10 October 1941, app. A, box 307, *Training.*

47. "Compendium of Tactical Exercises Conducted during Fiscal Year 1938, Destroyer Tactical Bulletin No. 4–38, Commander Destroyers Battle Force," VI-2 through VI-63, box 129, *TechPub.*

48. "Special Night Battle Practice, Commander Destroyer Squadron One," 2 July 1941, box 307, *Training.*
49. "Night Action off Savo Island (9th August 1942)—Remarks by C.T.G 62.6," 6, box 71, *Action.*
50. *Secret Information Bulletin No. 4, Battle Experience Solomon Islands Actions, November 1942,* United States Fleet, Headquarters of the Commander in Chief, 28-21, box 1, MC 207.
51. Morison, *History,* 5:148–49.
52. "Report of Night Action 11–12 October 1942, Commander Task Group 64.2," 22 October 1942, 2, box 17, *Action.*
53. "Report of Night Action 11–12 October 1942, the Commander South Pacific Area," 3 November 1942, box 19, *Action;* "Action off Savo Island, Night of 11–12 October; report of, U.S.S. *Helena,*" 20 October 1942, 2, box 1025, *Action.*
54. Bates, *Savo Island,* 169.
55. Morison, *History,* 5:149. Morison indicates that Scott instructed the cruisers to open fire without orders but that these instructions were not clear; see ibid., 5:157n13. Scott reported that he had instructed all captains to open fire without orders once the enemy was located; see "Report of Night Action 11–12 October 1942, Commander Task Group 64.2," 3. In a memorandum issued before the battle, Scott ordered the third and fourth cruisers in column to open fire on the disengaged flank without orders. Nothing is said about the other cruisers opening fire without orders; see "Memorandum for Task Group Sixty-Four Point Two, Commander Task Force Sixty Four," 9 October 1942, box 19, *Action.*
56. Scott used *San Francisco* as his flagship because she had the necessary facilities; *Helena* lacked them. Had Scott commanded the formation from *Helena,* he might have had a better sense of the battle, but he could not have embarked his staff and so would not have been able to command effectively.
57. Morison, *History,* 5:154.
58. Ibid., 5:157.
59. "Report of Night Action 11–12 October 1942, Commander Task Group 64.2," 3.
60. Morison, *History,* 5:161n15.
61. Quoted in ibid., 5:178.
62. *Tentative War Instructions and Battle Doctrine, Light Cruisers, 1938,* 11.
63. Capt. J. E. Bennet, USN (Ret.), "Callaghan Was Calm and Collected at Guadalcanal," *Shipmate* (April 1996): 18–19.
64. "Night Action between Task Force 67.4 and Japanese Forces, November 13, 1942, U.S.S. *Portland,*" 12 November 1942, box 1328, *Action.*

65. Grace, *Naval Battle of Guadalcanal*, 61.

66. Charles R. Haberlein Jr., *Reflections on Friday the Thirteenth: Daniel J. Callaghan's Naval Battle off Guadalcanal*, preliminary version for critical review, 30 August 1994, copy provided by Wayne Hughes.

67. *Secret Information Bulletin No. 4*, 28-20.

68. Grace's supposition that *Hiei* hit *Atlanta* with 14-inch bombardment shells, mistaken for 5.5-inch shells in her action report, is possibly correct. However, the timing of events and placement of the 8-inch hits makes it almost certain that *San Francisco* fired the shells that killed Scott and his staff. Grace, *Naval Battle of Guadalcanal*, 69; "Engagement with Japanese Surface Forces off Guadalcanal night of 12–13 November 1942, and Loss of U.S.S. *Atlanta*," 20 November 1942, box 23, *Action*.

69. *Secret Information Bulletin No. 4*, 28-20.

70. Hone, " 'Give Them Hell!' "

71. Commander Battleships, Battle Force, *Current Doctrine, Battleships, USF-17*, 1938, 6.

72. Robert Artigiani, "Chaos and Constitutionalism: Toward a Post Modern Theory of Social Evolution," *World Futures* 34 (1992): 131–56.

73. *Secret Information Bulletin No. 4*, 28-11.

74. "Preliminary Report of Action, 12–13 November 1942, Commander in Chief, U.S. Pacific Fleet," 28 December 1942, 8, box 19, *Action*.

75. Morison, *History*, 5:272, 274–75; *Battle of Guadalcanal, 11–15 November 1942*, 61.

76. Vice Adm. Lloyd Mustin had worked closely with Lee and recalled his extensive knowledge of technical matters. See Mustin, *Reminiscences*, 818–64.

77. "Action Report, Night of November 14–15, 1942, U.S.S. *Washington*."

78. Robert Lundgren, "*Kirishima* Damage Analysis," ed. Tony DiGiulian, 28 September 2010, http://www.navweaps.com/index_lundgren/Kirishima _Damage_Analysis.pdf (4 December 2016).

79. C. Raymond Calhoun, *Tin Can Sailor: Life aboard the USS* Sterett, *1939–1945* (Annapolis, Md.: Naval Institute Press, 1993), 74–89; Grace, *Naval Battle of Guadalcanal*, 88.

80. "Operation Plan No. 1-42, Commander Task Force Sixty-Seven," 27 November 1942, box 241, *Action*.

81. *Secret Information Bulletin No. 5, Battle Experience Solomon Islands Actions, December 1942—January 1943*, United States Fleet, Headquarters of the Commander in Chief, 31-4, box 1, MC 207.

82. Ibid., 31-6.

83. Ibid.

84. "Pacific Fleet Tactical Bulletin No. 4TB-42, Commander-in-Chief, Pacific Fleet," 26 November 1942, box 250, *WWII*.

Chapter 6. The CIC

1. For a detailed description of this concept, see Edwin Hutchins, *Cognition in the Wild* (Cambridge, Mass.: MIT Press, 1995).

2. Morison, *History,* 5:326.

3. "Radar Bulletin No. 1 (RADON), the Tactical Use of Radar," United States Fleet, Headquarters of the Commander in Chief, May 1942, *Classified Operational Archives,* box 266 [hereafter *Classified*]; "Detection Radar Doctrine, Atlantic Fleet, Commander-in-Chief, Atlantic Fleet," 5 June 1942, box 225, *WWII;* "Pacific Fleet Tactical Bulletin No. 6-41," 31 December 1941, box 250, *WWII;* "Radar Plot and Communications," 26 February 1942, box 211, *Records of the CNO Headquarters* [hereafter *CNO*].

4. "Pacific Fleet Tactical Bulletin No. 4TB-42." Note that the initial draft called for a "Combat Operations Center"; Admiral King changed "operations" to "information." See Timothy S. Wolters, *Information at Sea* (Baltimore, Md.: Johns Hopkins University Press, 2013), 206.

5. "Pacific Fleet Tactical Bulletin No. 4TB-42," 2.

6. Wolters, *Information at Sea,* 206.

7. "CIC Information Bulletin No. 2-43, Commander Destroyers Pacific Fleet," 15 December 1943, box 614, *CNO*.

8. "Gunnery Doctrine and Fire Control Procedures (C.P.T.B 1-43) Cruisers, Pacific Fleet, Commander Cruisers, Pacific Fleet," August 1943, 12, box 135, *TechPub*.

9. "Light Cruiser Doctrine, Light Cruiser Tactical Bulletin No. 2-39."

10. "Night Actions of Kula Gulf July 6–7, 1943, and Kolombangara July 12–13, 1943—Additional data on, Commander Task Force Thirty-Eight," 15 March 1944, box 140, *Action*.

11. "Action Report—Battle of Kula Gulf and Bombardment of Munda and Villa-Stanmore Areas, Night of 5–6 March, 1943, Commander Task Force Sixty-Eight," 9 March 1943, box 243, *Action*.

12. Ibid.

13. "Action Report—Night Engagement off Kula Gulf during Night of 5–6 July 1943, Commander Task Group Thirty-Six Point One," 1 August 1943, box 203, *World War II War Diaries* [hereafter *Diaries*].

14. "Surface Engagement with Enemy (Japanese) Forces off Kula Gulf, New Georgia Group, Solomon Islands on the Night of July 5–6, 1943; report of, Commander Task Unit 36.1.4," 20 July 1943, box 140, *Action*.

15. The exception to this was the destroyer *Nagatsuki,* lost when she ran aground after delivering supplies to Vila. See Morison, *History,* 6:172.

16. "Action Report—Night Engagement off Kula Gulf during Night of 5–6 July 1943, Commander Task Group Thirty-Six Point One," 1 August 1943, box 203, 6, *Diaries;* Morison, *History,* 6:166.

17. Morison, *History,* 6:166; "Action Report—Night Engagement off Kula Gulf during Night of 5–6 July 1943," 10.

18. "Action Report—Night Engagement off Kolombangara during Night of 12–13 July 1943, Commander Task Group Thirty-Six Point One," 3 August 1943, box 203, *Action.*

19. Ibid., 8.

20. ADM 199/1331, *Admiralty: War History Cases and Papers, Second World War,* National Archives of the United Kingdom.

21. "Action Report—Night Engagement off Kula Gulf during Night of 5–6 July 1943," 11.

22. "Surface Engagement with Enemy (Japanese) Forces off Kula Gulf, New Georgia Group, Solomon Islands on the Night of July 5–6, 1943."

23. "Pacific Fleet Confidential Memorandum 2CM-43," Commander-in-Chief Pacific Fleet, box 6593, *OpFor.*

24. Wolters, *Information at Sea,* 207–8.

25. *CIC Handbook for Destroyers, Pacific Fleet,* 24 June 1943, box 614, *CNO.*

26. Rear Adm. Joseph C. Wylie Jr., *The Reminiscences of Rear Admiral Joseph C. Wylie Jr.,* interview by Paul Stillwell (Annapolis, Md.: U.S. Naval Institute, 2003), 37.

27. *Tentative Radar Doctrine and CIC Instructions, Battleships, Pacific Fleet,* Commander Battleships, U.S. Pacific Fleet, 5 June 1944, box 1208, *CNO.*

28. Ibid., 3.

29. *CIC Handbook for Destroyers,* covering letter.

30. "Suggested Personnel, Duties, and Interior Communications of Combat Information Centers—Destroyers, Pacific Fleet, Commander Destroyers, Pacific Fleet," 16 January 1944, box 1162, *CNO;* "C.I.C. Information Bulletin No. 2-43, Commander Destroyers, Pacific Fleet," 15 December 1943, box 614, *CNO.*

31. "Battle Plan, Commander Destroyer Division Fourty-Four," 1 August 1943, copy provided by David Alan Rosenberg.

32. Quoted in E. B. Potter, *Admiral Arleigh Burke* (Annapolis, Md.: Naval Institute Press, 1990), 83.

33. David Alan Rosenberg, "Admiral Arleigh A. Burke," in *Men of War: Great Naval Leaders of World War II,* ed. Stephen Howarth (New York: St. Martin's Press, 1993), 511–12; Morison, *History,* 6:210.

34. "Action Report for Night of 6–7 August 1943, Commander Destroyer Division Fifteen," 12 August 1943, box 629, *Action.*

35. Potter, *Admiral Arleigh Burke,* 721n5, suggests that Burke wrote the plan before Moosbrugger took command. The plan Moosbrugger distributed followed Burke's ideas closely but differed in important respects. It was unique to the situation and composed immediately before battle, after

Burke had been relieved. See "Action Report for Night of August 6–7, 1943, Battle of Vella Gulf, Commander Destroyer Division Twelve," 16 August 1943, box 628, *Action*; "Battle Plan, Commander Destroyer Division Fourty-Four," 1 August 1943.

36. "Action Report for Night of 6–7 August 1943, Commander Destroyer Division Fifteen."

37. "Action Report for Night of August 6–7, 1943, Battle of Vella Gulf," 8.

38. "Vella Gulf Night Action of August 6–7, 1943—Report of, Commanding Officer U.S.S. *Craven*," 8 August 1943, box 73, *Action*.

39. Note, for example, the experience of Capt. Hara Tameichi recounted in his *Japanese Destroyer Captain: Pearl Harbor, Guadalcanal, Midway— The Great Naval Battles as Seen through Japanese Eyes* (Annapolis, Md.: Naval Institute Press, 2011).

40. "Pacific Fleet Confidential Letter 23CL-43," 25 August 1943, box 4679, *OpFor*; Wolters, *Information at Sea*, 213.

41. Wolters, *Information at Sea*, 214.

42. Ibid., 214–15.

43. "Outline of CIC Lectures for Destroyer PCOs and PXOs, COTCLANT," 1 May 1944, 1-1, box 1162, *CNO*.

44. Ibid., 1-4.

45. Ibid., 9; *CIC*, OPNAV, April 1945, box 1694, *CNO*.

46. Monthly OPNAV publications of *CIC* July–December 1944, box 982, *CNO*; Monthly OPNAV publications of *CIC* January–August 1945, box 1694, *CNO*.

47. USF-10A, part 6, sec. 6210, in *CIC*, OPNAV.

48. Ibid., part 6, sec. 6173.

49. Morison, *History*, 6:239–43.

50. "Advance Preliminary Report of Battle Action—SELFRIDGE, O'BANNON, and CHEVALIER with Enemy Forces off Sauka, Vella Lavella, Night 6–7 October 1943, Commander Destroyer Squadron Four," 13 October 1943, box 33, *Action*.

51. R. H. Roupe, "Hell and High Water," *Destroyer History*, http://destroyer history.org/fletcherclass/usschevalier/index.asp?r=45109&pid=45113 (13 August 2016).

52. "Advance Preliminary Report of Battle Action—SELFRIDGE, O'BANNON, and CHEVALIER," Commander Task Force Thirty-One, 19 November 1943, box 33, *Action*.

53. "Final Report of Battle Action—SELFRIDGE, O'BANNON, and CHEVALIER with Enemy Forces off Sauka Point, Vella Lavella Night of 6–7 October, 1943, Commander Destroyer Squadron Four," 26 October 1943, box 33, *Action*.

54. Ibid.
55. "Action Report—Battle of Kula Gulf and Bombardment of Munda and Villa-Stanmore Areas, Night of 5–6 March, 1943."
56. "Action Report of Night Surface Engagement off Bougainville Island, 2 November 1943, Commanding Officer *Charles Ausburne*," 2 November 1943, box 169, *Action*.
57. For contemporary knowledge of Japanese torpedoes, see "Night Actions of Kula Gulf July 6–7, 1943, and Kolombangara July 12–13, 1943—Additional data on, Commander Task Force Thirty-Eight."
58. "Action Reports—Task Force Thirty-Nine Covering Operations for Empress Augusta Bay and Treasury Island Echelons—Period 31 October to 3 November 1943, Commander Task Force Thirty-Nine," 3 November 1943, box 204, *Action*.
59. Ibid.
60. "Action Report of Night Engagement off Cape Moltke on the Night of November 1st–2nd, 1943, the Commander Destroyer Squadron Twenty-Three," 4 November 1943, 27, box 606, *Action*.
61. "Action Report; Battle of Empress Augusta Bay, Commanding Officer, U.S.S. *Montpelier*," 14 November 1943, copy provided by Keith Allan; "Action Report, U.S.S. *Denver*—The Night Engagement off Empress Augusta Bay," 4 November 1943, copy provided by Keith Allan.
62. "Action Report, U.S.S. Denver—The Night Engagement off Empress Augusta Bay."
63. Ibid.
64. "Action Report of Night Engagement off Cape Moltke on the Night of November 1st–2nd."
65. Ibid.
66. "Comments on Battles off Empress Augusta Bay, November 1–2, 1943, and off Cape St. George, November 24–25, 1943, President, Naval War College," 13 January 1944, box 752, *Action*.
67. "Action Report of Night Engagement off Cape St. George on the Night of November 24th—25th, 1943, Commander Destroyer Squadron Twenty-Three," 26 November 1943, box 606, *Action*.
68. "Action Report, Night Surface Engagement Surigao Straits, Leyte, PI, 24–25 October 1944, Commander Destroyer Squadron Twenty-Four," 30 October 1944, 5, box 610, *Action*.
69. "Action Report of Night Engagement off Cape Moltke on the Night of November 1st–2nd."
70. "Comments on Battles off Empress Augusta Bay, November 1–2, 1943, and off Cape St. George, November 24–25, 1943, President, Naval War College."

Chapter 7. Victory in the Pacific

1. "Memorandum for Secret Files: Courses of Action Open to Us in a Pacific Campaign, Attack, Capture and Occupation of the Mandated Islands," 1, box 153, *Strategic.*
2. Miller, *War Plan Orange,* 331–46.
3. "Preliminary Draft of Campaign—Granite," Commander-in-Chief, United States Pacific Fleet, 27 December 1943, 1–2, box 24, *Plans.*
4. Ibid, 6–7.
5. Thomas Wildenberg, *Gray Steel and Black Oil: Fast Tankers and Replenishment at Sea in the U.S. Navy, 1912–1992* (Annapolis, Md.: Naval Institute Press, 1996), 168–203; Morison, *History,* 7:100–13; Henry E. Eccles, *Operational Naval Logistics* (Honolulu, Hawaii: University Press of the Pacific, 2003).
6. Carrier task forces were generally formed around three carriers—two large fleet carriers and a small, light carrier. See Reynolds, *Fast Carriers,* 75–76.
7. "Revision of Pacific Fleet Cruising Instructions, Pacific Board to Revise Cruising Instructions," 18 May 1943, 1, box 22, *Plans.*
8. *Current Tactical Orders and Doctrine, U.S. Pacific Fleet,* PAC-10, Commander-in-Chief, U.S. Pacific Fleet, June 1943, IV-2, box 61, *OpPub.*
9. "1E3" indicated a normal action at extreme range with van light forces operating offensively and rear light forces defensively.
10. "Current Tactical Orders and Cruising Instructions, Task Force 10," 25 January 1943, box 231, *Plans.*
11. PAC-10, figures 6, 7, and 8; "Current Tactical Orders and Cruising Instructions, Task Force Ten," 25 January 1943, 3–4, box 231, *Plans*; "U.S. Pacific Fleet Tactical Bulletin No. 5–41, Light Forces in Night Search and Attack," 24 December 1941, box 6543, *Records of Naval Operating Forces* [hereafter *Forces*]; "U.S. Pacific Fleet Tactical Bulletin No. 5TB-42, Light Forces in Night Search and Attack," 14 November 1942, box 6543, *Forces.*
12. PAC-10, v.
13. See Trent Hone, "U.S. Navy Surface Battle Doctrine and Victory in the Pacific," *Naval War College Review* 62, no. 1 (Winter 2009): 67–105; *Current Tactical Orders and Doctrine, U.S. Fleet,* USF-10A, Commander-in-Chief, United States Fleet, 1 February 1944, box 16, *World War II Bates-Leyte Collection* [hereafter *Bates*]. Compare, for example, PAC-10, part IV, with USF-10A, part IV; *Current Tactical Orders and Doctrine, U.S. Fleet,* USF-10B, Commander-in-Chief, United States Fleet, 1 May 1945, Microfilm: NRS 1977–44, National Archives.
14. Morison, *History,* 5:71.
15. Reynolds, *Fast Carriers,* 87.

16. "Dater-Duckworth Memorandum," quoted in Ibid., 87–88.

17. Nimitz and Spruance expected the Japanese to oppose the movement into the Central Pacific with the bulk of their fleet. See Reynolds, *Fast Carriers*, 79–80; and "Operation Plan A2-43, Commander Task Force 54," 23 October 1943, box 161, *Plans*.

18. "Operation Plan 3-43, Commander Fifth Fleet," 24 October 1943, box 59, *Plans*.

19. "CATCHPOLE—Outline Plan, Commander-in-Chief, U.S. Pacific Fleet and Pacific Ocean Areas," 39, box 137, *Strategic*.

20. "GALVANIC Operation—General Instructions for, Commander Central Pacific Force," 29 October 1943, 1, box 59, *Plans*.

21. "Operation Plan 1–43, Commander Central Pacific Force," 25 October 1943, box 59, 9, *Plans*.

22. "Operation Plan 3-43, Commander Fifth Fleet."

23. "GALVANIC Operation—General Instructions for," 1.

24. "Battle Plan No. 1, Commander, Support Unit," 29 November 1943, box 260, *Plans*.

25. Reynolds, *Fast Carriers*, 115.

26. "Operation Plan No. 1-44, Commander Central Pacific Force," 6 January 1944, 14, box 60, *Plans*.

27. "Operation Plan 2-44, Commander Fifth Fleet," 6 January 1944, box 60, *Plans*; "Deployment and Battle Plan, Commander Support Group," 9 November 1943, box 260, *Plans*.

28. "Engagement off Truk, 16 February 1944—report of, Commanding Officer, U.S.S. *Iowa*," 26 February 1944, box 556, *Action*.

29. TG 50.9 faced similar challenges; although the destroyers and battleships had operated together, the cruisers *Minneapolis* and *New Orleans* had not operated with the other ships before. See Morison, *History*, 5:344, and "Operation Plan No. 1-44, Commander Central Pacific Force."

30. "Operations Order 5–44, Commander Task Force 58," Quoted in Morison, *History*, 8:36.

31. "Operation Plan 5-44, Commander Fast Carrier Task Force," 9 April 1944, Annex H, Operation Plan A, box 235, *Plans*; "Operation Plan 1-44, Commander Battleships, Pacific Fleet," 12 April 1944, box 224, *Plans*.

32. "Operation Plan 5-44, Commander Fast Carrier Task Force."

33. *Secret Information Bulletin No. 20: Battle Experience, Supporting Operations for the Capture of the Marianas Islands (Saipan, Guam, and Tinian), June–August 1944,* United States Fleet, Headquarters of the Commander-in-Chief, 21 December 1944, 74–23, box 444, *Records of Interservice Agencies,* RG 334, National Archives, Washington, D.C. [hereafter *Interservice*].

34. "Operation Plan 10-44, Commander Fifth Fleet," 21, box 61, *Plans*.

35. The plan called for strikes to start on 12 June. See ibid., Annex G, G-1. Explanation of the advanced date is from *Secret Information Bulletin No. 20*, 74–77.

36. *Redfin* reported the sortie of Ozawa's force from Tawi Tawi on 13 June; *Flying Fish* spotted the Japanese as they left San Bernardino on 15 June; and *Seahorse* reported the advance of the Japanese southern group the same day. See Morison, *History*, 8:237–41.

37. "Operation Plan 12-44, Commander Fifth Fleet," J-4, box 61, *Plans*.

38. "Research on Striking Force Tactics, Yokosuka Naval Air Group," 10 May 1943, copy provided by David Dickson.

39. "Operations of Task Force Fifty-Eight 11 June through 21 June 1944, Commander Task Force Fifty-Eight," 11 September 1944, 12–13, box 215, *Action*; Morison, *History*, 8:415.

40. "Operations of Task Force Fifty-Eight 11 June through 21 June 1944," 14.

41. Ibid., 17.

42. "Report of Night Action, Task Force Sixty-Four—November 14–15, 1942, Commander Task Force Sixty-Four," n.d., 8, copy provided by Keith Allan.

43. "Operations of Task Force Fifty-Eight 11 June through 21 June 1944," 17.

44. For the traditional interpretation, see Morison, *History*, 8:244.

45. "Research on Striking Force Tactics, Yokosuka Naval Air Group."

46. Capt. Wayne P. Hughes Jr., *Fleet Tactics and Coastal Combat* (Annapolis, Md.: Naval Institute Press, 2000), 105–8.

47. "Operations of Task Force Fifty-Eight 11 June through 21 June 1944," 13–20.

48. Ibid., 28.

49. Milan N. Vego, *The Battle for Leyte, 1944: Allied and Japanese Plans, Preparations, and Execution* (Annapolis, Md.: Naval Institute Press, 2006), 255–99, 335–36.

50. "Operation Plan 8–44, CINCPOA," 27 September 1944, quoted in ibid., 126.

51. "Battle Plan No. 1-44, Commander Third Fleet," 9 September 1944, box 57, *Plans*.

52. Ibid., Annex A, 2

53. Vego, *Battle for Leyte*, 155–60; Morison, *History*, 12:196, 426–27.

54. Kuasaka issued the order because Toyoda was on Formosa and had limited ability to communicate. See Vego, *Battle for Leyte*, 161–62, 212; Richard W. Bates, *The Battle for Leyte Gulf, October 1944, Strategical and Tactical Analysis*, vol. 3, *Operations from 0000 October 20th (D-Day) until 1042 October 23rd* (Newport, R.I.: Naval War College for Bureau of Naval Personnel, 1957), 150.

55. Bates, *Battle for Leyte Gulf*, 3:106, 567.

56. Ibid., 769–72.

57. "Report of Operations of Task Force Thirty-Four during the Period 6 October 1944 to 3 November 1944, Commander Task Force Thirty-Four," 14 December 1944, 5, box 135, *Action;* Richard W. Bates, *The Battle for Leyte Gulf, October 1944, Strategical and Tactical Analysis,* vol. 5, *Battle of Surigao Strait, October 24th–25th* (Newport, R.I.: Naval War College for Bureau of Naval Personnel, 1958), 169.

58. Bates, *Battle for Leyte Gulf,* 3:98.

59. "Action Report—Period 23–26 October 1944, Commander Third Fleet," 5, box 10, *Bates.*

60. Ibid., 5; *Secret Information Bulletin No. 22: Battle Experience, Battle for Leyte Gulf: A) Battle of Surigao Strait, B) Battle off Samar, C) Battle of Cape Engano, 23–27 October 1944,* 1 March 1945, 78–13—78–14, box 445, *Interservice;* Vego, *Battle for Leyte,* 278. Not all of Halsey's subordinates agreed with this decision.

61. "Report of Operations of Task Force Thirty-Four during the Period 6 October 1944 to 3 November 1944," 9–10; Morison, *History,* 12:318–19.

62. "Operation Plan 13-44, Commander Task Force Seventy-Seven," 26 September 1944, box 66, *Plans;* Morison, *History,* 5:346, 8:406, 409, and 12:416, 419. Australian ships served under Berkey; see Morison, *History,* 12:421.

63. Bates, *Battle for Leyte Gulf,* 5:122.

64. Ibid., 5:25.

65. "Action Report—Surface Engagement with Japanese Forces, Surigao Strait, Philippine Islands, Morning of 15 October 1944, Commander Task Group Seventy-Seven Point Three," 10 November 1944, 11, box 258, *Action.*

66. "Action in the Battle of Surigao Straits 25 October 1944, U.S.S. *West Virginia*—Report of," 1 November 1944, 6, box 1508, *Action.*

67. Myron J. Smith Jr., *The Mountain State Battleship: USS* West Virginia (Richwood: West Virginia Press Club, 1981), 129.

68. See Trent Hone, "Triumph of U.S. Navy Night Fighting," *Naval History* 20, no. 5 (October 2006): 54–59.

69. Bates, *Battle for Leyte Gulf,* 5:675.

70. "Report of Operations of Task Force Thirty-Four during the Period 6 October 1944 to 3 November 1944," 11. For plans concerning TG 34.5 and its operation, see "Operation Order 13-44, Commander Battleships Pacific Fleet," 6 October 1944, box 224, *Plans.*

71. "Action Report of San Bernardino Strait—Night Action by Task Group 34.5 on 25–26 October 1944, Commander Task Group Thirty Four Point Five," 7 November 1944, 2, box 136, *Action;* USF-10A, 4-11.

72. Weapons Systems Evaluation Group, *Operational Experience of Fast Carrier Task Forces in World War II,* WSEG Staff Study no. 4 (Washington, D.C.: Office of the Secretary of Defense, 15 August 1951), 208.

73. Norman Friedman, *Naval Antiaircraft Guns and Gunnery* (Yorkshire, U.K.: Seaforth, 2013), 273, caption.

74. See operation orders and battle plans October 1944–May 1945, box 232, *Plans,* and operation orders and battle plans January 1945, box 229 *Plans;* and "Battle Plan No. 1-44, Commander Task Group Fifty-Two Point Eight," 21 January 1944, box 260, *Plans.*

75. Halsey considered leaving TF 34 off San Bernardino Strait without air cover. This would have been a poor choice, and he appropriately dismissed it. Leaving TF 34 with TG 38.2, a more realistic option, was never seriously considered; see "Action Report—Period 23–26 October 1944, Commander Third Fleet," 5. Halsey had developed no plans for dispersal of his fighting strength; see "Battle Plan No. 1-44, Commander Third Fleet."

76. Quoted in Reynolds, *Fast Carriers,* 279–80.

Epilogue

1. B. Mitchell Simpson III, *Admiral Harold R. Stark: Architect of Victory, 1939–1945* (Columbia: University of South Carolina Press, 1989), 24.

2. Ibid., 20, 28.

3. Ibid., 32, 40.

4. Chisholm, *Waiting for Dead Men's Shoes,* 694, 726; Morison, *History,* 15:115.

5. Adm. James O. Richardson, *The Memoirs of Admiral James O. Richardson: On the Treadmill to Pearl Harbor* (Washington, D.C.: Naval History Division, Department of the Navy, 1974), 61.

6. Morison, *History,* 15:115.

7. G. C. Manning and M. S. Schumacher, *Principles of Warship Construction and Damage Control* (Annapolis, Md.: U.S. Naval Institute, 1935); Herrmann, *Exterior Ballistics.*

8. *Introduction to Engineering and Damage Control,* NAVPERS 16190, 1945; *Handbook of Damage Control,* NAVPERS 16191, 1945.

9. USF-2, *General Tactical Instructions,* United States Fleet, 1947, box 11, Bates; USF-4, *Carrier Task Force Tactical Instructions,* United States Fleet, 1946, box 11, Bates; USF-5, *Surface Action and Tactics,* United States Fleet, 1947, box 12, Bates; USF-15, *CIC Instructions,* United States Fleet, 1947, Bates, box 17.

10. USF-2, chap. 13, 13-8 to 13-10.

11. USF-5, 4-6, 4-7.

12. USF-2, 13-1.

13. USF-5, 4-2.

14. Richardson, *Memoirs,* 107.

15. Vice Adm. Edwin B. Hooper, *Oral History* (Annapolis, Md.: U.S. Naval Institute, 1978), 29.

16. Ibid., 57.
17. Ibid., 60–61.
18. Ibid., 75, 94.
19. Ibid., 93–94.
20. "Atlantic Fleet Memorandum 6M-41," 11–12, box 226, *Classified*.
21. Wylie, *Reminiscences*, 21.
22. Mustin, *Reminiscences*, 240.
23. Wylie, *Reminiscences*, app. "Letter to Peter, 8 October 1984," 4–5.
24. Hooper, *Oral History*, 112–13.
25. Ibid., 117–18.
26. "Annual Report of the Commander-in-Chief, United States Fleet for the Period 1 July 1928 to 21 May 1929," 48.
27. "Annual Report of the Commander-in-Chief, U.S. Fleet for the Period 1 July 1929 to 30 June 1930," box 256, *WWII*.
28. Capt. William Outerson, USN (Ret.), "Peacetime Admirals, Wartime Admirals," U.S. Naval Institute *Proceedings* 107, no. 4 (April 1981): 33–37.
29. Ibid.
30. Hughes, *Fleet Tactics and Coastal Combat*, 124–27.
31. Capt. Russell Crenshaw, USN (Ret.), *The Battle of Tassafaronga* (Baltimore, Md.: Nautical and Aviation, 1995), 199–200.

Conclusion

1. Sumida, *Inventing Grand Strategy*, xv.
2. Shmuel N. Eisenstadt, "The Axial Age: The Emergence of Transcendental Visions and the Rise of Clerics," *European Journal of Sociology* 23, no. 2, Watersheds (1982): 294–314.
3. Ibid.
4. Hendrix, *Theodore Roosevelt's Naval Diplomacy*, 133.
5. Cdr. A. T. Mahan, "Naval Education," U.S. Naval Institute *Proceedings* 5, no. 4 (1879): 353.
6. Ibid., 347.
7. Fiske, *Navy as a Fighting Machine*, 90.
8. Ibid., 93.
9. Reprinted in *Naval Essays of Service Interest* (Annapolis, Md.: U.S. Naval Institute, 1945), 117.
10. Richardson, *Memoirs*, 64.
11. Hooper, *Oral History*, 74.
12. Mustin, *Reminiscences*, 530–31.
13. Hooper, *Oral History*, 16.
14. Amy Edmondson, "Psychological Safety and Learning Behavior in Work Teams," *Administrative Science Quarterly* 44, no. 2 (June 1999): 350–83.
15. Lillard, *Playing War*, 33.

16. Wylie, *Reminiscences,* 18–19 [emphasis in original].
17. Mustin, *Reminiscences,* 126.
18. Richardson, *Memoirs,* 43.
19. Felker, *Testing American Sea Power,* 54.
20. Nofi, *To Train the Fleet for War,* 103.
21. Thomas Wildenberg, *All the Factors of Victory: Admiral Joseph Mason Reeves and the Origins of Carrier Air Power* (Washington, D.C.: Brassey's, 2003), 8, 145–47.
22. Nofi, *To Train the Fleet for War,* 157–59.
23. Felker, *Testing American Sea Power,* 137.
24. "Commander in Chief, United States Pacific Fleet and Pacific Ocean Areas, Command History, 7 December 1941—15 August 1945," 9, box 229, *WWII.*
25. Ibid., 11.
26. James G. March, "Exploration and Exploitation in Organizational Learning" *Organization Science* 2, no. 1 (February 1991): 71–87.
27. Boulton et al., *Embracing Complexity.*
28. Jurgen Appelo, *Management 3.0: Leading Agile Developers, Developing Agile Leaders* (Boston: Addison-Wesley, 2011).
29. Niels Pflaeging, *Organize for Complexity: How to Get Life Back into Work to Build the High-Performance Organization* (New York: Beta-Codex, 2014).
30. Dave Snowden, "Cynefin Framework: An Introduction," http://cognitive-edge.com/ (20 August 2016).
31. Thanks to David J. Anderson for bringing this to my attention.
32. "Strategic Readiness Review," Department of the Navy, 14 December 2017, http://s3.amazonaws.com/CHINFO/SRR+Final+12112017.pdf (21 December 2017).
33. Jon Tetsuro Sumida, *In Defence of Naval Supremacy: Finance, Technology, and British Naval Policy 1889–1914* (New York: Routledge, 1993); Sumida, "The Quest for Reach: The Development of Long-Range Gunnery in the Royal Navy, 1901–1912," in *Tooling for War: Military Transformation in the Industrial Age,* ed. Stephen Chiabotti (Chicago: Imprint, 1996), 49–96; Sumida, "A Matter of Timing: The Royal Navy and the Tactics of Decisive Battle, 1912–1916," *Journal of Military History* 67, no. 1 (January 2003): 85–137; Nicholas A. Lambert, *Sir John Fisher's Naval Revolution* (Columbia: University of South Carolina Press, 1999); John Brooks, *Dreadnought Gunnery and the Battle of Jutland: The Question of Fire Control* (New York: Routledge, 2005).
34. Gordon, *Rules of the Game;* Brooks, *Battle of Jutland.* Although he does not use the term, Brooks' description of the RN is illustrative of a lack of psychological safety.

35. Asada, *From Mahan to Pearl Harbor*, 26–46.
36. Evans and Peattie, *Kaigun*, 189–486.
37. Anthony Tully and Lu Yu, "A Question of Estimates: How Faulty Intelligence Drove Scouting at the Battle of Midway," *Naval War College Review* 68, no. 2 (Spring 2015): 85–99.
38. Hara, *Japanese Destroyer Captain*.

BIBLIOGRAPHY

ADM 199: *Admiralty: War History Cases and Papers, Second World War*, The National Archives of the United Kingdom.

Alger, Philip R. *The Groundwork of Practical Naval Gunnery: A Study of the Principles and Practice of Exterior Ballistics, as Applied to Naval Gunnery.* Annapolis, Md.: U.S. Naval Institute, 1915.

Allen, Peter M. "Modeling Evolution and Creativity in Complex Systems." *World Futures, the Journal of Evolution* 34, nos. 1–2 (June 1992): 105–24.

Annual Reports of the Navy Department. Washington, D.C.: Government Printing Office, 1902–1921.

Appelo, Jurgen. *Management 3.0: Leading Agile Developers, Developing Agile Leaders.* Boston: Addison-Wesley, 2011.

Artigiani, Robert. "Chaos and Constitutionalism: Toward a Post Modern Theory of Social Evolution." *World Futures* 34 (1992): 131–56.

———. "Leadership and Uncertainty: Complexity and the Lessons of History." *Futures* 37 (2005): 585–603.

Asada, Sadao. *From Mahan to Pearl Harbor: The Imperial Japanese Navy and the United States.* Annapolis, Md.: Naval Institute Press, 2006.

Bates, Richard W. *The Battle for Leyte Gulf, October 1944, Strategical and Tactical Analysis.* Volume 3, *Operations from 0000 October 20th (D-Day) until 1042 October 23rd.* Newport, R.I.: Naval War College for Bureau of Naval Personnel, 1957.

———. *The Battle for Leyte Gulf, October 1944, Strategical and Tactical Analysis.* Volume 5, *Battle of Surigao Strait, October 24th–25th.* Newport, R.I.: Naval War College for Bureau of Naval Personnel, 1958.

————. *The Battle of Savo Island, August 9th, 1942, Strategical and Tactical Analysis, Part 1.* Newport, R.I.: Naval War College for Bureau of Naval Personnel, 1950.

Battle Evaluation Group Records. Record Group 23, Naval War College Archives, Newport, R.I.

The Battle of Guadalcanal, 11–15 November 1942. Combat Narrative. Washington, D.C.: Naval Historical Center, Department of the Navy, 1994.

The Battles of Cape Esperance and Santa Cruz Islands. Combat Narrative. Washington, D.C.: Naval Historical Center, Department of the Navy, 1994.

The Battles of Savo Island, 9 August 1942, and the Eastern Solomons, 23–25 August 1942. Combat Narrative. Washington, D.C.: Naval Historical Center, 1994.

Beach, Edward L. *The United States Navy: 200 Years.* New York: Henry Holt, 1986.

Bennet, Capt. J. E., USN (Ret.). "Callaghan Was Calm and Collected at Guadalcanal." *Shipmate* (April 1996).

Bernstein, Marc D. "Tin Cans Raid Balikpapan." U.S. Naval Institute *Proceedings* 129, no. 4 (April 2003).

Bickel, Keith B. *Mars Learning: The Marine Corps' Development of Small Wars Doctrine, 1915–1940.* Boulder, Colo.: Westview, 2001.

Boslaugh, David L. *When Computers Went to Sea: The Digitization of the United States Navy.* Los Alamitos, Calif.: IEEE Computer Society, 1999.

Boulton, Jean G., Peter M. Allen, and Cliff Bowman. *Embracing Complexity: Strategic Perspectives for an Age of Turbulence.* Oxford, U.K.: Oxford University Press, 2015.

Brooks, Daniel R., and E. O. Wiley. *Evolution as Entropy: Toward a Unified Theory of Biology.* 2nd ed. Chicago: University of Chicago Press, 1988.

Brooks, John. *The Battle of Jutland.* Cambridge, U.K.: Cambridge University Press, 2016.

————. *Dreadnought Gunnery and the Battle of Jutland: The Question of Fire Control.* New York: Routledge, 2005.

Buell, Thomas B. *Master of Sea Power: A Biography of Fleet Admiral Ernest J. King.* Boston: Little, Brown, 1980.

Calhoun, C. Raymond. *Tin Can Sailor: Life aboard the USS Sterett, 1939–1945.* Annapolis, Md.: Naval Institute Press, 1993.

Campbell, Mark Allen. *The Influence of Air Power upon the Evolution of Battle Doctrine in the U.S. Navy, 1922–1941.* Master's thesis, University of Massachusetts, 1992.

Carneiro, Robert L. "Herbert Spencer as an Anthropologist." *Journal of Libertarian Studies* 5, no. 2 (Spring 1981): 153–210.

Chandonnet, Fern, ed. *Alaska at War: 1941–1945, the Forgotten War Remembered.* Fairbanks: University of Alaska Press, 2008.

Chisholm, Donald. *Waiting for Dead Men's Shoes: Origins and Development of the U.S. Navy's Officer Personnel System, 1793–1941*. Stanford, Calif.: Stanford University Press, 2001.

Classified Operational Archives. Washington, D.C.: Naval History and Heritage Command Archives.

Clymer, A. Ben. "The Mechanical Analog Computers of Hannibal Ford and William Newell." *IEEE Annals of the History of Computing* 15, no. 2 (1993).

Coletta, Paolo E., ed. *American Secretaries of the Navy*. Volume 1, *1775–1913*. Annapolis, Md.: Naval Institute Press, 1980.

———, ed. *American Secretaries of the Navy*. Volume 2, *1913–1972*. Annapolis, Md.: Naval Institute Press, 1980.

Commander Battleships, Battle Force. *Current Doctrine, Battleships*. USF-17. 1938.

Commander-in-Chief, United States Fleet. *Current Tactical Orders and Doctrine, U.S. Fleet*. USF-10B. 1 May 1945. Microfilm: NRS 1977–44, National Archives, Washington, D.C.

"Comments on the Battle of Guadalcanal, Nov. 11–15, 1942, the President, Naval War College." Serial 2238, 9 June 1943. Copy provided by Capt. Wayne P. Hughes Jr.

Confidential Correspondence. Record Group 80, General Records of the Department of the Navy, Office of the Secretary of the Navy, National Archives, Washington, D.C.

Cooke, Capt. A. P. "Naval Reorganization." U.S. Naval Institute *Proceedings* 12, no. 4 (1886): 491–526.

Crenshaw, Capt. Russell, USN (Ret.). *The Battle of Tassafaronga*. Baltimore, Md.: Nautical and Aviation, 1995.

Dupuy, Col. T. N., U.S. Army. *Understanding War: History and Theory of Combat*. New York: Paragon House, 1987.

Eccles, Henry E. *Operational Naval Logistics*. Honolulu, Hawaii: University Press of the Pacific, 2003.

Edmondson, Amy. "Psychological Safety and Learning Behavior in Work Teams." *Administrative Science Quarterly* 44, no. 2 (June 1999): 350–83.

Eisenstadt, Shmuel N. "The Axial Age: The Emergence of Transcendental Visions and the Rise of Clerics." *European Journal of Sociology*, Watersheds, 23, no. 2 (1982): 294–314.

Elias, Norbert. *The Genesis of the Naval Profession*. Dublin: University College Dublin Press, 2007.

"Estimate of the Situation, Lecture Delivered by Cdr. Frank H. Schofield, U.S.N. at the Summer Conference, U.S. Naval War College, Newport, R.I." June 1912, Naval History and Heritage Command Library.

The Estimate of the Situation, Plans and Orders. Newport, R.I.: Naval War College, 1929.

The Estimate of the Situation, Plans and Orders. Newport, R.I.: Naval War College, 1932.

Evans, David C., and Mark R. Peattie. *Kaigun: Strategy, Tactics, and Technology in the Imperial Japanese Navy, 1887–1941*. Annapolis, Md.: Naval Institute Press, 1997.

Felker, Craig C. *Testing American Sea Power: U.S. Navy Strategic Exercises, 1923–1940*. College Station: Texas A&M University Press, 2007.

Fire Control Installations. Annapolis, Md.: U.S. Naval Academy Postgraduate School, 1939.

Fire Control Notes, 1940, for U.S. Naval Reserve. Washington, D.C.: Government Printing Office, 1941.

Fiske, Bradley A. "American Naval Policy." U.S. Naval Institute *Proceedings* 31, no. 1 (March 1905): 1–80.

———. "The Naval Profession." U.S. Naval Institute *Proceedings* 33, no. 2 (April 1907): 477–578.

———. *The Navy as a Fighting Machine*. 2nd ed. New York: Charles Scribner's Sons, 1918. Reprint: Annapolis, Md.: Naval Institute Press, 1988.

Fleet Training Division Records. Entry 180, Record Group 38, Records of the Office of the Chief of Naval Operations, National Archives, Washington, D.C.

Friedman, Norman. *The British Battleship 1906–1946*. Annapolis, Md.: Naval Institute Press, 2015.

———. *Naval Antiaircraft Guns and Gunnery*. Yorkshire, U.K.: Seaforth, 2013.

———. *Naval Firepower: Battleship Guns and Gunnery in the Dreadnought Era*. Annapolis, Md.: Naval Institute Press, 2008.

———. *Network Centric Warfare: How Navies Learned to Fight Smarter through Three World Wars*. Annapolis, Md.: Naval Institute Press, 2009.

———. *U.S. Battleships: An Illustrated Design History*. Annapolis, Md.: Naval Institute Press, 1985.

———. *U.S. Naval Weapons*. Annapolis, Md.: Naval Institute Press, 1985.

Frost, Cdr. Holloway H. *The Battle of Jutland*. Annapolis, Md.: U.S. Naval Institute, 1936.

Furer, Rear Adm. Julius Augustus. *Administration of the Navy Department in World War II*. Washington, D.C.: Naval History Division, 1959.

General Board Records. Record Group 80, General Records of the Department of the Navy, National Archives, Washington, D.C.

Gordon, Andrew. *The Rules of the Game: Jutland and British Naval Command*. Annapolis, Md.: Naval Institute Press, 1996.

Grace, James W. *The Naval Battle of Guadalcanal*. Annapolis, Md.: Naval Institute Press, 1999.

Haberlein, Charles R., Jr. *Reflections on Friday the Thirteenth: Daniel J. Callaghan's Naval Battle off Guadalcanal*. Preliminary version for critical review, 30 August 1994. Copy provided by Capt. Wayne P. Hughes Jr.

Hammel, Eric. *Guadalcanal: Decision at Sea, the Naval Battle of Guadalcanal, November 13–15, 1942*. New York: Crown, 1988.

Handbook of Damage Control. NAVPERS 16191, 1945.

Hara, Capt. Tameichi. *Japanese Destroyer Captain: Pearl Harbor, Guadalcanal, Midway—The Great Naval Battles as Seen through Japanese Eyes*. Annapolis, Md.: Naval Institute Press, 2011.

Hayes, Mark L. "War Plans and Preparations and Their Impact on U.S. Naval Operations in the Spanish-American War." http://www.history.navy.mil /research/library/online-reading-room/title-list-alphabetically/s/spanish -american-war-war-plans-and-impact-on-u-s-navy.html (29 November 2015).

Hearings before the Committee on Naval Affairs, United States Senate, on the Bill S. 3335, to Increase the Efficiency of the Personnel of the Navy and Marine Corps of the United States. Washington, D.C.: Government Printing Office, 1908.

Hendrix, Henry J. *Theodore Roosevelt's Naval Diplomacy: The U.S. Navy and the Birth of the American Century*. Annapolis, Md.: Naval Institute Press, 2009.

Herrmann, Lt. Cdr. Ernest E. *Exterior Ballistics*. Annapolis, Md.: U.S. Naval Institute, 1935.

Hill, Howard C. *Roosevelt and the Caribbean*. Chicago: University of Chicago Press, 1927.

Hoag, Hannah. "Lyme Bacteria Show That Evolvability Is Evolvable." *Nature*, 14 November 2015, doi: 10.1038/nature.2013.14176 (18 December 2014).

Hone, Thomas C., Norman Friedman, and Mark D. Mandeles. *American and British Aircraft Carrier Development, 1919–1941*. Annapolis, Md.: Naval Institute Press, 2009.

Hone, Thomas C., and Trent Hone. *Battle Line: The United States Navy, 1919–1939*. Annapolis, Md.: Naval Institute Press, 2006.

Hone, Trent. "Building a Doctrine: USN Tactics and Battle Plans in the Interwar Period." *International Journal of Naval History* 1, no. 2 (October 2002).

———. "The Evolution of Fleet Tactical Doctrine in the U.S. Navy, 1922–1941." *Journal of Military History* 67, no. 4 (October 2003): 1107–48.

———. "'Give Them Hell!': The U.S. Navy's Night Combat Doctrine and the Campaign for Guadalcanal." *War in History* 13, no. 2 (April 2006): 171–99.

———. "Triumph of U.S. Navy Night Fighting." *Naval History* 20, no. 5 (October 2006): 54–59.

———. "U.S. Navy Surface Battle Doctrine and Victory in the Pacific." *Naval War College Review* 62, no. 1 (Winter 2009): 67–105.

Hooper, Vice Adm. Edwin B. *Oral History.* Annapolis, Md.: U.S. Naval Institute, 1978.

Hornfischer, James D. *The Last Stand of the Tin Can Sailors: The Extraordinary World War II Story of the U.S. Navy's Finest Hour.* New York: Bantam Books, 2009.

Howeth, Capt. L. S. *History of Communications-Electronics in the United States Navy.* Washington, D.C.: Bureau of Ships and Office of Naval History, 1963.

Hughes, Thomas. "Learning to Fight: Bill Halsey and the Early American Destroyer Force." *Journal of Military History* 77, no. 1 (January 2013): 71–90.

Hughes, Capt. Wayne P., Jr. (Ret.). *Fleet Tactics: Theory and Practice.* Annapolis, Md.: Naval Institute Press, 1986.

———. *Fleet Tactics and Coastal Combat.* Annapolis, Md.: Naval Institute Press, 2000.

Hutchins, Edwin. *Cognition in the Wild.* Cambridge, Mass.: MIT Press, 1995.

Intelligence and Technical Archives. Record Group 8, Naval War College Archives, Newport, R.I.

Introduction to Engineering and Damage Control. NAVPERS 16190, 1945.

Jacob, François. *The Possible and the Actual.* Seattle: University of Washington Press, 1982.

Jones, Jerry W. *U.S. Battleship Operations in World War I.* Annapolis, Md.: Naval Institute Press, 1998.

Juarrero, Alicia. *Dynamics in Action: Intentional Behavior as a Complex System.* Cambridge, Mass.: MIT Press, 1999.

Jurens, W. J. "The Evolution of Battleship Gunnery in the U.S. Navy, 1920–1945." *Warship International* 28, no. 3 (1991).

Kahneman, Daniel. *Thinking Fast and Slow.* New York: Farrar, Straus, and Giroux.

King, Ernest J., with Walter Muir Whitehill. *Fleet Admiral King: A Naval Record.* New York: W. W. Norton, 1952.

Kirschner, Marc, and John Gerhart. "Evolvability." *Proceedings of the National Academy of Sciences of the United States of America* 95.15 (1998): 8420–27, doi: 10.1073/pnas.95.15.8420 (15 August 2016).

Knox, Lt. Cdr. Dudley W. "Trained Initiative and Unity of Action: The True Bases of Military Efficiency." U.S. Naval Institute *Proceedings* 39, no. 1 (March 1913).

Kohnen, David. "The U.S. Navy Won the Battle of Jutland." *Naval War College Review* 69, no. 4 (Autumn 2016): 122–45.

Kuehn, John T. *Agents of Innovation: The General Board and the Design of the Fleet That Defeated the Japanese Navy.* Annapolis, Md.: Naval Institute Press, 2008.

Lambert, Nicholas A. *Sir John Fisher's Naval Revolution.* Columbia: University of South Carolina Press, 1999.

Laning, Adm. Harris (Ret.). *An Admiral's Yarn.* Newport, R.I.: Naval War College Press, 1999.

Laplace, Pierre-Simon, Marquis de. *Probabilities.* Translated by Frederick Wilson Truscott and Frederick Lincoln Emory. London: John Wiley & Sons, 1902.

Leeke, Jim. *Manila and Santiago: The New Steel Navy in the Spanish American War.* Annapolis, Md.: Naval Institute Press, 2009.

Li, Rong, and Bruce Bowerman. "Symmetry Breaking in Biology." *Cold Spring Harbor Perspectives in Biology* 2 no. 3 (March 2010), doi:10.1101/cshperspect.a003475 (21 July 2014).

Licht, Walter. *Industrializing America: The Nineteenth Century.* Baltimore, Md.: Johns Hopkins University Press, 1995.

Lillard, John M. *Playing War: Wargaming and U.S. Navy Preparations for World War II.* Lincoln, Neb.: Potomac Books, 2016.

Luce, Rear Adm. Stephen B. (Ret.). "On the Relations between the U.S. Naval War College and the Line Officers of the U.S. Navy." U.S. Naval Institute *Proceedings* 37, no. 3 (September 1911): 793–94.

Lundgren, Robert. "*Kirishima* Damage Analysis." Edited by Tony DiGiulian, 28 September 2010, http://www.navweaps.com/index_lundgren/Kirishima_Damage_Analysis.pdf (4 December 2016).

Lundstrom, John B. *Black Shoe Carrier Admiral: Frank Jack Fletcher at Coral Sea, Midway, and Guadalcanal.* Annapolis, Md.: Naval Institute Press, 2006.

Macy, Joanna. *Mutual Causality in Buddhism and General Systems Theory.* Albany: State University of New York, 1991.

Mahan, Cdr. A. T. *The Influence of Sea Power upon History, 1660–1783.* Reprint: New York: Dover, 1987.

———. *The Influence of Sea Power upon the French Revolution and Empire, 1793–1812.* London: Sampson, Low, Marston, 1892.

———. "Naval Education." U.S. Naval Institute *Proceedings* 5, no. 4 (1879).

Manning, G. C., and M. S. Schumacher. *Principles of Warship Construction and Damage Control.* Annapolis, Md.: U.S. Naval Institute, 1935.

Manuscript Collection 207. Papers of CDR Winston S. Brown, USN, Naval War College Archives, Newport, R.I.

March, James G. "Exploration and Exploitation in Organizational Learning." *Organization Science* 2, no. 1 (February 1991).

Miller, Edward S. *War Plan Orange: The U.S. Strategy to Defeat Japan, 1897–1945*. Annapolis, Md.: Naval Institute Press, 1991.

Mindell, David A. *Between Human and Machine: Feedback, Control, and Computing before Cybernetics*. Baltimore, Md.: Johns Hopkins University Press, 2002.

Ministry of Defense (Navy). *War with Japan*. Volume 3, *The Campaigns in the Solomons and New Guinea*. London: Her Majesty's Stationery Office, 1995.

Mitchell, Nancy. "The Height of the German Challenge: The Venezuela Blockade, 1902–03." *Diplomatic History* 20, no. 2 (1996):185–209.

Morison, Elting E. *Admiral Sims and the Modern American Navy*. Boston: Houghton Mifflin, 1942.

———. *Men, Machines, and Modern Times*. Cambridge, Mass.: MIT Press, 1966.

Morison, Samuel Eliot. *History of the United States Naval Operations in World War II*. Reprint: Boston: Little, Brown, 1984.

Mossio, Matteo, Leonardo Bich, and Alvaro Moreno. "Emergence, Closure and Inter-Level Causation in Biological Systems." *Erkenntnis* (2013).

Murray, Williamson, and Allan R. Millett, eds. *Military Innovation in the Interwar Period*. Cambridge, U.K.: Cambridge University Press, 1996.

Mustin, Vice Adm. Lloyd M. *The Reminiscences of Vice Admiral Lloyd M. Mustin*. Interviewed by John T. Mason Jr. Annapolis, Md.: U.S. Naval Institute, 2003.

"Naval Administration: Selected Documents on Navy Department Organization, 1915–1940." Washington, D.C.: Department of the Navy, 1940.

Naval Essays of Service Interest. Annapolis, Md.: U.S. Naval Institute, 1945.

Navy Ordnance Activities, World War, 1917–1918. Washington, D.C.: Government Printing Office, 1920.

Nofi, Albert A. *To Train the Fleet for War: The U.S. Navy Fleet Problems, 1923–1940*. Newport, R.I.: Naval War College Press, 2010.

O'Connell, Robert L. *Sacred Vessels: The Cult of the Battleship and the Rise of the U.S. Navy*. New York: Oxford University Press, 1993.

O'Hara, Vincent P. *The U.S. Navy against the Axis: Surface Combat, 1941–1945*. Annapolis, Md.: Naval Institute Press, 2007.

Outerson, Capt. William, USN (Ret.). "Peacetime Admirals, Wartime Admirals." U.S. Naval Institute *Proceedings* 107, no. 4 (April 1981): 33–37.

Paullin, Charles Oscar. *Paullin's History of Naval Administration: 1775–1911*. Annapolis, Md.: U.S. Naval Institute, 1968. Reprint 2012.

Pflaeging, Niels. *Organize for Complexity: How to Get Life Back into Work to Build the High-Performance Organization*. New York: BetaCodex, 2014.

Pierce, Terry C. *Warfighting and Disruptive Technologies: Designing Innovation*. New York: Frank Cass, 2004.

Posen, Barry R. *The Sources of Military Doctrine: France, Britain, and Germany between the World Wars*. Ithaca, N.Y.: Cornell University Press, 1984.

Potter, E. B. *Admiral Arleigh Burke*. Annapolis, Md.: Naval Institute Press, 1990.

Publications. Record Group 4, Naval War College Archives, Newport, R.I.

Range and Gunnery Tables, 1935. Annapolis, Md.: U.S. Naval Academy, 1935.

Reardon, Jeff. "Breaking the U.S. Navy's 'Gun Club' Mentality in the South Pacific." *Journal of Military History* 75, no. 2 (April 2011).

Records of Interservice Agencies. Record Group 334, National Archives, Washington, D.C.

Records of Naval Operating Forces. Entry 107, Record Group 313, National Archives, Washington, D.C.

Records of the Bureau of Ordnance. Record Group 74, National Archives, Washington, D.C.

Records of the CNO Headquarters. Records of the Office of the Chief of Naval Operations, Record Group 38, National Archives, Washington, D.C.

Records Relating to United States Navy Fleet Problems I to XXIII, 1923–1941. Washington, D.C.: National Archives, 1974. Microfilm.

Rentfrow, James C. *Home Squadron: The U.S. Navy on the North Atlantic Station*. Annapolis, Md.: Naval Institute Press, 2014.

"Report of Night Action, Task Force Sixty-Four—November 14–15, 1942, Commander Task Force Sixty-Four." N.d. Copy provided by Keith Allan.

"Research on Striking Force Tactics, Yokosuka Naval Air Group." 10 May 1943. Copy provided by David Dickson.

Reuterdahl, Henry. "The Needs of Our Navy." *McClure's Magazine* (January 1908).

Reynolds, Clark G. *Admiral John H. Towers: The Struggle for Naval Air Supremacy*. Annapolis, Md.: Naval Institute Press, 1991.

———. *The Fast Carriers: The Forging of an Air Navy*. Annapolis, Md.: Naval Institute Press, 1992.

Richardson, Adm. James O. *The Memoirs of Admiral James O. Richardson: On the Treadmill to Pearl Harbor*. Washington, D.C.: Naval History Division, Department of the Navy, 1974.

Rosenberg, David Alan. "Admiral Arleigh A. Burke." In *Men of War: Great Naval Leaders of World War II*, edited by Stephen Howarth, 506–27. New York: St. Martin's Press, 1993.

Roupe, R. H. "Hell and High Water." Destroyer History, http://destroyer history.org/fletcherclass/usschevalier/index.asp?r=45109&pid=45113 (13 August 2016).

Rules for the Conduct of the War Games. Newport, R.I.: Naval War College, 1903.

Rules for the Conduct of the War Games. Newport, R.I.: Naval War College, 1905.

Simpson, Mitchell B., III. *Admiral Harold R. Stark: Architect of Victory, 1939–1945.* Columbia: University of South Carolina Press, 1989.

Smith, Myron J., Jr. *The Mountain State Battleship: USS* West Virginia. Richwood: West Virginia Press Club, 1981.

Snowden, Dave. "Cynefin Framework: An Introduction." http://cognitive -edge.com/ (20 August 2016).

Sound Military Decision, Including the Estimate of the Situation and the Formulation of Directives. Newport, R.I.: Naval War College, 1938.

Spector, Ronald. *Professors of War: The Naval War College and the Development of the Naval Profession.* Newport, R.I.: Naval War College Press, 1977.

Sterling, Lt. Cdr. Yates, "The Nation's Defense—The Offensive Fleet: How Shall We Prepare It for Battle." U.S. Naval Institute *Proceedings* 34, no. 2 (June 1908): 393–428.

Strategic Plans Division Records. Record Group 38, Records of the Office of the Chief of Naval Operations, National Archives, Washington, D.C.

Stulberg, Adam N., and Michael D. Salomone. *Managing Defense Transformation.* Burlington, Vt.: Ashgate, 2007.

Sumida, Jon Tetsuro. "'The Best Laid Plans': The Development of British Battle-Fleet Tactics, 1919–1942." *International History Review* 14, no. 4 (November 1992): 681–700.

———. *In Defence of Naval Supremacy: Finance, Technology, and British Naval Policy 1889–1914.* New York: Routledge, 1993.

———. *Inventing Grand Strategy and Teaching Command: The Classic Works of Alfred Thayer Mahan Reconsidered.* Washington, D.C.: Woodrow Wilson Center Press, 1997.

———. "A Matter of Timing: The Royal Navy and the Tactics of Decisive Battle, 1912–1916." *Journal of Military History* 67, no. 1 (January 2003): 85–137.

———. "The Quest for Reach: The Development of Long-Range Gunnery in the Royal Navy, 1901–1912." In *Tooling for War: Military Transformation in the Industrial Age,* edited by Stephen Chiabotti. Chicago: Imprint, 1996.

Taleb, Nassim Nicholas. *Anti-Fragile: Things That Gain from Disorder (Incerto).* New York: Random House, 2014.

Taylor, Frederick Winslow. *The Principles of Scientific Management.* New York: Harper & Brothers, 1911.

Taylor, Capt. H. C. "Battle Tactics: The Value of Concentration." U.S. Naval Institute *Proceedings* 12, no. 2 (1886).

———. "Memorandum on General Staff for the U.S. Navy." U.S. Naval Institute *Proceedings* 26, no. 3 (1900).

Tritten, James J. *Doctrine and Fleet Tactics in the Royal Navy.* Norfolk, Va.: Naval Doctrine Command, 1994.

Tully, Anthony, and Lu Yu. "A Question of Estimates: How Faulty Intelligence Drove Scouting at the Battle of Midway." *Naval War College Review* 68, no. 2 (Spring 2015): 85–99.

Turner, Frederick Jackson. "The Significance of the Frontier." In *Rereading Frederick Jackson Turner: The Significance of the Frontier in American History and Other Essays by Frederick Turner.* Edited by John Mack Faragher. New Haven, Conn.: Yale University Press, 1998.

U.S. Navy. *Destroyer War Instructions, 1922.* WPL-6. Washington, D.C.: Government Printing Office, 1922.

———. *Notes on Fire Control, 1933.* FTP-135. Washington, D.C.: Government Printing Office, 1933.

U.S. Navy, Office of Naval Intelligence. *The Java Sea Campaign.* Combat Narrative. 1943. http://www.history.navy.mil/research/library/online-reading -room/title-list-alphabetically/j/java-sea-campaign.html (4 August 2015).

U.S. Navy and Related Operational, Tactical, and Instructional Publications. Entry 337, Record Group 38, Records of the Office of the Chief of Naval Operations, National Archives, Washington, D.C.

U.S. Navy Technical Publications. Entry 336A, Record Group 38, Records of the Office of the Chief of Naval Operations, National Archives, Washington, D.C.

Vego, Milan N. *The Battle for Leyte, 1944: Allied and Japanese Plans, Preparations, and Execution.* Annapolis, Md.: Naval Institute Press, 2006.

Weapons Systems Evaluation Group. *Operational Experience of Fast Carrier Task Forces in World War II.* WSEG Staff Study no. 4. Washington, D.C.: Office of the Secretary of Defense, 15 August 1951.

Wheeler, Gerald E. *Admiral William Veazie Pratt, U.S. Navy: A Sailor's Life.* Washington, D.C.: Naval History Division, Department of the Navy, 1974.

———. *Kinkaid of the Seventh Fleet: A Biography of Admiral Thomas C. Kinkaid, U.S. Navy.* Washington, D.C.: Naval Historical Center, 1995.

Wildenberg, Thomas. *All the Factors of Victory: Admiral Joseph Mason Reeves and the Origins of Carrier Air Power.* Washington, D.C.: Brassey's, 2003.

———. *Gray Steel and Black Oil: Fast Tankers and Replenishment at Sea in the U.S. Navy, 1912–1992.* Annapolis, Md.: Naval Institute Press, 1996.

———. "In Support of the Battle Line: Gunnery's Influence on the Development of Carrier Aviation in the U.S. Navy." *Journal of Military History* 65, no. 3 (July 2001).

Williams, Maj. Blair S., U.S. Army. "Heuristics and Biases in Military Decision Making." *Military Review* (September–October 2010): 40–52.

Wolters, Timothy S. *Information at Sea.* Baltimore, Md.: Johns Hopkins University Press, 2013.

World War II Action and Operational Reports. Record Group 38, Records of the Office of the Chief of Naval Operations, National Archives, Washington, D.C.

World War II Bates-Leyte Collection. Record Group 38, Records of the Office of the Chief of Naval Operations, National Archives, Washington, D.C.

World War II Command File. Washington, D.C.: Naval Historical Center Archives.

World War II Plans, Orders, and Related Documents. Record Group 38, Records of the Office of the Chief of Naval Operations, National Archives, Washington, D.C.

World War II War Diaries. Record Group 38, Records of the Office of the Chief of Naval Operations, National Archives, Washington, D.C.

Wright, Christopher C. "Questions on the Effectiveness of U.S. Navy Battleship Gunnery." *Warship International* 41, no. 1 (2004): 54–78.

———. "Questions on the Effectiveness of U.S. Navy Battleship Gunnery, Part II." *Warship International* 41, no. 3 (2004): 289–313.

Wylie, Rear Adm. Joseph C., Jr. *The Reminiscences of Rear Admiral Joseph C. Wylie Jr.* Interview by Paul Stillwell, Annapolis, Md.: U.S. Naval Institute, 2003.

INDEX

Abe Hiroaki, 190–91
Adams, Charles F., 129
adaptive systems. *See* complex adaptive systems
adaptive tactics, 215–22
Admiralty Fire Control Table (Britain), 87
aerial spotting, 85–86, 150
Agano (Japan), 237, 240, 271
aggressive action heuristic, 138–40
Agile software techniques, 340
Ainsworth, Warden L., 210, 215–17, 219–22, 225, 238, 307
Akiyama Teruo, 218, 219
Alabama (BB 8), 58, 61
Alabama (BB 60), 283, 284
Alaska, 311
Albacore, 279–80
Aldrich, Nelson, 18
Allen, Peter M., 3, 340
American Samoa, 25
American Society of Civil Engineering, 19
"anti-fragile" concept, 349n19
Aoba (Japan), 178, 188, 202
Appelo, Jurgen, 340
Arashi (Japan), 227
Arizona, 192
Arkansas, 74
Artigiani, Robert, 196
Asagumo (Japan), 288
A-scope, 170–71, 172, 205, 220
Astoria, 174, 175, 177, 178, 185

asymmetric warfare, 293–95
Atago (Japan), 283
Atlanta, 191, 194, 195, 328, 366n68
Atlantic Fleet, 103, 106–7, 111, 129, 341
Augusta, 168, 308, 310, 329, 331, 362n8
Ault, 310
Austin, Bernard L., 240, 241, 243, 244
Australia (Australia), 175, 177
Axial Age, 320–21
Ayanami (Japan), 199

Babcock, John V., 115
Badger, Charles J., 107–8
Badger, Oscar C., 290, 297
Balikpapan, Battle of, 179–80
Battle Fleet, 129, 131, 145, 313
Battle Fleet Fighting Instructions (1927), 145–51
Battle Instructions (1916), 111–12, 116, 123
Battle Plan 2E, 148
battle plans. *See* plans and doctrine development
Belknap, Reginald R., 34, 38
Belleau Wood, 261
Benham, 199
Benson, William S., 41, 53, 118, 138, 147
Berkey, Russell S., 286, 288
Birmingham, 114
Black Plan, 96
"black swan" events, 9
Blakely, Charles A., 127

ABOUT THE AUTHOR

Trent Hone is an authority on the U.S. Navy of the early twentieth century and a leader in the application of complexity science to organizational design. He studied religion and archaeology at Carleton College in Northfield, Minnesota. He works as a consultant in Arlington, Virginia, helping a variety of organizations improve their processes and techniques. He writes and speaks about tactical doctrine, organizational learning, and complexity.

The Naval Institute Press is the book-publishing arm of the U.S. Naval Institute, a private, nonprofit, membership society for sea service professionals and others who share an interest in naval and maritime affairs. Established in 1873 at the U.S. Naval Academy in Annapolis, Maryland, where its offices remain today, the Naval Institute has members worldwide.

Members of the Naval Institute support the education programs of the society and receive the influential monthly magazine *Proceedings* or the colorful bimonthly magazine *Naval History* and discounts on fine nautical prints and on ship and aircraft photos. They also have access to the transcripts of the Institute's Oral History Program and get discounted admission to any of the Institute-sponsored seminars offered around the country.

The Naval Institute's book-publishing program, begun in 1898 with basic guides to naval practices, has broadened its scope to include books of more general interest. Now the Naval Institute Press publishes about seventy titles each year, ranging from how-to books on boating and navigation to battle histories, biographies, ship and aircraft guides, and novels. Institute members receive significant discounts on the Press's more than eight hundred books in print.

Full-time students are eligible for special half-price membership rates. Life memberships are also available.

For a free catalog describing Naval Institute Press books currently available, and for further information about joining the U.S. Naval Institute, please write to:

Member Services
U.S. NAVAL INSTITUTE
291 Wood Road
Annapolis, MD 21402-5034
Telephone: (800) 233-8764
Fax: (410) 571-1703
Web address: www.usni.org